FOOTBALL PERIODIZATION
TO MAXIMISE PERFORMANCE

Session Design | The Training Week | Tapering Strategy | 102 Practices | Youth to Pro

Written by

ADAM OWEN Ph.D

UEFA Pro Coaching Licence

Published by

FOOTBALL PERIODIZATION
TO MAXIMISE PERFORMANCE

Session Design | The Training Week | Tapering Strategy | 102 Practices | Youth to Pro

First Published May 2022 by SoccerTutor.com

Info@soccertutor.com | www.SoccerTutor.com

UK: 0208 1234 007 | **US:** (305) 767 4443 | **ROTW:** +44 208 1234 007

ISBN: 978-1-910491-55-3

Copyright: SoccerTutor.com Limited © 2022. All Rights Reserved.

All rights reserved. No part of this publication may be reproduced, stored in a retrieval system, or transmitted in any form or by any means, electronic, mechanical, photocopy, recording or otherwise, without prior written permission of the copyright owner. Nor can it be circulated in any form of binding or cover other than that in which it is published and without similar condition including this condition being imposed on a subsequent purchaser.

Author
Adam Owen Ph.D

Editor
Alex Fitzgerald - SoccerTutor.com

Diagrams
Diagram designs by SoccerTutor.com. All the diagrams in this book have been created using SoccerTutor.com Tactics Manager Software available from www.SoccerTutor.com

Photos on pages 60, 66, 70, & 126 provided by **058 Sport**

Note: While every effort has been made to ensure the technical accuracy of the content of this book, neither the author nor publishers can accept any responsibility for any injury or loss sustained as a result of the use of this material.

CONTENTS

Dr. Adam Owen: Coach Profile 09
Dr. Adam Owen: Author of Bestselling Football Conditioning Book Set 12
Dr. Adam Owen: Career Overview of High Performance Expert 13
Introduction: Training Sessions for Peak Performance 14
Benefits of the "Football Periodization to Maximise Performance" Methodology 16
Foreword by Steve McClaren 17
Player and Content References 18

CHAPTER 1: Coaching Methodology to Maximise Performance 20

Coaching Methodology to Maximise Performance 21
Training Load, Adaptation, and Training Week (Microcycle) Tapering 22

CHAPTER 2: Developing a Game Model 25

Game Model: External Factors Influencing Game Model Development 26
Game Model: Positional, Unit, and Collective Principles Covered within the Microcycle (Training Week) 27
Game Model: The Development Process within the Phases of the Game 28
Game Model: Coaching Framework to Impact Players' Decision Making 29
Game Model: Phases of Play, Objectives, and the General, Operational, and Core Tactical Principles of the Game 31

CHAPTER 3: Training Load Management in Football 34

Training Load Management and Injury Prevention in Football 35

CHAPTER 4: Developing a Game Based Training Approach 40

Developing a Game Based Training Approach 41
Game Based Training: Small, Medium, and Large-Sided Games 42
Small vs. Medium vs. Large Sided Games 43
Physical and Technical Comparisons Between Various Sided Games within Professional Football 44
Heart Rate Responses and Technical Comparison of Small vs. Large-Sided Games in Elite Professional Football 45
Variables Significantly Influencing Training Intensity 46
Coaching Effects of Changing Pitch Sizes 47
Coaching Effects of Limited Touches 48
Considerations for Small Sided Games 49
Article: Multi-directional Sprints and Small Sided Games Training Effect on Agility and Changes of Direction (COD) Abilities in Youth Football 50
Age Category Performance Effects within Small Sided Games 51
Small-Sided Games: The Physiological and Technical Demands of Altering Pitch Size and Player Numbers ..52
Considerations for Large Sided Games 53

Large Sided Games - Coaching Effects of Increasing Bout Duration 54
Large 16 Minute Game: 10v10 + GKs (Box to Box) 55
Large 8 Minute Game: 10v10 + GKs (Box to Box) 56
Understanding Game Formats and Using a Mixed Approach 57
Justification for a Game Based Training Approach: Small, Medium, and Large Sided Game Areas 58

CHAPTER 5: Training Session Design 59

Training Session Design 60
Practice Design Considerations to Optimise Coaching Outcomes 62
The Tactical Objective 63
The Physical Objective 64
Workload Monitoring of Starters and Non-Starters 65
The Technical Objective 66
Skills Periodization 67
The Psychological Objective 68
Training Session Flow 69

CHAPTER 6: Planning the Training Week to Maximise Performance 71

Practical Coaching Model to Build the Training Week (Microcycle) 72
Periodization, Tapering Strategy and Maximising Performance 73
The Training Week: Professional Microcycle 74
Training Session Format Example for Professional Training Week (Microcycle) 75
The Training Week: Semi-professional Microcycle 76
The Training Week: Youth Academy Microcycle 77
The Training Week: Grassroots (Youth) Microcycle 1 78
The Training Week: Grassroots (Youth) Microcycle 2 79

CHAPTER 7: Practices for Tapering Strategy and Maximising Performance 80

The Benefit of the Data for Each Practice (Volume and Intensity Metrics) 81
Key Terms: Volume Metrics for All Practices 82
Key Terms: Intensity Metrics for All Practices 83

MONDAY Training Day: Recovery - 5 Days Until Match (MD +2/-5) 84

Recovery Day 85
1: Simple 40-Metre Recovery Strides @ 50-60% + Walking Rests 86
2: Basic Footwork and Movement Exercises + Football Tennis 87

TUESDAY Training Day: Resistance - 4 Days Until Match (MD +3/-4) 88

Positional Principle Training and Resistance 89
Physical and Physiological Focus 90
Physiology of Small Sided Games 92
Technical and Tactical Focus 93
Game Stimulus Response for Positional Principles Game Type 94

Fundamental Concepts of Positional Principle Training and Resistance..94

TUESDAY Training Day Practices: Resistance - 4 Days Until Match (MD +3/-4)...95

Resistance Warm-Up Practices...96
1: Circuit with Different Movements, Runs, and Jumps...................................97
2: Ball Control in a Square with Resting Outside Players................................98

Intensive Technical Practices...99
1: Quick Feet, One-Two, and Diagonal Passing in a Pass & Move Drill............100
2: Double Square Pass and Move Drill...101
3: Quick Footwork and Short Interplay in a Speed Passing Drill....................102
4: Support Play with One- Twos & Timing of Movement (Diamond Circuit).........103
5: Two-Sided Circuit with Timing of Movement for Through Pass..................104

Resistance Conditioning Practices..105
Football Specific Speed Training...106
1: Pass and Jockey, Zig-Zag Runs, Acceleration, and Deceleration..................107
2: Slalom Runs, Dribble + 1v1 Passive Jockey (Circuit).............................108
3: Passing + Speed and Agility Exercises in a Circuit...............................109
4: Maximum Sprints to Attack and Defend Crosses in 2v2 Situation................110
5: Speed and Agility Circuit with Finishing in Three Goals with GKs...............111
6: Speed and Agility Exercises + 2v2 (+GKs) Duel Game............................112
7: Dribble, Shoot & Sprint in a Group Finishing Practice...........................113

Small Sided Possession Practices..114
1: Playing Forwards in a Two Zone Directional Game................................115
2: Regain Possession in a 4v4 (+4) Three Team Competition Game................116

Small Sided Games..117
Small Sided Games - Example: 4 (+4) v 4 (+4) + GKs...............................118
1: Forward Movement to Break Lines in Intensive 2v2 (+6) +GK Game.............119
2: Resistance Conditioning Circuit and 3v3 (+6) +GKs Game.......................120
3: Using the Spare Man to Create Chances in a 4v4 (+1) Game....................121
4: High Intensity of Play in a 4v4 +GK Game.......................................122
5: Intensive Conditioning Game with 2 Mini Goals + Large Goal & GK.............123
6: Intensive Conditioning in a 4v4 (+4) +GK Game.................................124
7: Intensive Conditioning in a 4 (+4) v 4 (+4) +GK Game..........................125

WEDNESDAY Training Day:
Speed Endurance - 3 Days Until Match (MD +4/-3)..........................126
Collective Team Principle Training and Speed Endurance Development...............127
Physical and Physiological Focus..128
Technical and Tactical Focus..132
Game Stimulus Response for Collective Team Coaching Principles Game Type.......133
Fundamental Concepts of Collective Principle Training and Speed Endurance Development............133

WEDNESDAY Training Day Practices:
Speed Endurance - 3 Days Until Match (MD +4/-3) 134

Speed Endurance Warm-Up Practices 135
1: Slalom, Mobility, and Lunge Walk "Shuttles" with Poles & Hurdles 136
2: Dribble, Stop, Run, Turn, Accelerate and Pass Variations 137
3: Running with the Ball "Shuttles" with Variations 138
4: Dribble, Diagonal Passing, and Recover Warm-up Circuit 139

Extensive Technical Practices 140
1: Timing of Movement to Receive in a "Y" Shape (One-Two + Give & Go) 141
2: Quick Feet and Lay-offs in a Technical Pass and Move Drill 142
3: Pass Inside to Outside at Speed in a Practice with Middle Players 143
4: Fast Combination Play in a Pass & Move Drill with Final "Give & Go" 144
5: Quick Feet and Timing of Movement to Receive in a Passing Circuit 145
6: Switching Play Through Centre in a Square Drill with Middle Players 146
7: Progressive Passing with Lay-offs in a Positional Passing Practice 147
8: Speed Exercises and Patterns of Play in a Tactical Rotational Drill 148

Speed Endurance Conditioning Practices 149
Football Specific Conditioning 150
Technical / Tactical Conditioning 151
The Effect of Two Speed Endurance Training Regimes on the Performance of Football Players 152
1: Explosive Sprinting, Jogging and High Speed Running 153
2: Slalom Run or Dribble and Pass + 45m Sprints 154
3: Dribble and Pass, High Speed Run, and Recover 155
4: Crossing and Finishing + Dribble and Shoot 156
5: Agility, Running with Ball, Finish, Jog, and Final Sprint 157
6: Dribbling, Passing, and Finishing in a Sprinting Circuit 158
7: Attacking Wave in Pairs on a Full Pitch 159
8: 3-Player Passing Combination, Run in Behind & Finish 160
9: Continuous Sprints in a 2v2 Duel Transition Cycle 161
10: Pressing in Tactical Shape + 6-Second Counter Attack 162

Large Sided Possession Practices 163
1: Positional Shape Game with Mannequin Gates (9v9 +2) 164
2: Tactical 9v9 (+2) Directional Theme Game with 4 Progressive Zones 165
3: Positional and Directional Build-up Practice with Receiving GKs 166
4: Switch After Winning the Ball in a 10v10 Game with Split Halves 167
5: Build-up Play from Back to Front in an End to End Game with GKs 168
6: Tactical Three Zone Themed Game with Two Phases 169

Large Sided Games in Large Area 170
1: Fast Decision Making in a 9v9 (+GKs) Game within a Narrow Pitch 171
2: Tactical Three Zone Game with "Pushing Up" Rule 172
3: Box to Box Area Tactical Game 173
4: Tactical Game Focus on a Full Pitch 174

THURSDAY Training Day:
Reaction Speed - 2 Days Until Match (MD +5/-2) 175

Unit Principle Training and Reaction Speed Development 176
Physical and Physiological Focus 177
Technical and Tactical Focus 179
Game Stimulus Response for Unit Principle Game Type 180
Fundamental Concepts of Unit Principle Training and Reaction Speed Development 180

THURSDAY Training Day Practices:
Reaction Speed - 2 Days Until Match (MD +5/-2) 181

Reaction Speed Warm-Up Practices 182
1: Dead Leg & Lateral Runs, Rapid Feet, and Sprints Circuit 183
2: React to Signal, Fast Feet, and Sprint in a Speed Exercise 184

Intensive Technical Practices 185
6: One-Two Combinations and Timing of Third Man Run 186
7: Double "Give & Go" + Sprint Forward for Through Pass in a Diamond 187
8: Short Combinations with Lay-offs in an End to End Pass & Move Drill 188
9: Breaking the Lines in a Continuous End to End Pass & Move Drill 189
10: Incisive Diagonal Passing Circuit with Pattern Variations 190

Reaction Speed Conditioning Practices 191
1: Quick Reactions to Signals + Race to the Pole 192
2: Agility Work with Hurdles + React and Race to the Cone 193

Medium Sided Possession Practices 194
Small vs. Large Area Possession Comparison 195
1: Creating Space in a 5v5 Game with "No-Go" Middle Circle 196
2: Complete 6 Passes and Move in a Four Box Competition Game 197
3: Play Through the Middle in a 5v5 (+2) Game with Central Zone 198
4: Double 3v3 (+1) Two Zone Directional Possession Game 199
5: Secure Possession After Winning the Ball in a Transitional Game 200
6: Create Space and Play Through Press in a 6v6 Tactical Game 201
7: Breaking Lines in an End to End Two Zone Game with GKs 202
8: Beating the Press in a Transitional Three Team Game 203
9: Switch After Winning the Ball in an 8v8 Game with Split Halves 204
10: Intensive Possession Game with Progressively Increasing Numbers 205
11: Dynamic 8v8 (+2) Possession Game with Varying Conditions 206
12: Fast Defensive Transition to Press Ball in a Dynamic Game 207

Medium Sided Games 208
Medium Sided Games - Example: 5 (+5) v 5 (+5) + GKs - 30 x 35 m 209
1: Counter Attacking in a Three Team 5v5v5 (+GKs) Game 210
2: Playing Through the Thirds in a 6v6 (+2) +GKs Three Zone Game 211
3: Counter Attacking at Speed with Purpose in a 7v7v7 (+GKs) Game 212
4: Switching Play and Forward Passing with Outside Support Players 213

5: Maintain Possession and Fast Defensive Transition - 8v8 (+2) Game 214
6: Play Forward and Break the Lines - Narrow 7v7 (+2) +GKs Game........................... 215
7: Play Through the Thirds in a Progressive Three Zone Game.................................. 216
8: Create Space and Overloads for Crossing on a Wide Pitch 217

FRIDAY Training Day: Pre-Match Activation - 1 Day Until Match (MD +6/-1) 218

Pre-Match Activation Training Day.. 219
Pre-Match Activation.. 220
Fundamental Concepts of Pre-Match Activation Training 221
Analysis of a 6-Week Training Mesocycle & Positional Quantification in Elite European Football Players... 222

FRIDAY Training Day Practices:
Pre-Match Activation - 1 Day Until Match (MD +6/-1) 223

Resistance Warm-Up Practices 224
3: Lateral Hurdles, One-Two, In-and-Out Movements + Sprint Circuit 225
4: Hurdles, Slalom Runs, and Side-Shuffles in a Dynamic Circuit 226

Reaction Speed Conditioning Practices.. 227
3: Rebound Pass, Lateral Foot Speed + Sprint to Cone 228
4: Agility and 4-Player Reactive Speed Square 229
5: Reactive Sprints on the Coach's Signal 230

Large Sided Games in Small / Medium Area 231
LSG (Small Area) 1: Fast Decision Making in an 8v8 (+GKs) Game within a Narrow Pitch.................. 232
LSG (Small Area) 2: Positional Possession and Transitions in a 9v9 (+2) Tactical Game................... 233
LSG (Small Area) 3: Fast Decision Making in a 9v9 (+1) +GKs Game 234
LSG (Medium Area) 1: Build-up from Back to Front in a Four Zone 8v8 (+2) +GKs Game................. 235
LSG (Medium Area) 2: Positional Six Goal 9v9 (+2) Game with a Tactical Focus 236

Advance Your Career. Become a Better Coach with International Soccer Science & Performance Federation (ISSPF): Accredited & Endorsed Online Football Science & Performance Coaching Courses.... 237
Adam Owen Performance Consultancy 238
Additional Reading Reference 239

DR. ADAM OWEN: Coach Profile
UEFA Pro Coaching Licence

Dr. Adam Owen
PhD, MPhil, BSc HONS

@adamowen1980

www.aoperformance.co.uk

Credentials (Coaching and Academic):

- **UEFA Professional Coaching Licence**
  - Football Association of Wales (FAW)

- **FA Youth Trainers Award**
  - The England Football Association (FA)

- **Doctor of Philosophy (PhD) in Sport Science and Coaching** - Claude Bernard Lyon.1 University, Lyon, France

- **Master of Philosophy Degree (MPhil) in Sport and Exercise Science** - Glyndwr University, Wrexham, Wales, UK

- **BSc (HONS) Degree in Sport and Exercise Science**
  - Glyndwr University, Wrexham, Wales, UK

Football Positions:

- **Technical Director**, KKS Lech Poznań, Poland

- **High-Performance Director and Technical Advisor**, Seattle Sounders FC, USA (MLS)

- **High-Performance Director and Assistant Coach**, Hebei China Fortune FC, China

- **Head Coach**, KS Lechia Gdańsk, Poland

- **Sport Science and Fitness Coach**, Wales National Team

- **Assistant Manager**, FC Servette, Switzerland

- **High-Performance Director and Assistant Manager**, Sheffield United FC, England

- **Head of Sport Science and Performance**, Rangers FC, Scotland

- **Head of Sport Science and Fitness**, Sheffield Wednesday FC, England

- **Head of Academy Performance and Technical Coach**, Celtic FC, Scotland

- **Academy Head Coach**, Wrexham FC, Wales

- **Player**, Wrexham FC, Wales

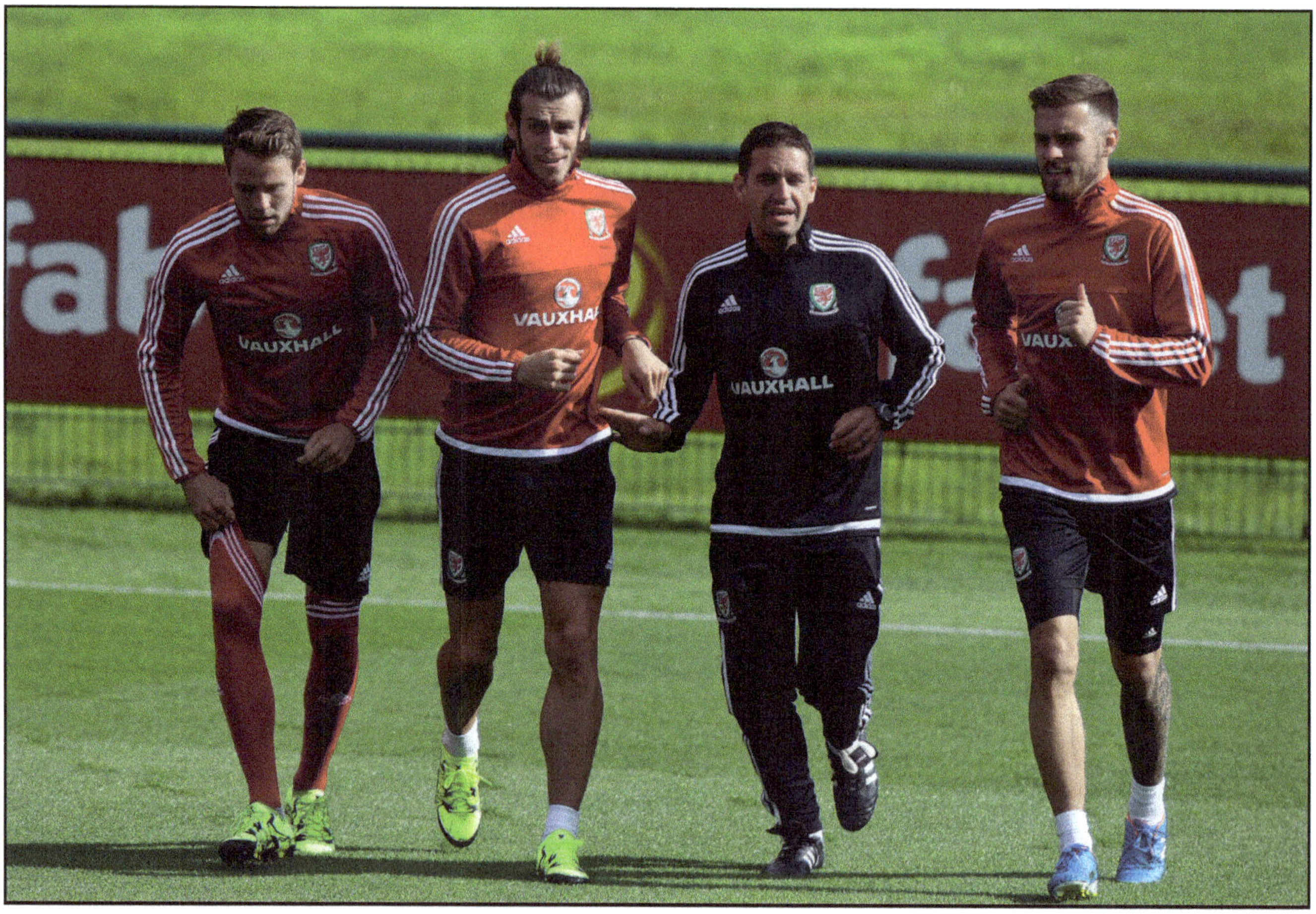
VAUXHALL
VAUXHALL
VAUXHALL

Energa
AO
ENERGY DRINK

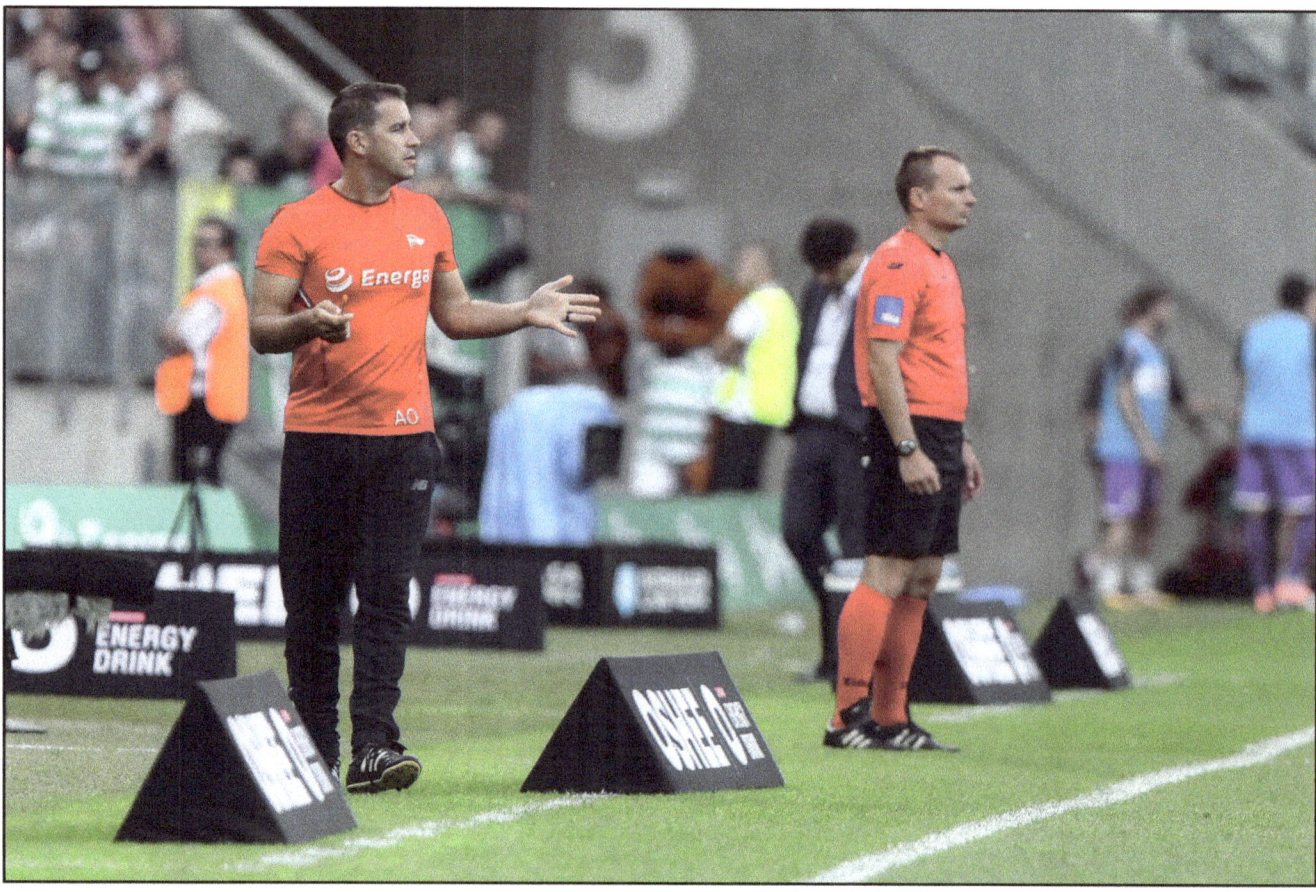

Further Roles, Development and Associations:

- **Associate Professorship** at Wrexham Glyndwr University, Wrexham, Wales

- **Associate Researcher (Football Science and Performance)** for Lyon.1 University, Lyon, France

- **UEFA Professional Licence and UEFA A Licence Coach Educator** for the England Football Association

- **UEFA Professional Licence Coach Educator and Coach Developer** for the Finland Football Federation

- **Faculty Member and Lecturer** for the International Soccer Science and Performance Federation (ISSPF) www.ISSPF.com

- **Over 85+ papers published in international peer-reviewed journals including:** Journals of Sport Sciences, International Journal of Sports Medicine, Journal of Strength and Conditioning Research, International Sport Science and Coaching Journal, and many more...

- **Football Consultant Role** with SL Benfica

- **Head of Research and Development** for 5 years at SL Benfica

- **Key Note Speaker** at various international level conferences and congresses

DR. ADAM OWEN: Author
Bestselling Football Conditioning Book Set

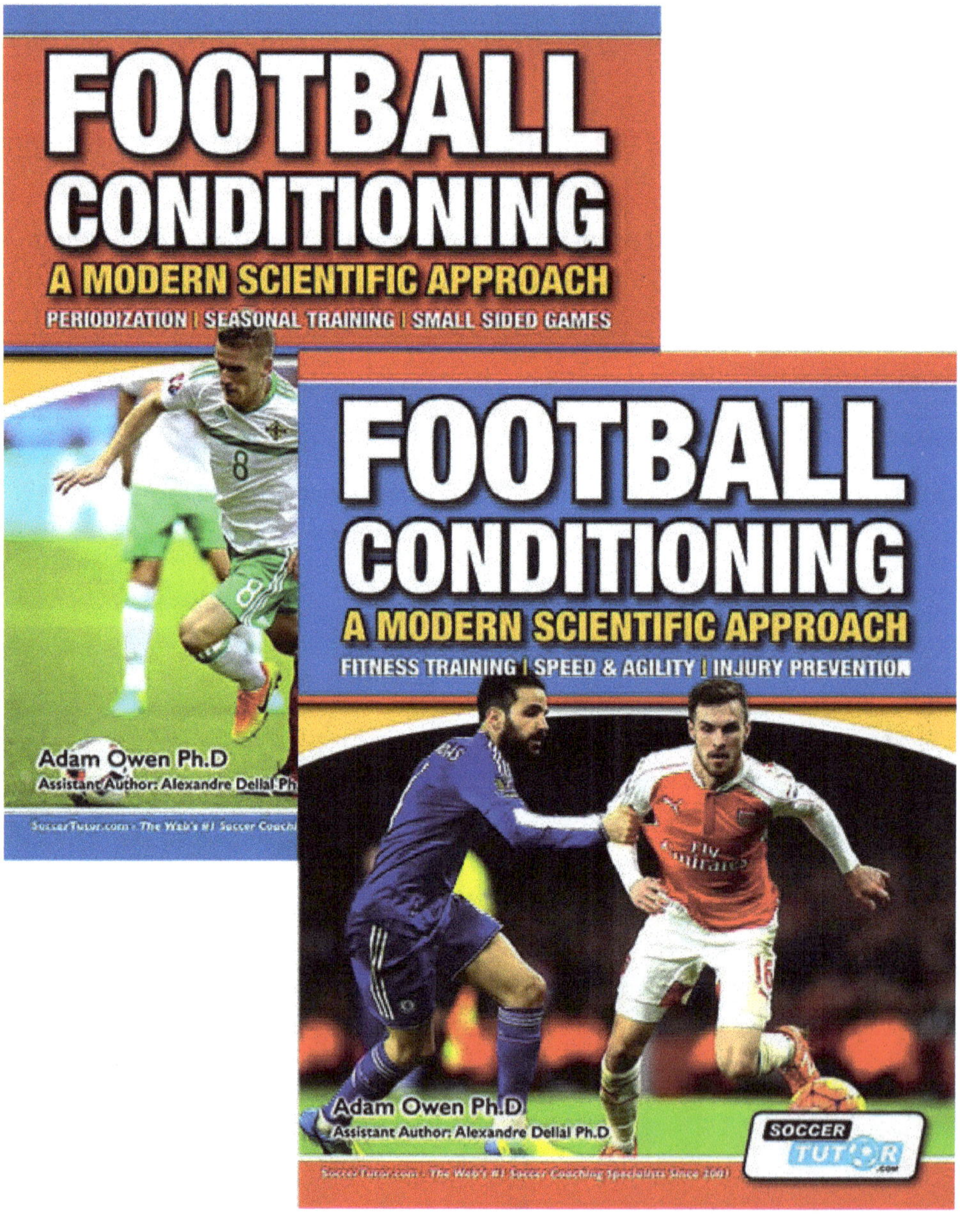

Available in English, German, and Spanish (Print & eBook)
Included: 130 Topics, 54 Practices, and 24 Exercises (U15-Pro)

www.SoccerTutor.com
info@soccertutor.com

DR. ADAM OWEN: Career Overview of High Performance Expert

Throughout his career, **Dr. Adam Owen** has developed a unique blend of practical coaching experience (**UEFA Pro Coaching Licence holder**) **with a very specific and high-level academic profile in Football Science and Coaching**. Obtaining a Ph.D in the field of Sport Science & Coaching from Lyon.1 University, France, he also holds an associate Professorship role with Glyndwr University, Wrexham in Wales, in addition to continuing as an associate researcher in France and working in the professional game.

Adam's previous **coaching roles** have seen him work across:

- Elite youth level
- Senior level
- UEFA Champions League
- UEFA Europa League
- European club football
- Elite level International football

At the age of 26, Adam was part of the **Rangers FC (Scotland)** management staff who reached the **UEFA Cup Final** in 2008 and remained at the club for seven and half years, gaining valuable experience preparing teams for successful league and cup campaigns in addition to several UEFA Champions League campaigns.

In the summer of 2014, Adam accepted the opportunity to move to **FC Servette (Switzerland)** and experience working abroad at a European club whilst also retaining his role with the **Wales National Team (2009-2018)**.

In 2016, Adam was part of the backroom and coaching staff that reached the **UEFA Euro 2016 Semi-Final** in France, before then becoming **Head Coach in Lechia Gdansk (Poland)**.

Following his experience as a Head Coach at the age of 37 in one of Europe's top leagues, Adam took the opportunity to move to the Chinese Superleague as a **High-Performance Director**. After a successful 2 year period, just missing out on the Asian Champions League position, Adam joined **MLS Champions Seattle Sounders FC (USA)** as **Technical Advisor** and **High-Performance Coaching Director**. After a 2 year coaching period in the USA, winning the **MLS Western Conference League Title** and reaching the MLS Cup Final, Adam returned to Europe to begin a **Technical Director** role at **Lech Poznań (Poland)**.

Working as an **elite coach educator at UEFA Professional level** within the **England FA** and **Finland FA** to name but a few, Adam has huge experience across many roles within the game:

- Playing
- Coaching
- High Performance Expert
- Manager
- Technical Director

Adam has been able to combine his practical and scientific understanding and experience of the game, in order to mould a specific coaching philosophy outlined in this book.

Adam has published over 90+ football science and coaching articles, book chapters and books, remaining very active in the development of football based research at the elite level, whilst also being a faculty member of the globally recognised International Soccer Science and Performance Federation (www.ISSPF.com), which delivers high-level international online football science and performance courses.

He has been able to utilise previous **European, Asian and North American domestic and inter-continental success to develop a justifiable, research based coaching method in order to maximise individual and group performance within elite professional football**.

INTRODUCTION:
Training Sessions for Peak Performance

Throughout the last decade or so, the training and match play demands imposed upon elite level football players have grown enormously in order to meet the high conditioning requirements of increased fixtures, travel and subsequent domestic, continental and international based competitions.

In order for players to cope with increased repetitive match related demands at near maximal performance levels during competition, the desire and need of coaches to understand, control, analyse, and eventually manipulate training sessions has increased.

As the modern game continues to rapidly evolve across various aspects of the game, a greater range of tactical understanding, situations and subsequent playing demands require players to have greater physiological capacity, in addition to an enhanced psychological understanding in and out of possession compared with previous decades (Križaj et al., 2019).

It is well-documented that **football is now played at a quicker pace** with the ball being in play ~12 minutes more than early reports in the 1990's, coupled with the fact **significantly more high-intensity actions and movements are performed during the game** (Mohr et al., 2003).

One such report (Barnes et al., 2014) in this area has shown how at the very elite level:

1. **High-intensity running distance has increased by 30% since the early 2000's**
2. **Sprint demands have nearly doubled since the early 2000's**

To positively influence performance levels, the most efficient methods to improve individuals or teams to the best of their ability must be used. To achieve this, the **training structure must be planned and prepared adequately through justifiable methodologies**, to therefore **maximise levels of performance**.

Coaches must ensure:

- **Players progress in-line with contemporary and innovative changes within the game**
- **Drive players to the next level from a technical, tactical and physical perspective (primary aim of a coach)**
- **Maximise the training time and efficiency of the coaching process**
- **Maximise the complex nature of football development in respect of technical and tactical abilities**

Psychosocial and cognitive skills place a huge multi-dimensional demand in the planning and training session design phase. Throughout the season, technical and performance practitioners consistently search for best practice in order to justify:

1. **Training objectives**
2. **Apply weekly tapering strategies**
3. **Apply specific training programs to achieve specific outcomes** (incorporating all the vital aspects of performance development)

When trying to apply a holistic coaching process (where every aspect of a player's development is taken into account), it is vitally important to select a coaching process or approach with the target of providing the best decisions for performance development.

When discussing a holistic coaching approach within the game and maximising player performance as a coach, it is necessary to continually expand the understanding of the game using research as a way of making better decisions, justifications and evolution. Not only can 'football science' research assist in making better coach-related decisions, but it can also lead to the development of new theory or methodologies to drive the game forward.

Various research into training methodology, nutrition, psychology, as well as the testing and monitoring of players, has recently led to managers, head coaches, performance coaches and technical support staff being able to produce much greater efficiency.

Irrespective of the level of players being coached within the game, all coaches face the very relevant question based on the various challenges needed to gain results:

- **What do I need to do in order to get the best possible performance from my group of players?**
- **What can I change or improve to maximise players collectively as individuals and subsequently as a team?**
- **What gives me the best possible chance of succeeding as a coach?**

Addressing these questions is something all individuals within the game want to achieve. In order to attempt to discuss this within a football environment, one of the most debated and hot topics include detailed discussions around:

- **Training Periodization**
- or **Tapering Strategies**
- and **Training Methodology**

The intentions behind this book are as follows:

- Utilise **applied football science and performance coaching** research, in collaboration with a football specific methodology **which can be used across a range of coaching levels**.
- Engage coaches with a thirst to evolve or understand more.
- This book provides a **unique blend of modern football coaching practices, with an innovative coaching theory and methodology**.
- Expose coaches to various topics such as the **development of a coaching methodology, understanding what is meant by 'game model'** in a football context, and teach a **game based training approach**.
- Show **how to build training sessions**.
- Teach to **practically apply the training content**.
- Consider and demonstrate **how each training aspect fits into the flow of the session and training week**.
- Show the actual demands imposed on players within the training and competitive environment (so you can adequately prepare the coaching process).
- **Training Load Management** - an overview of what coaches can do to ensure their players remain in the best state to **optimise performance, whilst reducing injury risk at the same time**.
- Gaining the balance of fitness vs. freshness to perform on a match-day.

Benefits of the "Football Periodization to Maximise Performance" Methodology

Key point

If the daily training content is poorly planned or managed through an insufficient methodological approach, poor performance occurs with the players insufficiently conditioned and significantly higher rates of injury.

What changes have there been in the last decade?

Individuals tasked with the development of football players have seen the understanding, progression and implementation of strength and conditioning, speed development and high-intensity football specific endurance training increase exponentially over the last decade. Furthermore, that has happened directly in accordance with growth in the players' tactical understanding of different systems of play.

What are the benefits?

- Enhancing the coaches' knowledge across a range of coaching and high-performance topics
- Maximising the use of specific training games and practices in the training week (microcycle)
- Understanding the benefits of tapering strategies = players arrive in optimal condition for competition!

The overall picture of the coaching process

Maximising the physical profile and status of players is only a part of the performance target, as from a coach's perspective, building an integrated training process to a level where the physical, technical and tactical outcomes seamlessly fit into the development of the player or team, is fundamental to obtain performance progression within the coaching process.

FOREWORD by Steve McClaren

- **FIFA Technical Advisor**
- **England National Team Head Coach**
- **Assistant Manager of Manchester United** (1 x Champions League, 3 x Premier League, 1 x FA Cup including 1999 Treble)
- **Middlesbrough FC Manager**
- **FC Twente Manager**
- **VfL Wolfsburg Manager**
- **Newcastle United FC Manager**
- **Derby County FC Manager**

"Throughout my career in the game as a coach, assistant manager or manager, one of the greatest shifts within the professional side of the game has come through the integration of performance science and training methodology.

Improving the performance of players and trying to gain a competitive advantage is something every coach desires.

The developments and evolution of **modern coaching education has been fundamental**, and becomes more evident amongst the elite teams when it comes to the **tactical and physical preparation, training methodology** and subsequent **match performance**.

Understanding the tactical demands of the game is significant to all individuals wanting to improve their work in the game. However, how we train or coach players to perform in the best possible condition should be the key target of all coaches.

Technical coaching staff, as well as performance specialists, will enjoy the applied coaching focus, methodology and topics discussed within this book.

Maximising the key coaching link between the technical, tactical and physical details of the game, **this book perfectly blends the research, coaching education and current trends within the game with practical integrated coaching details**.

As a result, this book provides a **great coaching resource for all individuals wanting to develop their knowledge of the game**."

Player and Content References

Javier Mascherano

- Current Argentina Under 20 National Team Manager
- Former FC Barcelona, Liverpool FC, and Argentina National Team player

"Adam and I started working together when he arrived in China. He is a great professional and person who shows a high level of passion and quality within his working methodology in football.

I am grateful to him for the time we were working together, as he was a great help to me both professionally and personally. We remain in contact, and I hope we will get the chance to work together again in the future."

Gareth Bale

- Real Madrid and Wales National Team player

"Adam is someone I have always trusted and whose opinion and advice I trust. We remained in constant communication between international duties and always had an excellent personal and professional relationship.

Having worked for so long together at the elite international level of the game, it shows his professional quality and worth.

Adam is someone who has helped me through my career and is someone I always enjoyed working with on a day-to-day basis."

Aaron Ramsey

- Juventus FC and Wales National Team player

"After knowing and working with Adam for many years internationally, I consider him to be a top professional in his area of expertise, and someone with whom I have been able to improve different areas of my game, due to his methodology and knowledge."

Nicolás Lodeiro

- Former Ajax, Boca Juniors and Uruguay player
- Current Seattle Sounders FC and MLS All-Star player

"Adam came to the MLS and implemented a first class training structure which was a big part of our club's success.

Adam's coaching approach was very detailed and one that I enjoyed working within due to it being very football specific and high-intensity. His integrated coaching methodology, training sessions and preparation helped me significantly through his time at the club."

Dr. Andreas Schlumberger, PhD

- Current Head of Recovery and Performance at Liverpool FC
- Former Head of Rehabilitation and Prevention at FC Bayern Munich

"Adam provides an outstanding mixture of applied research, practical application and tremendous experience in the world of high-performance football.

With this very unique approach, he will continue to have a big impact on criteria-based and functional work in all applied areas of performance development and coaching in football."

Dr. Jorge Candel, MD

- Currently Head of Medicine, Clinica Tecma, Spain
- Former Head of Medical Department and Club Doctor for CF Valencia

"Having worked with Adam for a number of years and seen his approach to both coaching and performance science, he is someone I feel will remain at the top of his profession for many years to come.

The contents of this book are of great interest to all individuals interested in increasing their knowledge of the game from a practical and academic perspective."

CHAPTER 1

Coaching Methodology to Maximise Performance

Chapter 1: Coaching Methodology to Maximise Performance

Coaching Methodology to Maximise Performance

Coaches, performance experts and physical specialists involved with the preparation of football players constantly research methods or ways to analyse and examine the training loads, **aiming to maximise performance**.

Maximising performance is determined by a great number of factors within football. However, at the elite level of the game, these are the <u>**3 key starting points**</u>:

1. **Balancing fitness vs. freshness**
2. **Encouraging physical robustness**
3. **Mental resilience**

Exposing players to key physical, psychological, technical and tactical demands across the training week is the fundamental aspect of player preparation.

This involves not only **assessing training periodization and tapering strategies**, but also recognising and justifying the distinct requirements and effects imposed on players through various training scenarios (Owen et al., 2014), the various positional demands, and the conditioning needs of the individual within competitive match-play (Owen et al., 2016).

Game Demands: Intersections and Fully Integrated Training Approach - Adapted from Bradley, et al., (2010)

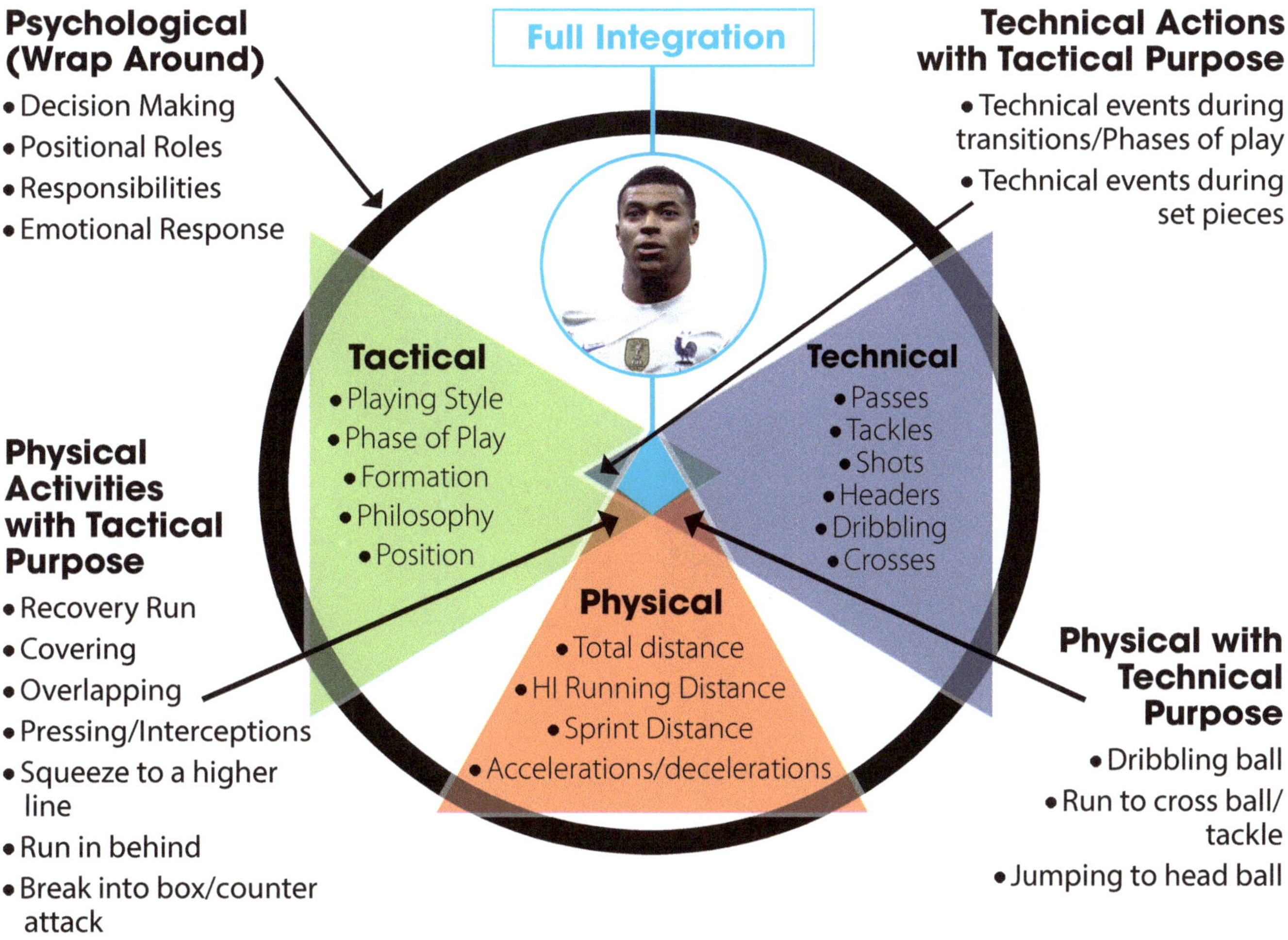

Psychological (Wrap Around)
- Decision Making
- Positional Roles
- Responsibilities
- Emotional Response

Full Integration

Technical Actions with Tactical Purpose
- Technical events during transitions/Phases of play
- Technical events during set pieces

Physical Activities with Tactical Purpose
- Recovery Run
- Covering
- Overlapping
- Pressing/Interceptions
- Squeeze to a higher line
- Run in behind
- Break into box/counter attack

Tactical
- Playing Style
- Phase of Play
- Formation
- Philosophy
- Position

Technical
- Passes
- Tackles
- Shots
- Headers
- Dribbling
- Crosses

Physical
- Total distance
- HI Running Distance
- Sprint Distance
- Accelerations/decelerations

Physical with Technical Purpose
- Dribbling ball
- Run to cross ball/tackle
- Jumping to head ball

Chapter 1: Coaching Methodology to Maximise Performance

Training Load, Adaptation, and Training Week (Microcycle) Tapering

Research surrounding the training session design and microcycle structuring has provided evidence of how players in different positions reveal varied outcomes in terms of key physical metrics monitored:

- Total Distance Covered (TDC)
- High Speed Running (HSR)
- Sprinting

It is **vitally important to understand how training sessions or coaching instructions influence these metrics, and this should be taken under consideration when programming the structure of the weekly microcycle** (Owen et al., 2017; Malone et al., 2018; Martin-Garcia et al., 2018).

Understanding that the **internal load responses of training is what causes significant adaptations is an integral foundation for any coach at any level of the game**, based on the impact of fatigue, recovery and the physiological adaptation process that occurs post-training.

Adaptation: The process of the body getting used to a particular training program through repeated exposure.

The microcycle and training structure is dictated by the physical recovery status and the conditioning requirements of the players in relation to the upcoming match. **Microcycle tapering strategies enable players to be in a better prepared physical, psychological and physiological state for competitive matches** (van Winkle et al., 2014; Malone et al., 2016; Fessi et al., 2016; Owen et al., 2017).

Load Management of the Weekly Microcycle (Training Week)

- Focus post-match = **Recovery**
- Research = **48hrs post-match key** to reduce physical, psychological, and biochemical fatigue
- Impact of **daily session** on the next day
- Cyclical basis and raised importance of **session design**

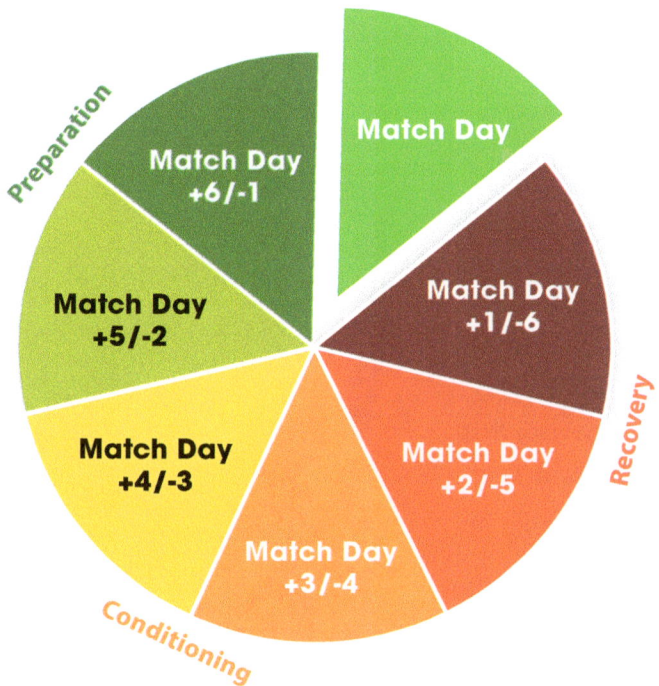

Correct loading strategy through the week employed to:

1. Cause adaptation
2. Recovery for match day

Chapter 1: Coaching Methodology to Maximise Performance

The Link Between Training Load and Recovery, and the Supercompensation Theory - www.pponline.co.uk/recovery

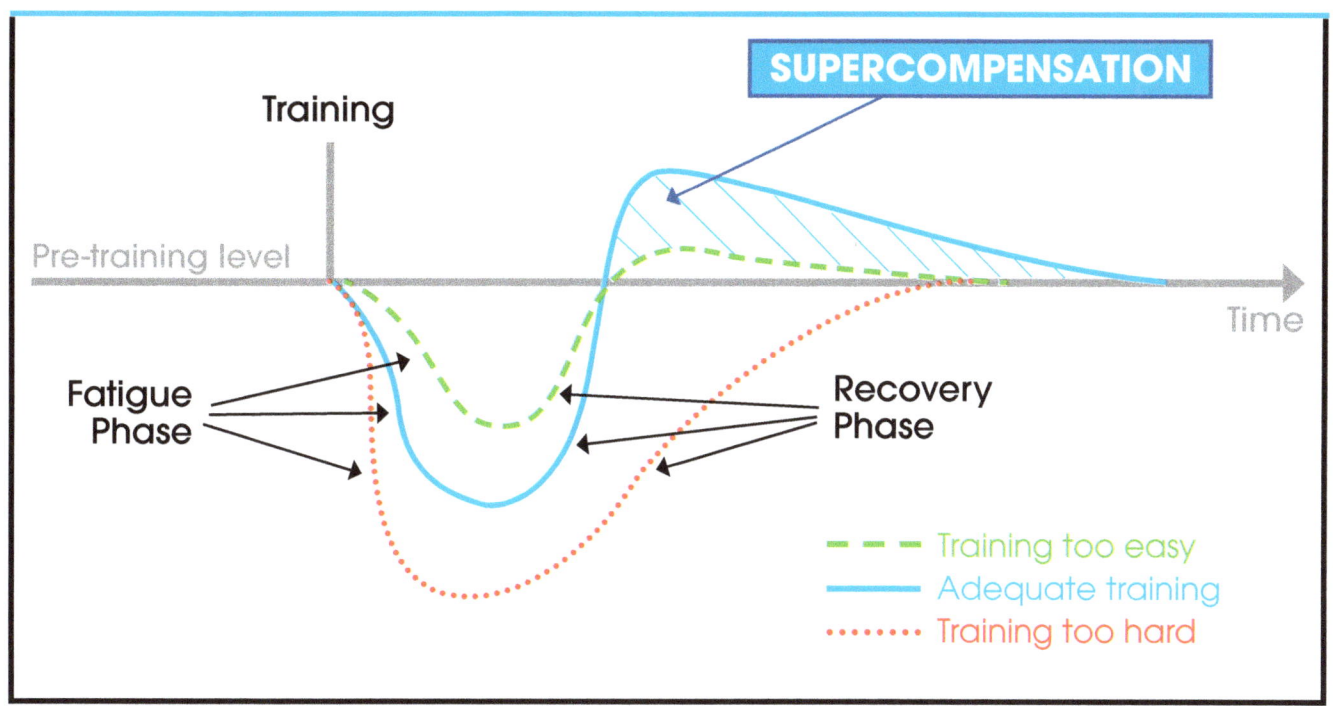

The Supercompensation Cycle

From a coaching perspective, and more importantly when developing a coaching methodology, there are many theories that are discussed within academic literature. However, one of the most fundamental concepts that should be understood irrespective of the coaching process employed is the **Supercompensation Theory**.

In a publication by Issurin (2010), it was indicated that in order to understand the concept of training methodology, planning and structure, the basic 'load-recovery' interaction shown in the figure above has to be a solid foundation.

Phase 1: The supercompensation cycle starts when the player performs a training session of adequate load (Phase 1) to cause a specific adaptation of physical load. This load serves as a stimulus which causes a reaction, which culminates in an element of fatigue. There is then a subsequent limitation of the player's work capability.

Phase 2: Having caused a specific stress to the player, the second step (Phase 2) is the direct knock on fatigue effect as shown above. It is here that the coach needs to have the knowledge, understanding and awareness to ensure sufficient recovery.

This **recovery period** is the direct link to the adaptation response, which **ensures an increase in the player's working capacity towards the end of this phase**, reaching pre-training levels.

Supercompensation Phase: If the stimulus has been at the right level for the individual's physical capacity, then their capability continues to grow and enhance, **progressing beyond their previous capacity** or pre-training level and achieving **'supercompensation' phase** (Issurin, 2010).

Developing further from the earlier reports of the supercompensation theory, it was concluded that a structure involving a number of workouts can be performed in close proximity with the athlete in a fatigued state (Matveyev, 1981).

Chapter 1: Coaching Methodology to Maximise Performance

We need to highlight that the supercompensation effect and training adaptation process only becomes prevalent if the balance between training load and recovery (as shown in the figure on the previous page) is sufficient.

The integrated approach utilises the on-pitch training details, testing and training load assessment, and physiological and sport science monitoring tools suggested in this book. It is based on a working methodology that has been employed and evolved over time. The successful implementation of this training model has been ingrained within different domestic, European, continental and international competitions (i.e. UEFA Champions League, UEFA Europa League, International competition, North American and Asian elite level competition).

This particular methodology described is based on an **Integrated Adaptation Cycle** (see figure below):

1. Football Training Stimulus ⇒
2. Adaptation ⇒
3. Improved Capacity ⇒
4. Improved Capability/Work Rate Potential ⇒
5. = Continuation of Adaptation Cycle

Adaptation Cycle Concept

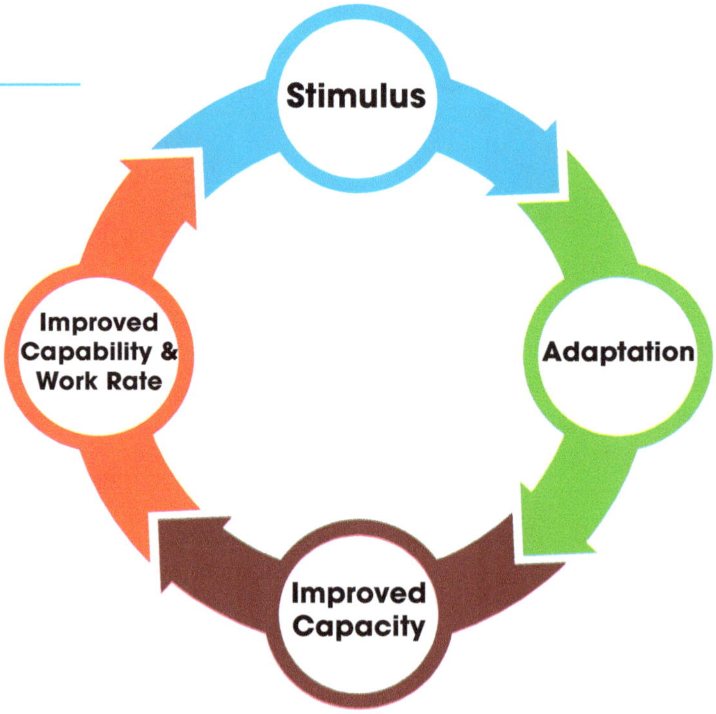

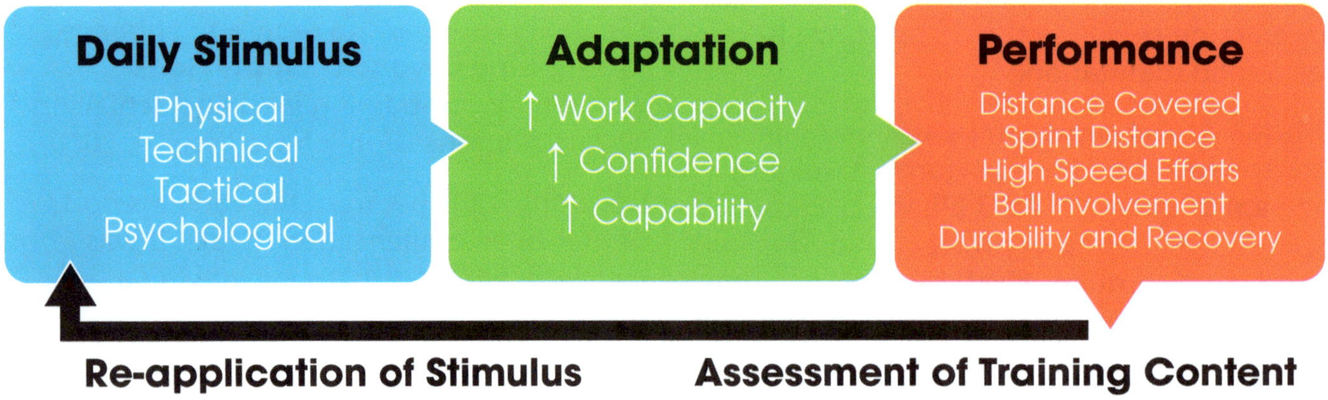

Stimulus → Adaptation → Improved Capacity → Improved Capability & Work Rate → (cycle)

Daily Stimulus	Adaptation	Performance
Physical Technical Tactical Psychological	↑ Work Capacity ↑ Confidence ↑ Capability	Distance Covered Sprint Distance High Speed Efforts Ball Involvement Durability and Recovery

Re-application of Stimulus ← → **Assessment of Training Content**

CHAPTER 2
Developing a Game Model

Chapter 2: Developing a Game Model

GAME MODEL: External Factors Influencing Game Model Development
- Adapted from Mallo, 2015

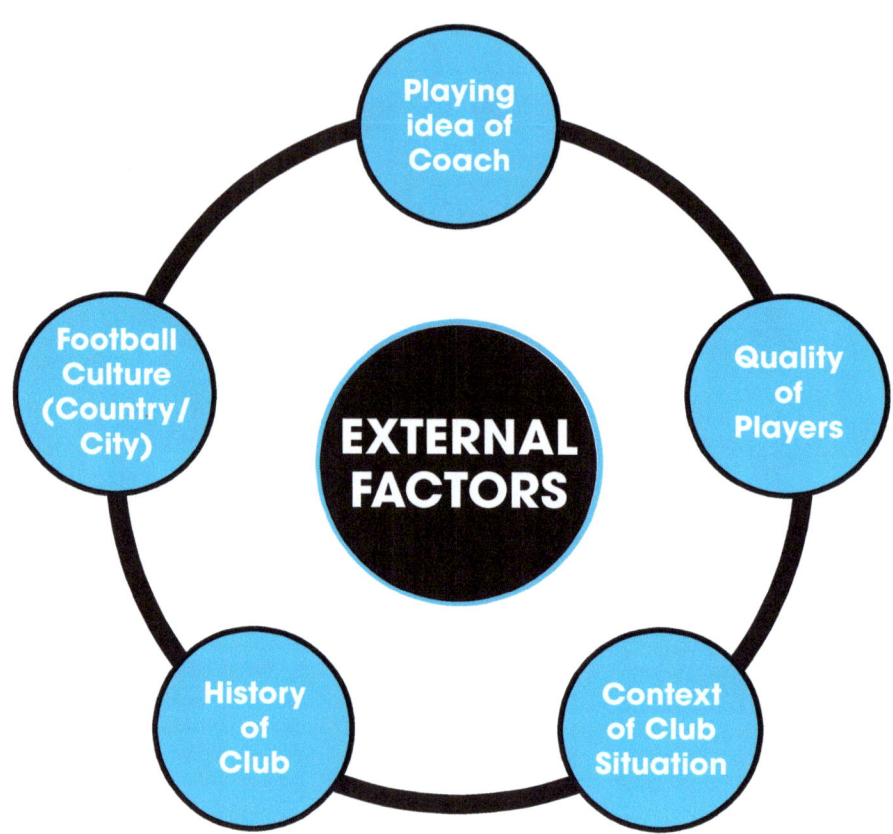

Playing Idea of the Coach: The playing strategy employed by the coach or coaching staff is generally based on the way they want the game to be played, or how they or the club view the game. The preferred style of play and formation (4-4-2, 3-4-3, 4-2-3-1, etc) outlines the perfect scenario when you don't have to consider external factors.

Football Culture (Country/Club): Mallo, (2015) described the cultural side of the game (where it is played) e.g. in Spain, it is about possession based football with high technical requirements for individuals.

History of Club: Tradition can create an expectancy around a team's chosen style of play and whether they should be playing a brand of football synonymous with the club.

Context of Club Situation: Other factors, such as the timing of a new management team taking over a club also has an effect. If it is pre-season, the coaching staff have a chance to develop a longer term process. If it is mid-season, quick results may be needed, which requires a change of philosophy and model to best suit the players at the club.

Quality of Players: The level of the players available for the coach on arrival may mean a change in the tactical strategy to best suit the players at that moment in time.

Developing the Game Model: After consideration of these external factors, it is from here that the head coach and coaching staff can develop the game model.

Chapter 2: Developing a Game Model

GAME MODEL: Positional, Unit, and Collective Principles Covered within the Microcycle (Training Week)

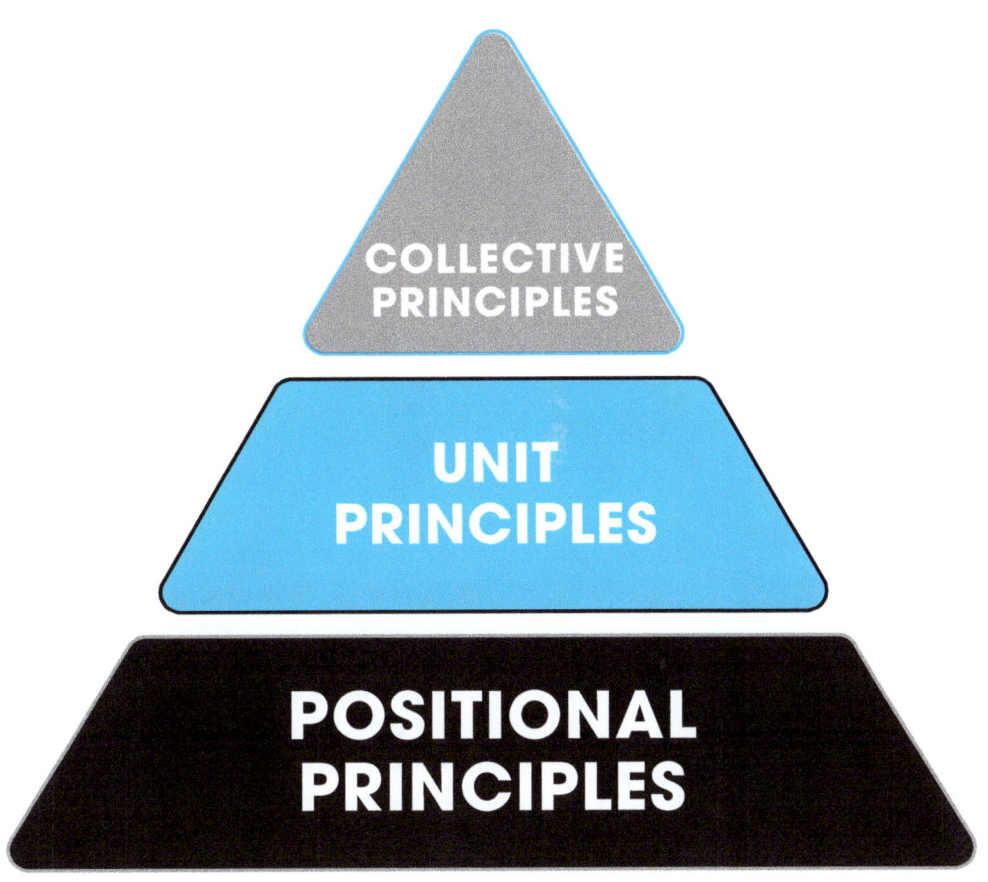

POSITIONAL PRINCIPLES

Key information around technical and tactical detail that will occur in **1v1, 2v2, and 3v3 scenarios** e.g. body shape, positional scanning requirements (defensive scanning vs. attacking scanning) angle of approach, opening passing lanes/closing passing lanes, supporting teammates, etc.

UNIT PRINCIPLES

Key information concerning the different **units (Defence-Midfield-Attack)** and the play that will occur in various game moments/situations e.g. distance between the lines, midfield rotations, switching play, counter movements to create space, etc.

COLLECTIVE PRINCIPLES

Key information for the **team approach** and what may be targeted as a collective e.g. rest or active defending, mid-block compactness, attacking transitions, tactical shape in and out of possession, having a clear vision depending on the area of the pitch, etc.

GAME MODEL: The Development Process within the Phases of the Game

The Game Phases

Within any competitive football game, ball possession changes hands and there are transitions between teams or individual players through possession related mistakes, interceptions, tackles, or set plays. As a direct consequence of this, every player within the game will find themselves within a specific situation defined as a 'game phase,' which includes attacking, defending, the attacking transition, the defensive transition, and set plays.

The **attacking and defensive phases can be very structured**, evident and with solid foundations, principals and conscious decision making objectives, set by the coaching staff as a collective or unit based function. However, the **transition phases of the game have been referred to as moments with no or minimal organisation**, and inclusive of chaotic behaviours (Cerezo, 2000). In addition, Barreira et al., (2010), suggests that transition periods in the game are chaotic with limited structure and made observations for how to improve them. He suggested that through training and by influencing key patterns of play, specific individual and collective movements, and decision making processes are a way of reducing the uncertainty in the transitions, and improving the effectiveness of managing the transition phases within games.

The Game Phases from a High Performance Perspective

As technical or performance related coaches, we now have a more detailed perception of an integrated coaching process, with a better understanding of the tactical dimensions of the game through a more teaching-learning-training (TLT) method (Garganta and Gréhaigne, 1999; Borges et al., 2017).

The training content should encompass an **integrated teaching, with guided understanding of the tactical requirements of positional, unit and collective principles** from the initiation of the coaching process in football. This is not to say training younger players should include detailed tactical information, but understanding basic defending and attacking principles may be an adequate starting point.

Developing an understanding of the game through the key positional roles and responsibilities as a collective organisation, whilst replicating the game phases to develop attacking/defensive decisions through tactical actions, is key for the integration of a specific game model.

In addition to a fuller understanding of the game phases, recent advancements through contemporary monitoring, analysis and testing equipment have been made. **Football coaching science has led to the evolution of a more research based way of maximising the efficiency of training.**

Chapter 2: Developing a Game Model

GAME MODEL: Coaching Framework to Impact Players' Decision Making

To master the key principles from a coaching and player perspective, in addition to clarifying the key decision making qualities and processes, we must assist the players with developing their capacity to:

1. Manage the game space
2. Understand other players' actions in certain similar scenarios
3. Impose a level of clarity to make better informed decisions
4. Problem solve in match-play scenarios based on training principles

Teoldo et al., (2021) proposed that as a result of defining specific principles within the training context, the tactical dimension of the game within a competitive environment can emerge from the interactions between key situations.

Based on these situations, **decision making demands team organisation, and will configure a collective identity over time** (Teoldo et al., 2021).

Defensive Principles (Out of Possession)

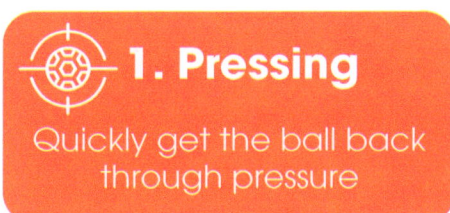

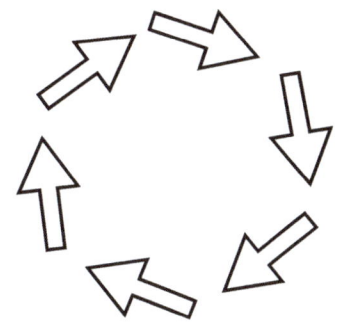

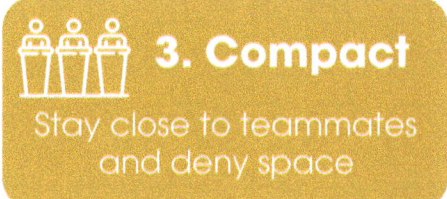

Chapter 2: **Developing a Game Model**

Attacking Principles (In Possession)

1. Creating Space
Create space for yourself and teammates

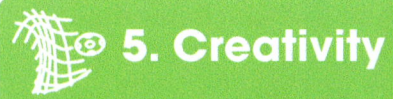
5. Creativity
"Magic" to create goal scoring opportunities

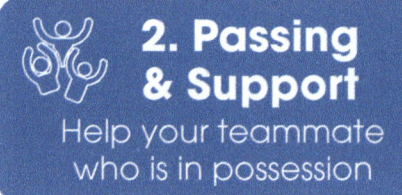
2. Passing & Support
Help your teammate who is in possession

5. Penetration
Play through gaps left by opponents

3. Movement & Mobility
Movement on & off ball

Chapter 2: Developing a Game Model

GAME MODEL: Phases of Play, Objectives, and the General, Operational, and Core Tactical Principles of the Game
- from Teoldo, et al., (2009)

GENERAL PRINCIPLES	Seek numerical superiority	Avoid numerical equality	Do not allow numerical inferiority
PHASES	**Attack (with the ball)**	*Transition from Attack to Defence and/or Defence to Attack*	**Defend (without the ball)**
OPERATIONAL PRINCIPLES	• Maintain ball possession • Build-up attacking actions • Progress through the opponent's half • Create shooting opportunities • Shoot on goal		• Prevent opponent's progression • Decrease opponent's playing space • Protect the team's goal • Deny shooting opportunities • Recover ball possession
CORE PRINCIPLES	**Penetration** • Destabilise the opponent's defensive organisation • Directly attack the opposite player or the opponent's goal • Create advantageous attacking situations in numerical and spatial terms **Attacking Coverage** • Support the player in possession by providing options to give sequence to the play • Decrease opponent's pressure on the player in possession • Create numerical superiority • Unbalance the opponent's defensive organisation • Ensure that ball possession is maintained **Depth Mobility** • Create actions to disrupt the opponent's defensive organisation • Positioning in a suitable space to score • Create in-depth passing options • Achieve ball control to give sequence to the attacking action (pass or shot)		**Delay** • Decrease the space the player in possession has for attacking action • Direct the progression of the player in possession • Block or delay the opponent's attack or counter-attack • Provide more time for defensive organisation • Restrict the ball carrier's passing options towards other opponents • Avoid dribbling moves that enable the opponent to progress in midfield towards the goal • Prevent shots on goal **Defensive Coverage** • Act as a new obstacle to the player in possession, in case he dribbles past the player trying to delay • Ensure and provide confidence to the player performing the delay tactic, in order to support his initiative in blocking the attacking actions of the player in possession

Chapter 2: Developing a Game Model

CORE PRINCIPLES		Transition from Attack to Defence and/or Defence to Attack	
	Width and Length • Use and increase the effective playing space of the team • Try to increase (extend) the distances between the opponent's positions • Make marking difficult for the opponents • Facilitate the attacking actions of the team • Move to a safer space • Win time to make adequate decision for a better subsequent action • Seek safe options through players in defensive positions to give sequence to the play		**Balance** • Ensure defensive stability in the area around the ball • Support teammates performing delays and defensive covering • Block potential passing options and mark potential players who could receive the ball • Press the player in possession and make an effort to recover the ball • Regain the ball and move it away from the zone where it was recovered quickly
	Attacking Unity • Midfield interplay and rotations to displace, move and disorganise the opponent's midfield • Allow team to attack in unity • Make the attacking actions performed in the key central area safer • Allow more players to play in the game's key central area		**Concentration** • Increase protection of the goal • Drive opponents attacking play towards safer areas • Increase pressure within the game's key central area
			Defensive Unity • Enable the team to defend in unity • Ensure the spacing, stability and dynamic synchronisation between the defensive, midfield, and attacking lines + between each player within those lines • Decrease the attacking possibilities of the opposition in width and depth • Ensure basic guidelines that influence the players' technical and tactical behaviours when positioned outside the game's key central area • Constantly balance or rebalance the relative strengths in the defensive organisation according to the game situation • Obstruct possible passing options for opponents that are in the key central area • Reduce the available playing space and utilise the offside rule • Enable involvement in a subsequent defensive action • Enable more players to move into the key central area

Chapter 2: Developing a Game Model

The specific principles shown in the table are based on the unique characteristics of a club or coaching staff game model, which influence the coaching process and vision of the playing strategy.

Depending upon the literature read, there are many reports defining these characteristics as "principles" due to them determining specific individual and small group actions. Furthermore, forming a collective team identity enables players to interact and combine individual actions to promote a team organisation.

According to Tee et al., (2018) who also promoted the benefits of a game model development through a 'principles of play' framework suggested how each moment of the game has a characteristic structure that presents teams with a performance problem. Players and teams **must make decisions for how best to achieve the team's tactical goal in that moment of the game within the constraints presented** by the opposition.

Additionally, it was clearly stated that because of the complex nature of sport, no two moments of play will ever be exactly identical, and as a result, it is impossible to practice for every scenario that players will experience on the pitch.

In order **to reduce the complexity and enhance player decision making processes in these scenarios, teams may apply training characteristics that are divided into 'larger principles' and 'smaller-principles,' to guide the tactical responses and player development through understanding** (Delgado-Bordonau & Mendez-Villanueva, 2012; Tee et al., 2018; Owen., 2022).

CHAPTER 3
Training Load Management in Football

Chapter 3: Training Load Management in Football

Training Load Management and Injury Prevention in Football

The Challenge: Coaches must improve the physical football performance as a whole without encroaching on the technical and tactical training time periods (Iaia et al., 2015).

Speed, **agility**, **acceleration**, **strength** and **endurance** are key attributes that must be continually developed across all levels of the game.

Developing more efficient training content does not always mean training more, or adding more volume and subsequent load to cover the bases, but instead is about making better and more informed decisions.

Injury Prevention

It is **widely accepted that appropriate planning of training is fundamental to optimal performance and reduction of injury risk** for players.

Although there is an obvious importance to keep a low injury burden within squads, the role of the coach is to continue to develop players and drive them to fulfil their capacity. Reducing injuries across a season is linked to successful levels of play, however that is not in direct relationship with reduced training load (TL) or intensity.

Within the planning process, arguably the most fundamental aspect that determines success or failure of any plan, strategy or methodology is not just training load, but the training load management of the players involved.

As a result of managing this process within football, **calculating the training load is considered crucial for the intricate process of accurate and effective training plans and evaluation, which may lead to improvements in physical fitness** (Jaspers et al., 2016; Bowen et al., 2016).

Players at all levels are subject to seemingly endless competitive periods on top of preseason preparation, match-play, international games and ever growing post-season demands involving national team fixtures and International tournaments. As a result of increased fixture and training demands, comes the limited accessibility of developmental training to prepare players accordingly. The continued accumulative load on muscles, ligaments and joints, will, if not correctly monitored, recovered or assessed, erode away the previous preparation work.

Injuries impair team performance, and any **injuries that are considered 'training load-related' are commonly viewed as 'preventable'** due to poor training session design, which can be an issue in regard to fatigue accumulation.

Key Point: Understanding the physical demands on specific training practices/drills and sessions, as shown by the data on the practice pages in this book, is a vitally important aspect of the modern coaching strategy to maximise all aspects of training.

Internal and External Load

Training Load (TL) management can be categorised into 2 different sections:

1. **INTERNAL** is related to the physiological aspects: Heart rate monitoring, biochemical (urine/blood profiles), and ratings of perceived exertion (RPE) scores - physical activity intensity level.

2. **EXTERNAL** is related to the actual physical and mechanical outputs: Global positioning data (GPS) metrics [total distance, sprint distance, etc], change of directions, maximum velocity achieved, accelerations and decelerations.

Chapter 3: Training Load Management in Football

Having a **greater knowledge of internal and external training load is suggested to help coaches balance the working capacity and employ a better tapering strategy across the weekly training week** (microcycle), in order to prevent high risk accumulative fatigue, and subsequent higher risk of illness and injury.

Additionally, it is suggested that training monitoring may help coaches design effective individual and group training content to provide the intended stimulus required to overload specific fitness parameters. Recent research in this area has shown how players with the appropriate fitness levels have the required resilience to both training and game demands, and therefore these players are at reduced injury risk (Malone et al., 2016).

Key Point: The main aim of any training load management process in football is to provide the individuals involved in the development of players to positively evaluate and interpret the data they have available to them.

If the same mistakes keep occurring without monitoring relationships between training load and the game, then we are just guessing, regressing the players development and providing poor quality to the players.

According to reports in the area of training load management, the best way to prevent injuries within team sports is to ensure players have developed the specific capacities required of them to participate within the training and match play environment, and ensure the appropriate application of training (Gabbett, 2016).

The primary aim in the physical preparation of elite athletes is to plan the **correct training load (volume x intensity) in order to maximise the performance outcome**:

- **Less than adequate training load =** limitations on the required level of physiological development

- **Overloading to higher levels than required =** predispose the athlete to a greater risk of injury and illness (Gabbett, 2007).

Main Aim: This section of the book provides key information on training load management to provide an overview of an extremely important aspect of session design construction, and generate the potential for the applied football coach to consider the importance of training load management within their own coaching practices.

The integration of research based practice in football and investigations brought over from other sports around the world have shown that when athletes or football players' training and competitive match playing load over a short period of time (1 week - acute training load) spikes above their average values from across a longer period (4 weeks - chronic training load), they are at greater risk of injury (Gabbett, 2007).

This rapid increase or training spike in the acute:chronic workload ratio may be from an unusual training load week where the coach decided to perform a double session, or even a change of coach who introduces a higher training load methodology.

Findings from the studies in this area, especially the **graph referenced and shown on the following page "Likelihood of Subsequent Injury vs. Workload Ratio" demonstrate a strong predictive relationship between acute:chronic workload ratio and injury likelihood**. Assessment of the training load management process as a result is an interesting approach for coaches and performance staff to monitor.

Chapter 3: **Training Load Management in Football**

Likelihood of Subsequent Injury vs. Workload Ratio

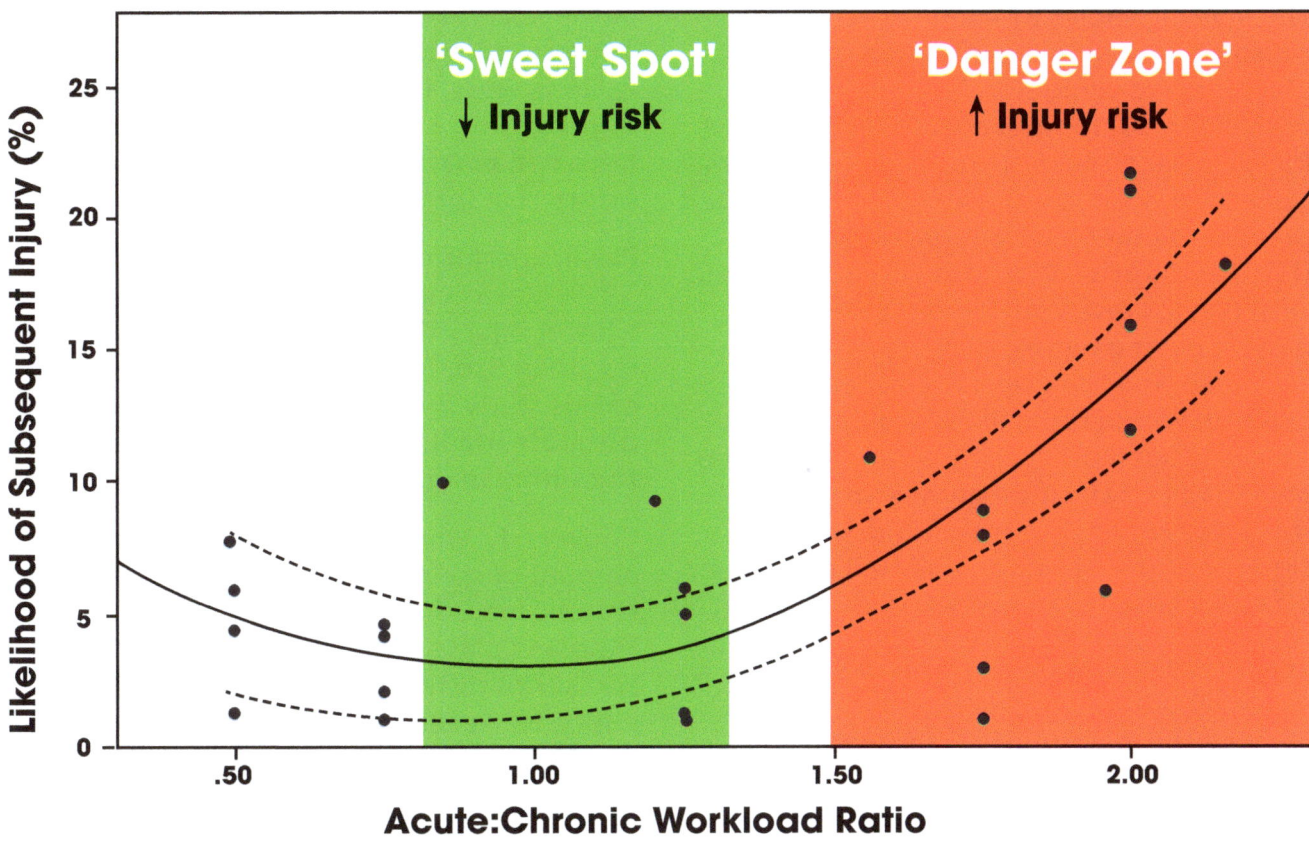

Fatigue, Recovery & Endurance

Adding significant training load to underprepared players within the training process or cycle inevitably leads to increased accumulation of fatigue. Based on the specific recovery needs generated by the fatigue, certain individuals may be affected in different ways due to several factors:

- Severity and type of exercises inducing the fatigue
- Training age
- Physical fitness and conditioning levels

Early research performed by Helgerud et al., (2001) using elite football players showed highly individual trained physical capacities are associated with significant performance benefits, such as **increased aerobic capacity leading to greater total distance covered (TDC), number of sprints, improved recovery and greater ball-involvement**.

In addition, recent research in this area have also described how relationships exist between endurance levels and **Total Distance Covered (TDC)** in competitive match-play, which also promoted an increased **Maximal Aerobic Speed** (Swaby et al., 2016).

Adding more credibility to these reports, it is suggested that aerobic endurance capacity is an important consideration with high maximal values correlating with match-play work rate. This results in significant benefits which aid the recovery periods between high intensity playing periods.

Furthermore, developing the training capacity of players offers a protective effect from subsequent injury risk, rather than limiting the training response in fear of injury (Gabbett, 2016).

Chapter 3: **Training Load Management in Football**

High Speed Running (HSR) and Sprinting (Maximal Velocity)

The investigation by Malone et al., (2018) into athletic capability of footballers found players performing significantly higher during the **30-15 Intermittent Fitness Test (IFT)** [30-second shuttle runs interspersed with 15-second walking recovery periods] tolerated greater volumes of **High Speed Running (HSR)** and **Sprint Distance** when compared with players revealing a reduced aerobic fitness. Having highlighted the importance of developing the players aerobic endurance capacity within football through practices/drills and sessions causing a **cardiovascular overload (small sided games and high-intensity resistance training drills)**, the significant role sprinting and HSR exercises play in reducing injury risk and developing all round-robust players should be considered.

An earlier study by Malone et al., (2016) examined the relationship between sprint exposures and injury risk in Gaelic footballers. The findings reported how **players who achieved >95% of their peak velocity had a reduced injury risk** when compared to players exposed to lower relative velocity. Further detailed analysis of the data revealed how **players who performed excessive loads of peak velocity actions were at increased risk of injury, highlighting a "U" shaped relationship between maximum velocity exposures and injury risk (please see the graph below)**.

Players performing between 6 to 10 sprints >95% Maximum Velocity (Vmax) capacity had a lower injury risk versus players performing less than 5, or more than 11 sprints. Results of this study therefore provide **evidence of a possible ideal sprint stimulus as a method to minimise injury risk in team sports**.

Conversely, when exposed to the same amount of sprinting, players with higher chronic loads had a lower injury risk. Exposing players to rapid increases in HSR and sprint distances increased the odds of injury. However, higher chronic training loads and better intermittent aerobic fitness off-set lower limb injury risk associated with these running distances (Malone et al., 2018).

Association Between Total Weekly Maximal Velocity Exposures and Likelihood of Injury - Taken from Malone et al., (2016)

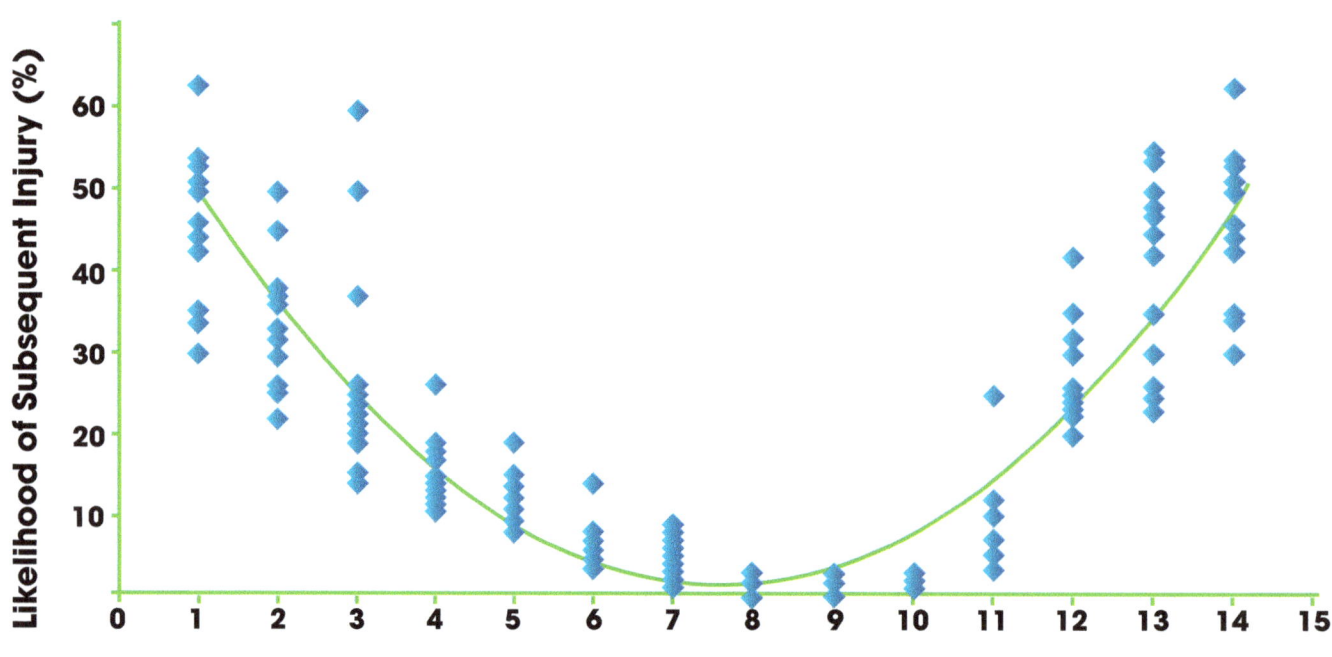

Chapter 3: Training Load Management in Football

From a coaching perspective, understanding the Training Load (TL) output and metrics influenced by coaching practices/drills or sessions creates more informed decisions. The importance of sprinting is compounded in a study by Morin et al., (2015) who confirmed the fact that through traditional strengthening exercises it is impossible to replicate or achieve sprint specific hamstring muscle activation, therefore highlighting that sprinting remains the only means of providing this specific stimulus required by sports athletes or football players.

Despite the obvious benefits of well-developed physical qualities, inappropriate high training loads may lead to injury. If the accumulated training load greatly exceeds a players' load capacity or tolerance for an extended period of time, the player may experience a reduction in performance and an increased injury risk. For this reason, **tapering phases coupled with rest and recovery are vital components of the planned training program**.

"Within football, the need for coaches and performance staff to maximise match performance is of paramount importance. The requirement to push players hard enough to progress in every element of the game whilst minimising the number of non-contact injuries is fundamental. However, using tapering models to navigate a way through the use of internal and external training load management methods has proved to be a capable way of enabling the maintenance of a uniformed, developmental training program."
(Dr. Adam Owen)

Key Point: Being able to utilise specific practices/drills and training sessions known to drive overloads in key physical stimulus, whilst engaging with technical and tactical development, can only assist in better coaching and maximise the efficiency of the training plan as proposed in this book.

CHAPTER 4

Developing a Game Based Training Approach

Developing a Game Based Training Approach

Interest and application of more specific training methods attempting to reproduce the technical and physical demands of competitive match play is becoming more evident through the amount of research performed in this area (Owen et al., 2011; Owen et al., 2012; Dellal et al., 2010; Koklu et al., 2012). Within both the applied and research domain, the integration of training games with the aim of applying specific overloads to induce specific outcomes are seen within the game across the world at every level.

Validation for **training games** stems from the **ability to develop the technical, psychological, tactical and physical ability of players all at once**, which leads to the enhancement of training efficiency (Dellal et al., 2012). By being able to manipulate key variables and add specific technical and tactical constraints (Abrantes et al., 2012), alter the pitch sizes (Casamichana and Castellano, 2010; Kelly and Drust, 2009), player numbers (Hill-Haas et al., 2009), bout duration (Fanchini et al., (2011), and number of individual touches per possession (Dellal et al., 2011), the physiological, tactical and technical responses of players can be influenced.

It is vital coaches have a clear objective for the planning process/session design, and an understanding of what variables are needed to be manipulated in order to achieve the targeted outcomes of the session. According to research in this area, physiological responses from training games within the course of the training week lend themselves to the philosophy outlined in this book.

The application of a game based training strategy at the centre of a weekly coaching methodology enables the stimulation of conditioning effects in coordination with high levels of reliable data (Jones & Drust, 2007; Owen et al., 2011; Owen et al., 2014; Coutts et al., 2009; Rampinini et al., 2007; Mallo et al., 2008).

Chapter 4: Developing a Game Based Training Approach

GAME BASED TRAINING:
Small, Medium, and Large Sided Games

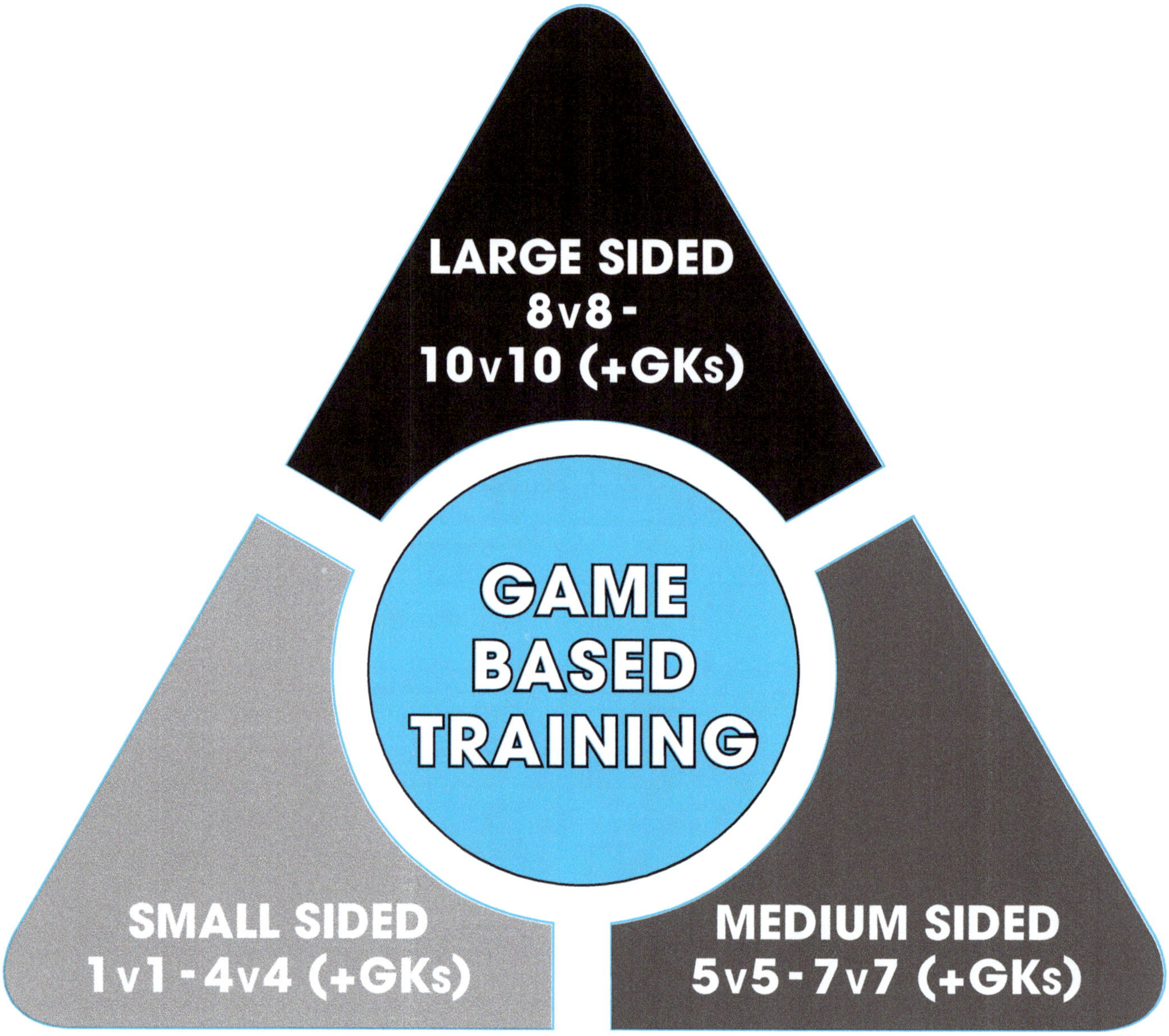

LARGE SIDED
8v8 - 10v10 (+GKs)

GAME BASED TRAINING

SMALL SIDED
1v1 - 4v4 (+GKs)

MEDIUM SIDED
5v5 - 7v7 (+GKs)

SMALL VS. MEDIUM VS. LARGE SIDED GAMES

*Data Below Based on 5 Minute Game Period Averages

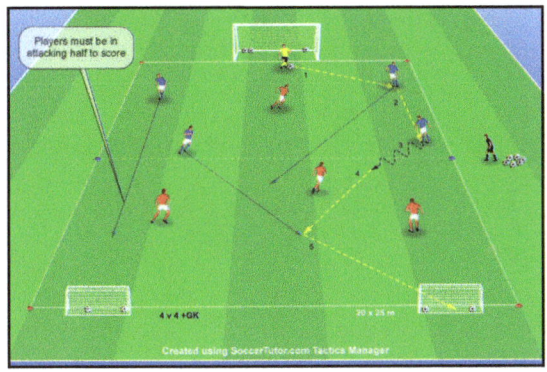

SMALL SIDED GAMES: 1v1-4v4 (+GKs)

- ↑ Speed of Thought - Closer Pressure from Opponents
- ↑ Cardiovascular Load - Higher Heart Rate Response
- ↑ Lower Body Strength Work - Change of Directions
- ↑ Technical Demand Per Player - Touches
- ↓ Sprint Distance - Reduced Area
- ↓ Tactical Focus

Total Distance	Speed of Play	Sprint Distance	Hi-Speed Running	Time > 85% HRM
580m	116m.min	0m	6m	3.2 min

MEDIUM SIDED GAMES: 5v5-7v7 (+GKs)

- ↑ Position Specific - Tactical Focus of Roles
- ↑ High Speed & Sprint Distance - Medium Size Area
- ↓ Possible Social Loafing Issues? - Relaxed Approach
- ↓ Technical Demand Per Player (More Players)

Total Distance	Speed of Play	Sprint Distance	Hi-Speed Running	Time > 85% HRM
520m	104m.min	4.5m	6m	3.5 min

LARGE SIDED GAMES: 8v8-10v10 (+GKs)

- ↑ Position Specific - Tactical Focus of Roles
- ↑ Sprint & High Speed Runs - Under Pressure to Cover Area!
- ↓ Cardiovascular Load - Less Pressure
- ↓ Technical Demand Per Player (More Players)
- • Acts as Injury Prevention 'Hamstring Primer'!

Total Distance	Speed of Play	Sprint Distance	Hi-Speed Running	Time > 85% HRM
589m	117m.min	7m	35m	2.1 min

@adamowen1980

Football Periodization to Maximise Performance

REFERENCE: Owen et al, (2004). Insight, FA Journal, spring, 2(7): 50-53. | Owen et al, (2005). J Strength Cond res. Jun; 29(6): 1705-12.

Chapter 4: Developing a Game Based Training Approach

PHYSICAL AND TECHNICAL COMPARISONS BETWEEN VARIOUS SIDED GAMES WITHIN PROFESSIONAL FOOTBALL

Reference: Owen, Wong, Paul & Dellal, IJSM 2014   Designed by @YLMSportScience

10 Elite Players Studied (3 x 5 min each game type)

SMALL (SSG) VS **MEDIUM (MSG)** VS **LARGE (LSG)**
1v1-4v4 +GKs   5v5-7v7 +GKs   8v8-10v10 +GKs

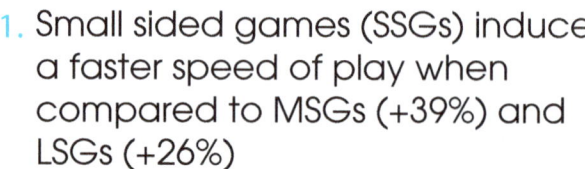

RESULTS

1. Small sided games (SSGs) induce a faster speed of play when compared to MSGs (+39%) and LSGs (+26%)

2. ... but induce less repeated high-intensity efforts (0.88 vs 4.40 m), high-intensity running (7 vs 39m) and sprint distance (0 vs 11m) when compared to large sided games (LSGs)

3. SSGs have more passing, receiving, dribbling, and shooting compared to medium sided games (MSGs) and LSGs

4. MSGs have more passing and shooting than LSGs

Conducting the correct type of sided game at specific times of the training week may enable you to optimally prepare players physically, technically and tactically, thus increasing the efficiency of your training sessions and the weekly schedule

Images provided by PresenterMedia

Chapter 4: **Developing a Game Based Training Approach**

Heart Rate Responses and Technical Comparison of Small vs. Large-Sided Games in Elite Professional Football

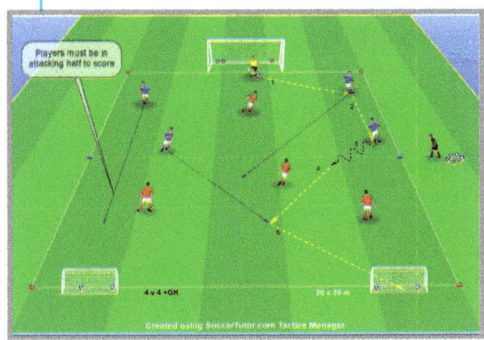

What?
Examine the difference in heart-rate (HR) responses and technical activities placed upon elite European players when exposed to two different sided games

When?
January during a 3-week period of the mid-season phase, to reflect players' in-season performance levels

How?
HR responses and players' technical actions recorded throughout 3x 5mins of small (3v3 + GKs - 25x30 m) and large (9v9 + GKs - 50x60 m) sided training games with 4 minute recovery bouts between

Who?
15 elite players competing at UEFA Champions League and international level

Findings?
- Small-sided games induce significantly higher HR responses than large-sided games
- Players spent more time **>85% HR max zone** in small-sided games
- Technical analysis = Large practical differences between the 2-game formats:
  - **SSGs** = *Higher number of dribbles, shots, and tackles*
  - **SSGs** = *Significantly greater number of ball touches per individual*
  - **LSGs** = *Higher number of blocks, headers, interceptions, passes, and receives*

Practical Application?
- Different technical requirements enable coaches to carry out training games suitable to specific playing positions
- **SSGs** = Stimulate more midfielder actions (dribbles, tackles and ball touches per player)
- **SSGs** = Strikers got more shots off!
- **LSGs** = Highlight more defensive actions (blocks, headers and interceptions)

Full Scientific Reference
Owen AL., Wong DP., McKenna M., Dellal A. (2011)
Heart rate responses and technical comparison between small vs. large-sided games in elite professional football.
Journal of Strength and Conditioning Research 25(8): 2104-10

Chapter 4: Developing a Game Based Training Approach

Variables Significantly Influencing Training Intensity

RPE = Rating of Perceived Exertion
bLa = Blood Lactate Concentration

Pitch Area or Player Density: Changing pitch sizes affects both physical and technical demands imposed on players e.g. high speed running, speed of play, sprint distance, etc.

Bout Duration: The shorter durations are generally used with reduced player numbers or SSGs, and as a result the intensity of the practices are higher. The LSGs generally include larger bout durations which drops the intensity over time.

Use of Goalkeepers: Research shows the inclusion of GKs reduces the intensity of play as the game slows down slightly. However, it is also suggested that motivation increases when different types of scoring are added to training games.

Verbal Encouragement: Consistent coach encouragement leads to significant increases in training intensity vs. non-encouragement with a greater Heart Rate response (*RPE & bLa**).

Scoring Options: Smaller goals or multiple goal scoring options require more possession maintenance or recycling of possession due to intense transitions. Furthermore, limited scoring chances also promote a greater intensity as a result.

Game Rules: Research has shown that increased *RPE & bLa* levels are found when Small Sided Games (SSGs) involved free play vs. 2-3 touch restrictions. Approximately 5% increases in *Heart Rate (HR)* response have been shown when using a man-marking rule within training games.

Player Numbers: Reducing player numbers involved in sessions leads to a greater technical exposure per player, significantly increased technical demand and decision making processing. Training games with reduced numbers per side leads to significantly greater *HR* response vs. Large Sided Games (LSGs).

COACHING EFFECTS OF CHANGING PITCH SIZES

*Physical Output Data based on 5 minute game period

LARGE SIDED GAME
9v9 (+ GKs) Tactical Game

SMALL SIDED GAME
4v4 (+4) + GKs Game

LSG

Passes	Dribbles	Headers	Shots	Speed of Play	Total Distance	Hi-Speed Running		
37	6	4	4	126m.min	580m	22m	Large Areas	More Tactical

SSG

Passes	Dribbles	Headers	Shots	Speed of Play	Total Distance	Hi-Speed Running		
52	8	1	15	114m.min	463m	2.2m	Small Areas	More Technical

KEY DIFFERENCES

- Varies the technical demand
- **Large Areas** = Greater high speed running; greater total distance covered; greater tactical emphasis (positional play)
- **Small Areas** = Greater technical load; more attacking based game scenarios (shots, dribbles, duels)

PITCH SIZE VARIATIONS

- Influence technical execution in "tighter areas"
- Influence players reaction or thinking speed in possession
- Influence the overall intensity and speed of play

@adamowen1980

@SoccerTutor.com

Football Periodization to Maximise Performance

REFERENCE • Williams & Owen. (2007). J sports sqi, 6, 100. • Owen AL et al., (2004). Insight, FA Journal, Spring.

COACHING EFFECTS OF LIMITED TOUCHES

FREE PLAY vs. 3-TOUCH

*Physical Output Data based on 5 Minute 7v7 (+GKs) Game Period

Players limited to 3 touches

7 v 7 +GKs

Created using SoccerTutor.com Tactics Manager

LIMITED TOUCHES:

- ↑ Total distance covered
- ↑ Speed and intensity of play
- ↑ High speed running distance
- ↑ Heart Rate response
- ↑ Cardiovascular Load
- ↑ Physiological demands

FREE PLAY
- Time > 85% HRM: 3 min
- Heart Rate Exertion: 17
- High Speed Distance: 12m
- Speed of Play: 107m.min
- Total Distance: 535m

3 TOUCH
- Time > 85% HRM: 4.4 min
- Heart Rate Exertion: 21
- High Speed Distance: 15m
- Speed of Play: 117m.min
- Total Distance: 585m

@adamowen1980

@SoccerTutor.com

Football Periodization to Maximise Performance

REFERENCE Casamichana et al., (2014). J Human Kinetics, Jul 8; 41:113-23 / Owen AL et al., (2014). Int J Sports Medicine, Apr 35(4): 286-92.

Chapter 4: Developing a Game Based Training Approach

Considerations for Small Sided Games

SSGs induce significant increases in heart rate, blood lactate concentrations and rate of perceived exertion in football players.

Formats between 2v2 and 4v4 are particularly demanding since they are close to or generally above 85% of max heart rate (> 85% HRM).

SSGs played in small areas generate increased movement demands due to the need to create space, move from opponents and form passing lanes. However, the findings reveal that minimal high speed efforts are created in SSGs.

SSGs (2v2 to 4v4 +GKs) reveal increased individual technical actions performed per player. The number of individual passes, dribbles, receptions or shots are significantly higher when compared to large sided game (LSGs).

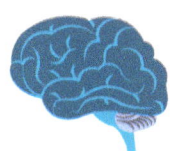

SSGs have been shown to increase the number of actions related to penetration attempts (passes to disrupt the opponent's defensive line) and defensive principles i.e. interceptions, tackles, 1v1 situations.

LSGs have revealed how they significantly increase the collective behaviours formed within game models in both defensive and attacking situations. This highlights the more tactical complexities involved in the LSG formats.

Chapter 4: Developing a Game Based Training Approach

ARTICLE: Multi-directional Sprints and Small Sided Games Training Effect on Agility and Changes of Direction (COD) Abilities in Youth Football

By Chaouachi et al. JSCR 2014

Design by @YLMSportScience

METHODS

- 36 football players were assigned to 2 groups during a 6 week training study: One group with pre-planned Change of Direction drills (**COD**) and one with Small Sided Games (**SSG**) vs. a Control Group (**CON**).

- Players completed a battery test before and after training involving straight line sprinting (15 and 30 metre (m) sprint), Change of Direction (COD) sprinting (COD 15m, Ball 15m, 10-8-8-10m, zig-zag 20m), reactive-agility tests, and vertical and horizontal jumping (CMJ Vertical Jump Test and 5JT 5-Jump Test).

RESULTS AND TRAINING IMPLICATIONS

- Increases in sprinting, agility without the ball, changes of direction and jumping performances were highest in the **COD**.

- The **SSG** tested higher than other groups in agility with the ball.

- The **CON** showed increases in straight line sprinting over distances longer than 10 metres and in all the agility and change of direction (COD) tests used in this study.

"It was concluded that in young male football players, agility can be improved either using purpose built Small Sided Games (SSGs) or pre-planned Changes of Direction (COD) sprints. However, the use of specifically designed SSGs may provide superior results in match relevant variables."

Chapter 4: Developing a Game Based Training Approach

Age Category Performance Effects within Small Sided Games

- Adapted Schematic from Nunes et al., (2021)

Smaller Playing Areas

Younger Players:
- More distance @ high speed running & sprinting
- Restricted positional technical development
- Development of aerobic endurance & individual participation

Older Players:
- More distance @ walking speeds
- Higher perception of intensity
- Greater variability in tactical actions
- Increased pressure on ball & decision making

NOTE: SSG playing areas reduce as players get older and experienced, in order to explore more possibilities

Larger Playing Areas

Younger Players:
- More distance @ high speed running & sprinting
- Performance of more tactical actions
- More time for decision making and performance of technical skills

Older Players:
- Increased tactical organisation and space exploitation
- More distance @ walking speeds
- Greater perception of intensity

This recent study explored the age-category effects on **external training workload** of 4v4 Small Sided Games (SSGs) across a range of age-groups (U11, U15, U23):

- Total distance covered.
- Distance covered while walking.
- Running and sprinting.
- Number of sprints and maximum sprint speed.
- Internal training load metrics through the use of rating of perceived exertion (**RPE**).
- Individual technical actions; passes with strong vs. weaker foot and passing speed within 3 different playing areas.

The results revealed substantial differences:

- U23 players covered more distance walking.
- U11 and U15 players covered more distance at faster speeds.
- U23 and U15 players showed increased RPE scores vs. U11 age group.
- **Conclusion:** 4v4 SSGs can provide different performance related stimuli to players, depending on age and playing area.
- Coaches should understand that different ages will deal differently with distinctive playing areas in SSGs. They should be aware of the key variables highlighted here before planning training practices/drills/sessions.

Chapter 4: Developing a Game Based Training Approach

SMALL-SIDED GAMES:
The Physiological and Technical Demands of Altering Pitch Size and Player Numbers

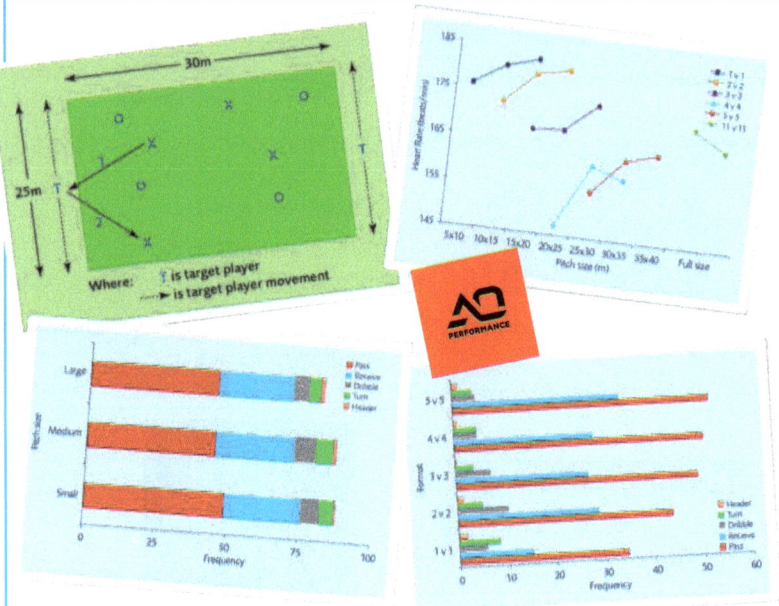

What?
Studying the physiological and technical effects of altering the pitch size and player numbers within various small-sided games (SSGs)

When?
Players took part in 5 separate training sessions performing each SSG format across the mid-session phase

How?
- Free-play, possession based SSG using teammates and target players to bounce pass
- Exercise-rest ratio of 1:4 used
- 3 minute period on each pitch size (small; medium; large) interspersed with a 4 minute recovery period

Findings?

- **Altering Pitch Size:**
  1. Enlarging the pitch size used for the SSGs by 10 metres generally caused increases in both the mean heart rates and mean peak heart rates
  2. Enlarging the pitch size used for the small-sided game by 10 metres had no effect on the technical actions the players performed.

- **Altering Player Numbers:** SSGs (3v3s) = Heart Rate (HR) similar to 11v11 match-play; SSGs (1v1 & 2v2s) = HRs > than 11v11 match-play; Adding an extra player to each team, but keeping the pitch size the same, generally reduced mean heart rates.

Who?
Professional football players from English League One (third tier) participated in the study

Pitch Sizes (m) used for Small Sided Games					
Type	1v1	2v2	3v3	4v4	5v5
Small	5x10m	10x15m	15x20m	20x25m	25x30m
Medium	10x15m	15x20m	20x25m	25x30m	30x35m
Large	15x20m	20x25m	25x30m	30x35m	35x40m

Practical Application?
- **Reducing player numbers** within SSGs has a significant impact on the physical demand of players
- **Increased number of players** increases the number of technical actions but reduces the individual technical demands
- Coach awareness in the **session design** for **player numbers and pitch areas** is of paramount importance to ensure the correct training load is provided

Full Scientific Reference
Owen AL., Twist C., Ford P. (2004)
Small-Sided Games: The Physiological & Technical Demands of Altering | Pitch Size & Player Number | INSIGHT - ISSUE, VOLUME 7, SPRING

Considerations for Large Sided Games

Larger pitches (mainly larger than 150+ m2) generally include larger-sided numbers and a reduced heart rate response vs. SSGs.

Larger pitches contribute to greater distances covered and cover more distances at higher speeds. This is linked to the playing density, which is greater for the larger numbers on the pitch in general and leads to players reaching greater velocities to cover the surface area.

Smaller pitches increase the number of accelerations and decelerations, but do not allow for high speed running or sprinting values.

Smaller pitches increase the number of individual technical actions performed by the players.

Larger pitches allow for ball possession to increase per side involved.

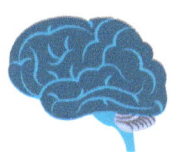

Larger pitches increase positional demands and position specific technical actions. Smaller length-to-width ratios are linked to a higher use of wide areas and enable specific tactical tasks, like switches of play, to become more visible.

Larger pitches also increase the distances/ space between teammates and lead to more extensive technical actions or passes.

LARGE SIDED GAMES
COACHING EFFECTS OF INCREASING BOUT DURATION
6 MINUTE vs. 10 MINUTE Game Periods (Box to Box)

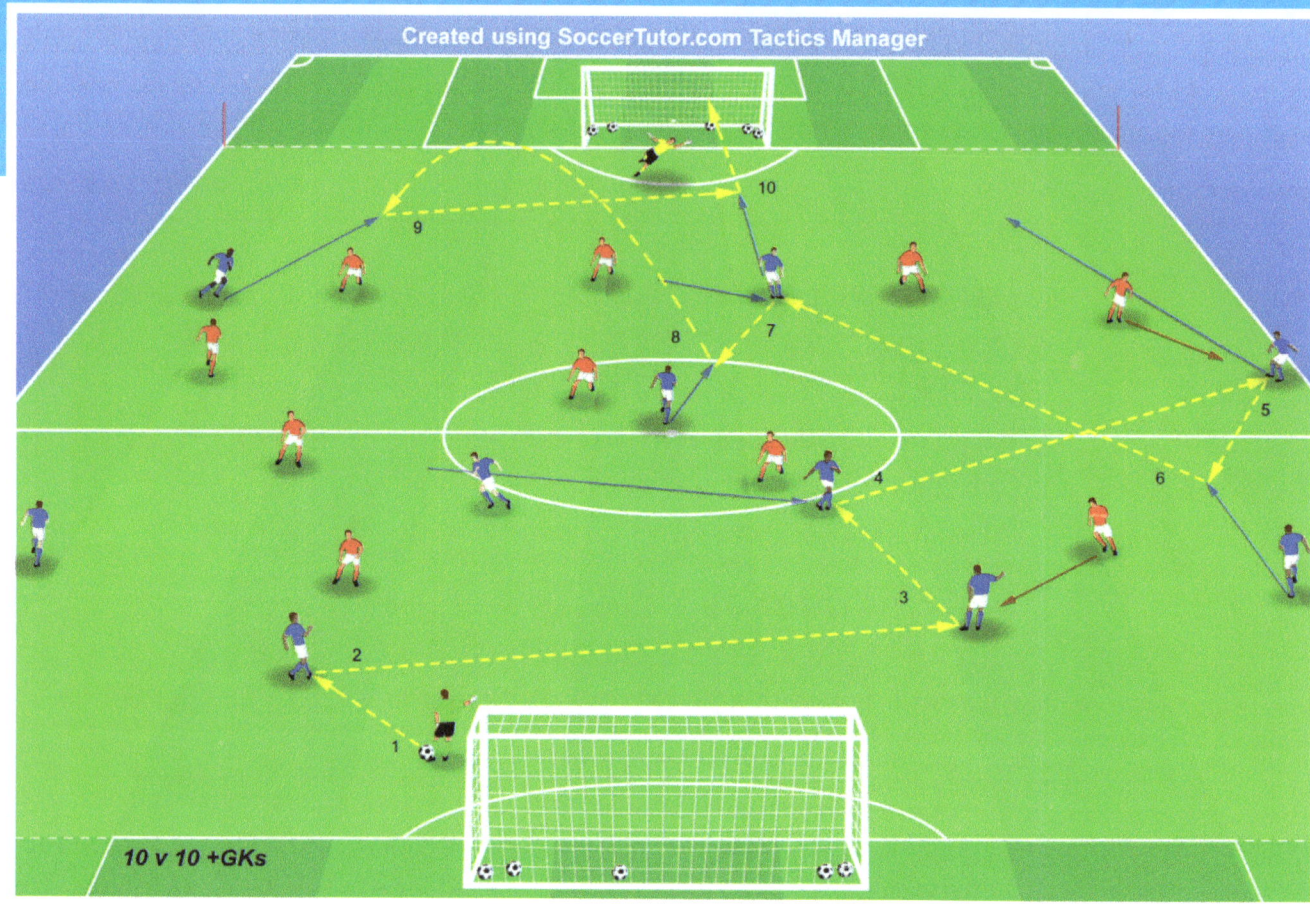

10 v 10 +GKs

Large Sided Games

- Prepares lower body muscles for high speed match demands
- Acts as an injury prevention 'primer'
- Increased high speed running distances
- Increased sprint distance/high intensity efforts
- Stimulation of positional physical demands
- Football specific training with tactical focus
- Increased positional technical exposure

Increasing Bout Durations

- Increases the training load (careful planning required to minimise risk)
- Significantly alters physical demand
- Stimulates progressive overloads
- Greater understanding of how bout duration affects fatigue rates
- Coaches must understand how extra bouts/durations affect physical demands imposed on players!

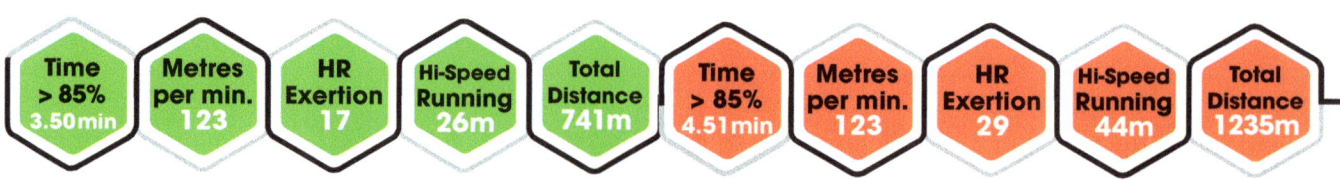

Time > 85%	Metres per min.	HR Exertion	Hi-Speed Running	Total Distance	Time > 85%	Metres per min.	HR Exertion	Hi-Speed Running	Total Distance
3.50min	123	17	26m	741m	4.51min	123	29	44m	1235m

@adamowen1980

REFERENCE: Owen AL et al (2014). Int J Sports Med. Apr; 35(4): 286-92

LARGE 16 MINUTE GAME
10v10 + GKs (Box to Box)
Data Below Based on 16 minute Directional Game

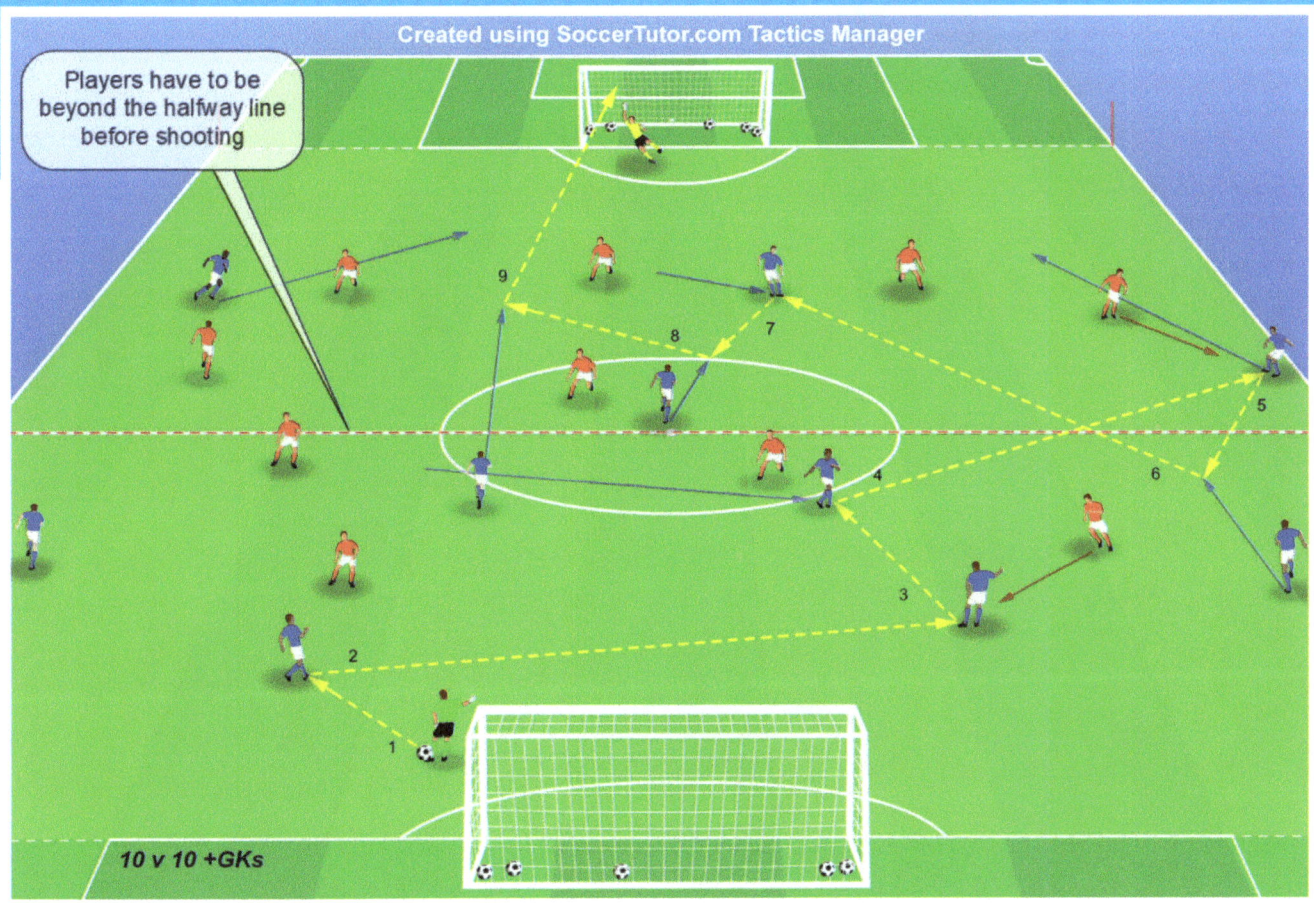

Players have to be beyond the halfway line before shooting

10 v 10 +GKs

Benefits of this Large Sided Game?

- ↑ High-speed running to support play in the final third of the pitch
- ↑ Preparation of lower body muscles for matches
- ↑ Tactical focus
- ↑ Positional and technical demands
- ↑ Realism of play within this LSG i.e. spatial awareness
- ↑ Focus on support play and driving in behind the defensive line

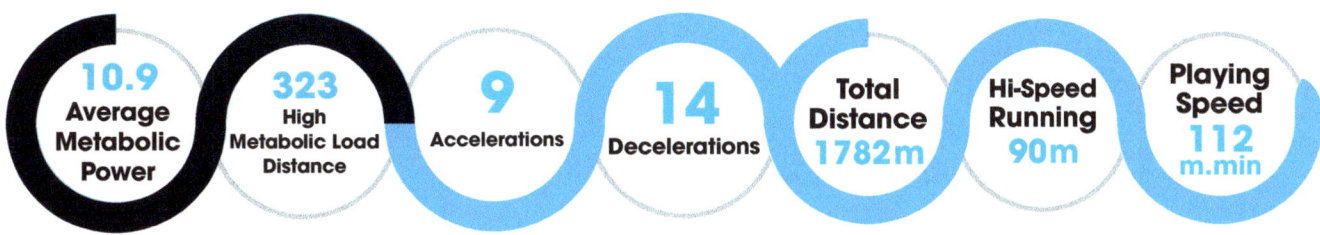

10.9 Average Metabolic Power | **323** High Metabolic Load Distance | **9** Accelerations | **14** Decelerations | **Total Distance 1782m** | **Hi-Speed Running 90m** | **Playing Speed 112 m.min**

@adamowen1980

@SoccerTutor.com | Football Periodization to Maximise Performance

REFERENCE Aguiar MV et al., (2013). J Strength Cond Res, May 27(5): 1287-94. | Owen AL et al., (2011). J Strength Cond Res, Aug;25(8);2104-10.

LARGE 8 MINUTE GAME

10v10 + GKs (Box to Box)

*Data Below Based on 8 Minute Directional 3 Zone Game

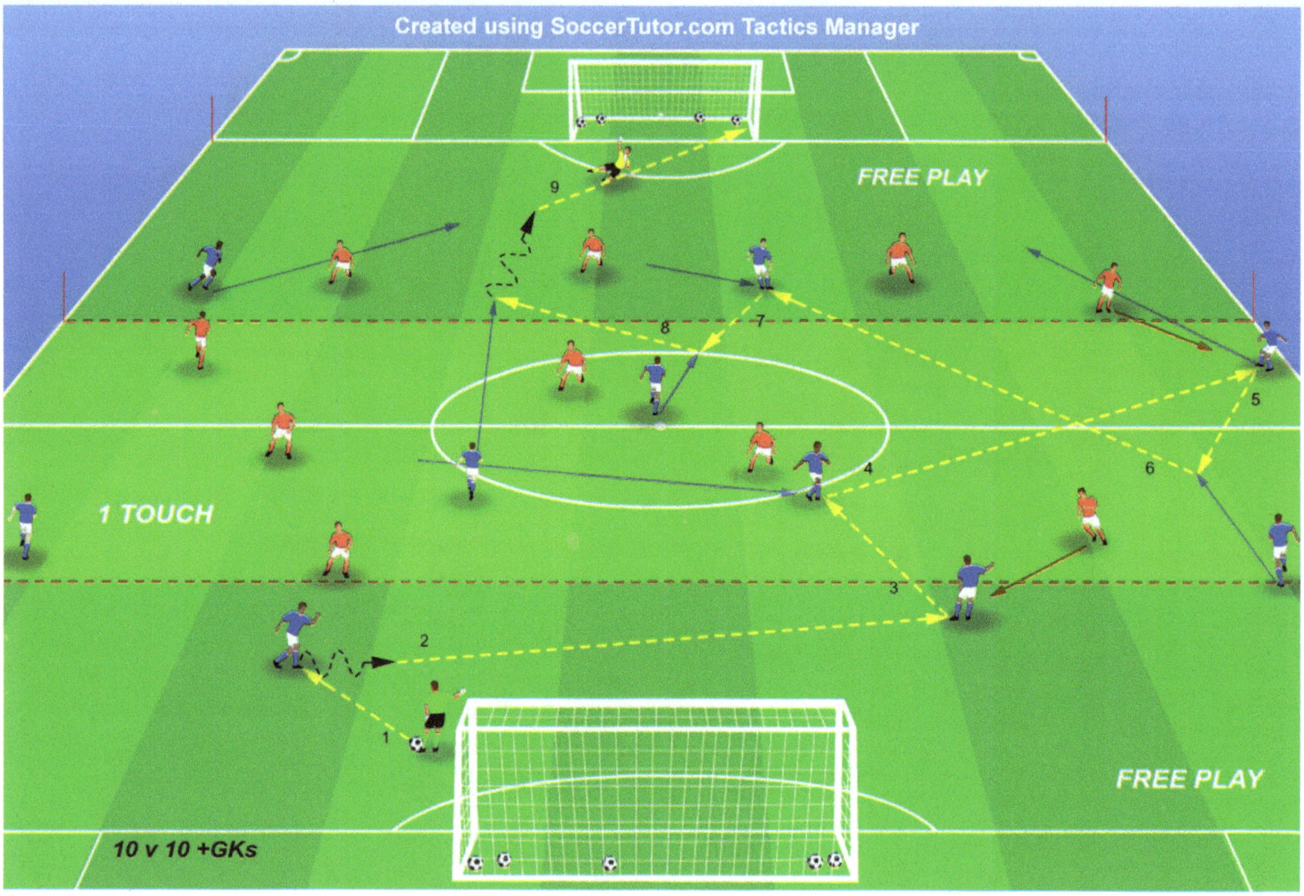

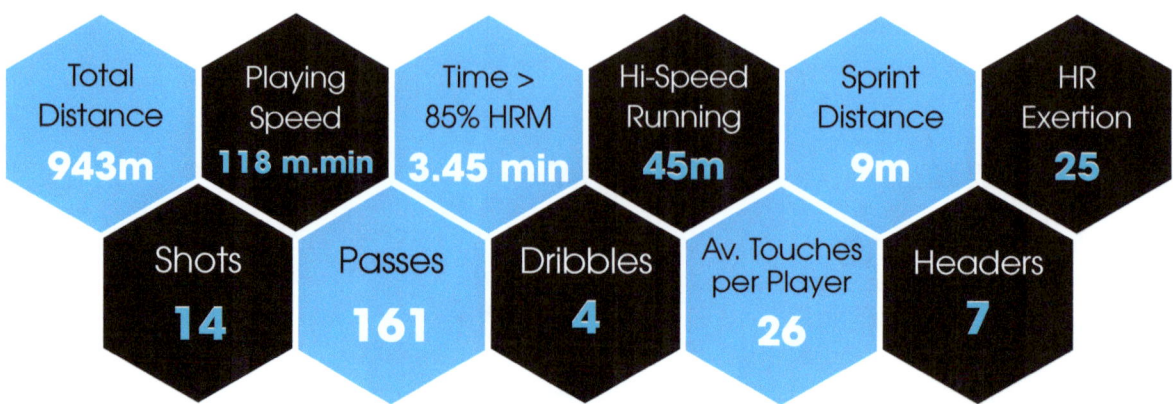

- ↑ **Speed of Play** through middle third
- ↑ **High Speed Running** to support play in the final third of the pitch
- ↑ **Realism of Play** within the LSG i.e. spatial awareness
- ↑ **Tactical Focus**
- ↑ Preparation of **Lower Body Muscles** for matches
- ↑ **Positional Specificity** and technical demands

Total Distance **943m**	Playing Speed **118 m.min**	Time > 85% HRM **3.45 min**	Hi-Speed Running **45m**	Sprint Distance **9m**	HR Exertion **25**
Shots **14**	Passes **161**	Dribbles **4**	Av. Touches per Player **26**	Headers **7**	

@adamowen1980

@SoccerTutor.com — Football Periodization to Maximise Performance

REFERENCE: Owen AI et al., (2012). J Strength Cond Res. Oct; 26(10):27 48-54. Dellal A et al., (2012). Hum Mov Sci. Aug; 31 (4):957-69.

Understanding Game Formats and Using a Mixed Approach

Limitations of Using Only Small Sided Games

Despite using games as a justifiable training method for aerobic-fitness and technical-tactical skill development (Hill-Haas et al., 2011), research has shown that when compared to actual match play, **certain game types used are unable to simulate repeated high speed and sprint demands** (Casamichana et al., 2012; Gabbett and Mulvey, 2008; Owen et al., 2014).

Although Small Sided Games (SSGs) are significantly utilised for cardiovascular and strength based overloads, these game formats **do not allow for players to achieve near Vmax (maximum velocity) levels**.

These findings are reinforced by the reported potential ceiling effect associated with a failure to achieve high exercise intensities in players retaining either high aerobic endurance capacities or technical competency respectively (Buchheit et al., 2009). However, this notion has been disputed by a number of authors working at the elite level (Owen et al., 2012; Dellal et al., 2011), based on the fact that manipulation of key variables within the games can lead to the desired training outcomes.

Large Sided Games

Identified within the research, **high-speed activity or movements and repeated-sprint demands are more commonly associated with match play when introducing larger sided games formats** (Hill-Hass et al., 2009). This is directly linked to the results of exposing players to LSGs within increased pitch sizes. As players in these LSG formats have less involvement with the ball and more lower intensity actions through the recovery phases, these game formats result in an **increased number of sustained high speed runs (HSR) and sprint bouts when working "off the ball"** in order to regain or retain possession.

As alluded to already within this section of the book, the challenge for coaches is not only to manipulate constraints for the design of challenging training tasks, but to identify the relationships between the manipulation of such constraints, the action capabilities of players, and the desired collective tactical goals of the team, in accordance to the individual player's stage of development (Owen et al., 2020).

The Mixed Approach

As a result of the research in this area, the variation of game formats Small Sided Games (SSGs), Medium Sided Games (MSGs), and Large Sided Games (LSGs) should be implemented across the training week.

The situations faced within the game itself in terms of the technical, tactical and psychological perspective are constantly in play across SSGs, MSGs and LSGs, so the implementation of these game formats across the weekly cycle can be advantageous. According to research, changing the playing area dimensions affects not only the intensity of the game and players actions, but it **significantly influences energy sources used** (Sangnier et al., 2019).

Larger playing areas are associated with greater distance covered (Silva et al., 2014) and an increase in the intensity of action or movement (Halouani et al., 2014; Sarmento et al., 2018) when compared to smaller areas. **Players' age and level influence their individual decision making and individual tactical actions**, which consequently has an effect on the collective behaviour of the team (Menuchi et al., 2018).

Chapter 4: **Developing a Game Based Training Approach**

Justification for a Game Based Training Approach: Small, Medium, and Large Sided Game Areas

The diagram above shows how the playing area sizes (dimensions) of the various sided games formats fit into a full 11v11 pitch size:

- **Small Sided Games** (SSGs: 1v1 - 4v4 +GKs)
- **Medium Sided Games** (MSGs: 5v5 - 7v7 +GKs)
- **Large Sided Games** (LSGs: 8v8 - 10v10 +GKs)

NOTE: The growing interest into the examination of Medium Sided Games (MSGs: 5v5-7v7 +GKs) and Large Sided Games (LSGs: 8v8-10v10 +GKs) may be a result of these game types being used more for technical and tactical purposes, rather than physical profile development.

However, not accounting for the potential physical and physiological stimulus during MSGs and LSGs may reduce the potential impact of the overall tapering strategy and subsequent program design. There are key varied central and peripheral benefits as part of a successful and multifunctional training plan influencing the acute variation of the microcycle.

CHAPTER 5
Training Session Design

Chapter 5: Training Session Design

Training Session Design

Today, many coaches struggle to meet all elements and demands of the game when preparing their team:

- **Physical**
- **Technical**
- **Psychological**
- **Tactical**

The coaching dilemma of achieving the right levels of training across each component is constantly at the forefront of youth and senior coaches, or managers thoughts.

Based on the increased understanding and analysis developments in all aspects of the game over the last few years, combined with the high-speed nature of the game progressing more rapidly, the questions continually asked are…

1. Have we progressed our training preparation and content in line with the game and player demands?

2. Do I coach in an integrated, modern methodology that enhances player development?

3. Do I maximise my time with the players during the session?

Elite level players are now more educated on their tactical roles, physical preparation and needs, as well as the technical requirements of training sessions.

Subsequently this leads to coaches and individuals involved in the player development and performance perspective of the game, having to continually enhance their skill-set and evolve/improve.

Chapter 5: Training Session Design

In recent years, team sports in general, and notably football has shifted towards a new trend in regard to physical training integration and coaching methodology. This is due to the result of improvements in the professionalism of coaching, as well as the **hugely positive impact and influence of sport and football science**.

According to highly respected football journalist Raphael Honigstein, Thomas Tuchel (Chelsea manager and Champions League winner) is, *"a superb developer of talent and a football scientist, delving deep into the game's microscopic details."*

One of the most debatable subjects among football science and technical coaching practitioners is the **importance of designing a structured weekly and daily coaching plan, to efficiently optimise the physical, technical, tactical and psychological game requirements**.

Efthymios, (2019) suggested an abundance of training methods and structures are consistently suggested by specialists in the football arena through videos, online drills/practices and research publications. However, in this section of the book, only the essential aspects determining the session design process are briefly outlined.

According to recent research in this area, **practice design or training session development is a concept measured by the degree to which skills acquired in practice transfer to the competitive environment**, and this is being supported increasingly through specific contextual research.

According to Otte et al., (2019) training session design displays certain dominant factors that can enhance the coaching process:

1. Providing players with relevant coordination between what they see and what they do, so that they enhance their perception of the realities faced within a competitive environment, and become attuned to critical information provided by specific situations

2. Facilitate the development of training that can integrate more than one element of the game with specific techniques, decision-making and tactical awareness

3. Developing specific session design formats that recreate players behavioural actions that emerge through training tasks and competitive games

4. Achievement of goals in the performance environment that are as a direct result of movements and technical executions influenced by specific and contextual constraints players have been exposed to in training

In addition, relevant research and literature in this area has reported how more advanced performers (across a range of different sports) perceive more relevant information (Travassos et al., 2012). This may well be as a result of the repetitive nature of specific situations faced in previous games, training, etc. This points to the fact that **higher level players are able to recall previous similar specific situations and make better decisions as a result of this**.

The flow chart on the following page displays key considerations when developing or designing a practice or training session...

Chapter 5: **Training Session Design**

Practice Design Considerations to Optimise Coaching Outcomes

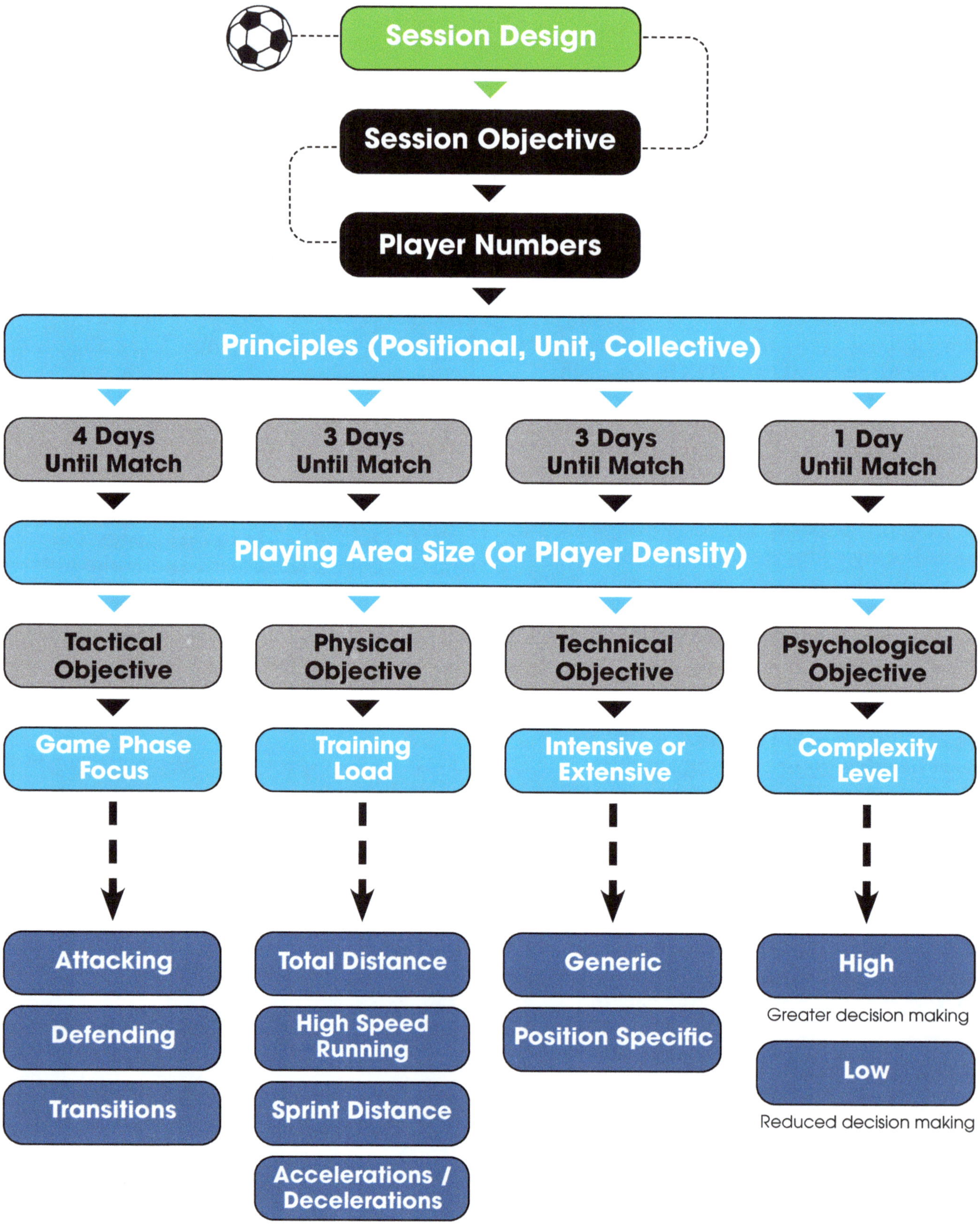

Session Design
↓
Session Objective
↓
Player Numbers
↓
Principles (Positional, Unit, Collective)

4 Days Until Match	3 Days Until Match	3 Days Until Match	1 Day Until Match

↓
Playing Area Size (or Player Density)

Tactical Objective	Physical Objective	Technical Objective	Psychological Objective
Game Phase Focus	Training Load	Intensive or Extensive	Complexity Level
Attacking	Total Distance	Generic	High — Greater decision making
Defending	High Speed Running	Position Specific	Low — Reduced decision making
Transitions	Sprint Distance		
	Accelerations / Decelerations		

Chapter 5: Training Session Design

The Tactical Objective

Determining the **Tactical Aspects** of the practice or session may be based upon the team's:

- **Tactical Priority**
- **Game Model**
- **Playing Philosophy**

The **Tactical Objective** may also be directly related to what the opposing team may do in the upcoming game and can change accordingly.

As shown, there are 5 different phases of the game - the **attacking phase**, the **defensive phase**, the **transition to attack**, the **transition to defence**, and **set plays** (free kicks, corners, goal kicks, throw-ins).

The Game Phase Focus

The coach or coaching team may develop a practice or session based on a specific phase of the game:

- When improvement is needed in a particular phase of the game
- Based around the strengths and weaknesses of the upcoming opponents in a particular phase of the game

Within a game or a training scenario, players are always within one of the 5 phases of the game we have outlined.

Chapter 5: Training Session Design

The Physical Objective

During the objective section of the session design phase, is where the holistic coaching approach takes shape, combining the physiological, psychological and biomechanical components to optimise performance.

Having considered the tactical objective of the design phase, understanding the physical requirements of the practice is vitally important in order to **balance the fitness vs. freshness aspects** as discussed previously. Overloading muscles or energy systems will result in an increased injury risk for players, so **being able to justify the physical targets to go after within the session will produce a better outcome for the session.**

The practices included in this book provide physical output metrics for coaches to understand how different drills/practices can influence different physical loads.

The **training load management** chapter in this book provides coaches with an understanding that different size areas, player density, player numbers and constraints within the session design phase will greatly influence player performance.

KEY POINT: We need to understand what the coaching focus is from a physical perspective, so here is an example:

1. Is the coach aiming for high levels of high speed running or sprint distance?
2. Or is the coach aiming for high levels of accelerations and decelerations?
3. Or is the aim to increase the number of changes of direction to increase the strength work of the lower limbs?

These will require different decisions from a coaching perspective.

Chapter 5: **Training Session Design**

WORKLOAD MONITORING OF STARTERS AND NON-STARTERS

During Congested Fixture Periods (Reference: Gualteri et al. IJSM 2020)

STUDY: 20 Serie A (Italy) football players were monitored during two mesocycles of 21 days, each to assess the internal and external workload players who started matches, and those who didn't (substitutes or unused)

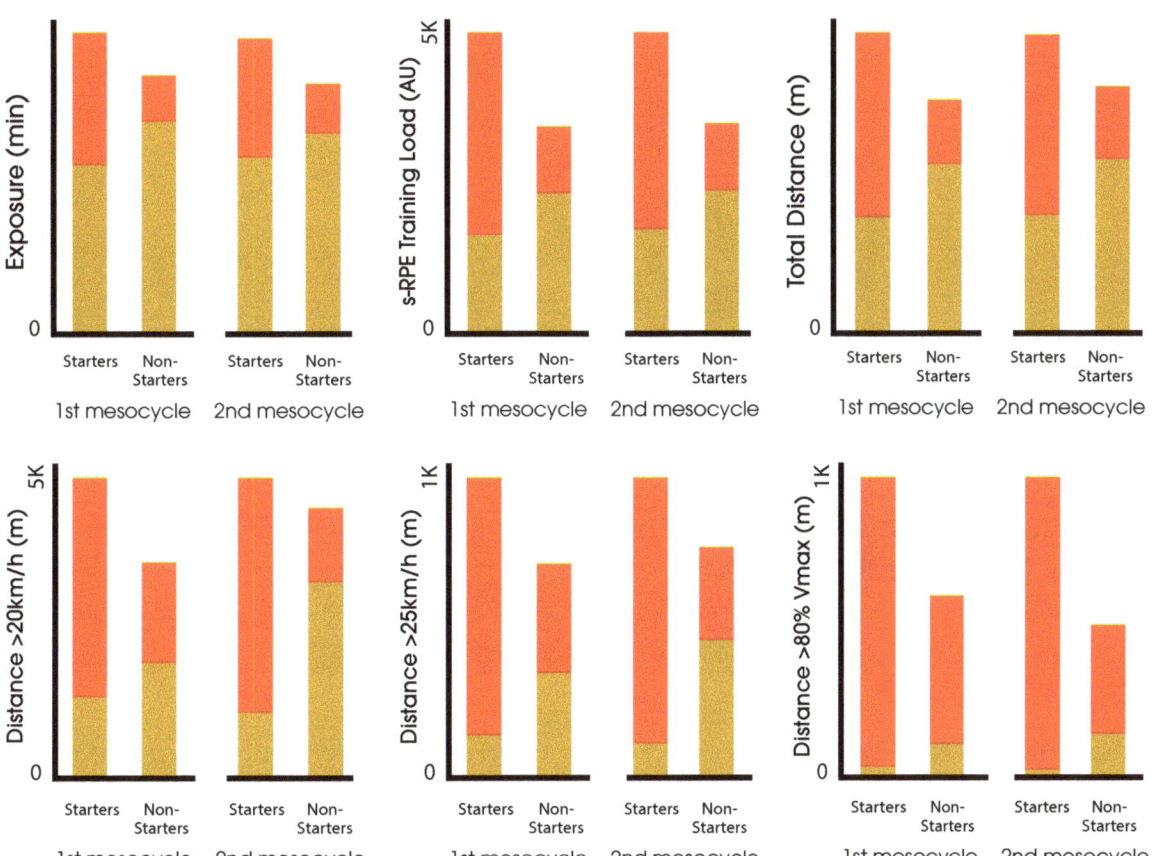

Match | **Training**

1. Starters demonstrated higher internal and external workload compared to non-starters during congested fixture periods when both training and match load were included.
2. Football matches are a critical training component of the week, where players can perform more very high-speed running and football-specific activities, which can be difficult to recreate during a congested fixture training week.

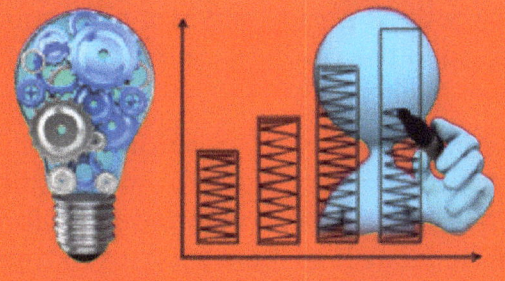

CONCLUSION: More tailored training strategies should be implemented for non-starter players to better compensate the lower workload experienced in comparison to starters.

Special attention should be paid to training strategies capable of promoting greater demands in terms of high-intensity activities.

Images provided by PresenterMedia

Designed by @YLMSportScience

Chapter 5: Training Session Design

The Technical Objective

The Technical Objective

The most important element within this section is whether or not there is a general technical feel or objective, or the coaching points are focused around positional based technical development in line with key objectives moving into the next game.

Intensive Technical Practices

Intensive technical practices focus on shorter sharper, explosive (intensive) based technical practices with a slightly reduced recovery time between each technical action.

Extensive Technical Practices

Extensive technical practices are used if the focus of the technical aspects are more around larger surface areas (extensive).

General Technical Practices

Thinking about this aspect, we consider the technical actions. General technical practices are made up of generic technical actions without any position specific executions.

Position Specific Technical Practices

Conversely, position specific technical practices contain the development of specific technical actions performed in specific areas of the pitch in the positions those players operate in a match.

For example, an intensive position specific technical practice for a full back may include a one-two pass around a mannequin before performing a cut-back for a forward to time his run and finish.

Chapter 5: Training Session Design

SKILLS PERIODIZATION

Reference: Mujika et al. IJSPP 2018

Designed by @YLMSportScience

SPECIFICITY

Specificity of the practice/s is an essential element of a periodized plan (specific time blocks)

The complexity of specificity could be manipulated through variations in the constraints applied e.g. amount of defensive pressure, time pressure, but some form of specificity is always present.

OVERLOAD

Cognitive effort usually indicates that the performer is required to actively engage in skill practice

Opportunities to unload the degree of cognitive effort is also critical, particularly when considered in connection (parallel) with the physical training load.

PROGRESSION

Progression in the complexity of the practiced skill and its interaction with the amount of repetitions (frequency) completed

Complexity and frequency can be manipulated (and recorded) to develop an overall load which brings about an optimal challenge point.

PREVENT REVERSIBILITY

Reversibility highlights the importance of systematically recording skill performance to determine the degree of learning achieved

Identifying how long a skill can be left without practice before reversibility effects appear is useful in periodized high performance programs often overcrowded with competing practice needs and limited practice time.

PREVENT BOREDOM

Boredom due to monotony is detrimental to any skill development

Increased practice variability is useful for reducing the likelihood of boredom. Higher practice variability is associated with suppressed practice performance but superior transfer performance and increased cognitive effort. These interactive features need to be understood for skill development periodization.

Images provided by PresenterMedia

Chapter 5: Training Session Design

The Psychological Objective

I would suggest that the psychological aspects are the most untapped aspects of coaching development. The psychological objectives in this book are determined through the level of complexity.

Increasing or decreasing the psychological demand on players will generally be in line with the fatigue state of the player.

For example, if the session is during the highest load day of the training week (microcycle), when players are at their freshest, the level of complexity can be increased.

If the levels of fatigue are higher on the first day of the training week, then the level of complexity should therefore be reduced in consideration.

NOTE: The periodized/tapered session plans and training week for peak physical performance are fully outlined in the next chapter for different levels of the game.

Training Session Flow

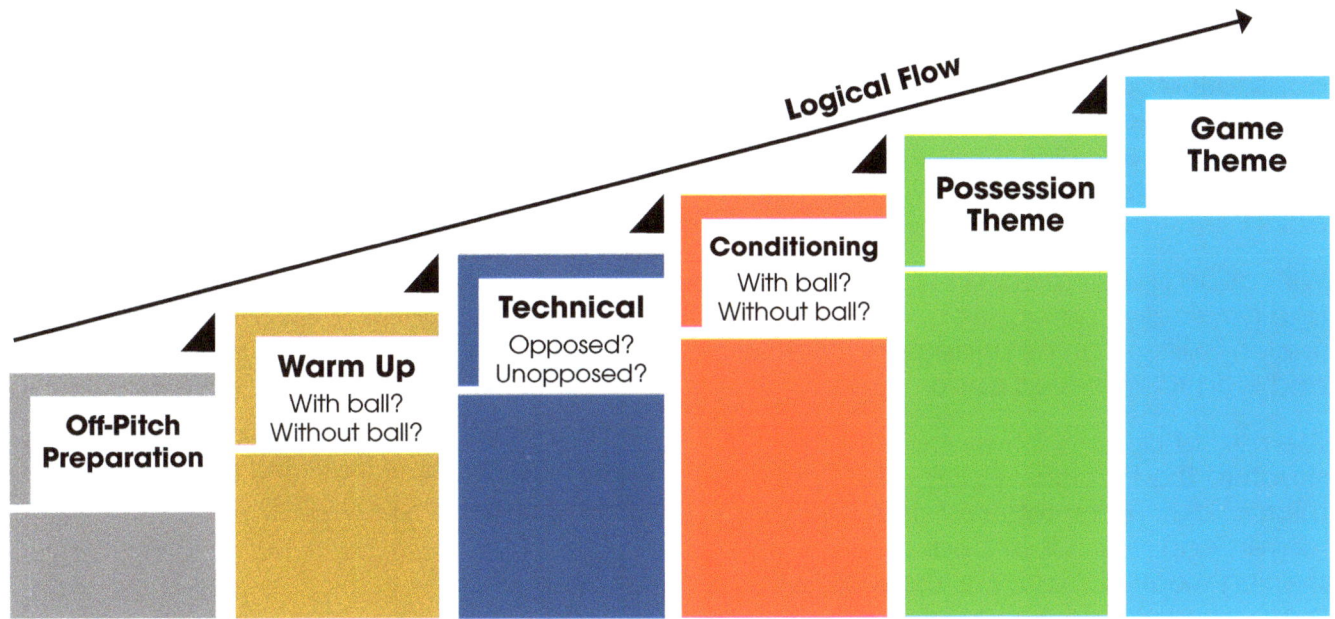

- Ensure logical flow through session – physical, technical, and tactical
- Intelligent and efficient coaching – maintain focus and intensity
- Be concise and direct with coaching points – maintain clarity
- Use natural breaks to coach and get points across
- Don't break the rhythm and reduce intensity
- Sessions should flow!

Warm-up

- Don't just use as a time filler!
- Physically prepare for session demands
- Psychological preparation (tactical)

Technical

- Continue flow of the session
- Gradually increase intensity and demand from warm-up phase
- Influence technical, tactical, psychological and physical outcomes
- Expansion or limitation of area size depending on physical requirements

Conditioning

- Overload the physical focus of session
- Induce key physical stimulus of session
- Ensure opportunity for players to develop specific physical qualities
- Prepare players fully for the upcoming intensity demands

Possession

- Continue flow and demand of the session
- Ensure coaching within the phase is concise and intelligent
- Ensure match intensity is attained to achieve competition transfer and realism
- Coaching within natural recovery breaks is key to minimise influencing the intensity and direction of the session

Chapter 5: Training Session Design

Planning the Training Week with Tapering Strategy to Maximise Performance

To assist in the practical application of the content, the flow of the training session is vitally important to increase the intensity, application and engagement of the players. This can be done through administering the content of the session through a logical flow, focussing on some simple key coaching points.

With good preparation, both tactically and physically, the players' roles and responsibilities can be understood further and lead to improved performances.

The next chapter 6 shows you how to structure the training week (periodized microcycle) with a tapered strategy so your players can reach their peak performance. Training week plans for Professional, Semi-professional, Youth Academy, and Grassroots (Youth) football are all included.

The following chapter 7 is **"Periodized Practices to Maximise Performance"** which shows you all the different types of practices organised into their different sections:

- » **Recovery**
- » **Warm-ups** (Resistance, Speed Endurance, Reaction Speed)
- » **Technical** (Intensive, Extensive)
- » **Conditioning** (Resistance, Speed Endurance, Reaction Speed)
- » **Possession** (Small, Medium, Large)
- » **Games** (Small, Medium, Large)

You can then drop these practice types into the applicable day and session on the training week session plans.

CHAPTER 6

Planning the Training Week with Tapering Strategy to Maximise Performance

Practical Coaching Model to Build the Training Week (Microcycle)

Using the training sessions within this book, the tables to follow provide a framework for coaches of various coaching levels or categories to utilise as a guide in order to structure their training week. Following this specific training methodology, it is possible to implement an integrated training concept. Being able to understand the physical, technical and tactical outcomes of the session are key to maximising the coaching time with the players involved.

Selecting from the various categorised practices in this book in the correct order provides assistance with the fundamentally important session design phase.

Furthermore, based on the understanding of the physical outcomes of each practice, coaches will be able to enhance their knowledge of how **the session design phase can be tailored to meet the session objectives from a physical, technical and tactical perspective**.

Key Point: Selection of practices in the book will generate a better understanding for coaches of the physical demands imposed by individual practices and accumulative total sessions over a period of time.

It should be noted that the physical data provided in these practices and sessions within this book has been generated from elite professional players, so it is suggested that practice durations, repetitions and area sizes are adapted to best suit the age groups being coached.

The data values give the readers an understanding of the demands imposed on players at the level assessed. The physical output metrics are for coaches to understand how different practices can influence different physical loads.

The 5 different training week examples (microcycles) outlined on the following pages are as follows:

1. **Professional Microcycle**
   (4 Training Sessions per week + Match + Compensatory Session)

2. **Semi-professional Microcycle**
   (3 Training Sessions per week + Match)

3. **Youth Academy Microcycle**
   (2 Training Sessions per week + Match)

4. **Grassroots (Youth) Microcycle 1 - Small Sided Game Focus**
   (1 Training Session per week, which alternates with Grassroots Microcycle 2)

5. **Grassroots (Youth) Microcycle 2 - Large Sided Game Focus**
   (1 Training Session per week, which alternates with Grassroots Microcycle 1)

NOTE: In the next chapter of the book, we have presented the practices in the format of the **Professional 4 Training Sessions + Match training week**, but you can adapt it and select the practices required for your relevant 3, 2 or 1 session training week.

Periodization, Tapering Strategy and Maximising Performance

Bringing together the previous sections in this book enables the development of a specific and integrated coaching approach to the training week, otherwise known as the **microcycle tapering strategy**.

It is well documented that placing various but contextual stressors on individual athletes or football players as a way of developing them from a physical, tactical and technical perspective is imperative.

As previously reported, this is done through variation and changing of the training load but also ensuring the balance between work and recovery is apparent.

Periodization and Tapering is a process of structuring and forward planning that involves the manipulation of key variables in order to cause a balanced approach to both overload and regeneration periods causing optimal performance (Mallo, 2015).

Manipulating key variables as described previously through **various constraints such as player numbers, surface area, training game types, bout duration, frequency and intensity, will significantly affect training load variables and outcomes, which conjunctively lead to performance enhancement** (Bosquet et al., 2007).

The strategy discussed and employed will be highlighted through **daily objectives or themes directly linked to their physiological focus**, whilst highlighting some of the key manipulated variables used to cause energy system and muscular overloads through football training concepts.

Each section will provide practical coaching principles that can be influenced by various game-model development or playing philosophies, and where possible, justify the content through published scientific work.

Please note that the training week (microcycle) overview is predominantly focussing on those starting players accumulating >45 to 60 minutes in competitive match-play.

Non-starters or squad players within the group obviously follow a program ensuring compensatory 'top-up' training is performed.

In order to understand the daily formatting, the content is titled by the number format of training days following the previous match (+), in addition to the number of days until the next fixture (-).

For example, in the Professional Microcycle, the Tuesday training day is 3 days after the previous match and 4 days before the next match, so is therefore named **MD +3/-4**.

Chapter 6: Planning the Training Week with Tapering Strategy to Maximise Performance

THE TRAINING WEEK:
Professional Microcycle

4 Training Sessions per Week + Match + Compensatory Session

DAY OF THE WEEK		MONDAY	TUESDAY	WEDNESDAY	THURSDAY	FRIDAY	SATURDAY	SUNDAY
Post-Game + / Pre-Game -		MD +2/-5	MD +3/-4	MD +4/-3	MD +5/-2	MD +6/-1	Match	MD +1/-6
Game Focus		Recovery	Intensive	Extensive	Balanced	Intensive	Extensive	Non-Starters
Tactical Focus		Evaluate	Defending	Attacking	Balanced	Review	Execute	-
PHYSICAL FOCUS		RECOVERY	RESISTANCE	SPEED END.	REACTION SPEED	ACTIVATION	MATCH	COMPEN-SATORY
Warm-up	Recovery	■						
	Resistance		■			■		
	Speed Endurance			■				
	Reaction Speed				■			
Technical	Intensive		■					
	Extensive			■				
Conditioning	Resistance		■					
	Speed Endurance			■				
	Reaction Speed				■	■		
Possession	Small Sided		■					
	Medium Sided				■			
	Large Sided			■				
Game	Small Sided		■					
	Medium Sided				■			
	Large Sided			■		■		

This shows how the colour-coded practices to follow in the book can form the training week based on periodized training sessions to optimise performance.

This example shows a specific methodology of work across the microcycle for professional or full-time training teams. Obviously, this is a template to work from because every coach has their own individual way of working when it comes to session flow, tactical focus, etc. The compensatory based training content is left blank for the coach to fill in.

Training Session Format Example for Professional Training Week (Microcycle)

SUNDAY/MONDAY - 1/2 Days Until Match = Recovery

TUESDAY (70-75 min) - 4 Days Until Match (MD +3/-4)
Positional Principle Training and Resistance:

1. Resistance Warm-up (10-12 min)
2. Intensive Technical Practice (10-15 min)
3. Resistance Conditioning Practice (10-20 min)
4. Small Sided Possession (10-12 min)
5. Small Sided Game (10-25 min)

WEDNESDAY (85-95 min) - 3 Days Until Match (MD +4/-3)
Collective Team Principle Training and Speed Endurance:

1. Speed Endurance Warm-up (10-12 min)
2. Extensive Technical Practice (12-15 min)
3. Speed Endurance Conditioning Practice (5-15 min)
4. Large Sided Possession (10-15 min)
5. Large Sided Game in Large Area (10-50 min)

THURSDAY (60-70 min) - 2 Days Until Match (MD +5/-2)
Unit Principle Training and Reaction Speed Development:

1. Reaction Speed Warm-up (5-7 min)
2. Intensive Technical Practice (10-15 min)
3. Reaction Speed Conditioning Practice (5-15 min)
4. Medium Sided Possession (6-15 min)
5. Medium Sided Game (10-25 min)

FRIDAY (45-60 min) - 1 Day Until Match (MD +6/-1)
Pre-Match Activation Training Day:

1. Resistance Warm-up (10-12 min)
2. Reaction Speed Conditioning Practice (5-15 min)
3. Large Sided Game in Small/Medium Area (10-50 min)

Chapter 6: Planning the Training Week with Tapering Strategy to Maximise Performance

THE TRAINING WEEK:
Semi-professional Microcycle

3 Training Sessions per Week + Match

DAY OF THE WEEK		MONDAY	TUESDAY	WEDNESDAY	THURSDAY	FRIDAY	SATURDAY	SUNDAY
Post-Game + / Pre-Game -		MD +2/-5	MD +3/-4	MD +4/-3	MD +5/-2	MD +6/-1	Match	MD +1/-6
Game Focus		Recovery	Intensive	Extensive	Recovery	Intensive	Extensive	Recovery
Tactical Focus		Free Evening	Defending	Attacking	Free Evening	Review	Execute	Free Evening
PHYSICAL FOCUS		RECOVERY	RESISTANCE	SPEED END.	RECOVERY	ACTIVATION	MATCH	RECOVERY
Warm-up	Recovery							
	Resistance		■			■		
	Speed Endurance			■				
	Reaction Speed							
Technical	Intensive		■					
	Extensive			■				
Conditioning	Resistance		■					
	Speed Endurance			■				
	Reaction Speed					■		
Possession	Small Sided		■					
	Medium Sided							
	Large Sided			■				
Game	Small Sided			■				
	Medium Sided					■		
	Large Sided			■				

This shows how the colour-coded practices to follow in the book can form the training week based on periodized training sessions to optimise performance.

This example shows a specific methodology of work across the microcycle for semi-professional teams training 3 times per week.

Obviously, this is a template to work from because every coach has their own individual way of working when it comes to session flow, tactical focus, etc.

Chapter 6: Planning the Training Week with Tapering Strategy to Maximise Performance

THE TRAINING WEEK:
Youth Academy Microcycle

2 Training Sessions per Week + Match

DAY OF THE WEEK		MONDAY	TUESDAY	WEDNESDAY	THURSDAY	FRIDAY	SATURDAY	SUNDAY
Post-Game + / Pre-Game -		MD +2/-5	MD +3/-4	MD +4/-3	MD +5/-2	MD +6/-1	Match	MD +1/-6
Game Focus		Recovery	Intensive	Recovery	Extensive	Recovery	Extensive	Recovery
Tactical Focus		Free Evening	Defending	Free Evening	Attacking	Free Evening	Execute	Free Evening
PHYSICAL FOCUS		RECOVERY	RESISTANCE	RECOVERY	SPEED END.	RECOVERY	MATCH	RECOVERY
Warm-up	Recovery							
	Resistance		●					
	Speed Endurance				●			
	Reaction Speed							
Technical	Intensive		●					
	Extensive				●			
Conditioning	Resistance		●					
	Speed Endurance				●			
	Reaction Speed							
Possession	Small Sided		●					
	Medium Sided							
	Large Sided				●			
Game	Small Sided		●					
	Medium Sided							
	Large Sided				●			

This shows how the colour-coded practices to follow in the book can form the training week based on periodized training sessions to optimise performance.

This example shows a specific methodology of work across the microcycle for youth academy teams training 2 times per week.

Obviously, this is a template to work from because every coach has their own individual way of working when it comes to session flow, tactical focus, etc.

Chapter 6: Planning the Training Week with Tapering Strategy to Maximise Performance

THE TRAINING WEEK:
Grassroots (Youth) Microcycle 1

SSG / Resistance Focus - Alternates with Grassroots (Youth) Microcycle 2

DAY OF THE WEEK		MONDAY	TUESDAY	WEDNESDAY	THURSDAY	FRIDAY	SATURDAY	SUNDAY
Post-Game + / Pre-Game -		MD +2/-5	MD +3/-4	MD +4/-3	MD +5/-2	MD +6/-1	Match	MD +1/-6
Game Focus		Recovery	Recovery	Intensive	Recovery	Recovery	Extensive	Recovery
Tactical Focus		Free Evening	Free Evening	Attacking	Free Evening	Free Evening	Execute	Free Evening
PHYSICAL FOCUS		**RECOVERY**	**RECOVERY**	**RESISTANCE**	**RECOVERY**	**RECOVERY**	**MATCH**	**RECOVERY**
Warm-up	Recovery							
	Resistance			■				
	Speed Endurance							
	Reaction Speed							
Technical	Intensive			■				
	Extensive							
Conditioning	Resistance			■				
	Speed Endurance							
	Reaction Speed							
Possession	Small Sided			■				
	Medium Sided							
	Large Sided							
Game	Small Sided			■				
	Medium Sided							
	Large Sided							

This shows how the colour-coded practices to follow in the book can form the training week based on periodized training sessions to optimise performance.

Grassroots (Youth) Microcycle 1 has a small sided game focus and alternates with **Grassroots (Youth) 2 - see next page**, which has a large sided game focus

Obviously, this is a template to work from because every coach has their own individual way of working when it comes to session flow, tactical focus, etc.

Chapter 6: Planning the Training Week with Tapering Strategy to Maximise Performance

THE TRAINING WEEK:
Grassroots (Youth) Microcycle 2

LSG / Speed Endurance Focus - Alternates with Grassroots (Youth) Microcycle 1

DAY OF THE WEEK		MONDAY	TUESDAY	WEDNESDAY	THURSDAY	FRIDAY	SATURDAY	SUNDAY
Post-Game + / Pre-Game -		MD +2/-5	MD +3/-4	MD +4/-3	MD +5/-2	MD +6/-1	Match	MD +1/-6
Game Focus		Recovery	Recovery	Extensive	Recovery	Recovery	Extensive	Recovery
Tactical Focus		Free Evening	Free Evening	Defending	Free Evening	Free Evening	Execute	Free Evening
PHYSICAL FOCUS		RECOVERY	RECOVERY	SPEED END.	RECOVERY	RECOVERY	MATCH	RECOVERY
Warm-up	Recovery							
	Resistance							
	Speed Endurance			■				
	Reaction Speed							
Technical	Intensive							
	Extensive			■				
Conditioning	Resistance							
	Speed Endurance			■				
	Reaction Speed							
Possession	Small Sided							
	Medium Sided							
	Large Sided			■				
Game	Small Sided							
	Medium Sided							
	Large Sided			■				

This shows how the colour-coded practices to follow in the book can form the training week based on periodized training sessions to optimise performance.

Grassroots (Youth) Microcycle 2 has a large sided game focus and alternates with Grassroots (Youth) Microcycle 1 - <u>see previous page</u>, which has a small sided game focus

Obviously, this is a template to work from because every coach has their own individual way of working when it comes to session flow, tactical focus, etc.

CHAPTER 7

Periodized Practices to Maximise Performance

NOTE: In this chapter, we have presented the practices in the format of the **Professional 4 Training Sessions + Match training week (see pages 74-75)**, but you can adapt it and select the practices required for your relevant 3, 2 or 1 session training week (please see relevant tables in the previous chapter).

Chapter 7: Periodized Practices to Maximise Performance

The Benefit of the Data for Each Practice
(Volume and Intensity Metrics)

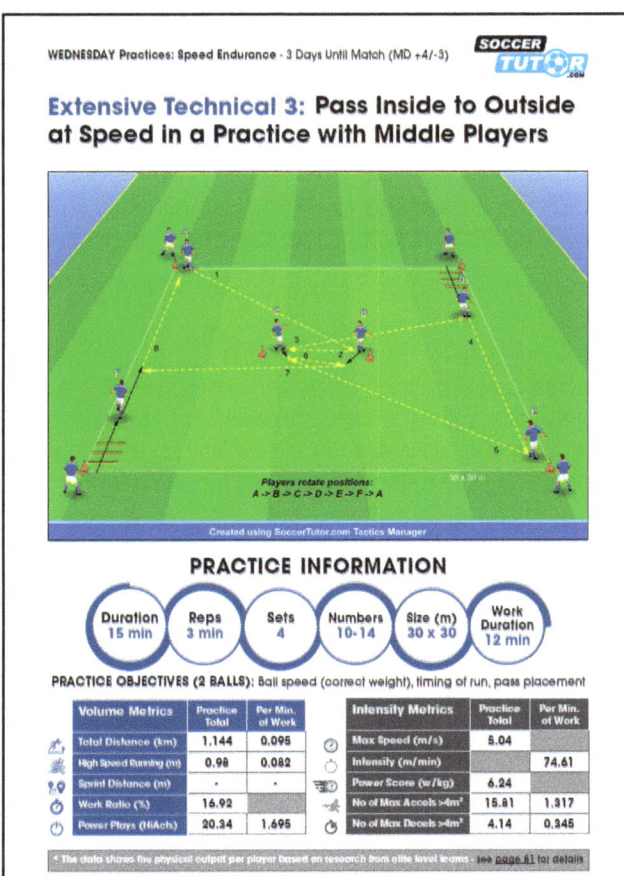

Where does the data come from?

The data is collected from the elite professional level using GPS tracking equipment.

How can coaches of all levels learn from this data?

In my role as a **coach educator** for Level 2, **UEFA B, UEFA A** and **UEFA Pro Licence**, all of the coaches have been extremely excited to have access to the data included in this book.

The information provides a method for all coaches tasked with the performance development of players. The data provides key information from the professional level (average per player), in order to educate the differences between different types of practices and their specific physical loads for coaching at all levels.

It is extremely important to understand how different practices produce specific outcomes and physical development stresses to the players within those sessions. This is key for **tapering sessions and weekly training plans to reduce the risk of injury and for optimising the specific coaching focus from a physical conditioning perspective**.

Why are the volume and intensity metrics useful information to have for each practice?

The values give the readers an understanding of the demands imposed on players. It is extremely important to understand how different practices produce different physical outcomes and stresses. The data figures show you this e.g. Total Distance Covered (m), Work Ratio (%), Sprint Distance (m), etc.

How can this data help me optimise my training plan to produce maximum (peak) level performances?

Selection of practices in the book will generate a better understanding of the physical demands imposed by individual practices and accumulative total sessions over a period of time.

Understanding the physical demands on specific training practices and sessions is a vitally important aspect of the modern coaching strategy to maximise all aspects of training.

The main aim of any training load management process is to provide the individuals involved in the football development of players to positively evaluate and interpret the data they have available to them.

The main point is that all coaches need to now be aware of this information and data, so they can produce the best possible results.

If the same mistakes keep occurring without monitoring relationships between training load and the game, then we may just be guessing, potentially regressing the players development, and providing poor quality training to our players...

Chapter 7: **Periodized Practices to Maximise Performance**

KEY TERMS

VOLUME METRICS FOR ALL PRACTICES

Total Distance (km)
Total distance provides a full representation of volume of exercise (walking, running, sprinting, jogging) and is a very simple way of assessing individual effort within the practice or game.

High Speed Running (m)
HSR is distance travelled above speeds of 5.5 metres per second. Greater amounts of high speed running signify a high level of the game or football fitness, however different playing surface areas influence this metric assessed within training. Players will commonly cover HSR distances above 1000-1500m depending on position, maximum speed and fitness levels.

Sprint Distance (m)
Sprint distance is calculated as total distance covered above 7 metres per second. The capacity of players to achieve this is generally higher amongst elite professional players. The playing area significantly influences this value as small sided, reduced areas lower the sprint opportunities. Greater amounts of sprinting signify a high level of game or sport fitness.

Work Ratio (%)
This is defined as the percentage of time the player was performing work or movements. The work is defined as walking or running at speeds higher than 1.5 metres per second (slow to moderate walk for most people). Work ratio in general can be associated with the amount of time a player is working compared to resting during a training session, or game phase.

High Metabolic Load Distance (HMLD)
HMLD measures the total amount of high speed running performed, coupled with the total distance of accelerations and decelerations throughout a session.

Power Plays (HiActs)
This is defined as a significant action (such as acceleration or high speed running event) in which the power output performed by the player was above 20 watts per kg of body weight. Counting power plays gives you an indication of the number of intense actions the players performed in the practice or game. These are obviously far more physically demanding.

Player Density (m²)
The quantity per unit of playing space per player, which is calculated as follows:
Length of pitch x width of pitch, divided (÷) by the number of players on the pitch.

Chapter 7: Periodized Practices to Maximise Performance

INTENSITY METRICS FOR ALL PRACTICES

Max Speed (m/s)
Max speed is defined in this book as the fastest maximum speed achieved and sustained for at least half a second. They are represented as metres per second (m/s). For most players, 8.5m/s can be considered quick, but when we compare to elite level sprinters such as world record holder and legendary athlete Usain Bolt, he achieved regular speeds ~11.1m/s.

Intensity (m/min)
Distance per minute provides the coaches and players with an overall representation of how hard, or how intense they have worked. Professional players within competitive match play can achieve between 112-135 m/min, however these results are different depending on the tactical strategy played, and positional differences of the individual players.

Power Score (w/kg)
Calculated as watts (w) divided by your body weight in kilograms (kg) = w/kg. This provides an insight into the power output used per kg of the player's weight and is used to gauge the intensity of training practices with high work-rates within a small area e.g. Small sided games. Practices are considered intense when the power score is above 10 w/kg. Amongst amateur football players, values of 7-8 w/kg are normal.

Number of Max Accelerations >4m^2
Number of accelerations performed in the practice/drill or session that are greater than 4 metres per second^2. These are the higher, more explosive accelerations that demand significant energy, strength and power.

Number of Max Decelerations >4m^2
Number of decelerations performed in the practice/drill or session that are greater than 4 metres per second^2. These are the higher, more explosive decelerations that demand significant energy, strength and power.

Max Acceleration Distance (m)
Total distance accumulated within the session through accelerations performed greater than 4 metres per second^2. These are the higher, more explosive acceleration distances.

Max Deceleration Distance (m)
Total distance accumulated within the session through decelerations performed greater than 4 metres per second^2. These are the higher, more explosive deceleration distances.

MONDAY: RECOVERY DAY

5 DAYS UNTIL MATCH (MD +2/-5)

MONDAY - 5 DAYS UNTIL MATCH (MD +2/-5):
Recovery Day

What are Recovery Practices?

- Low speed.
- Very light movements with or without the ball as a way of increasing heat rate.
- Recover the overloaded muscle groups.
- Stimulate a slightly elevated heart rate response to aid blood flow and recovery without adding fatigue.

Why are they used on this day of the training week (MD +2/-5)?

- To assist in the recovery of players with minimal amounts of high-speed work, no sprinting, no aggressive accelerations, or changes of direction.

MONDAY Training Day: Recovery - 5 Days Until Match (MD +2/-5)

Recovery 1: Simple 40-Metre Recovery Strides @ 50-60% + Walking Rests

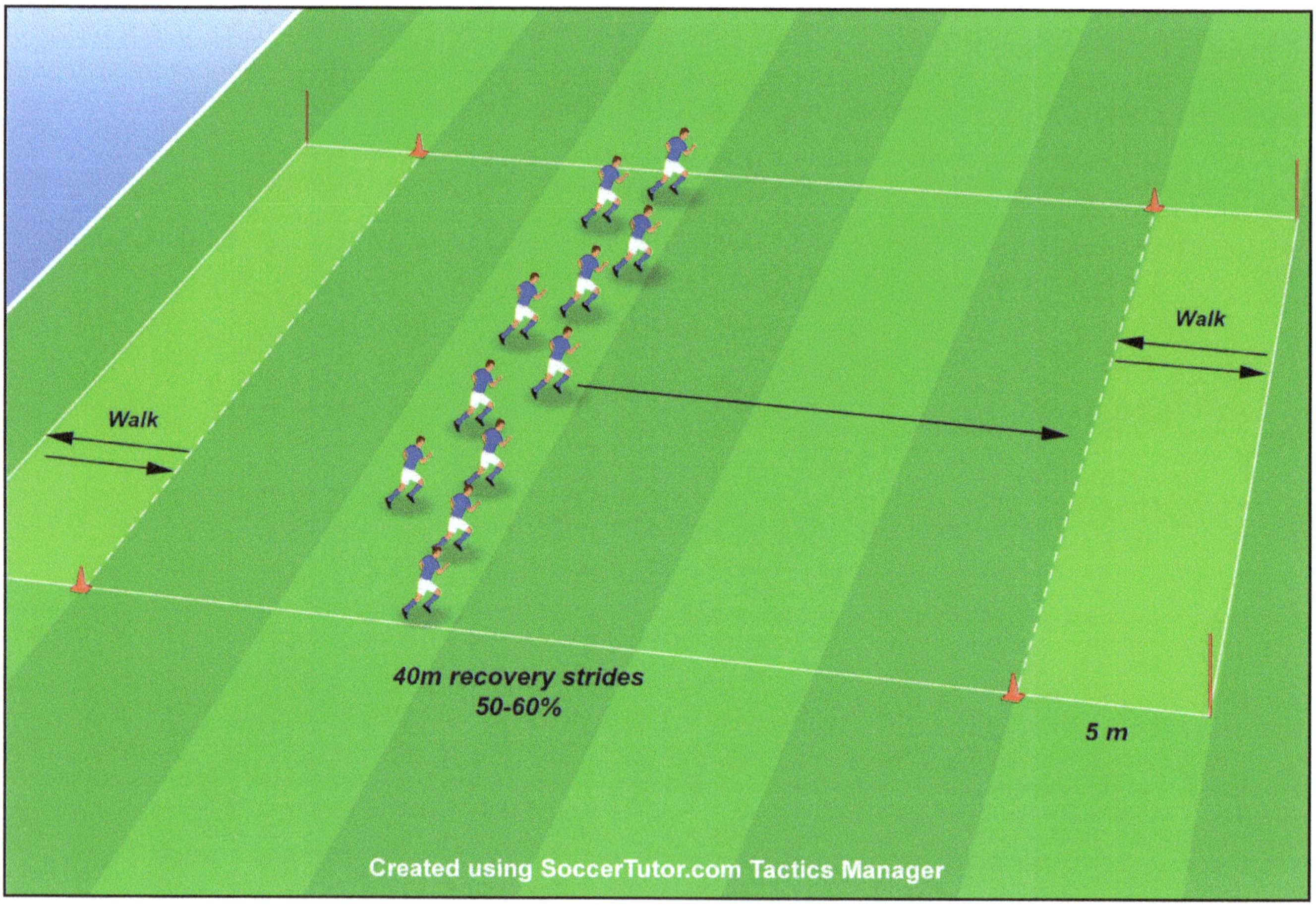

PRACTICE INFORMATION

Duration	Reps	Sets	Numbers	Size (m)	Work Duration
7 min	4 x 10 sec	2 sets @ 60%	N/A	50	80 sec

OBJECTIVES: To assist in the recovery of the key muscle groups required for football performance

Volume Metrics	Practice Total	Per Min. of Work
Total Distance (km)	0.549	0.41
High Speed Running (m)	44.19	33.14
Sprint Distance (m)	-	-
Work Ratio (%)	34.8	
Power Plays (HiActs)	7.59	5.7

Intensity Metrics	Practice Total	Per Min. of Work
Max Speed (m/s)	6.02	
Intensity (m/min)		88.86
Power Score (w/kg)	7.02	
Max Accel. Distance (m)	4.46	3.35
Max Decel. Distance (m)	0.48	0.36

* The data shows the physical output per player based on research from elite level teams - see pages 81-83 for details

MONDAY Training Day: Recovery - 5 Days Until Match (MD +2/-5)

Recovery 2: Basic Footwork and Movement Exercises + Football Tennis

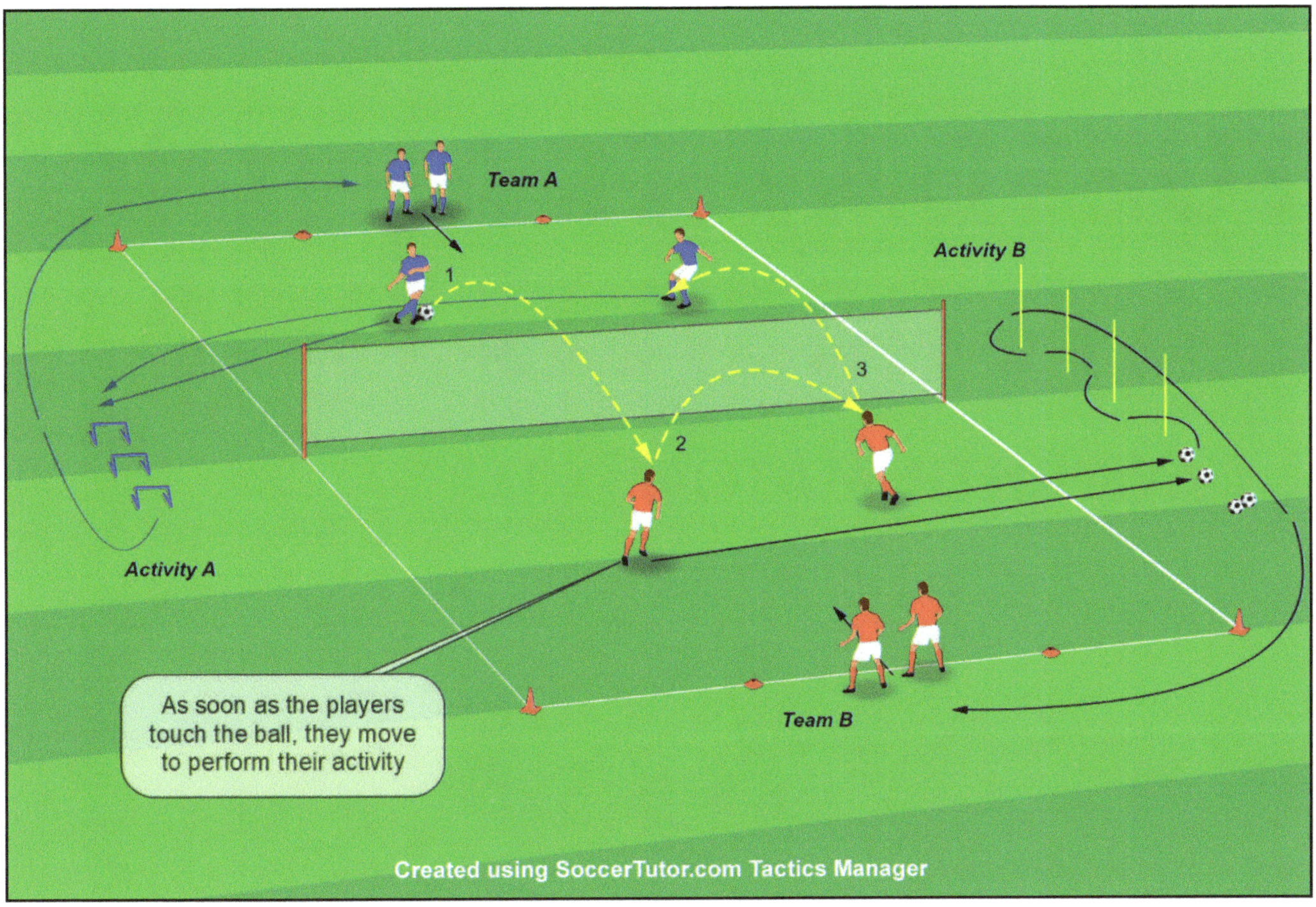

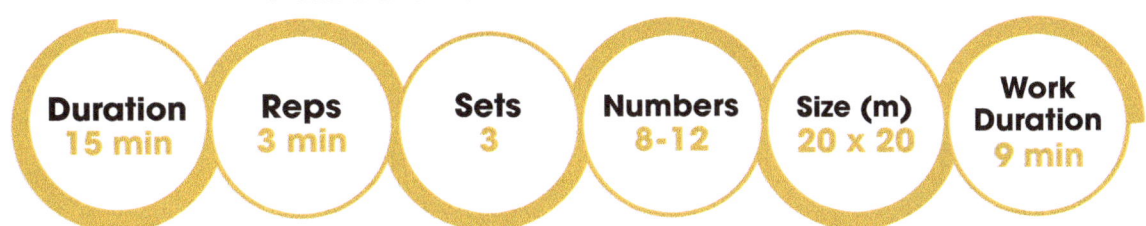

As soon as the players touch the ball, they move to perform their activity

Created using SoccerTutor.com Tactics Manager

PRACTICE INFORMATION

Duration	Reps	Sets	Numbers	Size (m)	Work Duration
15 min	3 min	3	8-12	20 x 20	9 min

OBJECTIVES: To assist in the recovery of the key muscle groups required for football performance

Volume Metrics	Practice Total	Per Min. of Work
Total Distance (km)	0.6	0.07
High Speed Running (m)	-	-
Sprint Distance (m)	-	-
Work Ratio (%)	9.2	
Power Plays (HiActs)	-	-

Intensity Metrics	Practice Total	Per Min. of Work
Max Speed (m/s)	4.2	
Intensity (m/min)		53
Power Score (w/kg)	3.2	
Max Accel. Distance (m)	-	-
Max Decel. Distance (m)	-	-

The data shows the physical output per player based on research from elite level teams - see pages 81-83 for details

Football Periodization to Maximise Performance

TUESDAY TRAINING DAY: RESISTANCE

4 DAYS UNTIL MATCH (MD +3/-4)

TUESDAY Training Day: Resistance - 4 Days Until Match (MD +3/-4)

4 DAYS UNTIL THE MATCH (MD +3/-4):
Positional Principle Training and Resistance

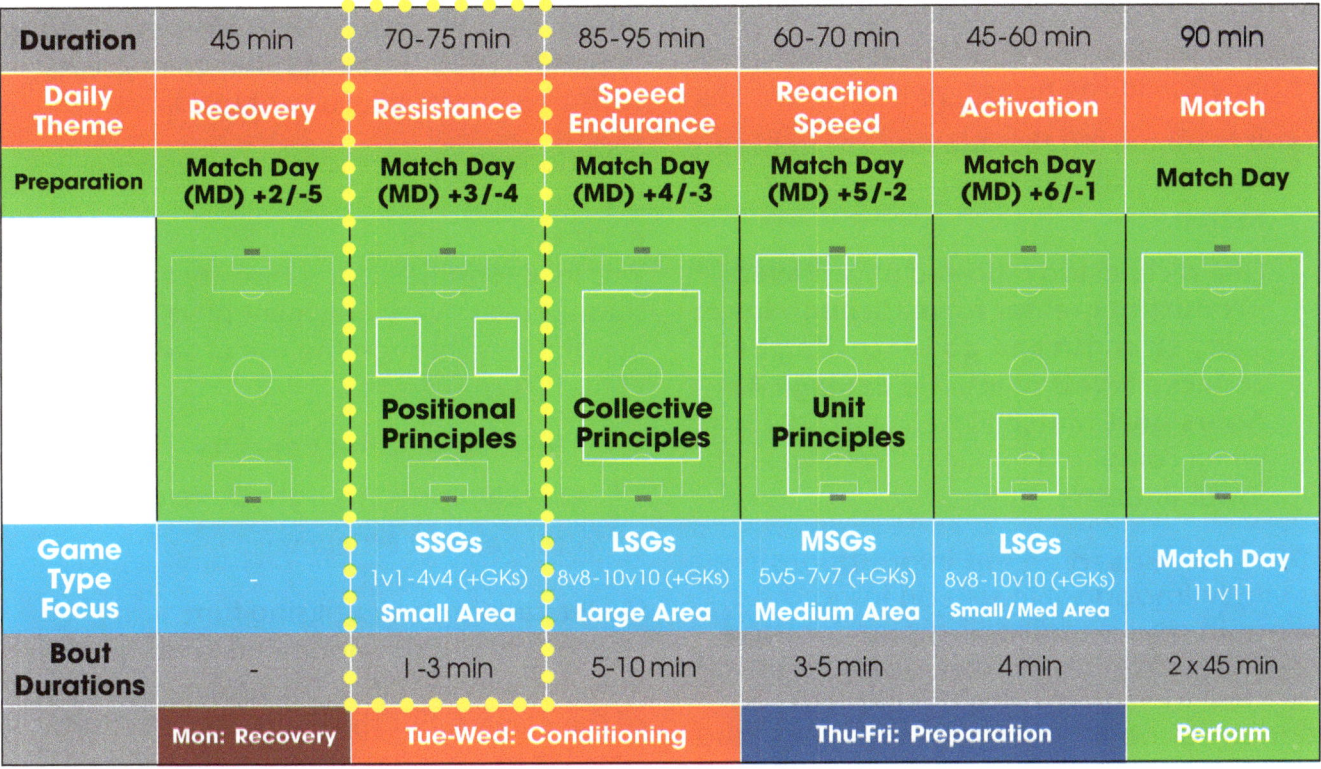

Duration	45 min	70-75 min	85-95 min	60-70 min	45-60 min	90 min
Daily Theme	Recovery	Resistance	Speed Endurance	Reaction Speed	Activation	Match
Preparation	Match Day (MD) +2/-5	Match Day (MD) +3/-4	Match Day (MD) +4/-3	Match Day (MD) +5/-2	Match Day (MD) +6/-1	Match Day
		Positional Principles	Collective Principles	Unit Principles		
Game Type Focus	-	SSGs 1v1-4v4 (+GKs) Small Area	LSGs 8v8-10v10 (+GKs) Large Area	MSGs 5v5-7v7 (+GKs) Medium Area	LSGs 8v8-10v10 (+GKs) Small/Med Area	Match Day 11v11
Bout Durations	-	1-3 min	5-10 min	3-5 min	4 min	2 x 45 min
	Mon: Recovery	Tue-Wed: Conditioning		Thu-Fri: Preparation		Perform

* **Training Week based on Professional Microcycle Example** - see pages 74-75.

Key Focus on:
- **Positional Principles**
- **Higher Muscle Resistance**
- **Changes of Direction** (CODs)
- **Accelerations and Decelerations** (A:D)

TUESDAY Training Day: Resistance - 4 Days Until Match (MD +3/-4)

TUESDAY (MD +3/-4) TRAINING DAY:
Physical and Physiological Focus

Physical Conditioning

As this is the first training day back on the training pitch after the match, it is important to understand the recovery processes:

- It is suggested that **players are in high levels of fatigue for 48 hours post-match**.

- One recent study showed how **players producing greater force through lower body strength and power testing had reduced levels of muscle damage 48 hours post-match** (Owen et al., 2015), when compared to players with weaker lower limb strength.

Key Point: Based on this information, it is vitally important to use an integrated strength and conditioning plan focused on increasing lower body strength levels, as it will lead to an improvement in performance for the physical aspect, and aid in assisting recovery after matches.

Focussing on the key micro or positional principles (i.e. **1v1 or 2v2 Duels**) faced in the system or style of play, reducing the training area size or playing density per player is key to:

- **Increasing Changes of Direction** (CODs)
- **Increasing Accelerations/Decelerations** (A:Ds)
- **Increasing Overall Physical Demands** on players
- **Driving the Cardiovascular System into an Overload State** >90% of maximum heart rate [HRmax]

Small Sided Games (SSGs)

Research into the use of small sided games (SSGs) have highlighted **significant benefits to football players across all levels** of play. Owen et al., (2011) revealed that a group of Champions League level players spent **significantly more time above the adaptation threshold (85%HRmax) playing in Small Sided Games (SSGs)** compared with a comparative study of LSGs.

Additionally, in another study involving the regular use of SSGs within the training microcycle (training week), SSGs were tested within a periodized structure. It concluded that there are very prevalent physical adaptations through the use of SSGs (Owen et al., 2012):

- > **Repeated Sprint Capacity**
- > **Lower Body Strength Development**
- > **Movement Efficiency**

Understanding and utilising functional strength based developments through SSGs may not only enhance the physical capacity of the players, but the suggested strength benefits of SSGs on player recovery could also be significant to coaches.

An earlier study into SSGs (Owen et al., 2014) and the subsequent reduced playing area revealed how the obvious need to evade or create space away from opponents causes more:

- **Individual Technical Demands**
- **Body Contacts** and **Duel Scenarios**
- **Football Specific Strength Demands**, maybe as a result of holding off opponents

From a physiological and psychological point, it may be important that players understand:

- The physical demands imposed on this training day (MD +3/-4) through SSGs.
- How the reduced playing areas help **develop muscle capacity** to withstand the increased levels of A:Ds and CODs.

TUESDAY Training Day: Resistance - 4 Days Until Match (MD +3/-4)

Football Resistance and Intensive Game Focus (SSGs)

Ligament, tendon, joint strength	Eccentric loading
Battle of the arms/legs - body position	Agility based movements
Ability to reproduce football strength actions	Small pitch sizes, small group numbers
> % Tight space TDC vs. linear speed distance	**Key Coaching Themes:** Pressing, transition work, body contacts (arms, legs, ball protection), duels, 1v1s, 2v2s, low level plyometrics
Short explosive Hi-Intensity Efforts & Changes of Direction	
Body contact, football strength/power	

Fatigue and Recovery

The key physical coaching perspectives on this training day should ensure the content is developed to enable the game model or playing details to be included. Although this day is classed as a "conditioning" or "overloading" day, there is the possibility of some residual fatigue remaining from the previous game. Taking this into consideration, the **exposure to large pitch densities should be avoided as a way to reduce the risk of exposing players to high sprint demands or high-speed running efforts** that engage hamstring and maximal sprinting forces.

One study in this area investigating fatigue in differing muscle fibre types revealed how distinctive muscle groups fatigue differently during post-sprint related activities, with a higher degree of fatigue shown with fast twitch (FT) groups vs. groups categorised into slow twitch (ST) muscle typology (Lievens et al., 2020). Furthermore, it was revealed that only 90 seconds of high-intensity exercise induced long-lasting fatigue and muscle impairment in the muscle function after these types of activities.

Fast twitch (FT) exercises delay recovery, so we want to **promote the reduction of High Speed Running (HSR) activities in the post-match recovery phase (within 48-72 hours)** as a result of accumulated fatigue and potential injury (Lievens et al., 2020).

Positional Principles

Training of the positional principles on this day is in conjunction with core-principles of the game, previously highlighted by Teoldo et al., (2020). Focusing on muscle contractions with significant increases in tension through directional changes rather than high-speed linear content, has shown excellent results in the balancing of recovery vs. work at the elite level.

The practice design element of this methodology has shown the existence of SSGs and such practices inclusive of low level plyometrics, duels, accelerations and decelerations (A:Ds), body contacts and change of directions (CODs), not only stimulate and overload the required physical components, but are obtained through reduced density positional drills in the micro-form: 2v2 in centre of goal [centre forwards vs. centre backs]; 1v1 in wide areas to cross or stop cross [full back vs. winger].

These resistance conditioning drills and SSGs stimulus are generally loading not only the strength in the lower limbs, but also the cardiovascular system which leads to an improved endurance capacity of the players.

TUESDAY Training Day: Resistance - 4 Days Until Match (MD +3/-4)

Physiology of Small Sided Games

By Hill-Haas, Dawson, Impelizeri & Coutts - Sports Medicine 2011

Small sided games (SSGs) are played on reduced pitch areas, often using modified rules and involving a smaller number of players than traditional football. These games are less structured than traditional fitness training methods but are very popular for players of all ages and levels.

ADJUSTABLE VARIABLES

Many prescriptive variables controlled by the coach can influence the exercise intensity during small sided games (SSGs)

 **Pitch Area**

 **Training Regimen** Continuous vs Interval

 **Rules**

 **Coach Motivation**

 **Player Numbers**

 **Use of Goalkeeper**

KEY POINTS

1 In general, it appears that SSG exercise intensity is increased with the concurrent reduction in player numbers and increase in relative pitch area per player

2 However, the inverse relationship between the number of players in each SSG and exercise intensity does not apply to the time-motion characteristics

3 Consistent encouragement can increase training intensity, but most rule changes do not strongly affect exercise intensity

4 SSGs with fewer players can exceed match intensity and create similar intensities to long and short high intensity interval running

5 Fitness and football-specific performance can be improved equally with SSGs and generic training drills

TUESDAY (MD +3/-4) TRAINING DAY:
Technical and Tactical Focus

Small Format Duels

The main component of this training day is ensuring all players are exposed to **individual positional based content** situated around the key principles, which are defined by Delgado-Bordonau and Mendez-Villanueva, (2012) in the adapted Tactical Periodization methodology. These principles have further evolved within the coaching framework as the **details required or encountered within 2v2 to 4v4 situations**. These key messages are replicated in direct line with the game model or playing system and style of the coaching team, placing a huge emphasis on the practice design element of the session, as previously described.

Impact of Constraints

It has been well documented that a number of **coaching constraints (e.g. player numbers, pitch sizes and rule changes) involved within a training session influence the physical and technical demands on each player** (Owen et al, 2011; Dellal et al, 2011; Owen et al, 2004; Kaits and Kellis, 2009):

- Clemente et al., (2012) described how **lower player numbers provide increased overloads** within certain games to prepare for competitive match play, as it reduces the variability and potential possibilities of passing options.

- The **size of the pitch or playing density is significant if trying to expose or target certain individuals with more specific positional technical aspects.** For example, small sided games (SSGs) reduce the chances of centre backs heading the ball, or full-backs playing longer passes into forwards due to pitch density limitations.

- Specific **SSGs deliver a more effective intensive or technical training stimulus, due to the overload in technical actions** being increased in accordance with the decrease in player numbers (Owen et al, 2013; Katis and Kellis, 2009; Owen et al, 2004).

- By manipulating the number of touches allowed, the technical and physical demands can be significantly altered. This shows that coaches should carefully implement game rules (e.g. 1-Touch, 2-Touch or free play) to achieve a specific purpose from their training sessions. Exposing players to more technical actions or limitations throughout the training session may lead to technical and decision making improvements (Dellal et al., 2011).

Small Sided Game Benefits

As SSGs provide fewer passing options based on the limited number of players involved, the **increased need for players to dribble past opponents to create space** when trying to maintain possession is a key component of these lesser numbered game formats.

Goal scoring options should be carefully considered by coaches in their organization, session design and periodized approach to the training week structure. Research has suggested how the use of smaller goals over traditional sized goals limits players' scoring opportunities (reduced target size). As a result, it **forces players to recycle possession more often to create better goal scoring opportunities**, therefore maintaining possession for longer periods of time. This leads to **increased ball possession**, **speed of play**, and **decision making processes**.

If players do not have any tactical limitations and are not maintaining possession to build towards a specific target or goal scoring direction, a lower technical demand and cognitive stimulation may be shown. However, further research is needed in order to fully justify these claims. The suggestions of reduced intensity and subsequent technical demands due to no specific directional purpose, directly links to similar findings from Mallo and Navarro (2008). Their research and analysis revealed that the technical outcomes of the sessions inclusive of goalkeepers lowered the number of total technical actions for outfield players. This highlights the lower technical demand in games including goalkeepers (maybe due to a lower intensity of play).

TUESDAY Training Day: Resistance - 4 Days Until Match (MD +3/-4)

TUESDAY (MD +3/-4) TRAINING DAY:
Game Stimulus Response for Positional Principles Game Type

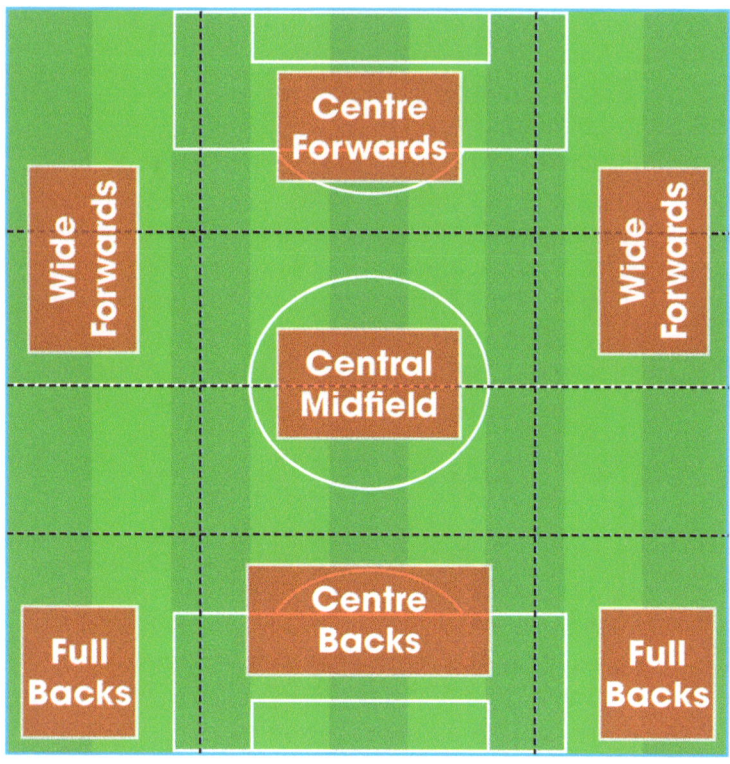

POSITIONAL TRAINING PRINCIPLES

- **Positional Principles** (Individual Focus)
- **Apply Tactical Positional Principles** in small density areas
- **Positional Technical Skills** in small areas
- **Fast Cognitive Situations** — attacking and defensive learning
- Develop the **Decision Making Process**

TUESDAY (MD +3/-4) TRAINING DAY: Fundamental Concepts of Positional Principle Training and Resistance

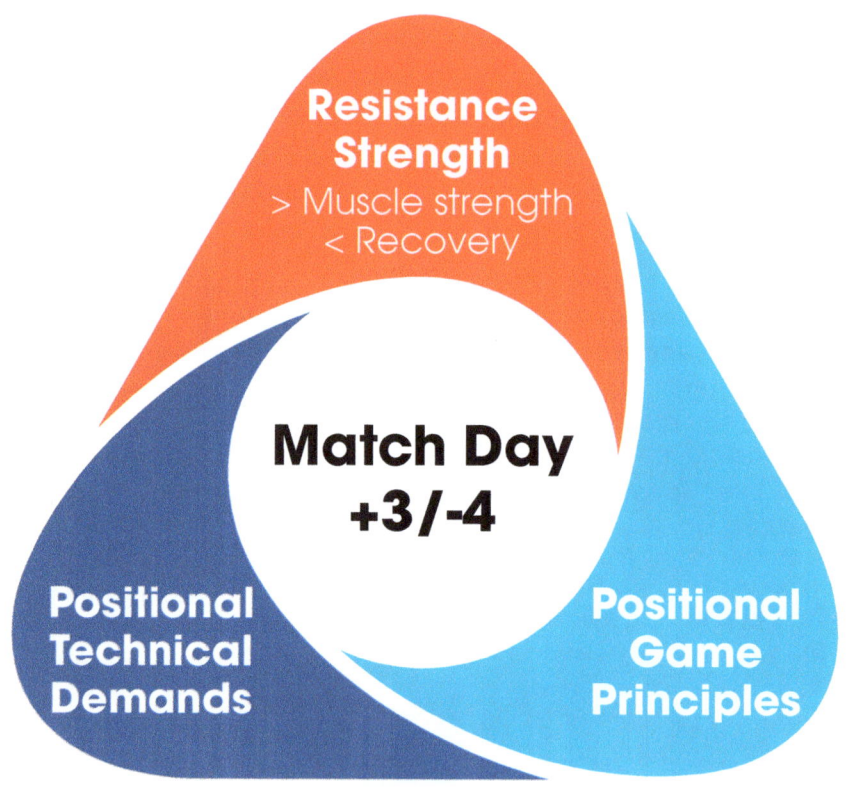

TUESDAY TRAINING DAY PRACTICES: RESISTANCE

4 DAYS UNTIL MATCH (MD +3/-4)

TUESDAY TRAINING SESSION (70-75 min)

Positional Principle Training and Resistance:

1. Resistance Warm-up (10-12 min)
2. Intensive Technical Practice (10-15 min)
3. Resistance Conditioning Practice (10-20 min)
4. Small Sided Possession (10-12 min)
5. Small Sided Game (10-25 min)

TUESDAY Training Day Practices: Resistance - 4 Days Until Match (MD +3/-4)

TUESDAY - 4 DAYS UNTIL MATCH (MD +3/-4):
Resistance Warm-Up Practices

INTENSITY: All practices are performed at full intensity

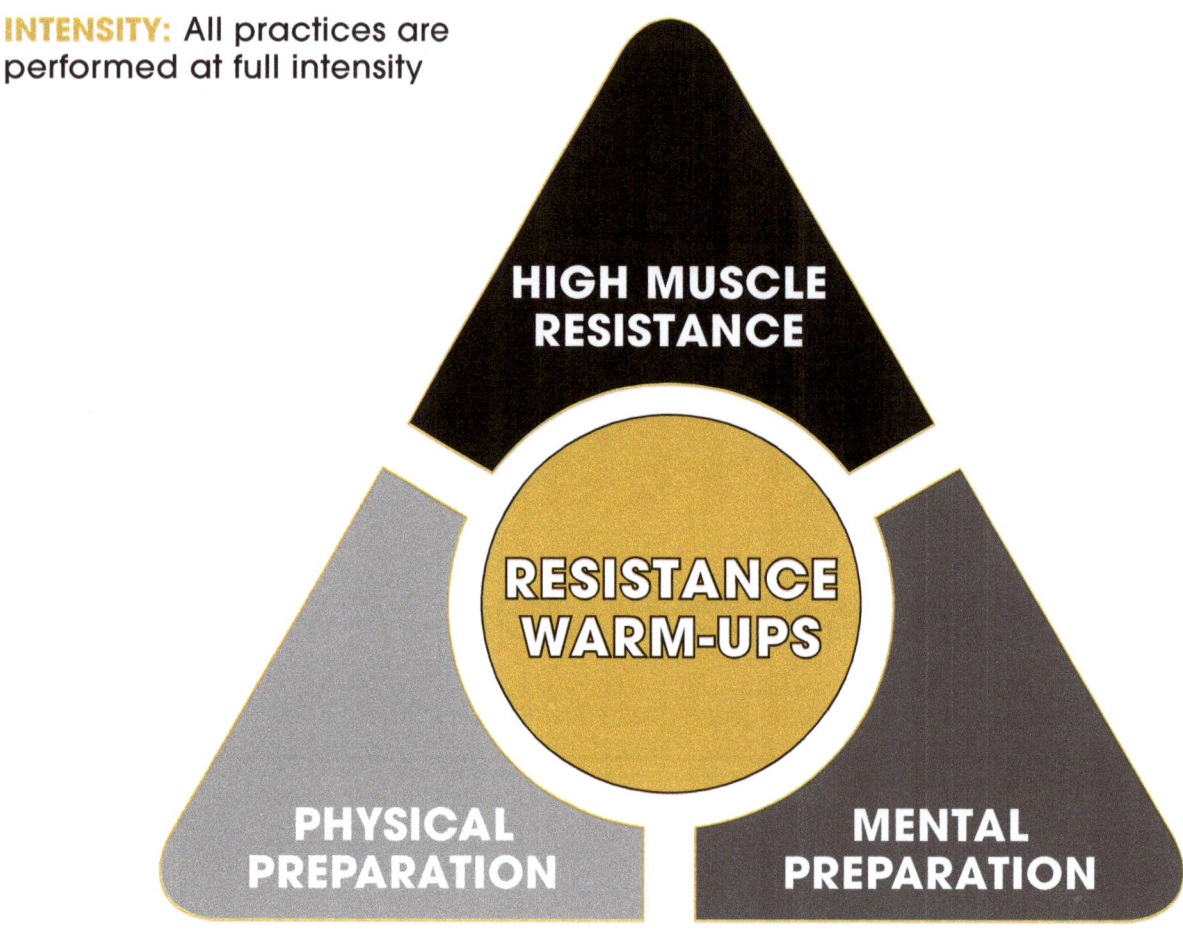

What are Resistance Warm-ups?

- Include many stop and start actions, and directional changes.
- Include many lower level accelerations and decelerations in tight spaces.
- Activate the muscle groups for the explosive maximum accelerations and decelerations later in the session.
- Provide more resistance to the working muscles through explosive actions in small spaces.

Why are they used on this day of the training week (MD +3/-4)?

- To prepare the players for the smaller surface area type work developed through the course of the session.

How does this help to maximise performance?

- Resistance warm-ups are used on this day as a way of preparing the players muscles used for changing directions, acceleration and deceleration efforts.
- Resistance warm-ups also generally ready the body for the session ahead (small sided games).

TUESDAY Training Day Practices: Resistance - 4 Days Until Match (MD +3/-4)

Resistance Warm-up 1: Circuit with Different Movements, Runs, and Jumps

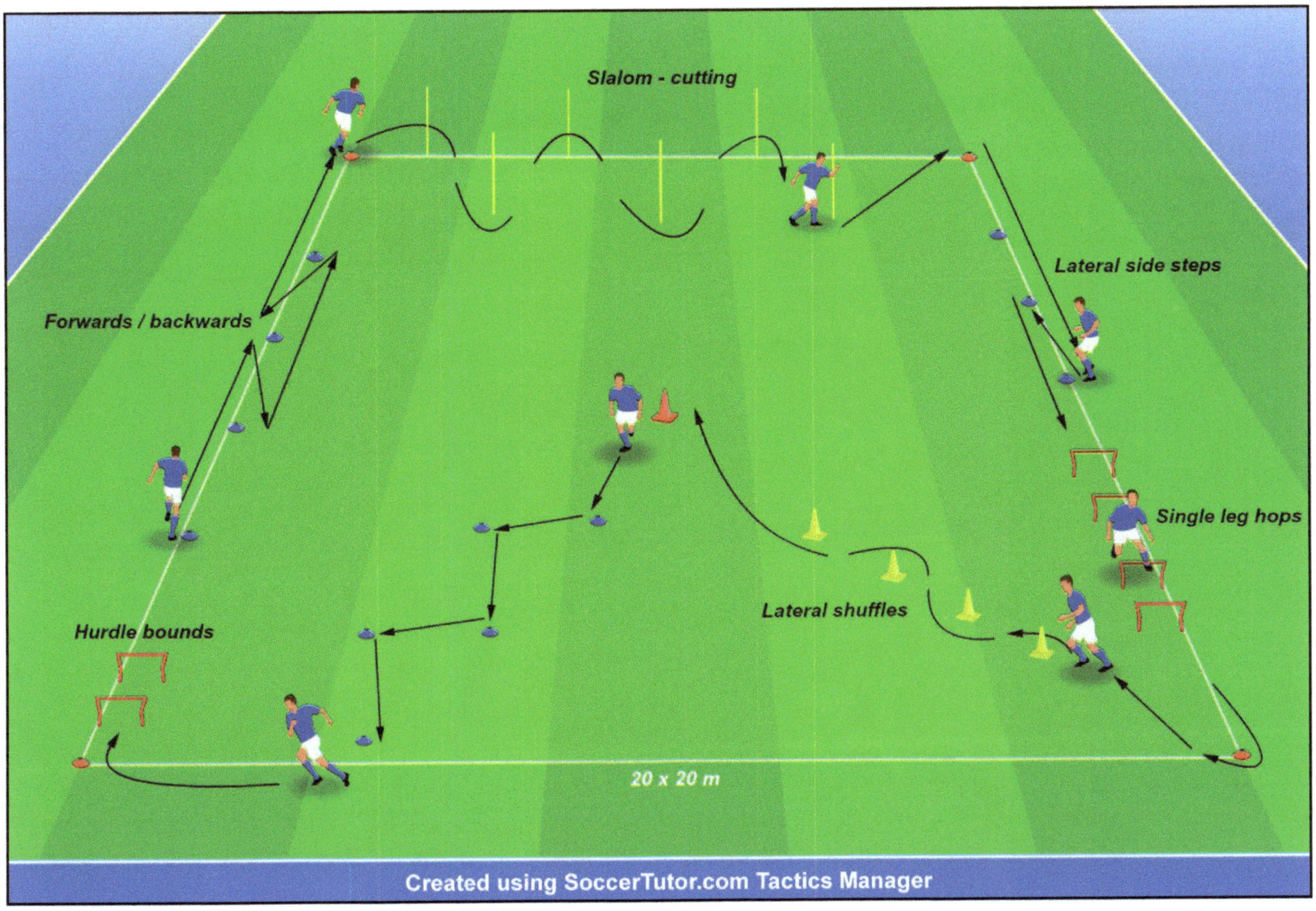

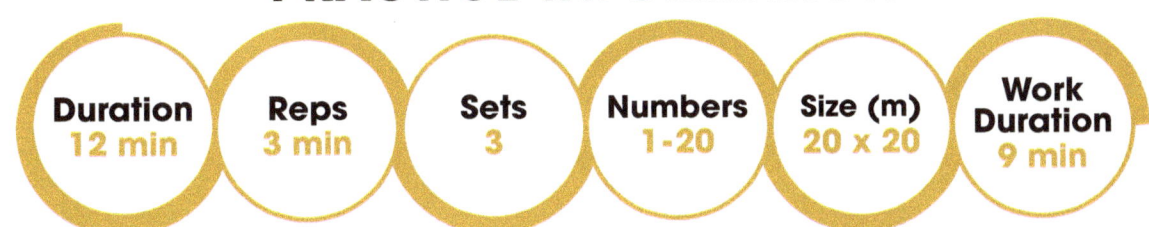

PRACTICE INFORMATION

Duration	Reps	Sets	Numbers	Size (m)	Work Duration
12 min	3 min	3	1-20	20 x 20	9 min

OBJECTIVE: Physically and mentally prepare the players for the training session (without the ball)

Volume Metrics	Practice Total	Per Min. of Work
Total Distance (km)	1.023	0.11
High Speed Running (m)	-	-
Sprint Distance (m)	-	-
Work Ratio (%)	66.72	
Power Plays (HiActs)	-	-

Intensity Metrics	Practice Total	Per Min. of Work
Max Speed (m/s)	3.59	
Intensity (m/min)		113.6
Power Score (w/kg)	6.77	
No. of Max Accels >4m²	1.44	0.16
No. of Max Decels >4m²	3.33	0.37

* The data shows the physical output per player based on research from elite level teams - see **pages 81-83** for details

TUESDAY Training Day Practices: Resistance - 4 Days Until Match (MD +3/-4)

Resistance Warm-up 2: Ball Control in a Square with Resting Outside Players

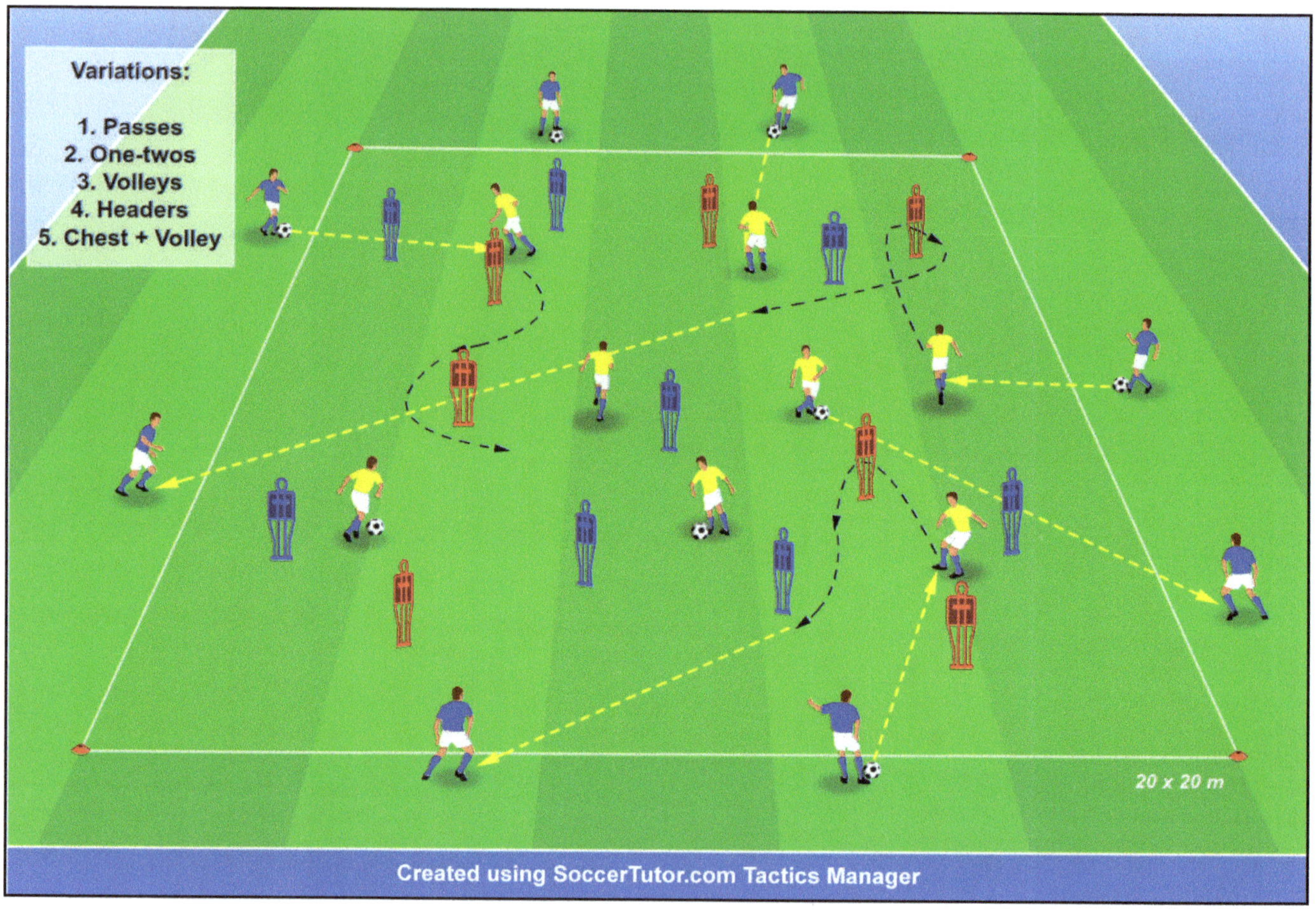

Variations:
1. Passes
2. One-twos
3. Volleys
4. Headers
5. Chest + Volley

Created using SoccerTutor.com Tactics Manager

20 x 20 m

PRACTICE INFORMATION

Duration	Reps	Sets	Numbers	Size (m)	Work Duration
10 min	30 sec	7	10-24	20 x 20	3.5 min

OBJECTIVE: Physically and mentally prepare the players for the training session (with the ball)

Volume Metrics	Practice Total	Per Min. of Work
Total Distance (km)	0.524	0.15
High Speed Running (m)	0.06	0.017
Sprint Distance (m)	-	-
Work Ratio (%)	38.8	
Power Plays (HiActs)	-	-

Intensity Metrics	Practice Total	Per Min. of Work
Max Speed (m/s)	4.03	
Intensity (m/min)		149.7
Power Score (w/kg)	4.74	
No. of Max Accels >4m²	1	0.29
No. of Max Decels >4m²	1.4	0.4

* The data shows the physical output per player based on research from elite level teams - see **pages 81-83** for details

Football Periodization to Maximise Performance

TUESDAY Training Day Practices: Resistance - 4 Days Until Match (MD +3/-4)

TUESDAY - 4 DAYS UNTIL MATCH (MD +3/-4):
Intensive Technical Practices

INTENSITY: All practices are performed at full intensity

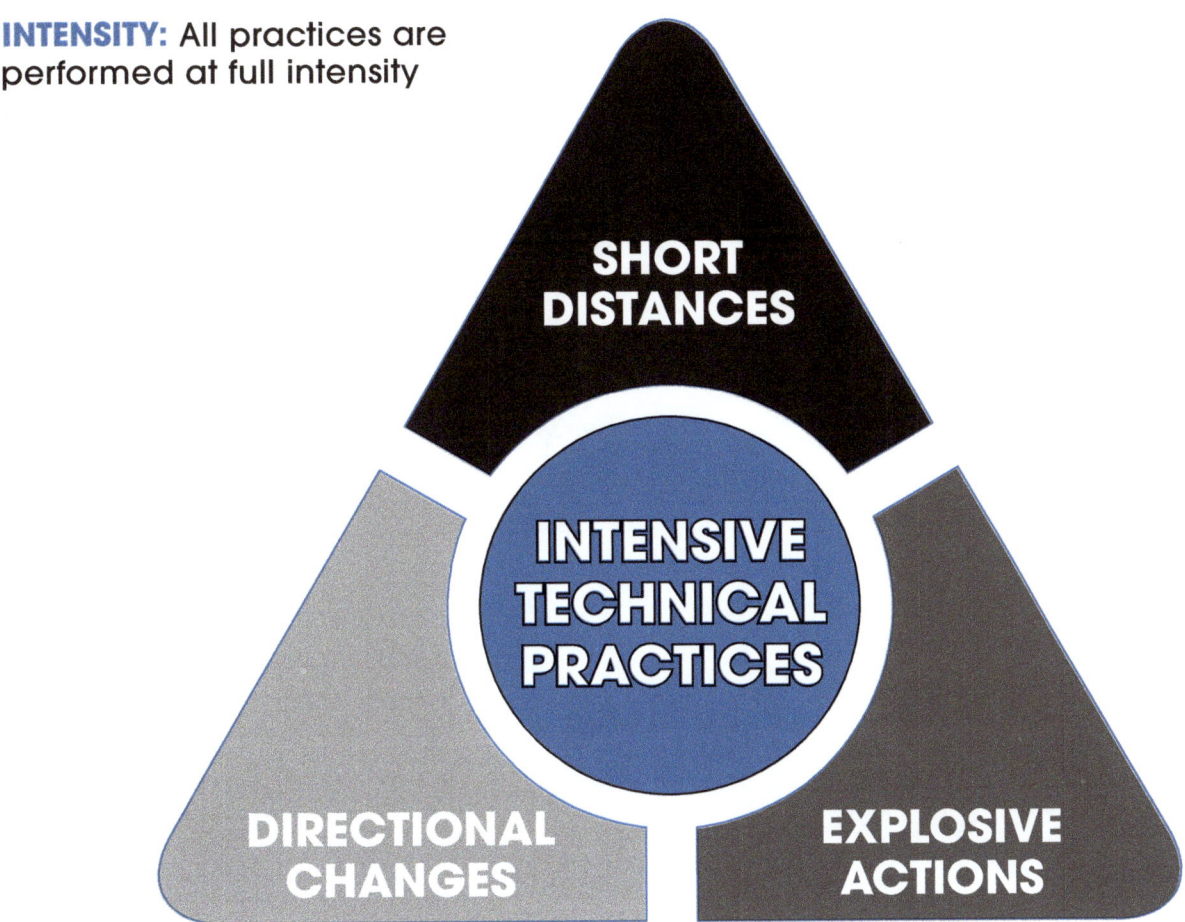

What are Intensive Technical Practices?

- Short passing distances (10-15 metres).
- Lots of directional changes, accelerations and decelerations in tighter spaces rather than big surface training areas.
- Provide more resistance to the working muscles through explosive actions in small spaces.
- Focused and in-keeping with the flow of the training day and working muscle groups on this particular training day.

Why are they used on this day of the training week (MD +3/-4)?

- To prepare the players for the smaller surface area type work developed through the course of the session.

How does this help to maximise performance?

- These intensive technical practices are used on this training day as a way of preparing the players' muscles used for changing direction, acceleration and deceleration efforts.
- Generally ready the body for the session ahead (small sided games).

TUESDAY Training Day Practices: **Resistance** - 4 Days Until Match (MD +3/-4)

Intensive Technical 1: Quick Feet, One-Two, and Diagonal Passing in a Pass & Move Drill

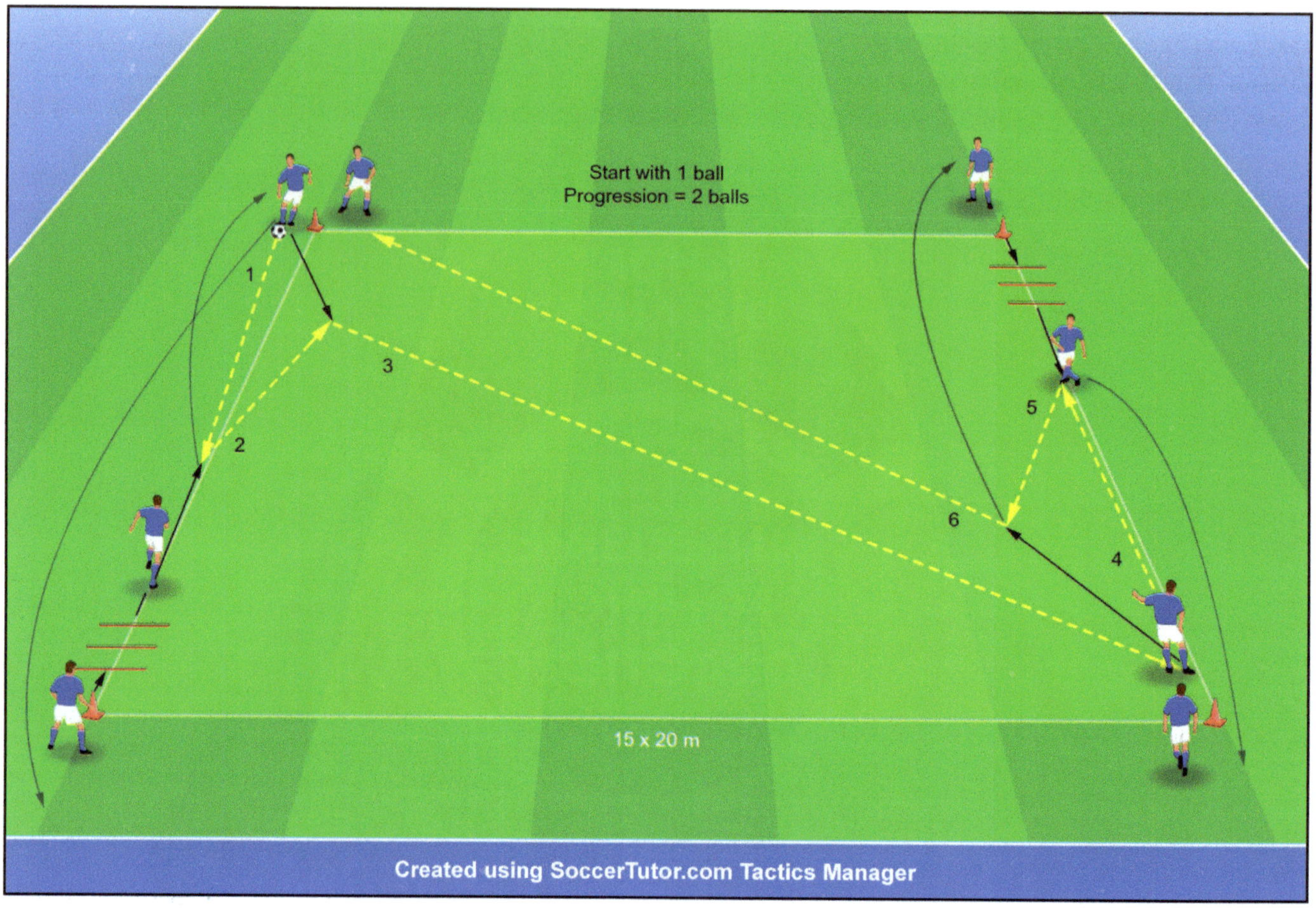

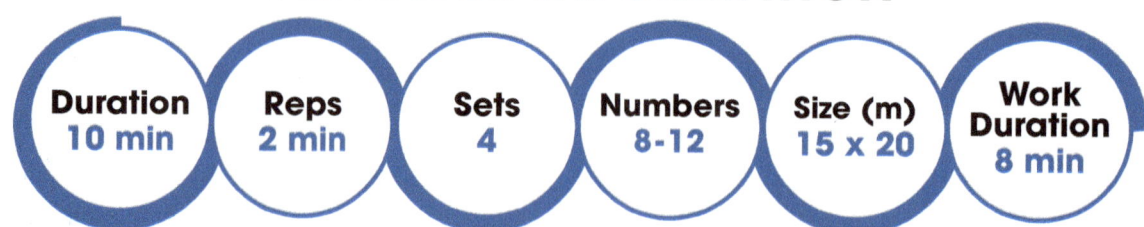

PRACTICE INFORMATION

Duration	Reps	Sets	Numbers	Size (m)	Work Duration
10 min	2 min	4	8-12	15 x 20	8 min

PRACTICE OBJECTIVES: Ball speed (correct weight), timing of run, pass placement

Volume Metrics	Practice Total	Per Min. of Work
Total Distance (km)	0.917	0.115
High Speed Running (m)	0.09	0.01
Sprint Distance (m)	-	-
Work Ratio (%)	38.57	
Power Plays (HiActs)	0.67	0.08

Intensity Metrics	Practice Total	Per Min. of Work
Max Speed (m/s)	4.43	
Intensity (m/min)		80.23
Power Score (w/kg)	6.48	
No. of Max Accels >4m²	7.63	0.95
No. of Max Decels >4m²	2.29	0.29

* The data shows the physical output per player based on research from elite level teams - see **pages 81-83** for details

@SoccerTutor.com   Football Periodization to Maximise Performance

REFERENCE   @adamowen1980

TUESDAY Training Day Practices: **Resistance** - 4 Days Until Match (MD +3/-4)

Intensive Technical 2: Double Square Pass and Move Drill

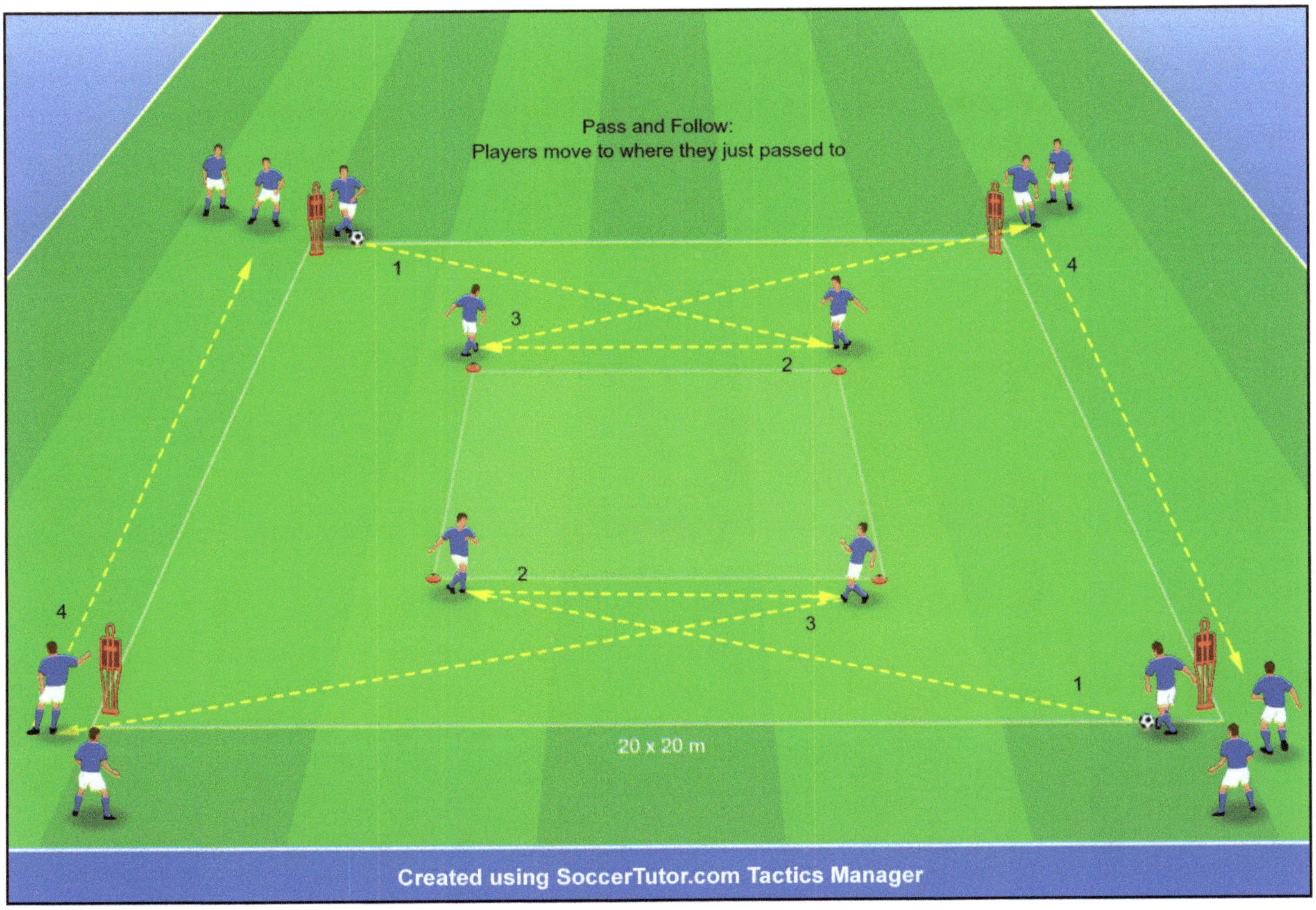

[Diagram: Pass and Follow - Players move to where they just passed to. 20 x 20 m area.]

PRACTICE INFORMATION

Duration	Reps	Sets	Numbers	Size (m)	Work Duration
10 min	2 min	4	12-16	20 x 20	8 min

PRACTICE OBJECTIVES (2 BALLS): Ball speed (correct weight), timing of run, pass placement

Volume Metrics	Practice Total	Per Min. of Work
Total Distance (km)	0.859	0.1
High Speed Running (m)	0.81	0.1
Sprint Distance (m)	-	-
Work Ratio (%)	33.88	
Power Plays (HiActs)	0.8	0.1

Intensity Metrics	Practice Total	Per Min. of Work
Max Speed (m/s)	4.71	
Intensity (m/min)		77.62
Power Score (w/kg)	6.34	
No. of Max Accels >4m²	11.86	1.48
No. of Max Decels >4m²	2.65	0.33

* The data shows the physical output per player based on research from elite level teams - see **pages 81-83** for details

TUESDAY Training Day Practices: Resistance - 4 Days Until Match (MD +3/-4)

Intensive Technical 3: Quick Footwork and Short Interplay in a Speed Passing Drill

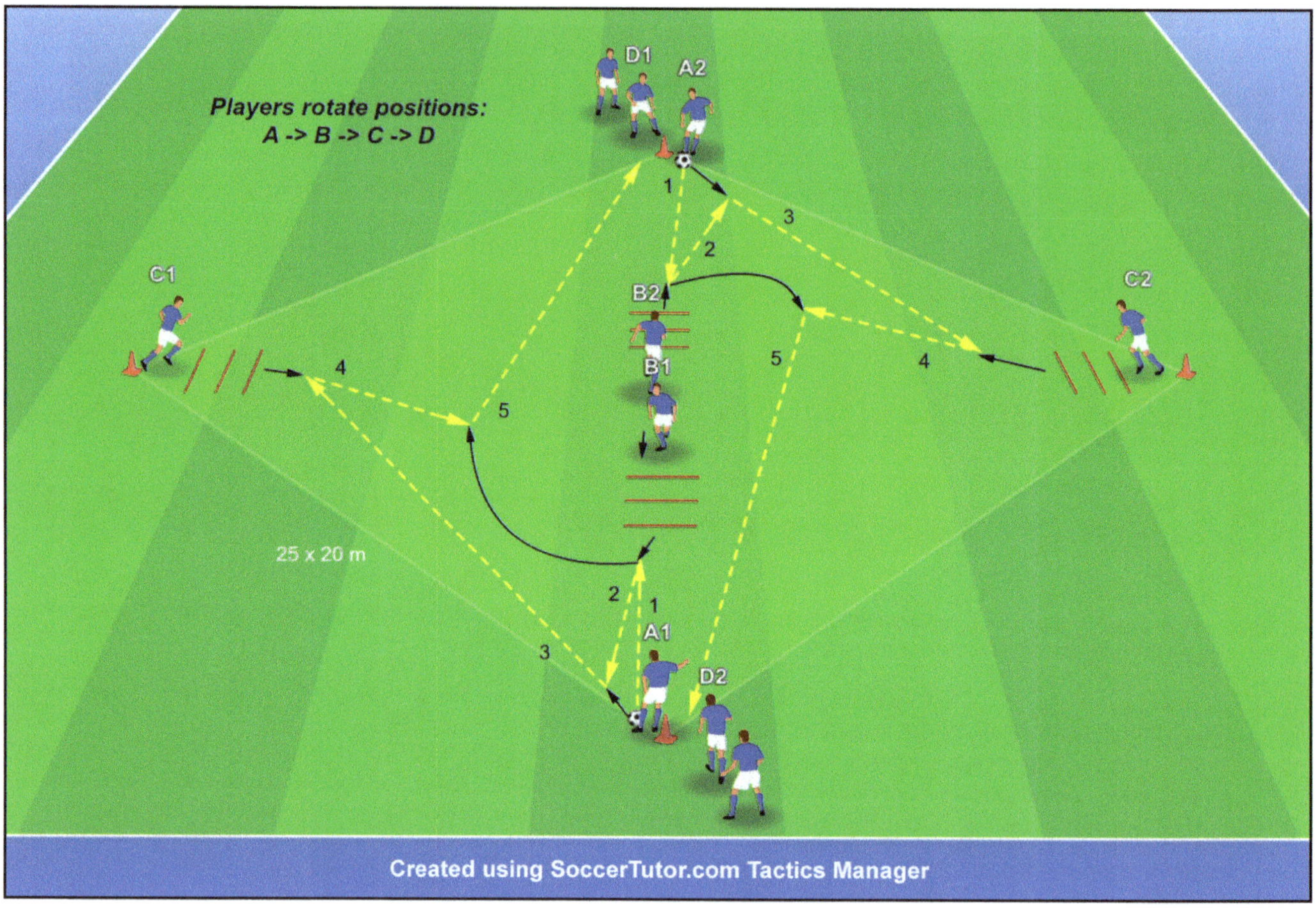

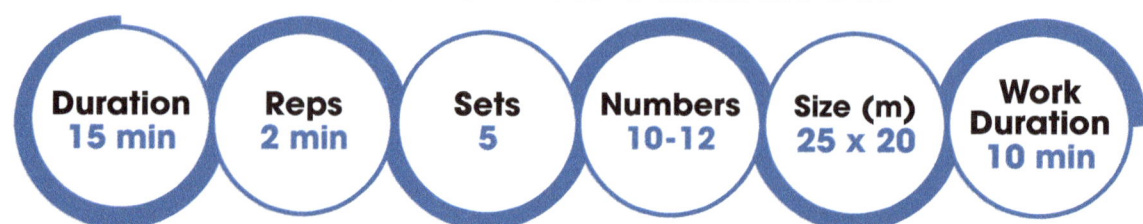

PRACTICE INFORMATION

Duration	Reps	Sets	Numbers	Size (m)	Work Duration
15 min	2 min	5	10-12	25 x 20	10 min

PRACTICE OBJECTIVES (2 BALLS): Ball speed (correct weight), timing of run, pass placement

Volume Metrics	Practice Total	Per Min. of Work
Total Distance (km)	1.376	0.14
High Speed Running (m)	1.52	0.15
Sprint Distance (m)	-	-
Work Ratio (%)	47.47	
Power Plays (HiActs)	3.07	0.3

Intensity Metrics	Practice Total	Per Min. of Work
Max Speed (m/s)	5.2	
Intensity (m/min)		93.39
Power Score (w/kg)	7.82	
No. of Max Accels >4m²	11.96	1.2
No. of Max Decels >4m²	8.19	0.82

* The data shows the physical output per player based on research from elite level teams - see pages 81-83 for details

TUESDAY Training Day Practices: **Resistance** - 4 Days Until Match (MD +3/-4)

Intensive Technical 4: Support Play with One-Twos & Timing of Movement (Diamond Circuit)

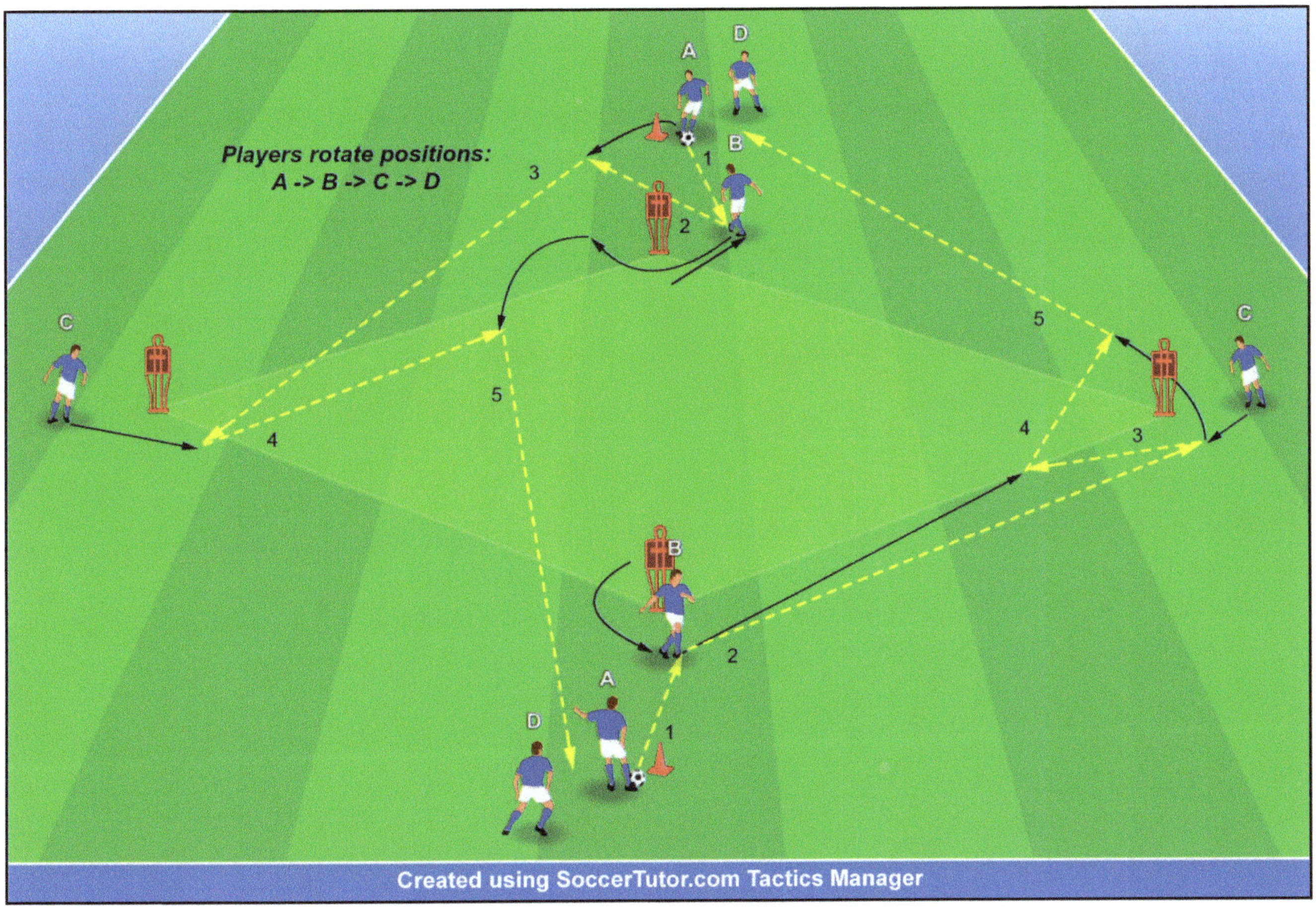

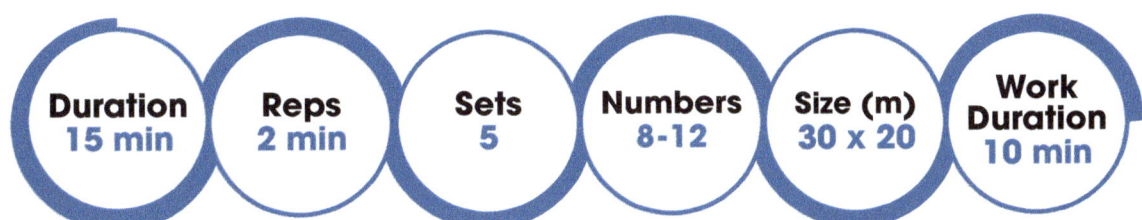

PRACTICE INFORMATION

Duration	Reps	Sets	Numbers	Size (m)	Work Duration
15 min	2 min	5	8-12	30 x 20	10 min

PRACTICE OBJECTIVES (2 BALLS): Ball speed (correct weight), timing of run, pass placement

Volume Metrics	Practice Total	Per Min. of Work
Total Distance (km)	1.073	0.1
High Speed Running (m)	1.42	0.14
Sprint Distance (m)	-	-
Work Ratio (%)	43.60	
Power Plays (HiActs)	0.86	0.09

Intensity Metrics	Practice Total	Per Min. of Work
Max Speed (m/s)	4.70	
Intensity (m/min)		87.58
Power Score (w/kg)	6.83	
No. of Max Accels >4m^2	4.71	0.47
No. of Max Decels >4m^2	0.58	0.06

* The data shows the physical output per player based on research from elite level teams - see **pages 81-83** for details

TUESDAY Training Day Practices: Resistance - 4 Days Until Match (MD +3/-4)

Intensive Technical 5: Two-Sided Circuit with Timing of Movement for Through Pass

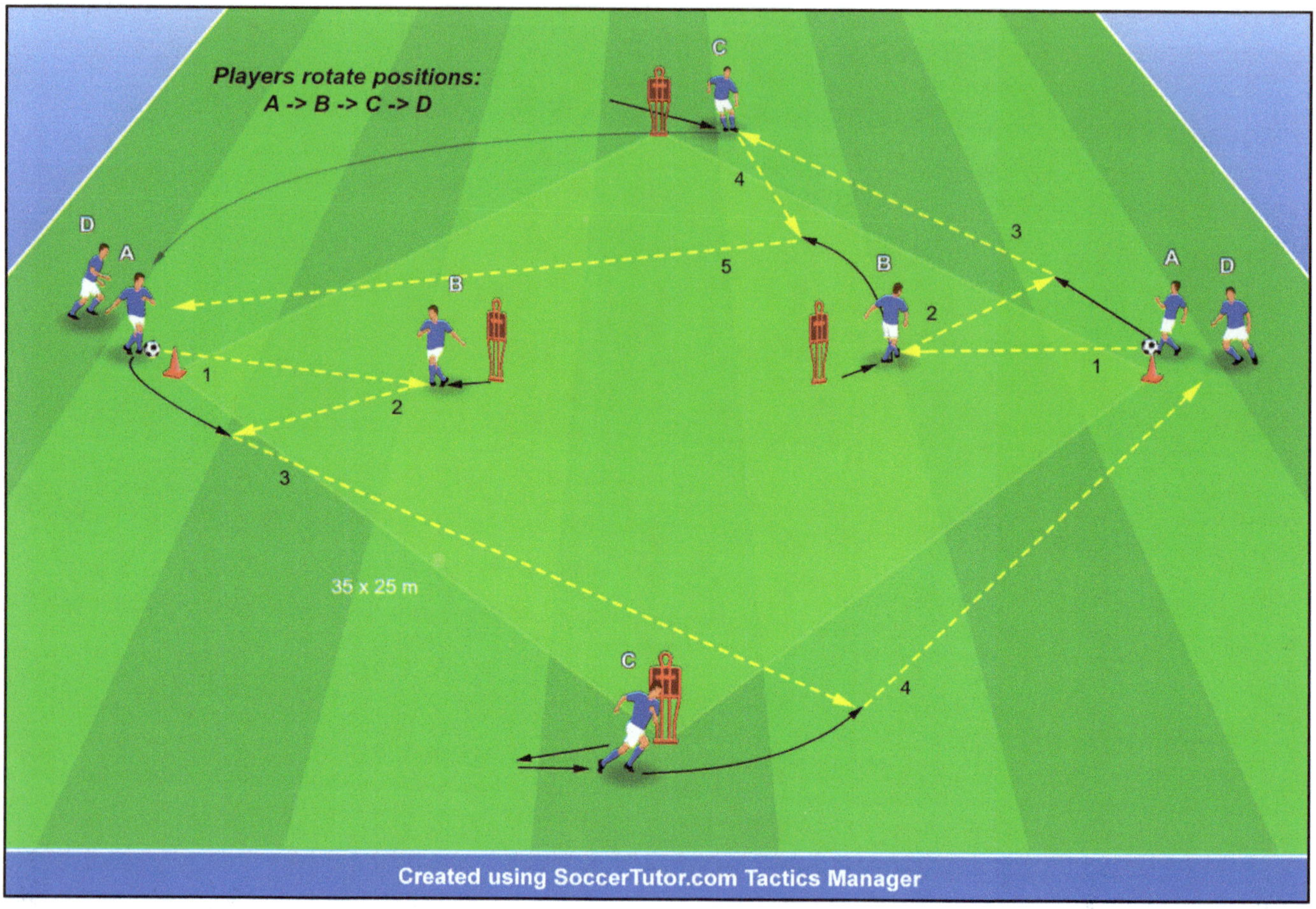

Players rotate positions: A -> B -> C -> D

35 x 25 m

Created using SoccerTutor.com Tactics Manager

PRACTICE INFORMATION

Duration	Reps	Sets	Numbers	Size (m)	Work Duration
15 min	2 min	6	8-12	35 x 25	12 min

PRACTICE OBJECTIVES (2 BALLS): Ball speed (correct weight), timing of run, pass placement

Volume Metrics	Practice Total	Per Min. of Work
Total Distance (km)	1.296	0.1
High Speed Running (m)	1.64	0.14
Sprint Distance (m)	-	-
Work Ratio (%)	41.6	
Power Plays (HiActs)	1.7	0.14

Intensity Metrics	Practice Total	Per Min. of Work
Max Speed (m/s)	5.89	
Intensity (m/min)		86.43
Power Score (w/kg)	7.08	
No. of Max Accels >4m²	12.92	1.08
No. of Max Decels >4m²	3.53	0.29

* The data shows the physical output per player based on research from elite level teams - see **pages 81-83** for details

@SoccerTutor.com   Football Periodization to Maximise Performance

TUESDAY - 4 DAYS UNTIL MATCH (MD +3/-4):
Resistance Conditioning Practices

INTENSITY: All practices are performed at full intensity

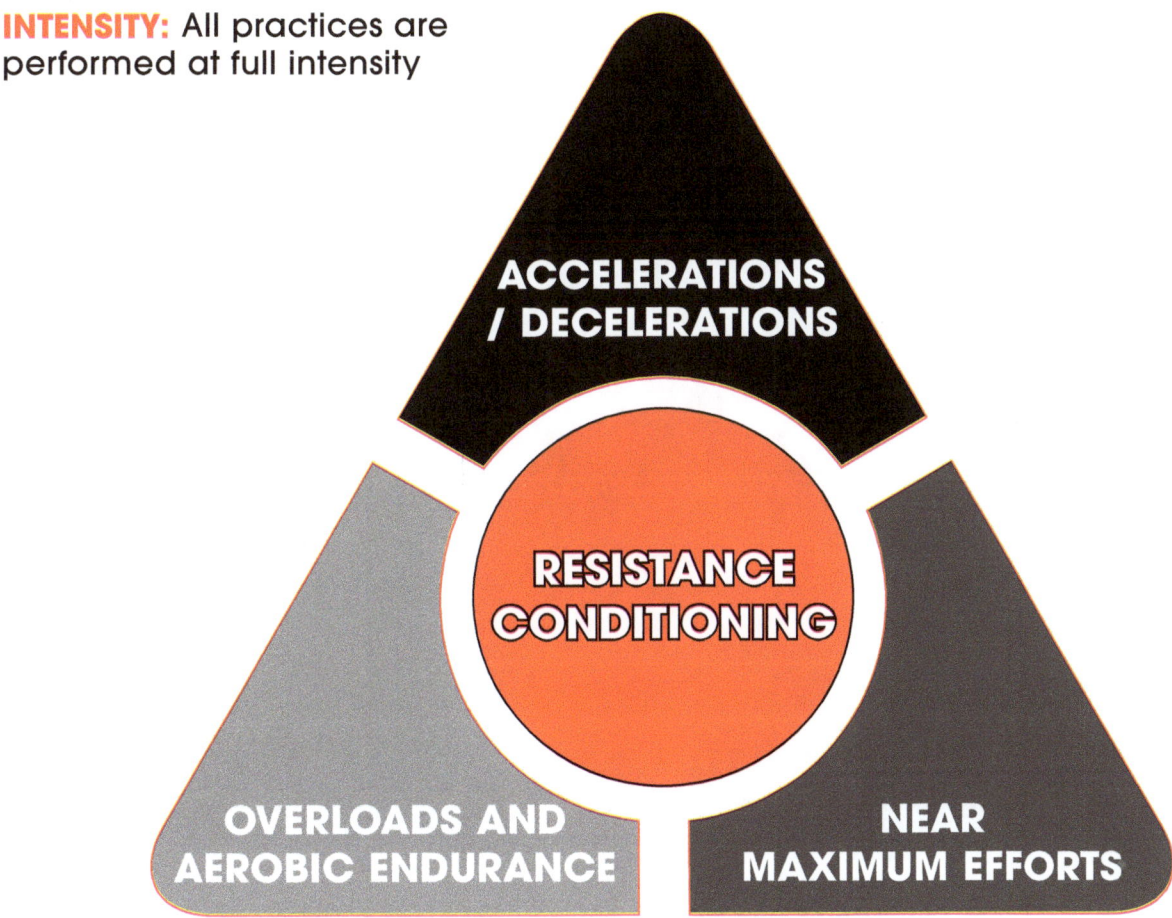

What are Resistance Conditioning Practices?

- Expose players to high levels of accelerations, decelerations, directional changes, and increased aerobic endurance.

- Include smaller surface areas with maximum or near maximum efforts to attain a high cardiovascular overload.

Why are they used on this day of the training week (MD +3/-4)?

- To overload the key muscle groups and endurance system required on a day that is far enough away from the match day to recover but elicits a stimulus in order to progress the players' capability to improve their conditioning.

How does this help to maximise performance?

- These 'resistance' based conditioning practices are used on this day as a way of preparing and developing the players' muscles and capacity to perform this type of work in training and matches.

FOOTBALL SPECIFIC SPEED TRAINING

RESISTANCE CONDITIONING: 4 Sets of 3 x 30m with Full Recovery

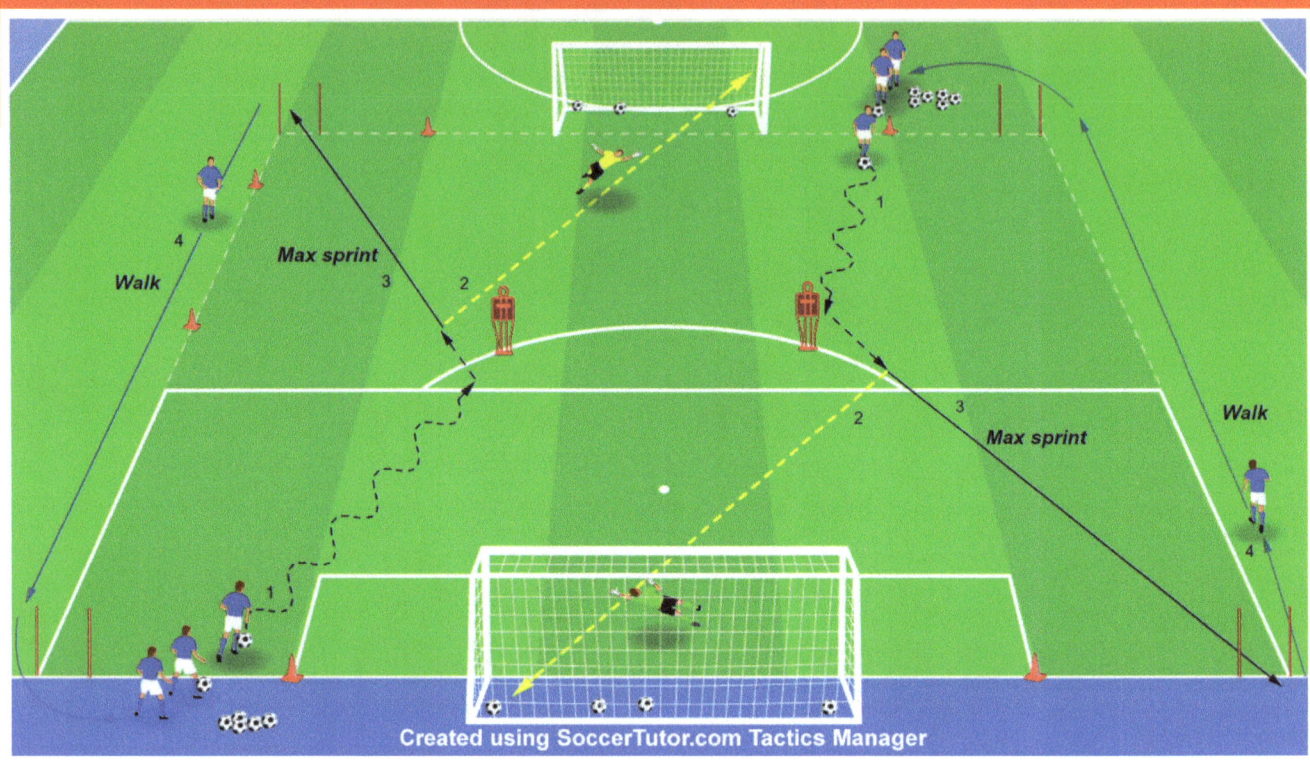

Benefits of this Resistance Conditioning Practice?

- Balance between speed with and without the ball
- High specific muscle overload
- Increase number of sets and reps as players become conditioned
- Allows players to receive high-speed stimulus to assist in injury prevention
- Provides a maximum acceleration stimulus relative to game movement
- Improving players' capability to perform a technical action and sprint
- Ensure a technical focus within the practice
- Improved motivation of players due to the inclusion of technical elements

Total Distance	Max Decel. Distance	HSR % TDC	Max Accel. Distance	Power Plays	High Speed Running	Max Speed Av.
886m	15m	15%	22m	11	132m	6.7 m/s

@adamowen1980

Football Periodization to Maximise Performance

TUESDAY Training Day Practices: Resistance - 4 Days Until Match (MD +3/-4)

Resistance Conditioning 1: Pass and Jockey, Zig-Zag Runs, Acceleration, and Deceleration

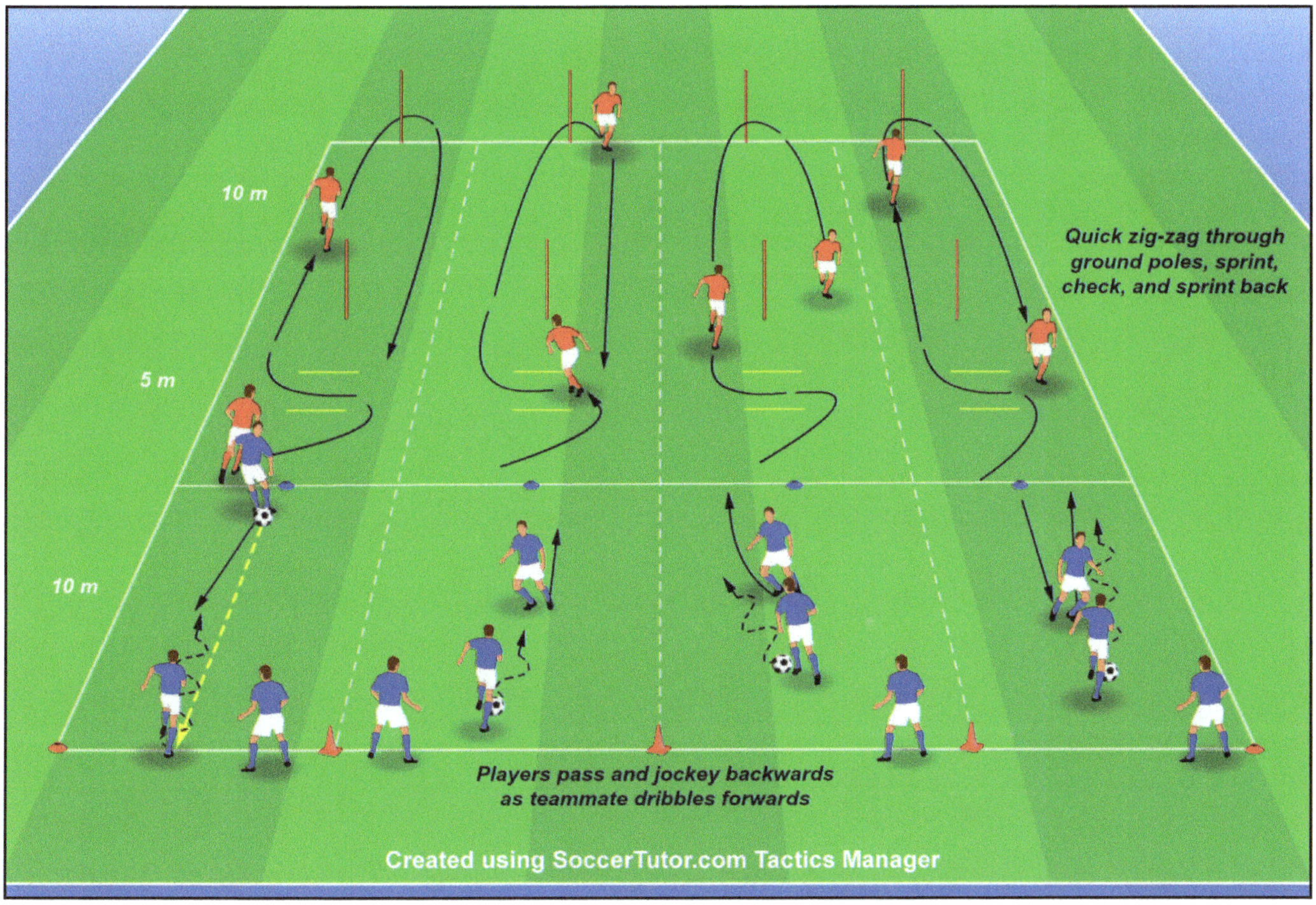

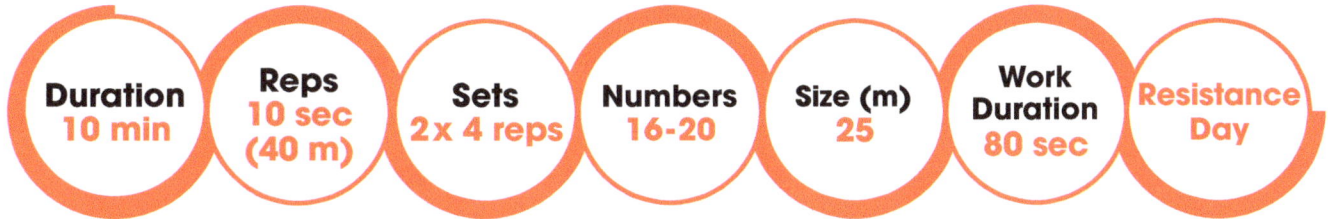

Quick zig-zag through ground poles, sprint, check, and sprint back

Players pass and jockey backwards as teammate dribbles forwards

Created using SoccerTutor.com Tactics Manager

PRACTICE INFORMATION

- **Duration**: 10 min
- **Reps**: 10 sec (40 m)
- **Sets**: 2 x 4 reps
- **Numbers**: 16-20
- **Size (m)**: 25
- **Work Duration**: 80 sec
- **Resistance Day**

OBJECTIVES: Overloads, movements (accelerations/decelerations), lower body strength and power

Volume Metrics	Practice Total	Per Min. of Work
Total Distance (km)	0.563	0.42
High Speed Running (m)	0.9	0.68
Sprint Distance (m)	-	-
Work Ratio (%)	21.12	
Power Plays (HiActs)	1.08	0.81

Intensity Metrics	Practice Total	Per Min. of Work
Max Speed (m/s)	5.1	
Intensity (m/min)		59.84
Power Score (w/kg)	5.24	
Max Accel. Distance (m)	11.43	8.57
Max Decel. Distance (m)	19.37	14.53

* The data shows the physical output per player based on research from elite level teams - see pages 81-83 for details

TUESDAY Training Day Practices: Resistance - 4 Days Until Match (MD +3/-4)

Resistance Conditioning 2: Slalom Runs, Dribble + 1v1 Passive Jockey (Circuit)

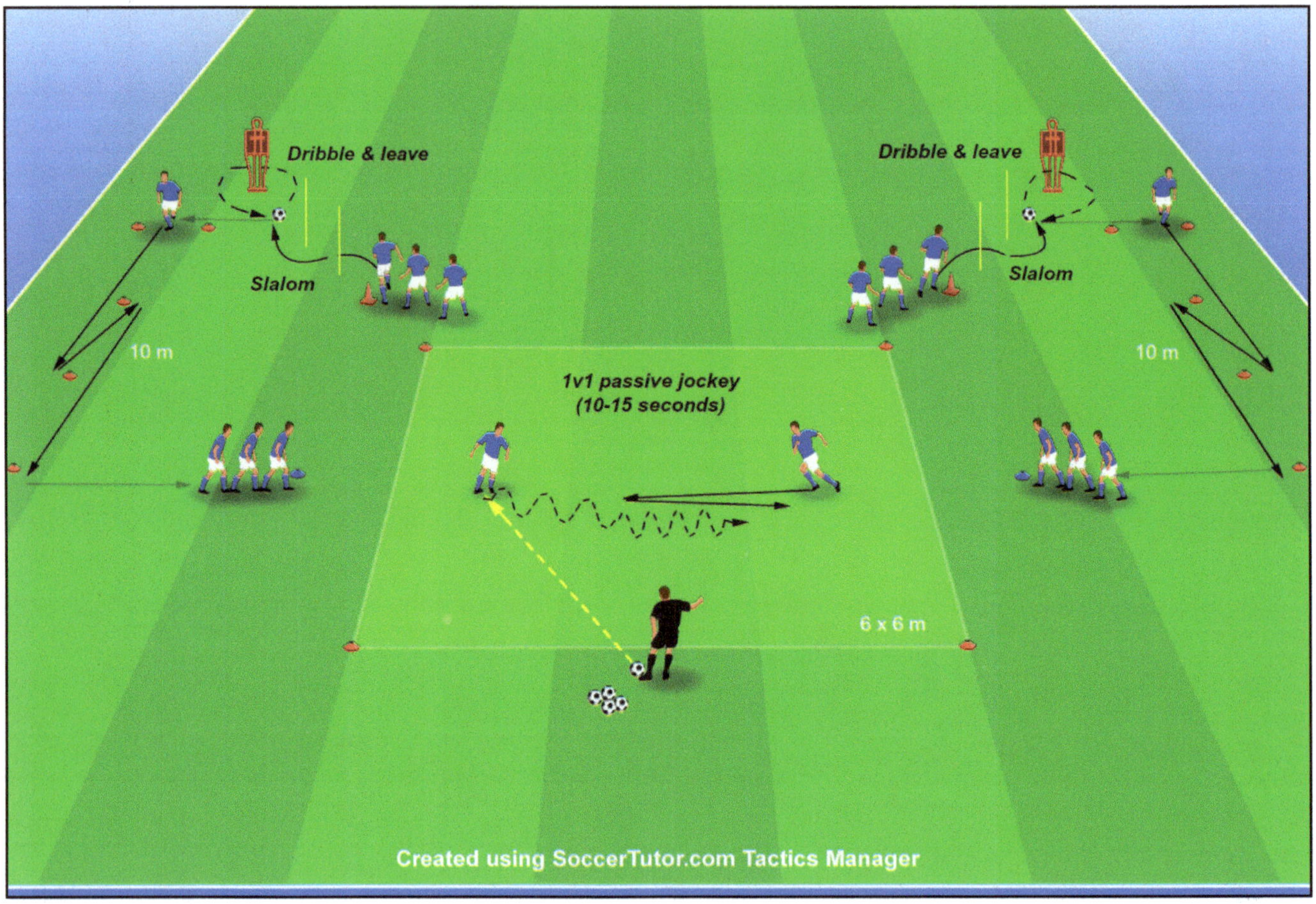

PRACTICE INFORMATION

Duration	Reps	Sets	Numbers	Size (m)	Work Duration	Explosive Actions
10 min	4 min	2	8-16	20 x 20	8 min	Throughout

OBJECTIVES: Overloads, movements (accelerations/decelerations), lower body strength and power

Volume Metrics	Practice Total	Per Min. of Work
Total Distance (km)	0.624	0.08
High Speed Running (m)	-	-
Sprint Distance (m)	-	-
Work Ratio (%)	33.3	
Power Plays (HiActs)	12	1.5

Intensity Metrics	Practice Total	Per Min. of Work
Max Speed (m/s)	4.44	
Intensity (m/min)		64
Power Score (w/kg)	5.56	
No. of Max Accels >4m²	6	0.75
No. of Max Decels >4m²	7	0.88

* The data shows the physical output per player based on research from elite level teams - see pages 81-83 for details

TUESDAY Training Day Practices: Resistance - 4 Days Until Match (MD +3/-4)

Resistance Conditioning 3: Passing + Speed and Agility Exercises in a Circuit

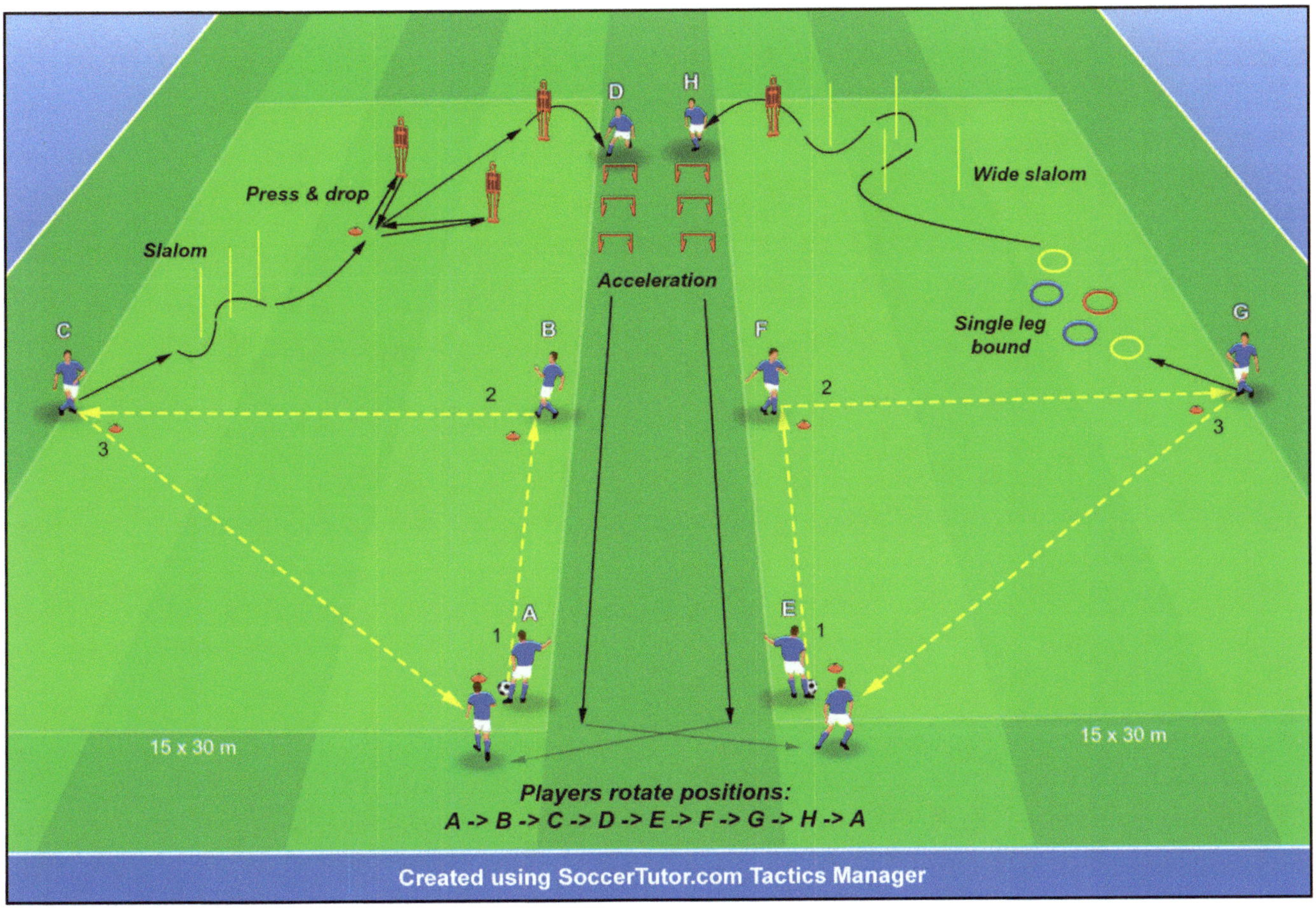

PRACTICE INFORMATION

- **Duration:** 10 min
- **Reps:** 4 min (8 reps)
- **Sets:** 2 x 4 min (16 reps)
- **Numbers:** 10-16
- **Size (m):** 35 x 30
- **Work Duration:** 8 min
- **Work Through:** Figure 8

OBJECTIVES: Overloads, movements (accelerations/decelerations), lower body strength and power

Volume Metrics	Practice Total	Per Min. of Work
Total Distance (km)	1.095	0.14
High Speed Running (m)	20.83	2.6
Sprint Distance (m)	-	-
Work Ratio (%)	46.5	
Power Plays (HiActs)	17	2.13

Intensity Metrics	Practice Total	Per Min. of Work
Max Speed (m/s)	5.67	
Intensity (m/min)		113
Power Score (w/kg)	9.87	
No. of Max Accels >4m²	7.7	0.96
No. of Max Decels >4m²	3.82	0.48

* The data shows the physical output per player based on research from elite level teams - see **pages 81-83** for details

TUESDAY Training Day Practices: Resistance - 4 Days Until Match (MD +3/-4)

Resistance Conditioning 4: Maximum Sprints to Attack and Defend Crosses in 2v2 Situation

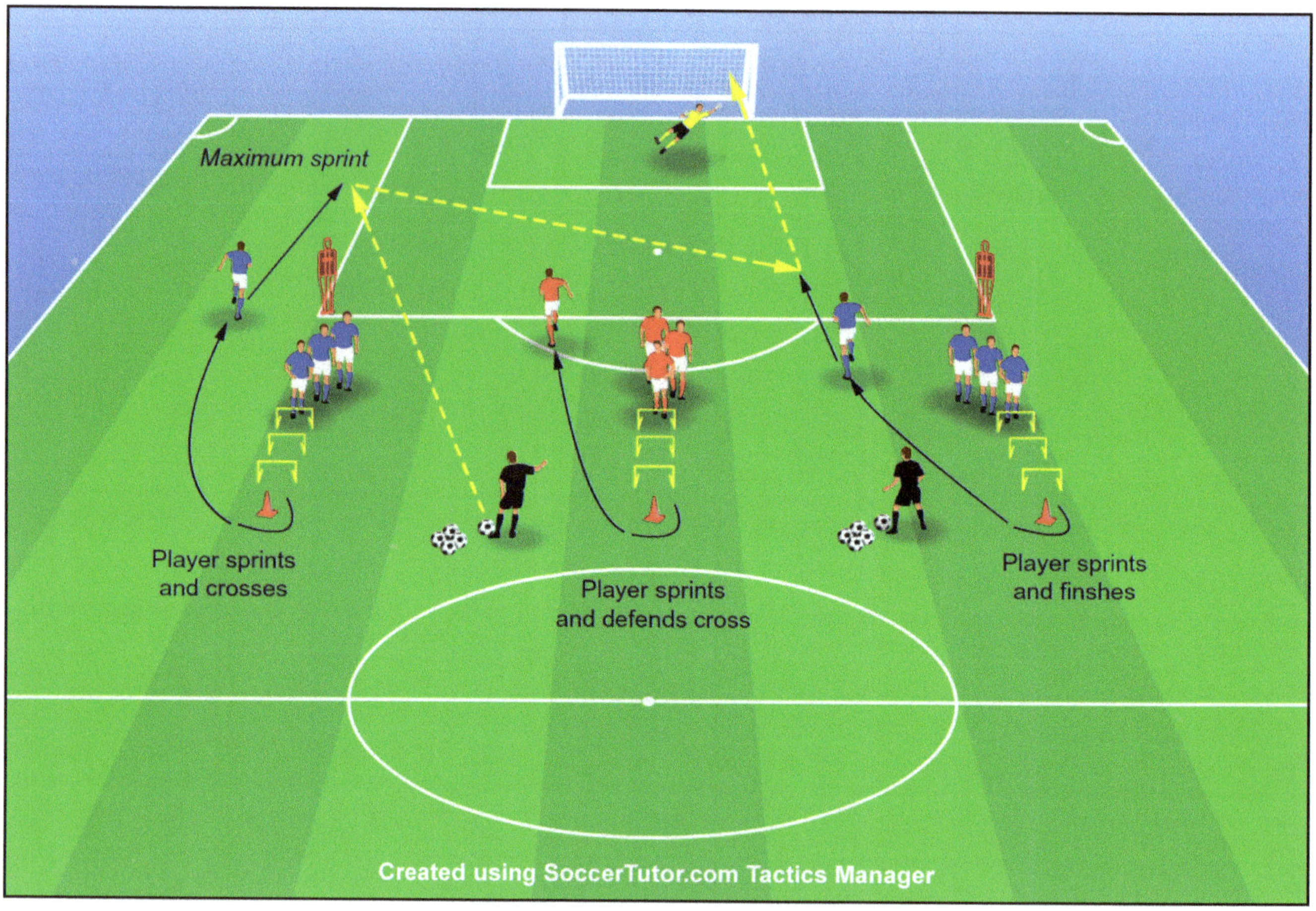

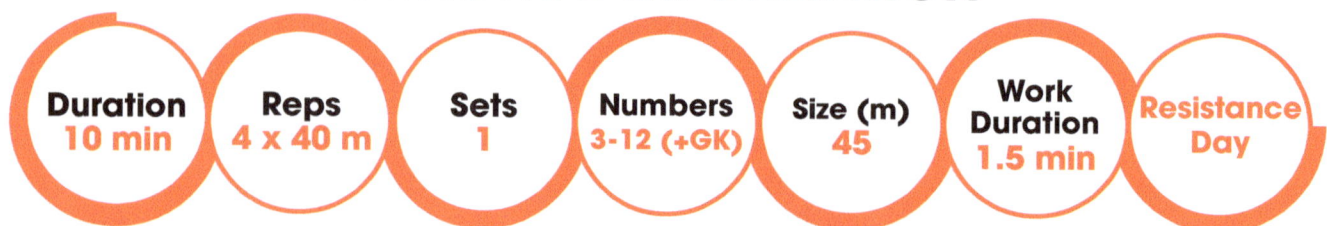

PRACTICE INFORMATION

- **Duration**: 10 min
- **Reps**: 4 x 40 m
- **Sets**: 1
- **Numbers**: 3-12 (+GK)
- **Size (m)**: 45
- **Work Duration**: 1.5 min
- **Resistance Day**

OBJECTIVES: Overloads, movements (accelerations/decelerations), lower body strength and power

Volume Metrics	Practice Total	Per Min. of Work
Total Distance (km)	0.438	0.29
High Speed Running (m)	64.16	42.77
Sprint Distance (m)	20	13.33
Work Ratio (%)	25.1	
Power Plays (HiActs)	3.53	2.35

Intensity Metrics	Practice Total	Per Min. of Work
Max Speed (m/s)	7.33	
Intensity (m/min)		41.58
Power Score (w/kg)	3.36	
Max Accel. Distance (m)	4	2.67
Max Decel. Distance (m)	4	2.67

* The data shows the physical output per player based on research from elite level teams - see **pages 81-83** for details

TUESDAY Training Day Practices: Resistance - 4 Days Until Match (MD +3/-4)

Resistance Conditioning 5: Speed and Agility Circuit with Finishing in Three Goals with GKs

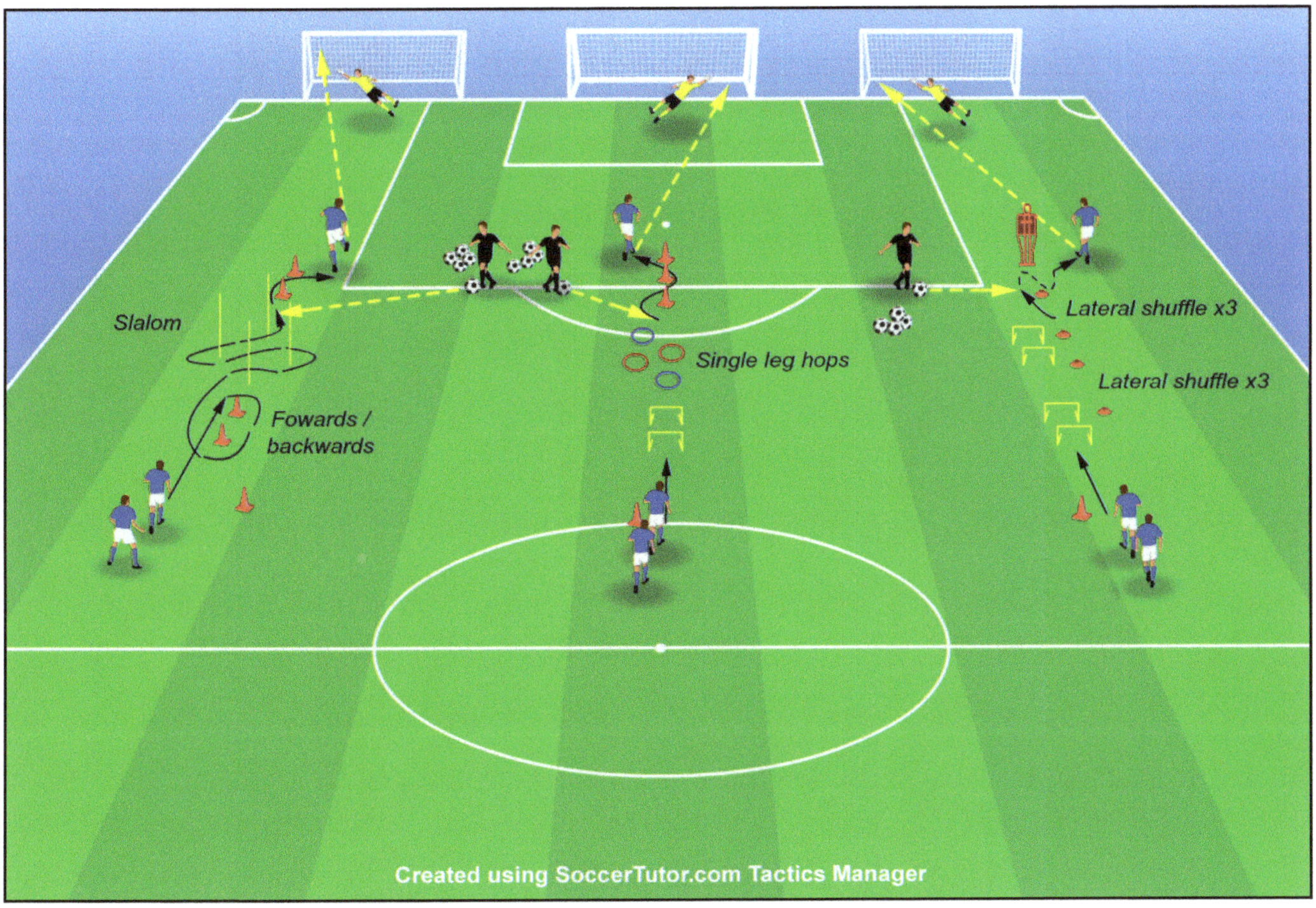

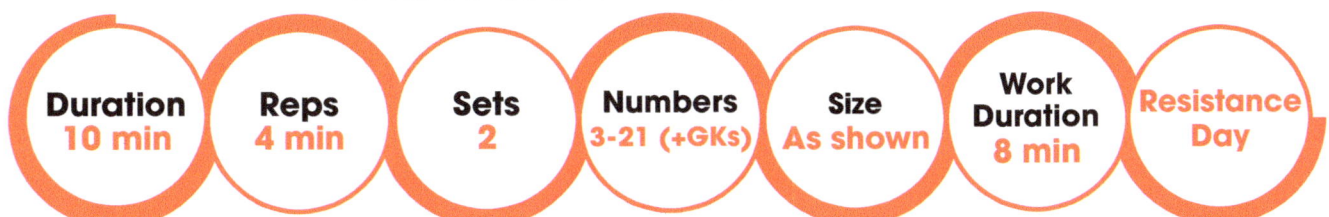

PRACTICE INFORMATION

Duration 10 min | **Reps** 4 min | **Sets** 2 | **Numbers** 3-21 (+GKs) | **Size** As shown | **Work Duration** 8 min | **Resistance Day**

OBJECTIVES: Overloads, movements (accelerations/decelerations), lower body strength and power

Volume Metrics	Practice Total	Per Min. of Work
Total Distance (km)	0.754	0.09
High Speed Running (m)	27.33	3.42
Sprint Distance (m)	-	-
Work Ratio (%)	31.96	
Power Plays (HiActs)	7.62	0.95

Intensity Metrics	Practice Total	Per Min. of Work
Max Speed (m/s)	5.97	
Intensity (m/min)		83.49
Power Score (w/kg)	6.79	
Max Accel. Distance (m)	0.91	0.11
Max Decel. Distance (m)	1.07	0.13

*The data shows the physical output per player based on research from elite level teams - see pages 81-83 for details

Football Periodization to Maximise Performance

TUESDAY Training Day Practices: Resistance - 4 Days Until Match (MD +3/-4)

Resistance Conditioning 6: Speed and Agility Exercises + 2v2 (+GKs) Duel Game

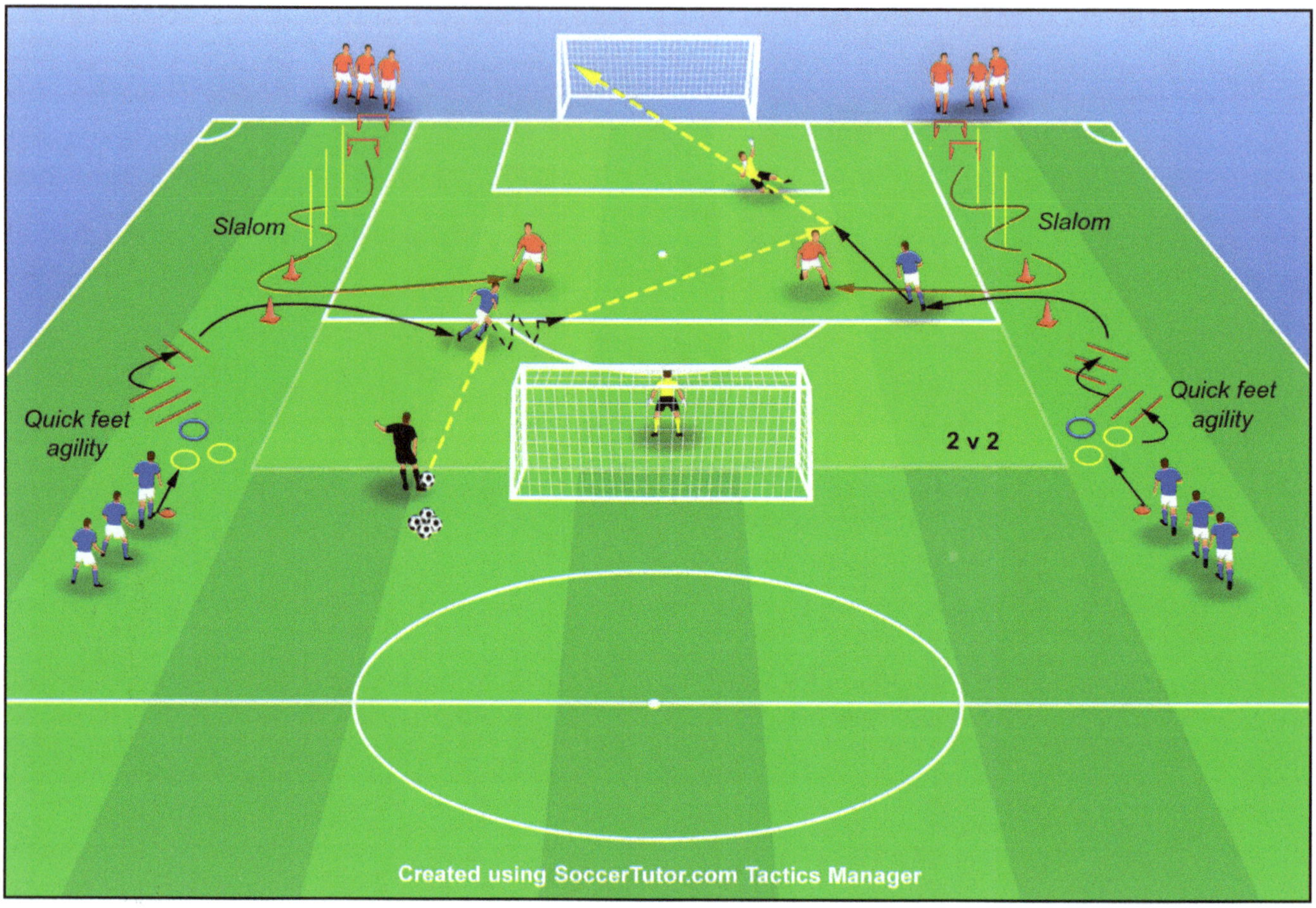

PRACTICE INFORMATION

- **Duration:** 32 min
- **Reps:** 1.5 min
- **Sets:** 5
- **Numbers:** 16 +GKs
- **Size:** As shown
- **Work Duration:** 7.5 min
- **Resistance Day**

OBJECTIVES: Overloads, movements (accelerations/decelerations), lower body strength and power

Volume Metrics	Practice Total	Per Min. of Work
Total Distance (km)	0.926	0.12
High Speed Running (m)	13.89	1.85
Sprint Distance (m)	-	-
Work Ratio (%)	13.28	
Power Plays (HiActs)	5.75	0.77

Intensity Metrics	Practice Total	Per Min. of Work
Max Speed (m/s)	5.84	
Intensity (m/min)		123.4
Power Score (w/kg)	3.47	
Max Accel. Distance (m)	15.66	2.08
Max Decel. Distance (m)	23.78	3.17

* The data shows the physical output per player based on research from elite level teams - see pages 81-83 for details

TUESDAY Training Day Practices: Resistance - 4 Days Until Match (MD +3/-4)

Resistance Conditioning 7: Dribble, Shoot & Sprint in a Group Finishing Practice

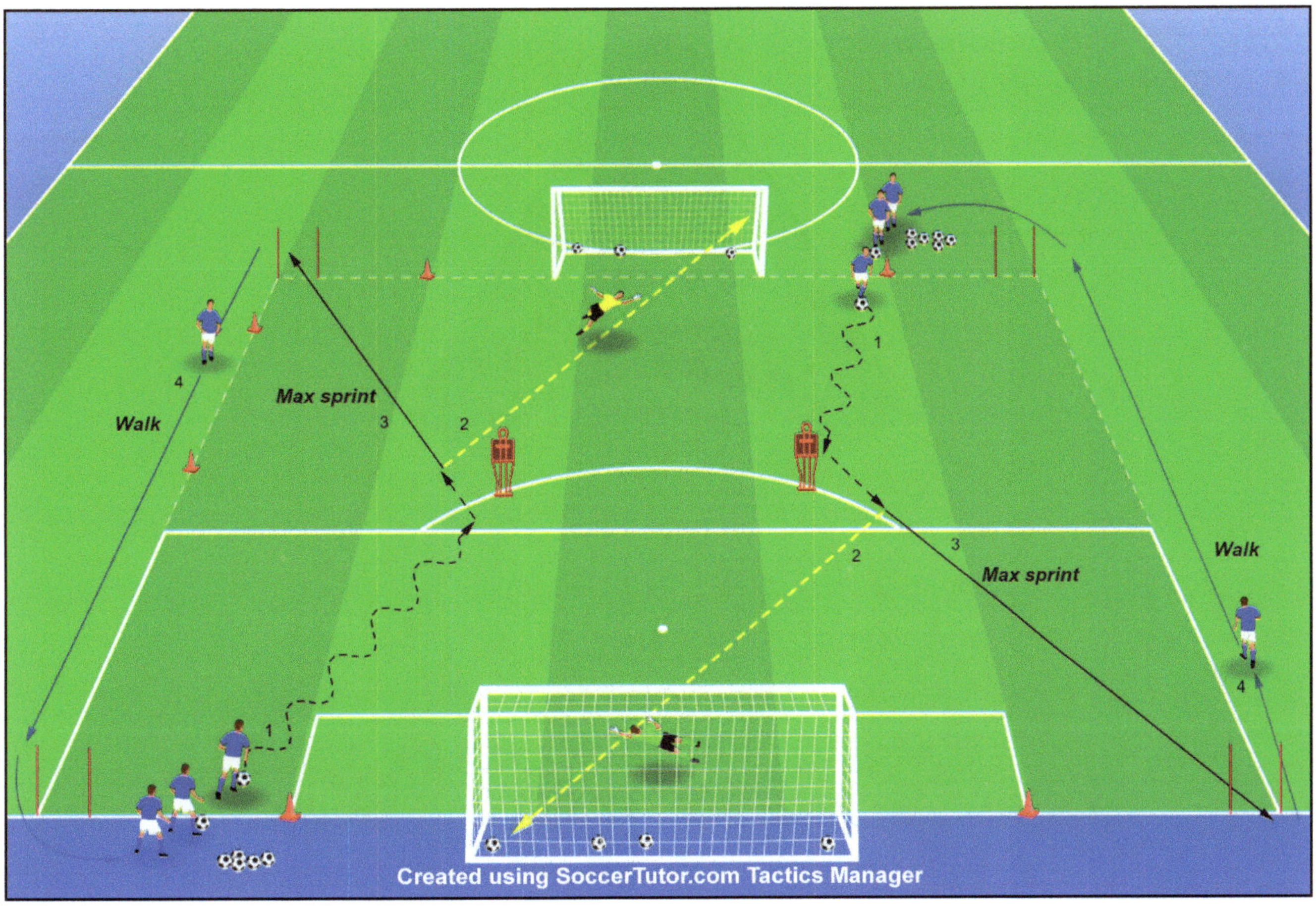

PRACTICE INFORMATION

Duration	Reps	Sets	Numbers	Size (m)	Work Duration	React / Activate
15 min	3 x 30 m	4	5-10 per Group	45	1.5 min	

OBJECTIVES: Overloads, movements (accelerations/decelerations), lower body strength and power

Volume Metrics	Practice Total	Per Min. of Work
Total Distance (km)	0.886	0.59
High Speed Running (m)	131.73	87.82
Sprint Distance (m)	5.31	3.54
Work Ratio (%)	16.05	
Power Plays (HiActs)	11.13	7.42

Intensity Metrics	Practice Total	Per Min. of Work
Max Speed (m/s)	6.74	
Intensity (m/min)		58.83
Power Score (w/kg)	5.17	
Max Accel. Distance (m)	22	14.67
Max Decel. Distance (m)	15.53	10.35

* The data shows the physical output per player based on research from elite level teams - see **pages 81-83** for details

TUESDAY Training Day Practices: Resistance - 4 Days Until Match (MD +3/-4)

TUESDAY - 4 DAYS UNTIL MATCH (MD +3/-4):
Small Sided Possession Practices

INTENSITY: All practices are performed at full intensity

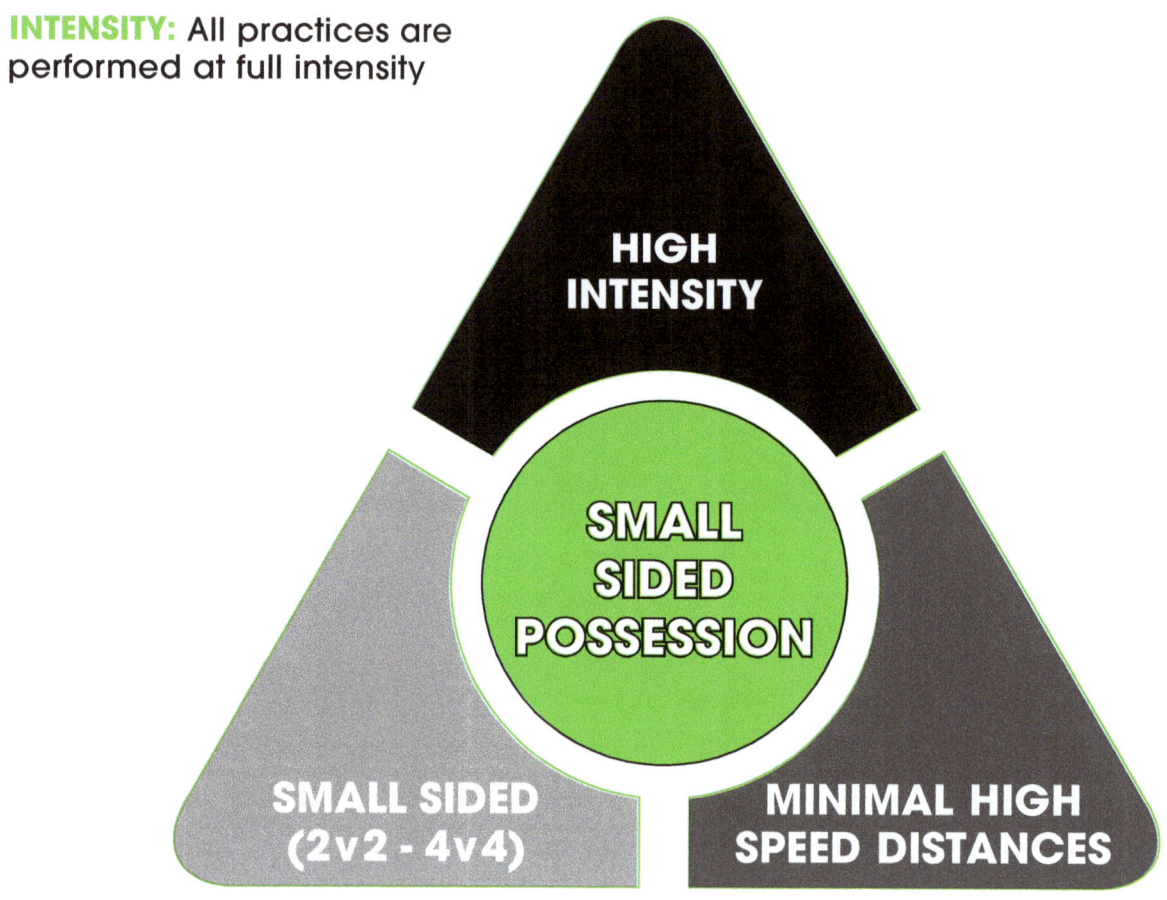

What are Small Sided Possession Practices?

- Small sided possession games are defined as including 2 to 4 players per side = 2v2 - 4v4 +GKs.

Why are they used on this day of the training week (MD +3/-4)?

- Small sided possession games can be used in different periods of the training week but within this framework they are focused around the MD +3/-4 training day with reduced or small playing areas as a way of training the positional principles.

- They are also performed in this part of the training week to ensure specific muscle groups are not overloaded for the remaining training days of the week.

How does this help to maximise performance?

- Small sided possession games result in minimal high-speed running and sprint distance vs. medium or larger game types but expose players to increased cardiovascular loads when compared.

- They also provide players with significantly greater technical demands, increased numbers of changes of direction, accelerations, and decelerations.

TUESDAY Training Day Practices: Resistance - 4 Days Until Match (MD +3/-4)

Small Sided Possession 1: Playing Forwards in a Two Zone Directional Game

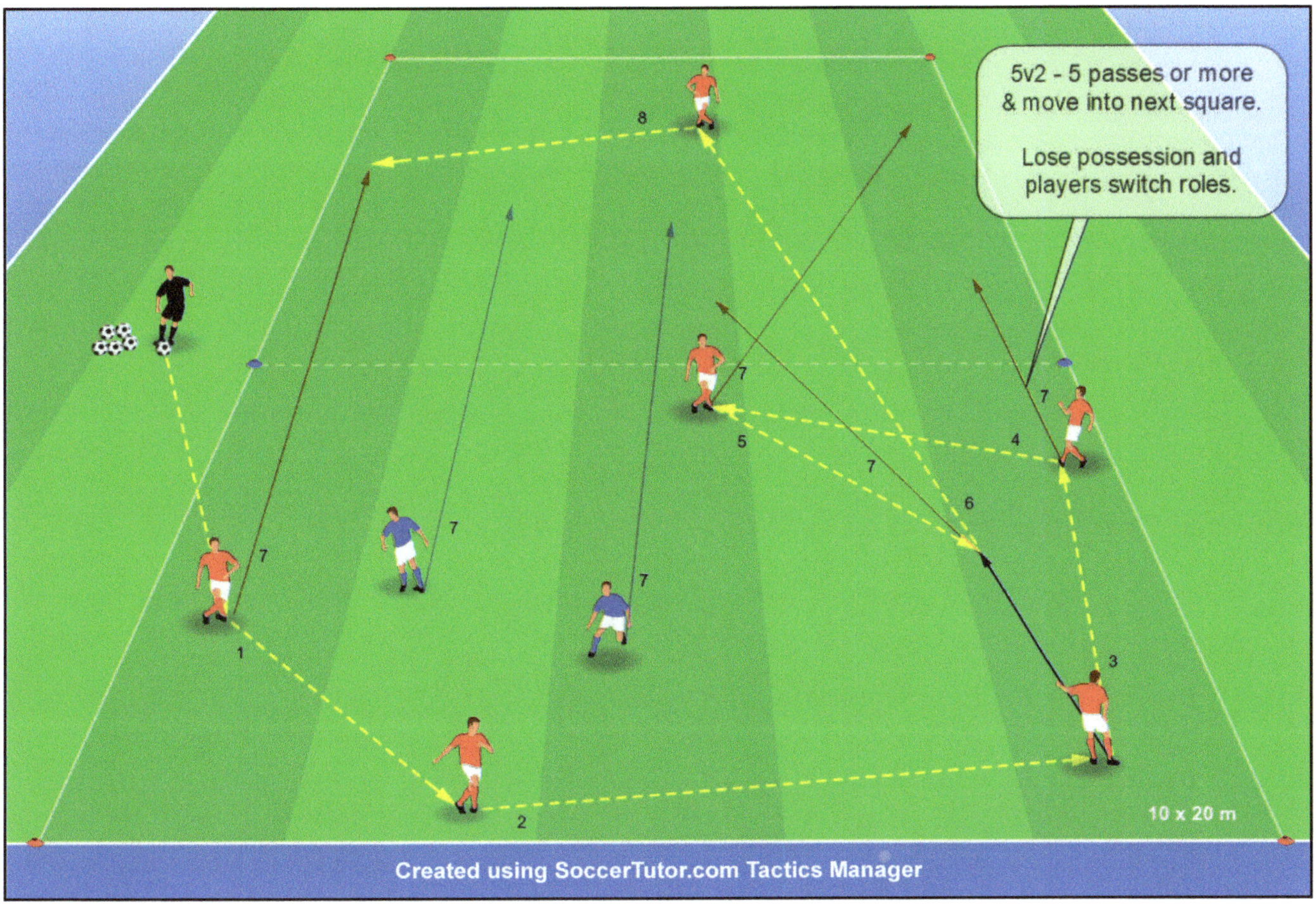

![Diagram showing a 5v2 possession exercise in a 10 x 20 m area with players. Annotation: "5v2 - 5 passes or more & move into next square. Lose possession and players switch roles."]

PRACTICE INFORMATION

- Duration: 12 min
- Reps: 3 min
- Sets: 3
- Numbers: 8
- Size (m): 10 x 20
- Work Duration: 9 min
- Player Density: 13 m²

OBJECTIVE: Directional based possession with focus on playing forwards when possible

Volume Metrics	Practice Total	Per Min. of Work
Total Distance (km)	0.733	0.08
High Speed Running (m)	0.7	0.08
Sprint Distance (m)	-	-
Work Ratio (%)	20.39	
Power Plays (HiActs)	0.56	0.06

Intensity Metrics	Practice Total	Per Min. of Work
Max Speed (m/s)	4.71	
Intensity (m/min)		59.6
Power Score (w/kg)	4.92	
Max Accel Distance (m)	7	0.78
Max Decel Distance (m)	9	1

* The data shows the physical output per player based on research from elite level teams - see pages 81-83 for details

Football Periodization to Maximise Performance

TUESDAY Training Day Practices: Resistance - 4 Days Until Match (MD +3/-4)

Small Sided Possession 2: Regain Possession in a 4v4 (+4) Three Team Competition Game

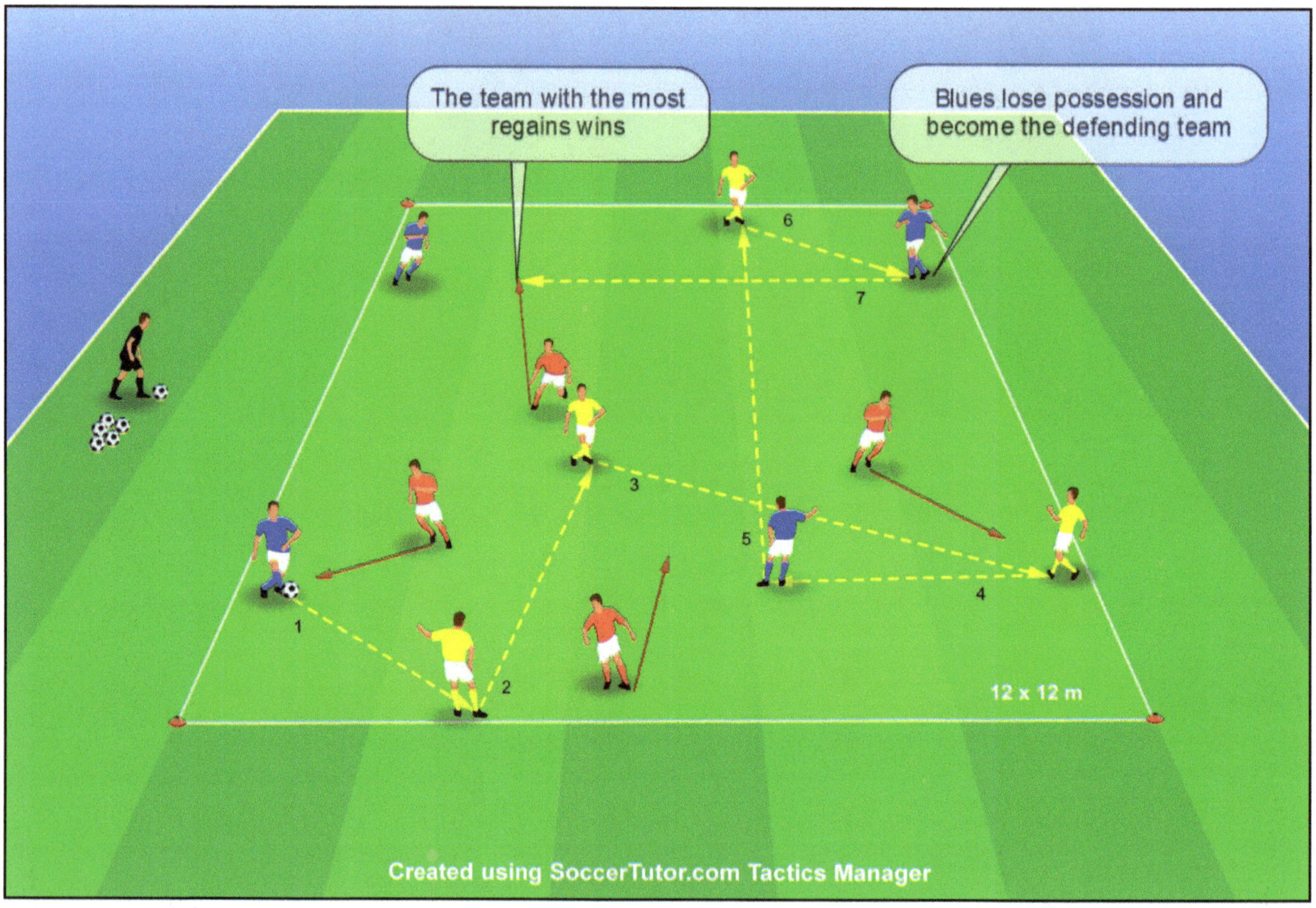

PRACTICE INFORMATION

- **Duration:** 12 min
- **Reps:** 2 min; 1 min
- **Sets:** 3 x 2 min; 3 x 1 min
- **Numbers:** 12
- **Size (m):** 12 x 12
- **Work Duration:** 9 min
- **Player Density:** 12 m²

OBJECTIVE: Transition based possession with focus on regaining possession as quickly as possible

Volume Metrics	Practice Total	Per Min. of Work
Total Distance (km)	0.870	0.1
High Speed Running (m)	-	-
Sprint Distance (m)	-	-
HML Distance (m)	84.42	9.38
Power Plays (HiActs)	-	-

Intensity Metrics	Practice Total	Per Min. of Work
Max Speed (m/s)	4.33	
Intensity (m/min)		49.1
Power Score (w/kg)	3.95	
No. of Max Accels >4m²	4.79	0.53
No. of Max Decels >4m²	5.47	0.6

* The data shows the physical output per player based on research from elite level teams - see **pages 81-83** for details

TUESDAY Training Day Practices: Resistance - 4 Days Until Match (MD +3/-4)

TUESDAY - 4 DAYS UNTIL MATCH (MD +3/-4):
Small Sided Games

INTENSITY: All practices are performed at full intensity

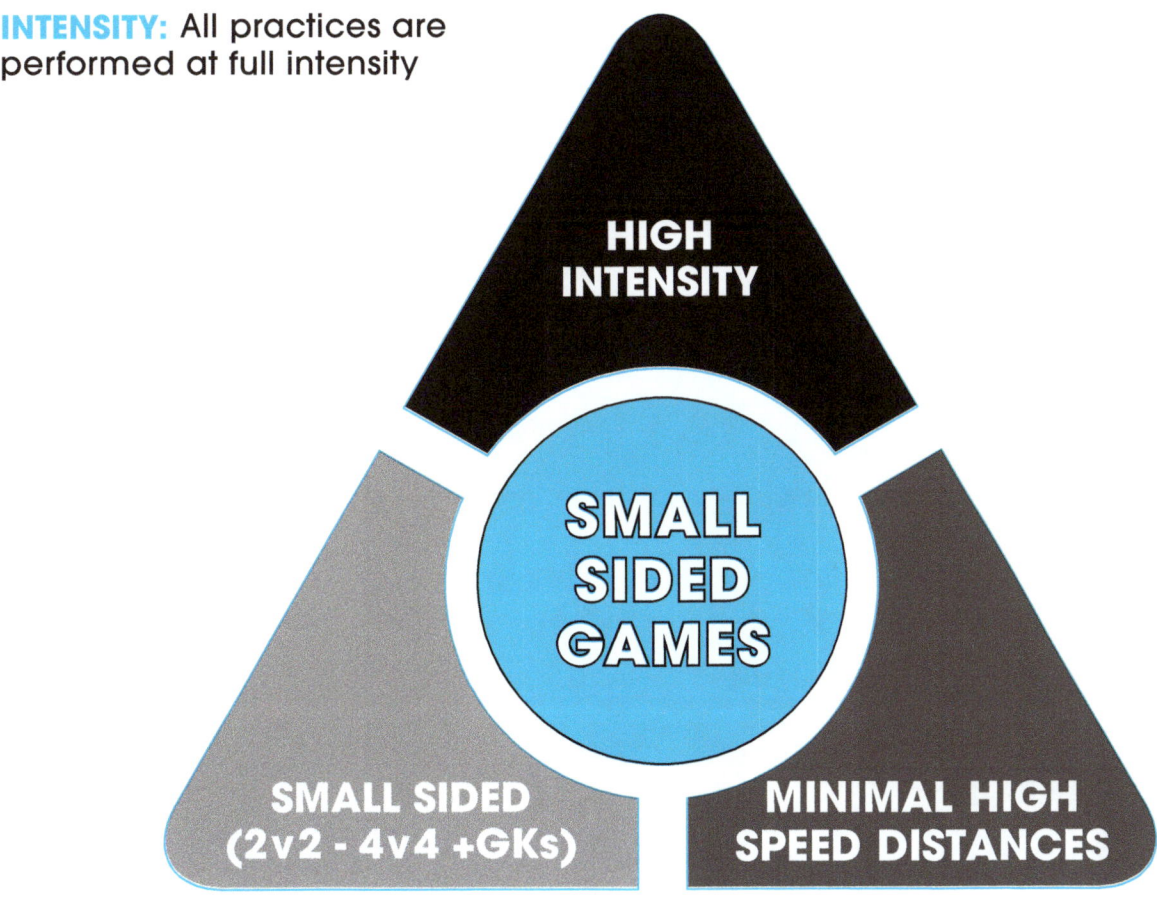

What are Small Sided Games?
- Small sided games are defined as including 2 to 4 players per side = 2v2 - 4v4 (+GKs if applicable).

Why are they used on this day of the training week (MD +3/-4)?
- Small sided games can be used in different periods of the training week but within this framework they are focused around the MD +3/-4 training day with reduced or small surface areas as a way of training the positional principles.

- They are performed in this part of the training week to ensure specific muscle groups are not overloaded for the remaining training days of the week.

How does this help to maximise performance?
- Small sided games result in minimal high-speed running and sprint distance vs. medium or larger game types but expose players to increased cardiovascular loads when compared.

- They also provide players with significantly greater technical demands, increased numbers of changes of direction, accelerations, and decelerations.

SMALL SIDED GAMES

EXAMPLE: 4 (+4) v 4 (+4) + GKs

Data based on 6 x 1.5 minute sets (9 minute work duration)

⬆ **Speed of Play and Thought**
Closer pressure from opponents

⬆ **Cardiovascular Load**
Higher heart rate response

⬆ **Lower Body Strength Work**
Changes of direction

⬆ **Technical Demand per Player**
Touches

⬆ **Goal Scoring Opportunities**
More shots at goal

⬆ **1 v 1 Situations**
Attacking and defending

⬇ **Sprint Distance**
Reduced area

⬇ **Tactical Focus**

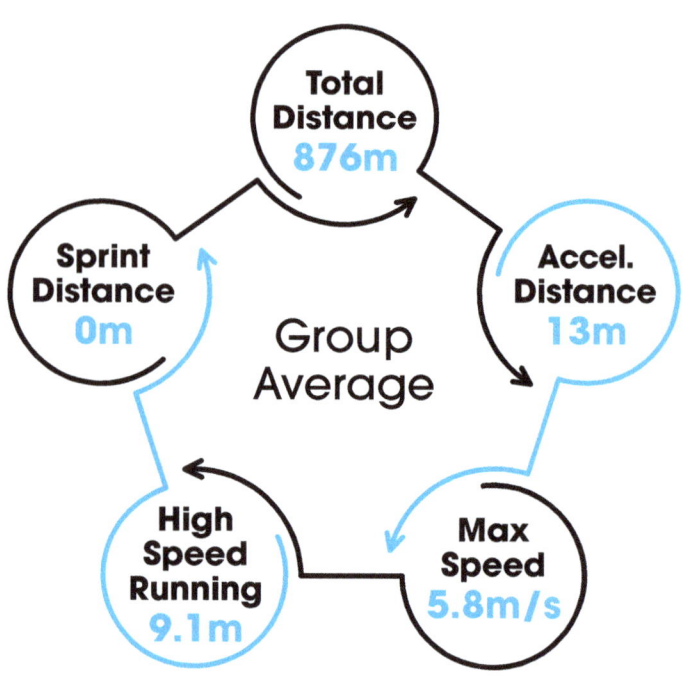

Group Average
- Total Distance: 876m
- Accel. Distance: 13m
- Max Speed: 5.8m/s
- High Speed Running: 9.1m
- Sprint Distance: 0m

@adamowen1980

@SoccerTutor.com | 118 | Football Periodization to Maximise Performance

REFERENCE: Owen AL et al (2011). J Strength Cond Res. Aug; 25(8): 2104-10. | Owen AL et al (2012). J Strength Cond Res. Oct; 26(10): 2748-54

TUESDAY Training Day Practices: Resistance - 4 Days Until Match (MD +3/-4)

Small Sided Game 1: Forward Movement to Break Lines in Intensive 2v2 (+6) +GK Game

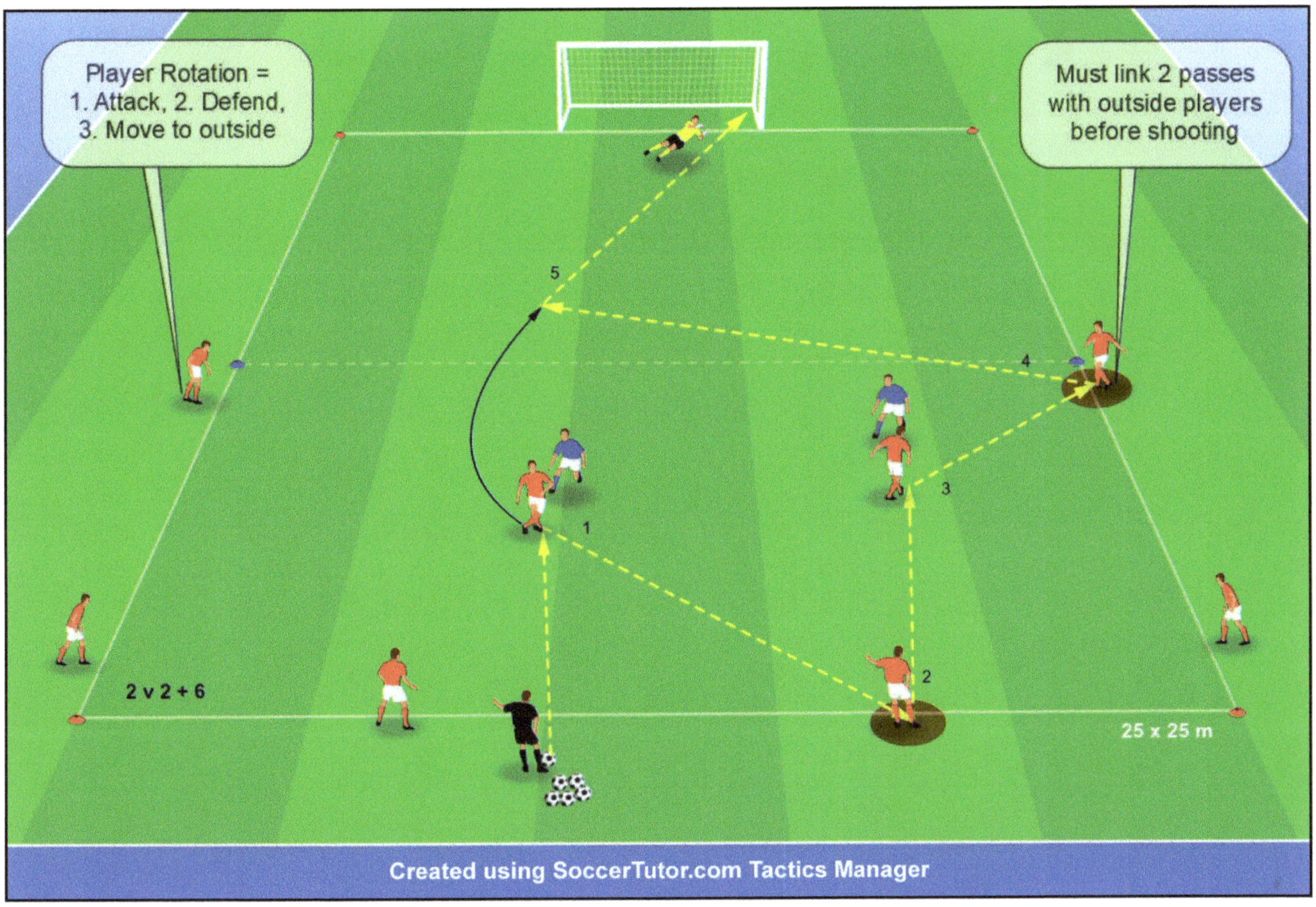

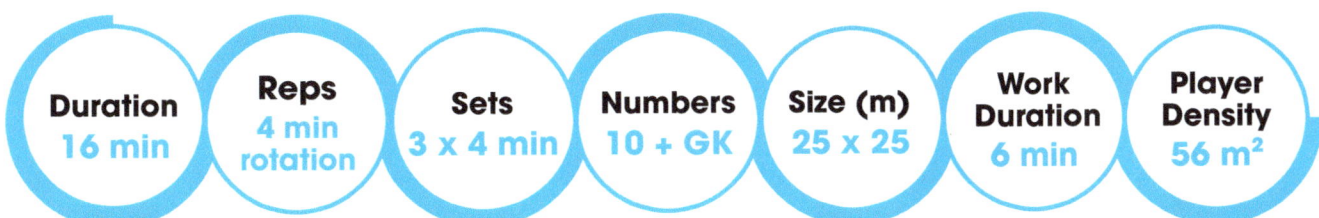

Player Rotation =
1. Attack, 2. Defend,
3. Move to outside

Must link 2 passes with outside players before shooting

2 v 2 + 6

25 x 25 m

Created using SoccerTutor.com Tactics Manager

PRACTICE INFORMATION

Duration	Reps	Sets	Numbers	Size (m)	Work Duration	Player Density
16 min	4 min rotation	3 x 4 min	10 + GK	25 x 25	6 min	56 m²

OBJECTIVE: Intensive SSG with focus on forward movement to break lines in attacking play

Volume Metrics	Practice Total	Per Min. of Work
Total Distance (km)	1.467	0.24
High Speed Running (m)	31.84	5.3
Sprint Distance (m)	0.2	0.03
HML Distance (m)	208	34.67
Power Plays (HiActs)	14	2.33

Intensity Metrics	Practice Total	Per Min. of Work
Max Speed (m/s)	6.34	
Intensity (m/min)		70.14
Power Score (w/kg)	6.04	
No. of Max Accels >4m²	10.43	1.74
No. of Max Decels >4m²	8.71	1.45

* The data shows the physical output per player based on research from elite level teams - see pages 81-83 for details

TUESDAY Training Day Practices: Resistance - 4 Days Until Match (MD +3/-4)

Small Sided Game 2: Resistance Conditioning Circuit and 3v3 (+6) +GKs Game

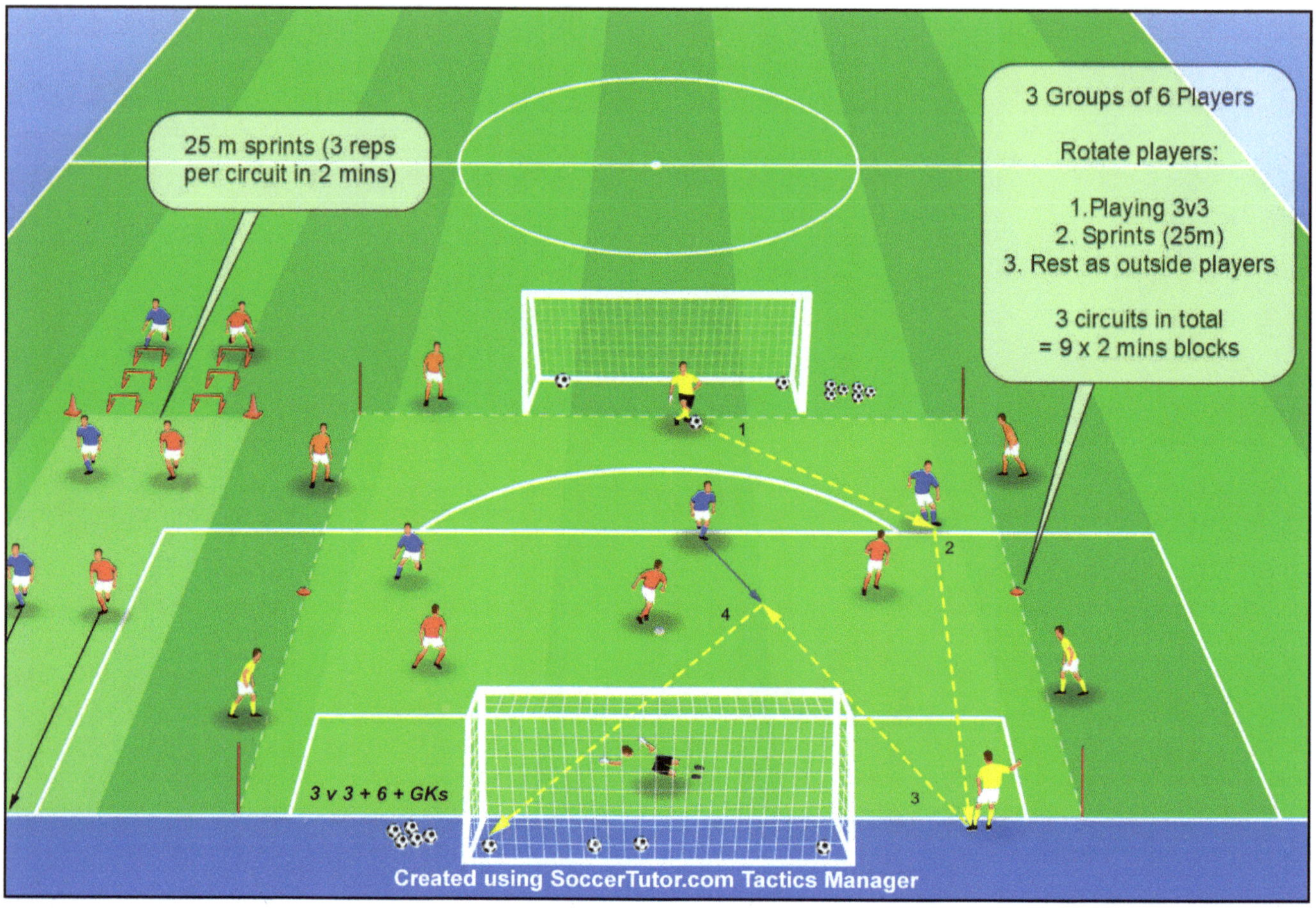

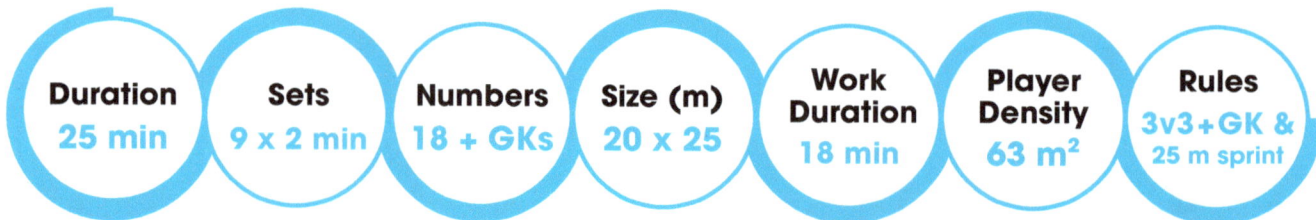

Callouts in diagram:
- 25 m sprints (3 reps per circuit in 2 mins)
- 3 Groups of 6 Players
  Rotate players:
  1. Playing 3v3
  2. Sprints (25m)
  3. Rest as outside players
  3 circuits in total = 9 x 2 mins blocks
- 3 v 3 + 6 + GKs

Created using SoccerTutor.com Tactics Manager

PRACTICE INFORMATION

Duration	Sets	Numbers	Size (m)	Work Duration	Player Density	Rules
25 min	9 x 2 min	18 + GKs	20 x 25	18 min	63 m²	3v3+GK & 25 m sprint

OBJECTIVE: SSG + resistance conditioning circuit for lower body strength and resistance capacity

Volume Metrics	Practice Total	Per Min. of Work
Total Distance (km)	1.081	0.06
High Speed Running (m)	163.46	9.08
Sprint Distance (m)	36	2
HML Distance (m)	390	21.67
Power Plays (HiActs)	4.81	0.27

Intensity Metrics	Practice Total	Per Min. of Work
Max Speed (m/s)	7.38	
Intensity (m/min)		61.12
Power Score (w/kg)	5.24	
No. of Max Accels >4m²	16	0.89
No. of Max Decels >4m²	11	0.61

* The data shows the physical output per player based on research from elite level teams - see **pages 81-83** for details

Football Periodization to Maximise Performance

@SoccerTutor.com | REFERENCE | @adamowen1980

TUESDAY Training Day Practices: Resistance - 4 Days Until Match (MD +3/-4)

Small Sided Game 3: Using the Spare Man to Create Chances in a 4v4 (+1) Game

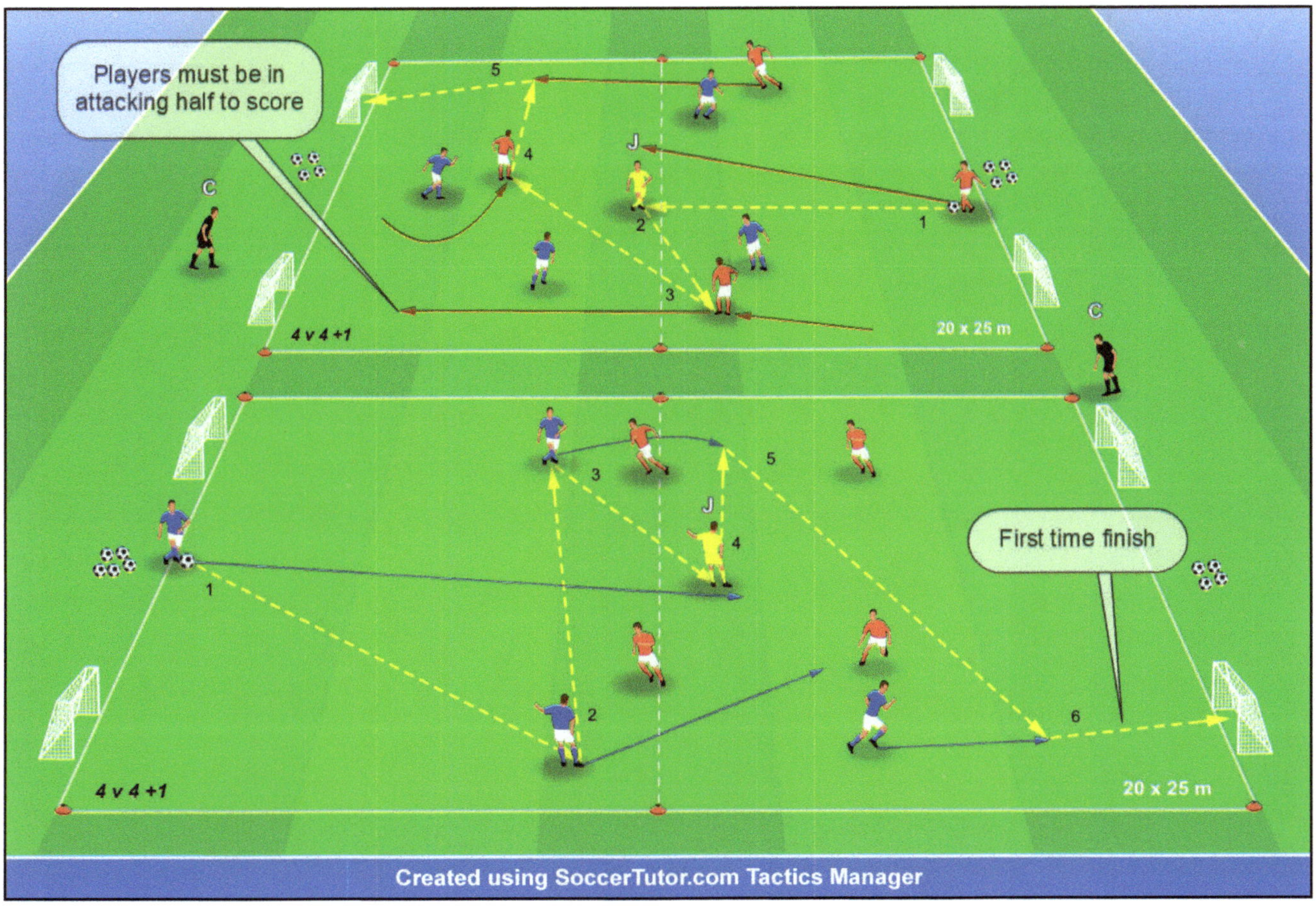

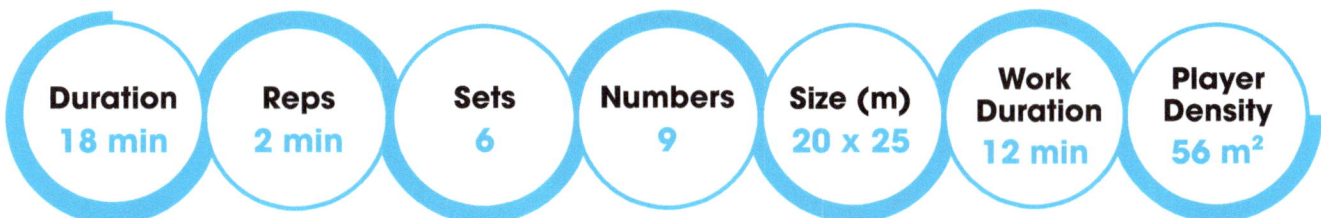

PRACTICE INFORMATION

Duration	Reps	Sets	Numbers	Size (m)	Work Duration	Player Density
18 min	2 min	6	9	20 x 25	12 min	56 m²

OBJECTIVE: Intensive SSG with focus on using spare man to create goalscoring opportunities

Volume Metrics	Practice Total	Per Min. of Work
Total Distance (km)	1.467	0.12
High Speed Running (m)	9.15	0.76
Sprint Distance (m)	-	-
HML Distance (m)	185	15.42
Power Plays (HiActs)	4.35	0.36

Intensity Metrics	Practice Total	Per Min. of Work
Max Speed (m/s)	5.79	
Intensity (m/min)		69.45
Power Score (w/kg)	5.91	
No. of Max Accels >4m²	11.17	0.93
No. of Max Decels >4m²	8.59	0.72

* The data shows the physical output per player based on research from elite level teams - see **pages 81-83** for details

TUESDAY Training Day Practices: Resistance - 4 Days Until Match (MD +3/-4)

Small Sided Game 4: High Intensity of Play in a 4v4 +GK Game

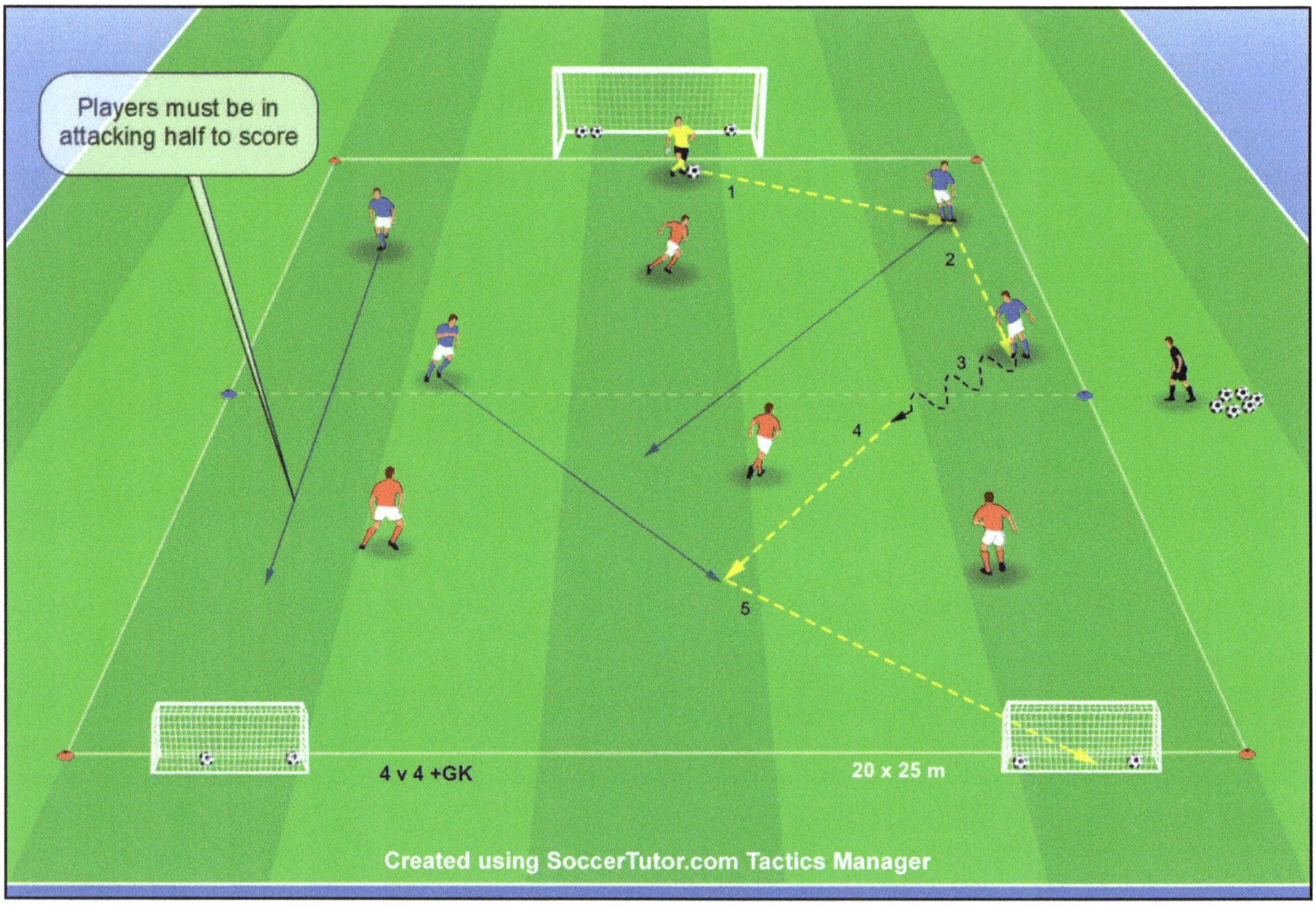

PRACTICE INFORMATION

Duration	Reps	Sets	Numbers	Size (m)	Work Duration	Player Density
16 min	4 min	3	8 + GK	20 x 25	12 min	56 m²

OBJECTIVE: Intensive small sided game with the focus on a high intensity of play

Volume Metrics	Practice Total	Per Min. of Work
Total Distance (km)	1.369	0.11
High Speed Running (m)	28	2.33
Sprint Distance (m)	2	0.17
HML Distance (m)	282	23.5
Power Plays (HiActs)	7	0.58

Intensity Metrics	Practice Total	Per Min. of Work
Max Speed (m/s)	5	
Intensity (m/min)		86
Power Score (w/kg)	5.55	
No. of Max Accels >4m²	4	0.33
No. of Max Decels >4m²	6	0.5

* The data shows the physical output per player based on research from elite level teams - see **pages 81-83** for details

@SoccerTutor.com   Football Periodization to Maximise Performance

TUESDAY Training Day Practices: Resistance - 4 Days Until Match (MD +3/-4)

Small Sided Game 5: Intensive Conditioning Game with 2 Mini Goals + Large Goal & GK

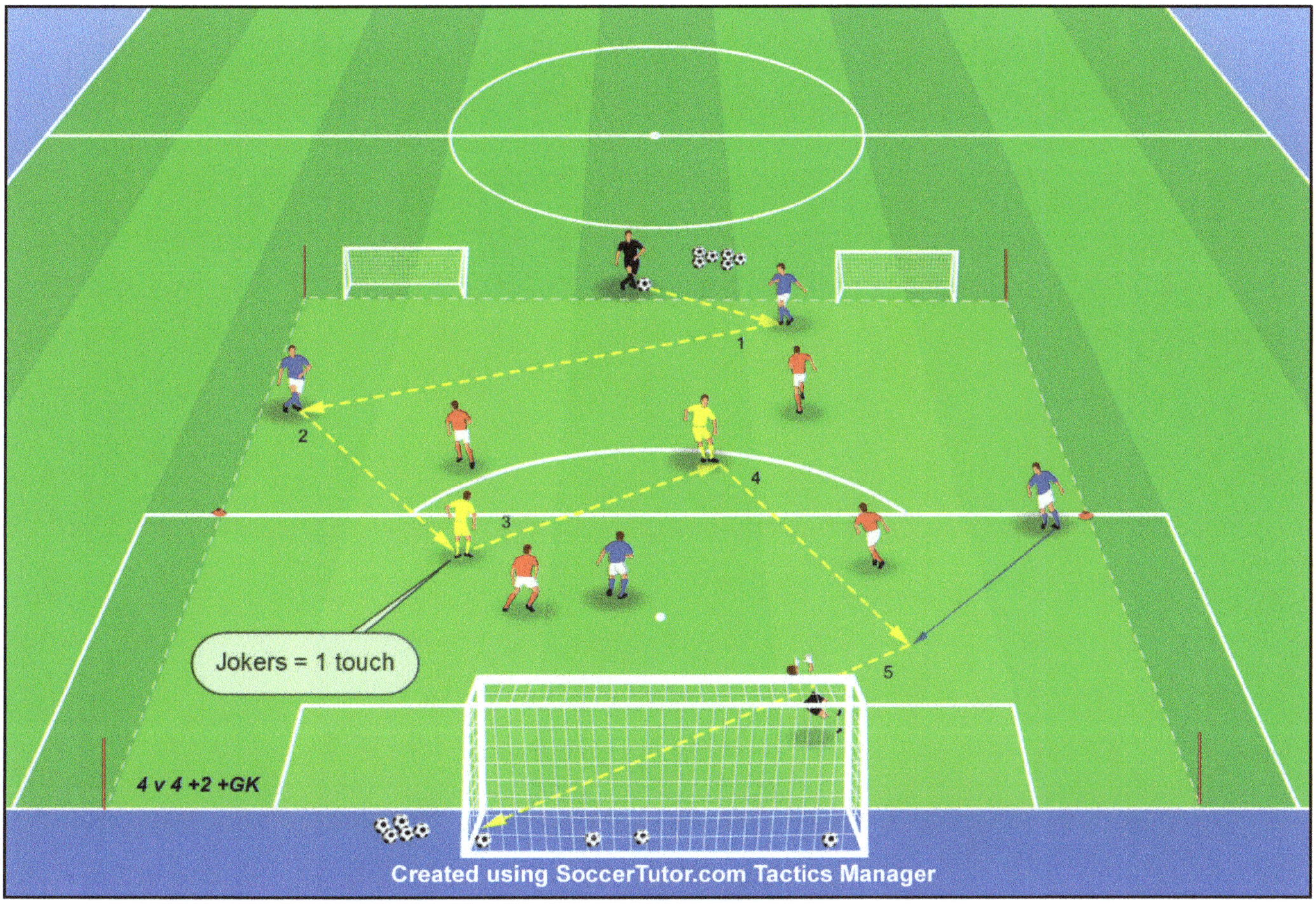

![Diagram: 4 v 4 +2 +GK small sided game with Jokers = 1 touch]

PRACTICE INFORMATION

Duration	Reps	Sets	Numbers	Size (m)	Work Duration	Player Density
10 min	3 min	3	10 + GK	30 x 35	9 min	96 m²

OBJECTIVE: Small sided game with the focus on conditioning and a high intensity of play

Volume Metrics	Practice Total	Per Min. of Work
Total Distance (km)	1.036	0.115
High Speed Running (m)	12.11	1.35
Sprint Distance (m)	0.10	0.01
HML Distance (m)	132.88	14.76
Power Plays (HiActs)	3.44	0.38

Intensity Metrics	Practice Total	Per Min. of Work
Max Speed (m/s)	5.95	
Intensity (m/min)		79.99
Power Score (w/kg)	6.85	
No. of Max Accels >4m²	9.88	1.1
No. of Max Decels >4m²	7.55	0.84

* The data shows the physical output per player based on research from elite level teams - see pages 81-83 for details

TUESDAY Training Day Practices: Resistance - 4 Days Until Match (MD +3/-4)

Small Sided Game 6: Intensive Conditioning in a 4v4 (+4) +GK Game

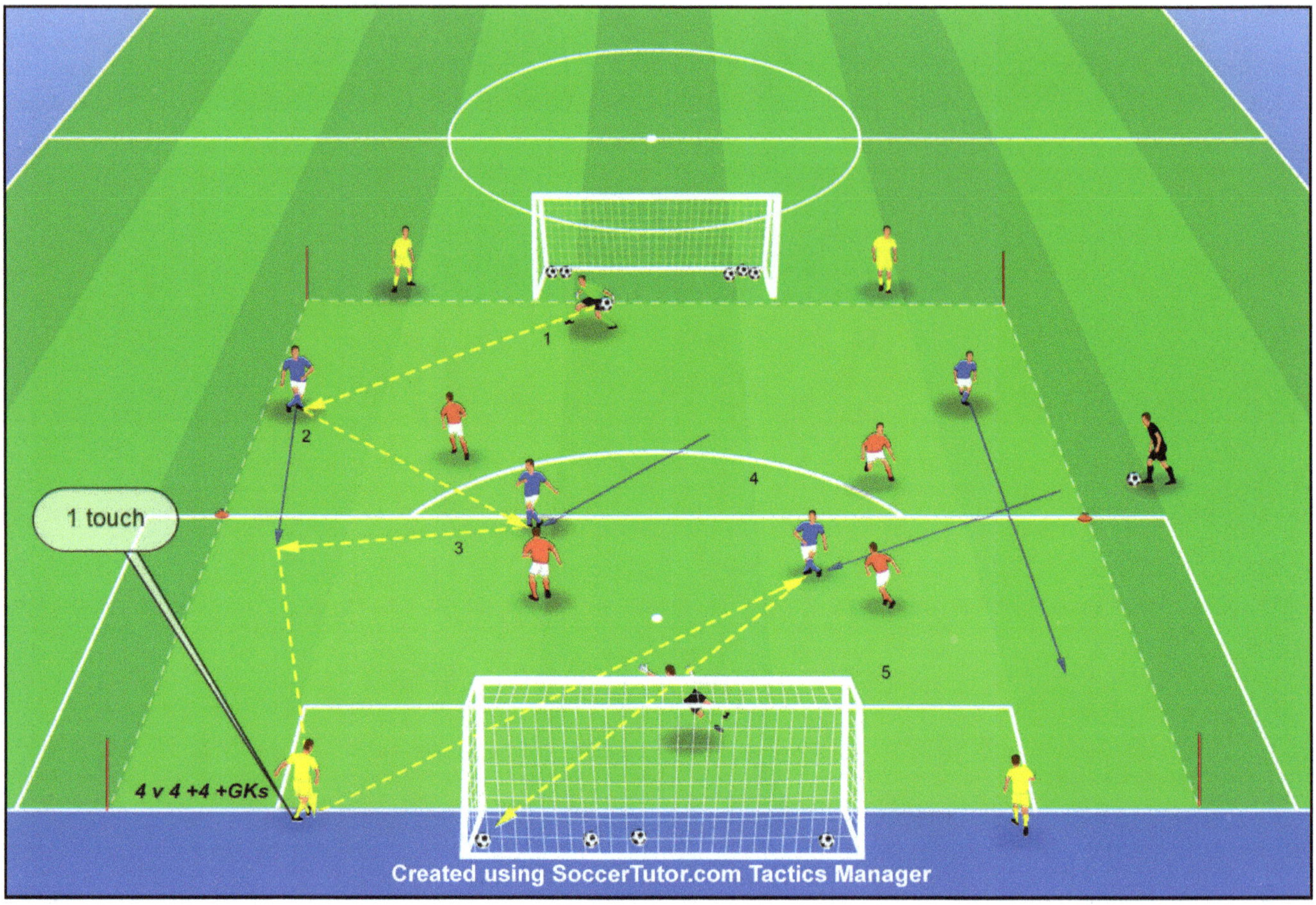

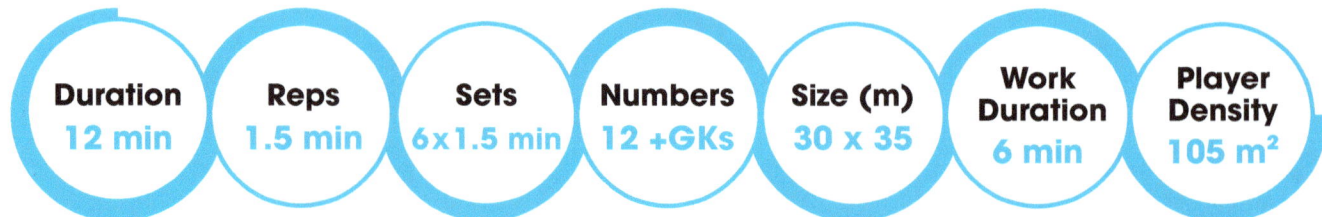

PRACTICE INFORMATION

Duration	Reps	Sets	Numbers	Size (m)	Work Duration	Player Density
12 min	1.5 min	6 x 1.5 min	12 +GKs	30 x 35	6 min	105 m²

OBJECTIVE: Small sided game with the focus on conditioning and a high intensity of play

Volume Metrics	Practice Total	Per Min. of Work
Total Distance (km)	0.834	0.14
High Speed Running (m)	3.9	0.65
Sprint Distance (m)	-	-
Work Ratio (%)	20.66	
Power Plays (HiActs)	2.36	0.39

Intensity Metrics	Practice Total	Per Min. of Work
Max Speed (m/s)	5.15	
Intensity (m/min)		58.27
Power Score (w/kg)	4.95	
Max Accel. Distance (m)	12.77	2.13
Max Decel. Distance (m)	16.13	2.69

* The data shows the physical output per player based on research from elite level teams - see **pages 81-83** for details

@SoccerTutor.com — Football Periodization to Maximise Performance

TUESDAY Training Day Practices: Resistance - 4 Days Until Match (MD +3/-4)

Small Sided Game 7: Intensive Conditioning in a 4(+4) v 4(+4) +GK Game

4 v 4 +4 +GKs

Created using SoccerTutor.com Tactics Manager

PRACTICE INFORMATION

Duration	Reps	Sets	Numbers	Size (m)	Work Duration	Player Density
12 min	1.5 min	6 x 1.5 min	16 + GKs	25 x 30	4.5 min	90 m²

OBJECTIVE: Small sided game with the focus on conditioning and a high intensity of play

Volume Metrics	Practice Total	Per Min. of Work
Total Distance (km)	0.876	0.2
High Speed Running (m)	9.12	2.03
Sprint Distance (m)	-	-
Work Ratio (%)	22.56	
Power Plays (HiActs)	2.54	0.56

Intensity Metrics	Practice Total	Per Min. of Work
Max Speed (m/s)	5.83	
Intensity (m/min)		62.45
Power Score (w/kg)	5.3	
Max Accel. Distance (m)	13.26	2.95
Max Decel. Distance (m)	19.45	4.32

* The data shows the physical output per player based on research from elite level teams - see **pages 81-83** for details

WEDNESDAY TRAINING DAY:
SPEED ENDURANCE

3 DAYS UNTIL MATCH (MD +4/-3)

WEDNESDAY Training Day: Speed Endurance - 3 Days Until Match (MD +4/-3)

3 DAYS UNTIL THE MATCH (MD +4/-3):
Collective Team Principle Training and Speed Endurance Development

Duration	45 min	70-75 min	85-95 min	60-70 min	45-60 min	90 min
Daily Theme	Recovery	Resistance	Speed Endurance	Reaction Speed	Activation	Match
Preparation	Match Day (MD) +2/-5	Match Day (MD) +3/-4	Match Day (MD) +4/-3	Match Day (MD) +5/-2	Match Day (MD) +6/-1	Match Day
		Positional Principles	Collective Principles	Unit Principles		
Game Type Focus	-	SSGs 1v1-4v4 (+GKs) Small Area	LSGs 8v8-10v10 (+GKs) Large Area	MSGs 5v5-7v7 (+GKs) Medium Area	LSGs 8v8-10v10 (+GKs) Small/Med Area	Match Day 11v11
Bout Durations	-	1-3 min	5-10 min	3-5 min	4 min	2 x 45 min
	Mon: Recovery	Tue-Wed: Conditioning		Thu-Fri: Preparation		Perform

* **Training Week based on Professional Microcycle Example** - see pages 74-75.

Key Focus on:

- **Collective Principles and Game Principles** at near maximum speed
- **Speed Endurance**
- **Physical Overloads** within larger training areas per player (density) and positional/tactical structure

WEDNESDAY Training Day: Speed Endurance - 3 Days Until Match (MD +4/-3)

WEDNESDAY (MD +4/-3) TRAINING DAY:
Physical and Physiological Focus

This **Wednesday (MD +4/-3) Training Day** is the second "conditioning" training day within the professional microcycle and is vitally important from a session design perspective. It addresses some of the key physiological, technical and psychological components of match preparation.

This specific training day focusses around the game model through **Collective Principles** (or Macro-Principles) that the **players will face in competitive 11v11 matches**.

These football actions should be inclusive of:

- **Near Maximum Speed Exposures**
- **Speed Endurance Based Conditioning Overloads**

Large Sided Games (LSGs)

These principles should be constructed and overloaded within a tactical structure, based on the future game references demanded. This **session structure should be focused around letting the blocks of work run for longer durations whilst minimising stoppages or interferences**. This drives the intensity and volume through large sided games and extensive (long) based possession phases.

Based around the key collective principles players are exposed to through the technical instruction forming the coaching system or style, it's important to note that **the playing area and density is substantially greater**.

Research concerning this provides confidence to the coaching community through intelligent practice design phases significantly eliciting **greater high speed running (HSR) and sprint distances**, which accumulate as a result of the greater distances players cover in these session types (**8v8 to 10v10 +GKs**).

Furthermore, in addition to the more forceful accelerations and decelerations (A:Ds) in these larger game types, the **greater recovery periods between technical actions** due to the increased number of players involved, means the players are far **more recovered with greater spatial density per player to recreate higher, more forceful, repetitive, explosive actions**.

This was shown in a study (Owen et al., 2011) which produced the following results concerning large sided games (LSGs):

- Significantly lower cardiovascular responses were reported in LSGs, when compared with SSGs or MSGs
- Significant increases in High Speed Running (HSR) and sprint exposures

WEDNESDAY Training Day: Speed Endurance - 3 Days Until Match (MD +4/-3)

Fatigue & Injury Prevention

Based on my own unpublished data surrounding accumulative fatigue, it has shown that the MD +4/-3 training sessions can fully integrate maximum high speed running (HSR) efforts and sprinting overloads without increased risk of injury. A recent investigation by Malone et al., (2018a) revealed how **well-developed physical qualities inclusive of HSR and sprint actions through progressive training, are paramount as a way of reducing muscle injuries within team sports**. According to further research, limiting player exposure to the near maximal velocity bouts in the microcycle may have a debilitating effect on the body's preparedness to compete.

Key Point: Coaches who regularly conduct training in reduced player densities (**see graph below**) do not provide the stimulus required to prepare or recover sufficiently from competitive matches: not enough high speed running!

Furthermore, recent research in this area from Campos-Vasquez et al., (2021) showed how distances covered at high and very high velocity during La Liga training sessions following a specific training microcycle, still did not simulate the values recorded during competitive matches.

It has also been suggested that **if training sessions in the preparation of games do not simulate or even intensify the high-speed efforts demanded by competitive matches, the physical performance during matches could be compromised** (Di Salvo et al., 2007), **as well as enhancing the risk of injury** (Gabbett, 2016).

High Speed Running (HSR) per Minute of Work vs. Player Density

* Density = Numbers of players on the pitch / (length x width of playing area)
* m2/player = Metres squared per player used for the density of the pitch area
* High Speed Running (HSR) per minute of work = Per minute of play (practice or game)

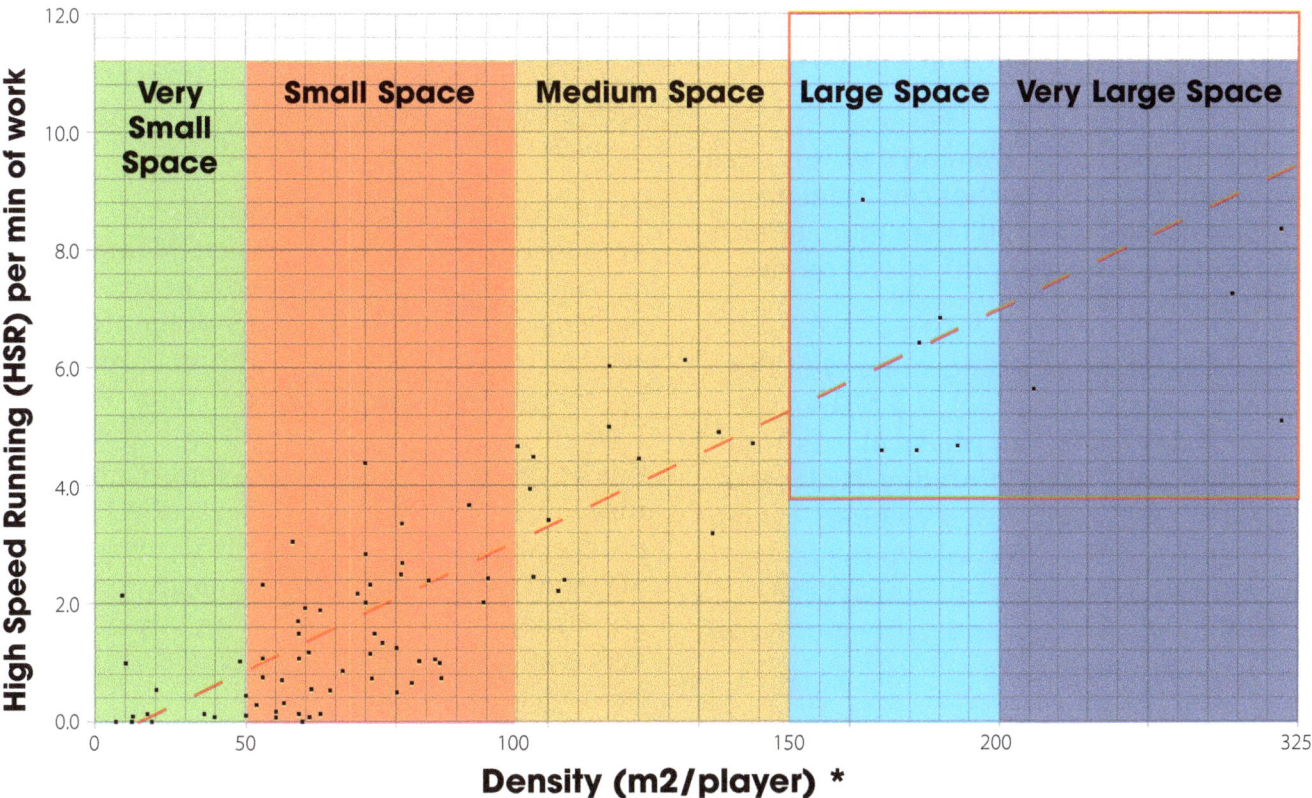

WEDNESDAY Training Day: Speed Endurance - 3 Days Until Match (MD +4/-3)

The Physiological Perspective

From a physiological perspective, it is paramount to understand that having previously overloaded the players from an accelerations and decelerations (A:Ds) and change of directions (CODs) movement profile (Tuesday MD +3/-4 training day focus), the content behind the **Wednesday MD +4/-3 loading day is exposing players to more high speed running (HSR) and sprint activity with greater volumes than any other time in the microcycle**.

This physical stimulus is achieved through the playing density and size of the playing areas being significantly greater, coupled with increased bout durations to elicit the overload required. With this type of movement and exposure through the careful consideration of session design development, the coaching staff can successfully provide a **key physical stimulus replicating near match play speed** and contractions in a football context, as shown in the practices/sessions in this book.

The training sessions for this MD +4/-3 training day should be very similar to the competition (matches) in terms of collective/team tactics and technical interactions, as well as demands.

During this particular training day, it is vitally important that the coaches can induce a physical overload and full maximum effort in terms of sprinting and high speed running (HSR) exposures.

Looking across the loading strategy of the training week (microcycle), the **MD +4/-3 training day is classed physically as the most demanding training day**. It places a large demand on increased volumes, higher-speed and sprint actions within the larger pitch density. This must encompass the tactical focus, strategy and game model for the upcoming match.

Emotional fatigue is greater on this training day as a result of the implementation of training drills/practices with greater complexity and all round multifunctional aspects. Utilising more complex tactical practices and sessions with a larger-game focus (LSGs = 8v8-10v10 +GKs) evidently leads to a greater volume of training and longer session duration.

Preparing for Match-Play

Within this training day (MD +3/-4), there is a necessity to ensure the players are exposed to training practices in larger areas to prepare for competitive match demands from a generic perspective, but also, they are enabling specific positional movements within competitive games. As a result of these games and specific movements, **similar rapid muscular contractions and movements required during match-play can be performed in preparation**.

From a practical perspective, positive results have been elicited when elite level players are exposed to 4-5 repetitions of >95% maximal speed (Vmax) in each microcycle. These are considered positive results because they resulted in achieving high training availability levels (>90%), gradual and progressive maximal speed development increments and Vmax hit over the course of the season. Consequentially, it also showed very good soft-tissue injury rates versus the general injury rates in football.

This is not a unique notion, as it is demonstrated by more research (Malone et al., 2018a) which describes how near maximal velocity exposures integrated within the weekly 'microcycle' improved preparation for competition, as discussed in *Chapter 3: Training Load Management in Football* of this book. According to some reports, these running exposures may be prescribed as potential 'vaccines against soft-tissue injuries' if performed at the correct intensity, duration and distance within the training microcycle. This is all in conjunction with the correct training load for the group.

WEDNESDAY Training Day: Speed Endurance - 3 Days Until Match (MD +4/-3)

Players should hit near maximal velocity (>95%Vmax) on this MD+4/-3 training day. If not (i.e. as a result of poor training session design and coaching process), then players should be subsequently exposed to 'top-up' drills, or football specific practices focussing on attaining the required stimulus post-training as a way of protecting or increasing their capacity to perform such actions.

This is a thought process also justified by Campos-Vasquez et al., (2021) who as mentioned previously indicates that it is necessary to induce additional training tasks within the microcycle incorporating high-velocity maximal efforts, in order to replicate the velocities achieved in official competition (matches) and optimally prepare elite players.

Speed Endurance and Extensive Game Focus (LSGs)

Repeated High Speed Running (HSR) - Increased HSR as % of Total Distance Covered (TDC)	**Repeated Sprint Ability (RSA)** function and recovery between bouts
Longer acceleration distance	Increase player ability to reproduce high speed football movements
Extensive LSGs (large areas & numbers)	Positional roles?
Greater % of linear speed distance **vs.** tight space distance	**Key Coaching Themes:** • Extensive games • LSGs = 8v8 to 10v10 (+GKs) • Positional roles • High intensity
Ability to reproduce high speed football actions	
High speed running >5.5m/s	

WEDNESDAY (MD +4/-3) TRAINING DAY:
Technical and Tactical Focus

From a technical-tactical perspective, the **Wednesday MD +4/-3 Training Day** should be concentrated around **"Collective Team Principles,"** and the relationship between them. Concerning the game model training concept by Teoldo & Silvino, coaches within this method of work can try to ensure all the "coaching principles" are engaged in a synchronised way across the different units (i.e. defence, midfield, attack), maximising positional roles through the incorporation of the tactical strategy.

Research by Clemente et al., (2018) recommends that small, half-size pitch dimensions are more appropriate for lower-intensity training sessions and field exploration for players in different positions, which adds more credibility to the methodology in this section of the book. Alternatively, the larger pitch density is more appropriate for greater physically demanding training sessions with players focused on tactical positional behaviours that also fit directly into this microcycle tapering approach.

Large Sided Games (LSGs)

Investigations are very concise about differing demands of various-sided games (SSGs, MSGs, LSGs) with respect to technical outputs (Owen et al, 2014). One such study in this area performed with UEFA Champions League level players revealed how the greater number of players on the pitch (e.g. 8v8, 9v9, 10v10) significantly reduced the individual technical demands imposed.

The different technical demands imposed upon players with variations in playing surface area and player numbers highlight how **coaches are able to provide more position specific training through the use of the large sided games (LSGs)** format.

When discussing the additional benefits of LSGs from a coaching perspective, the potential for the defensive units to evolve technically and tactically has been reported, based on suggestions that these game types offer more opportunities to improve the capacity to read game situations and oppositional build-up play, perform more blocks, interceptions and aerial challenges. These suggestions also concur with other studies in this topic area comparing the differences between medium sided games (MSGs) and small sided games (SSGs). Jones and Drust, (2007) performed a research study revealing significant technical differences with an increased number of ball touches within the SSGs due to lower player numbers. To conclude, concurrent changes of pitch size and player numbers generally leads to a significant variation of physical, tactical and technical demands imposed upon players. This further highlights the need for coaches to clarify key outcomes in the pre-session design and planning phase.

Key Point: One of the fundamental aspects of this section of the book addresses the misconception that all physical qualities can be developed within the game itself.

As long as the training session design phase is maximised utilising the key concepts, constraints and manipulation of key variables (i.e. rules per possession, player density, player numbers and durations), a lot of the physical overloads or stimulus may be possible. However, coaches should take note that in order to take players' physical and footballing capacity to the next level, isolating specific energy systems, high acceleration:deceleration overloads (A:D), and near maximal velocity exposures through positional specific work may need to be performed to achieve the desired outcome for the individual's profile.

WEDNESDAY Training Day: Speed Endurance - 3 Days Until Match (MD +4/-3)

WEDNESDAY (MD +4/-3) TRAINING DAY: Game Stimulus Response for Collective Team Coaching Principles Game Type

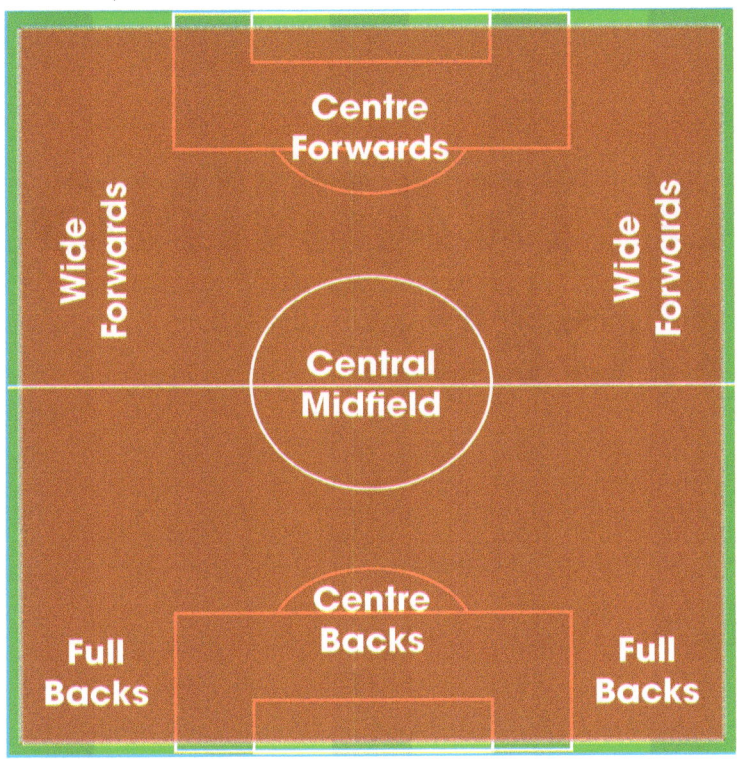

COLLECTIVE TRAINING PRINCIPLES

- **Team Based Principles** (collective)
- Apply **Tactical Unit Principles** in large density areas
- **Positional Technical Skills** in full game area
- **Game Based Situations** - attacking and defensive learning

WEDNESDAY (MD +4/-3) TRAINING DAY: Fundamental Concepts of Collective Principle Training and Speed Endurance Development

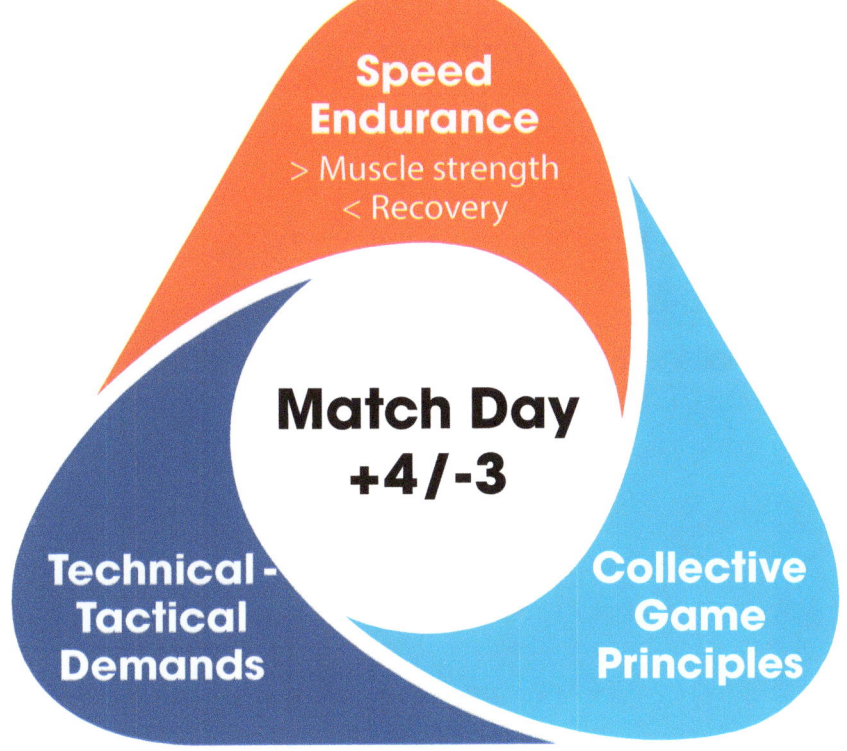

@SoccerTutor.com — Football Periodization to Maximise Performance

WEDNESDAY TRAINING DAY PRACTICES: SPEED ENDURANCE

3 DAYS UNTIL MATCH (MD +4/-3)

WEDNESDAY TRAINING SESSION (85-95 min)

Collective Team Principle Training and Speed Endurance Development:

1. Speed Endurance Warm-up (10-12 min)
2. Extensive Technical Practice (12-15 min)
3. Speed Endurance Conditioning Practice (5-15 min)
4. Large Sided Possession (10-15 min)
5. Large Sided Game in Large Area (10-50 min)

WEDNESDAY - 3 DAYS UNTIL MATCH (MD +4/-3):
Speed Endurance Warm-Up Practices

INTENSITY: All practices are performed at full intensity

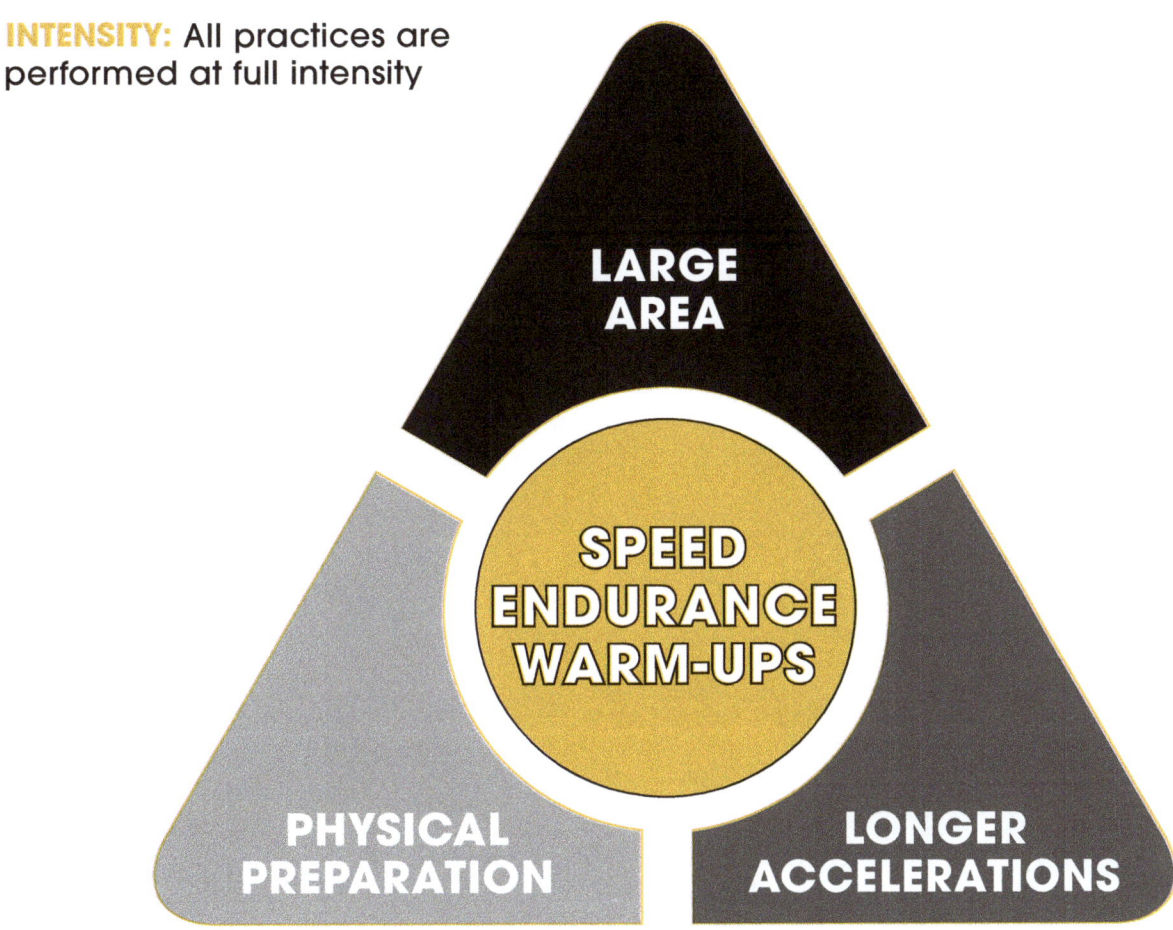

What are Speed Endurance Warm-ups?

- These warm up types are inclusive of less aggressive or explosive directional changes but include more longer acceleration based work in more expansive (larger) spaces.

- The bigger surface area provides the opportunity to engage the hamstrings through more high-speed running exposures.

Why are they used on this day of the training week (MD +4/-3)?

- These types of warm ups are used around the MD +4/-3 training day to prepare the players for the larger surface area type work developed through the course of the session.

How does this help to maximise performance?

- These warm up types are used on this day as a way of preparing the players' muscles used for larger, high speed and sprinting based efforts.

- Generally readying the body for the session ahead (large sided games).

WEDNESDAY Practices: Speed Endurance - 3 Days Until Match (MD +4/-3)

Speed Endurance Warm-up 1: Slalom, Mobility, and Lunge Walk "Shuttles" with Poles & Hurdles

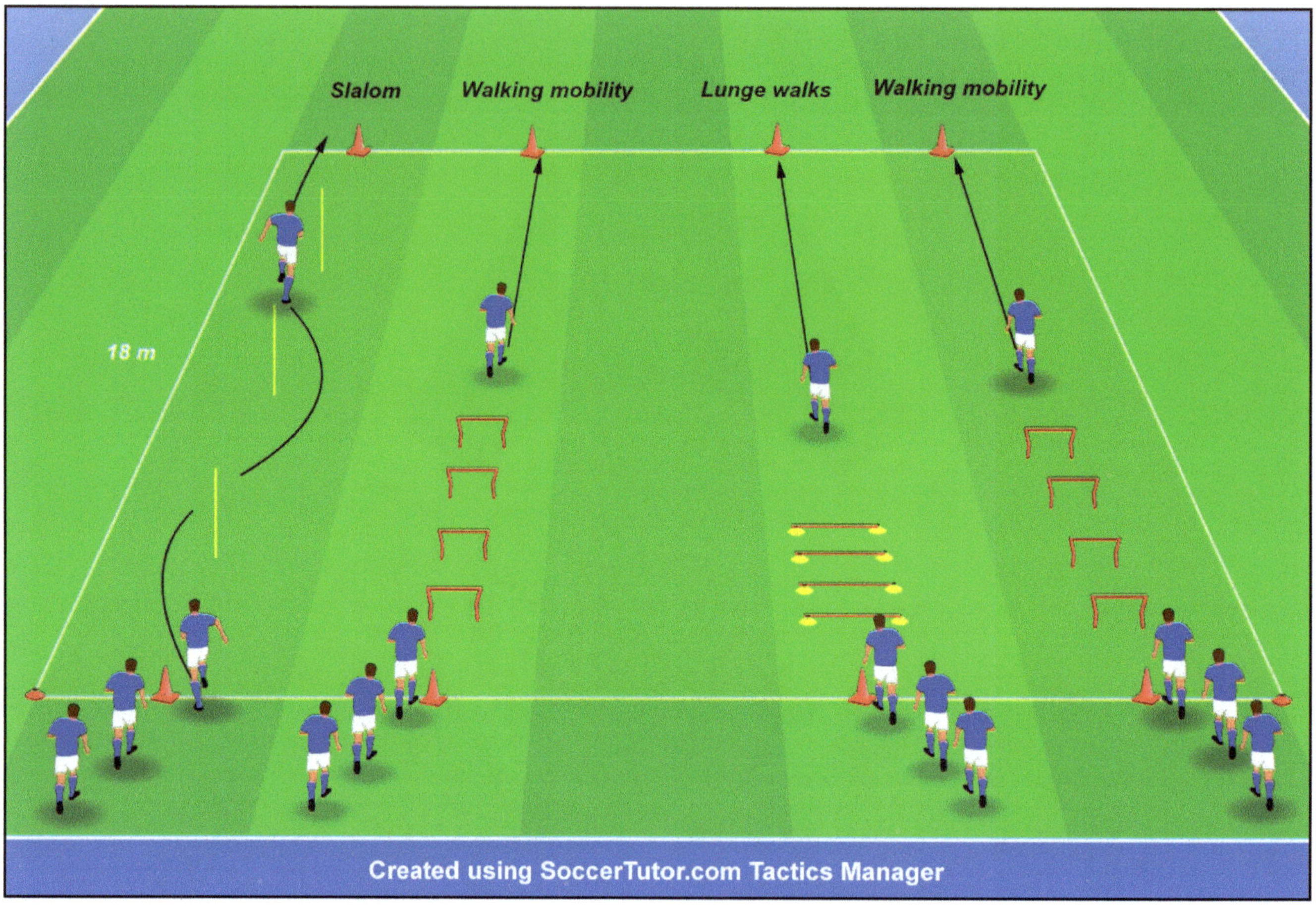

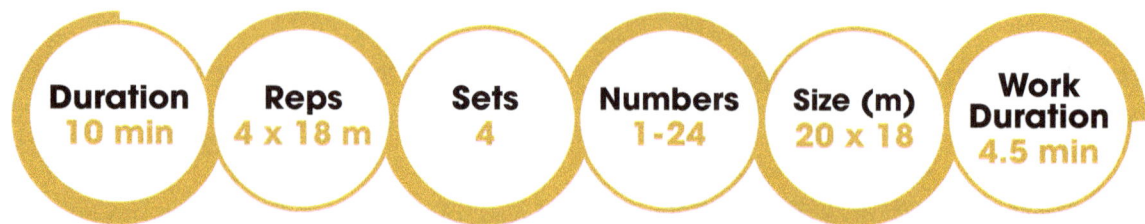

PRACTICE INFORMATION

Duration	Reps	Sets	Numbers	Size (m)	Work Duration
10 min	4 x 18 m	4	1-24	20 x 18	4.5 min

OBJECTIVE: Physically and mentally prepare the players for the training session (without the ball)

Volume Metrics	Practice Total	Per Min. of Work
Total Distance (km)	1.1	0.24
High Speed Running (m)	7	1.56
Sprint Distance (m)	-	-
Work Ratio (%)	89.57	
Power Plays (HiActs)	5	1.11

Intensity Metrics	Practice Total	Per Min. of Work
Max Speed (m/s)	5.40	
Intensity (m/min)		80
Power Score (w/kg)	5	
No. of Max Accels >4m²	-	-
No. of Max Decels >4m²	-	-

* The data shows the physical output per player based on research from elite level teams - see **pages 81-83** for details

WEDNESDAY Practices: Speed Endurance - 3 Days Until Match (MD +4/-3)

Speed Endurance Warm-up 2: Dribble, Stop, Run, Turn, Accelerate and Pass Variations

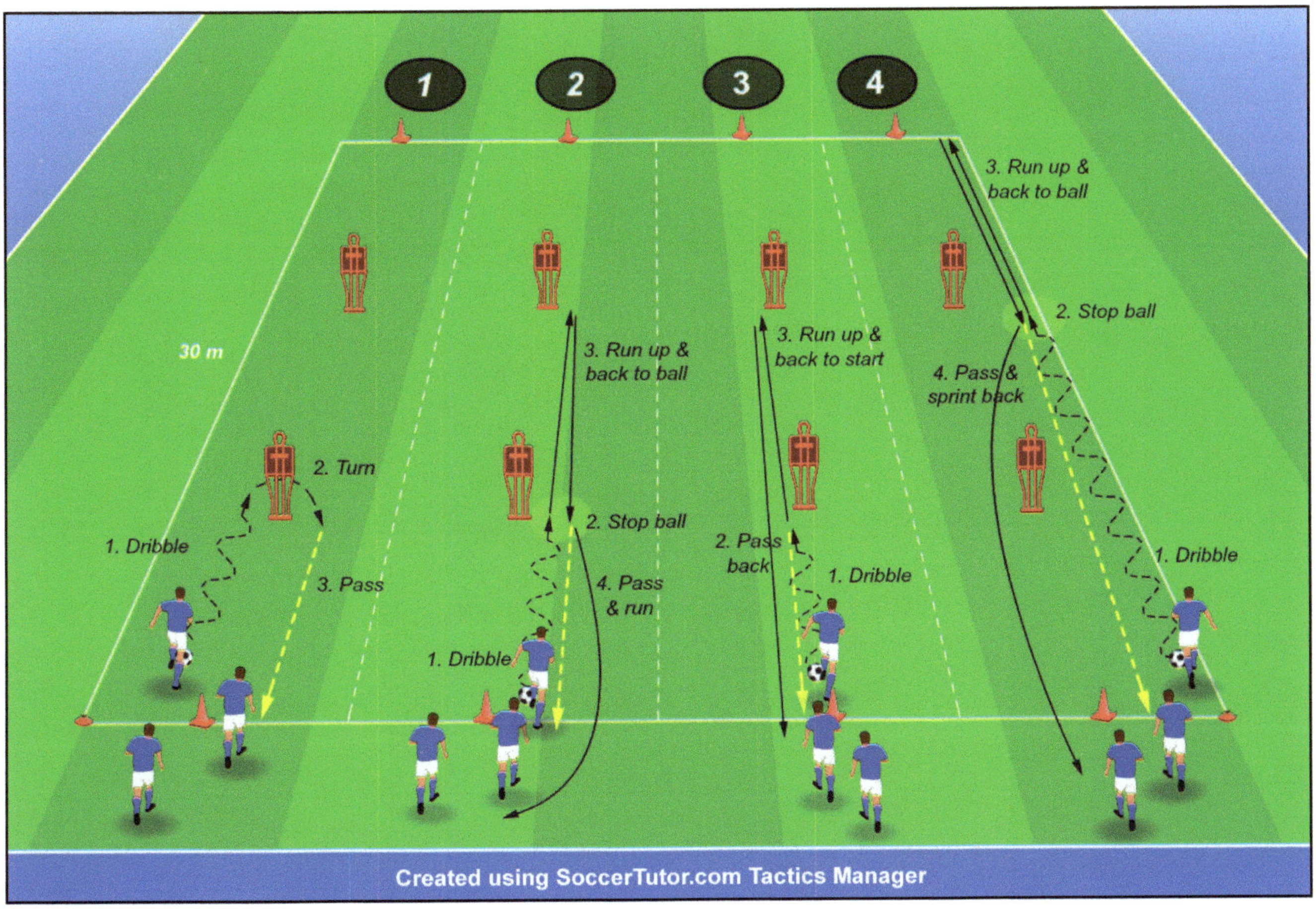

[Diagram: 30 x 30 m area with 4 stations (1, 2, 3, 4) each featuring mannequins and cones]

Station 1: 1. Dribble, 2. Turn, 3. Pass
Station 2: 1. Dribble, 2. Stop ball, 3. Run up & back to ball, 4. Pass & run
Station 3: 1. Dribble, 2. Pass back, 3. Run up & back to start
Station 4: 1. Dribble, 2. Stop ball, 3. Run up & back to ball, 4. Pass & sprint back

Created using SoccerTutor.com Tactics Manager

PRACTICE INFORMATION

Duration	Reps	Sets	Numbers	Size (m)	Work Duration
12 min	16	4 x 10; 20; 20; 30 m	3-16	30 x 30	5 min

OBJECTIVE: Physically and mentally prepare the players for the training session (with the ball)

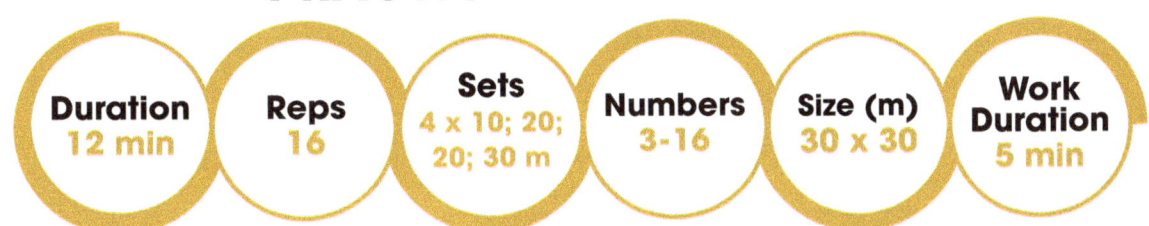

Volume Metrics	Practice Total	Per Min. of Work
Total Distance (km)	0.785	0.16
High Speed Running (m)	15.87	3.17
Sprint Distance (m)	-	-
Work Ratio (%)	29.98	
Power Plays (HiActs)	7.63	1.53

Intensity Metrics	Practice Total	Per Min. of Work
Max Speed (m/s)	5.79	
Intensity (m/min)		73.05
Power Score (w/kg)	6.33	
No. of Max Accels >4m²	14.68	2.94
No. of Max Decels >4m²	19.04	3.8

* The data shows the physical output per player based on research from elite level teams - see **pages 81-83** for details

Football Periodization to Maximise Performance

WEDNESDAY Practices: Speed Endurance - 3 Days Until Match (MD +4/-3)

Speed Endurance Warm-up 3: Running with the Ball "Shuttles" with Variations

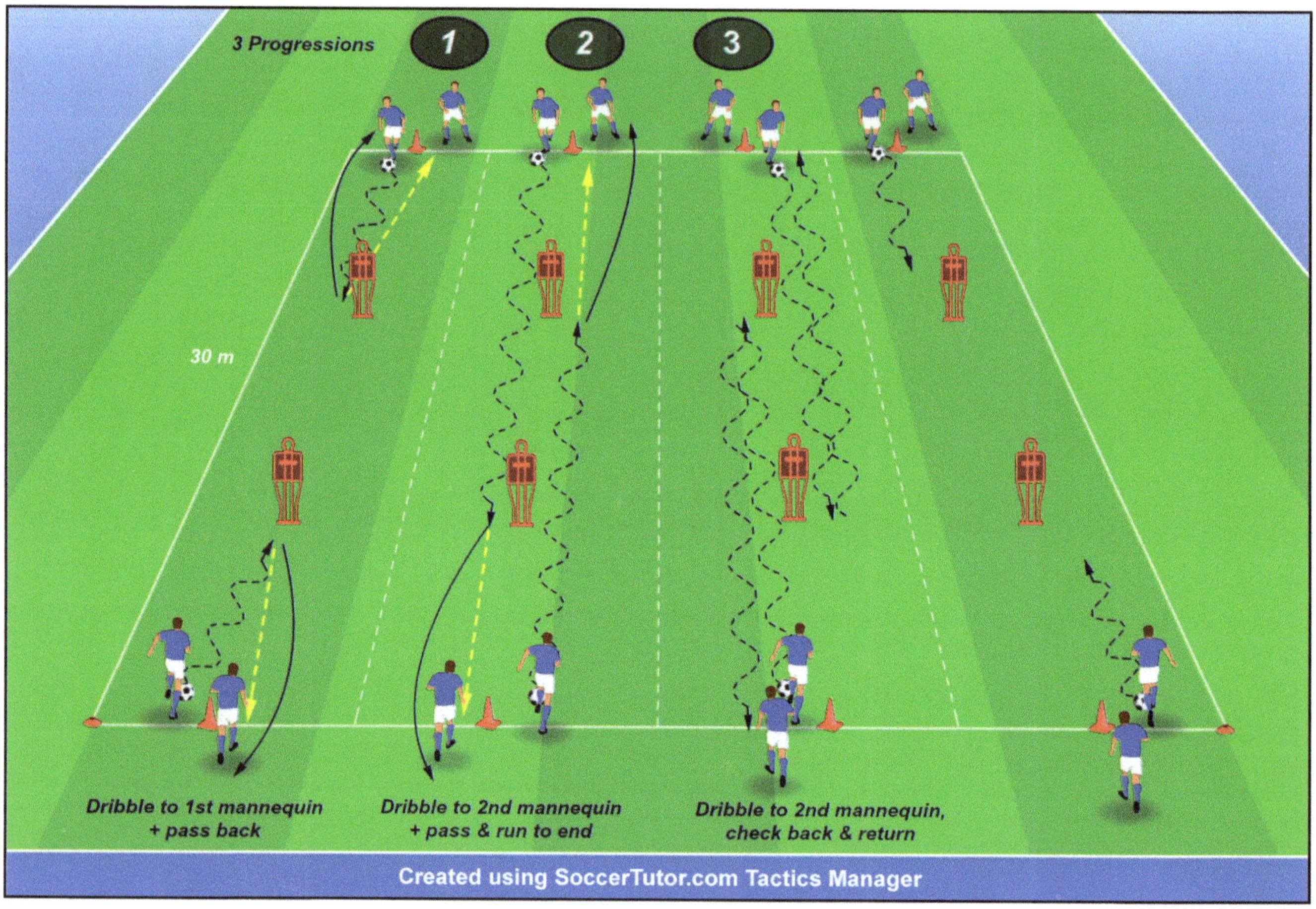

![Diagram showing 3 Progressions with mannequins and players dribbling: (1) Dribble to 1st mannequin + pass back, (2) Dribble to 2nd mannequin + pass & run to end, (3) Dribble to 2nd mannequin, check back & return. 30 m field.]

PRACTICE INFORMATION

Duration	Reps	Sets	Numbers	Size (m)	Work Duration
10 min	x 4 per block	3 x 4 reps	4-24	30 x 30	5 min

OBJECTIVE: Physically and mentally prepare the players for the training session (with the ball)

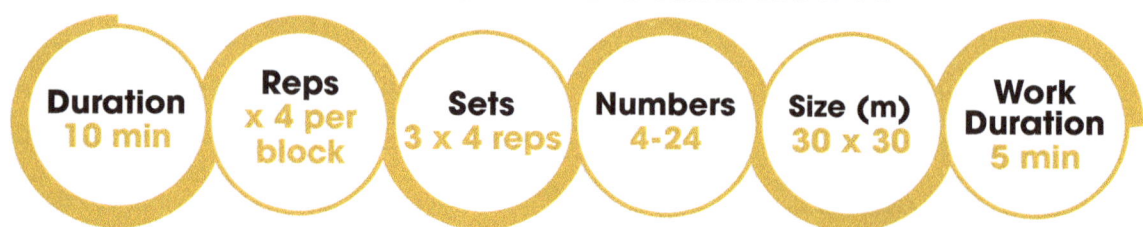

Volume Metrics	Practice Total	Per Min. of Work
Total Distance (km)	0.752	0.15
High Speed Running (m)	10	2
Sprint Distance (m)	-	-
Work Ratio (%)	48.55	
Power Plays (HiActs)	6	1.2

Intensity Metrics	Practice Total	Per Min. of Work
Max Speed (m/s)	5.02	
Intensity (m/min)		75
Power Score (w/kg)	4.33	
No. of Max Accels >4m²	12.2	2.44
No. of Max Decels >4m²	14.6	2.92

* The data shows the physical output per player based on research from elite level teams - see **pages 81-83** for details

WEDNESDAY Practices: Speed Endurance - 3 Days Until Match (MD +4/-3)

Speed Endurance Warm-up 4: Dribble, Diagonal Passing, and Recover Warm-up Circuit

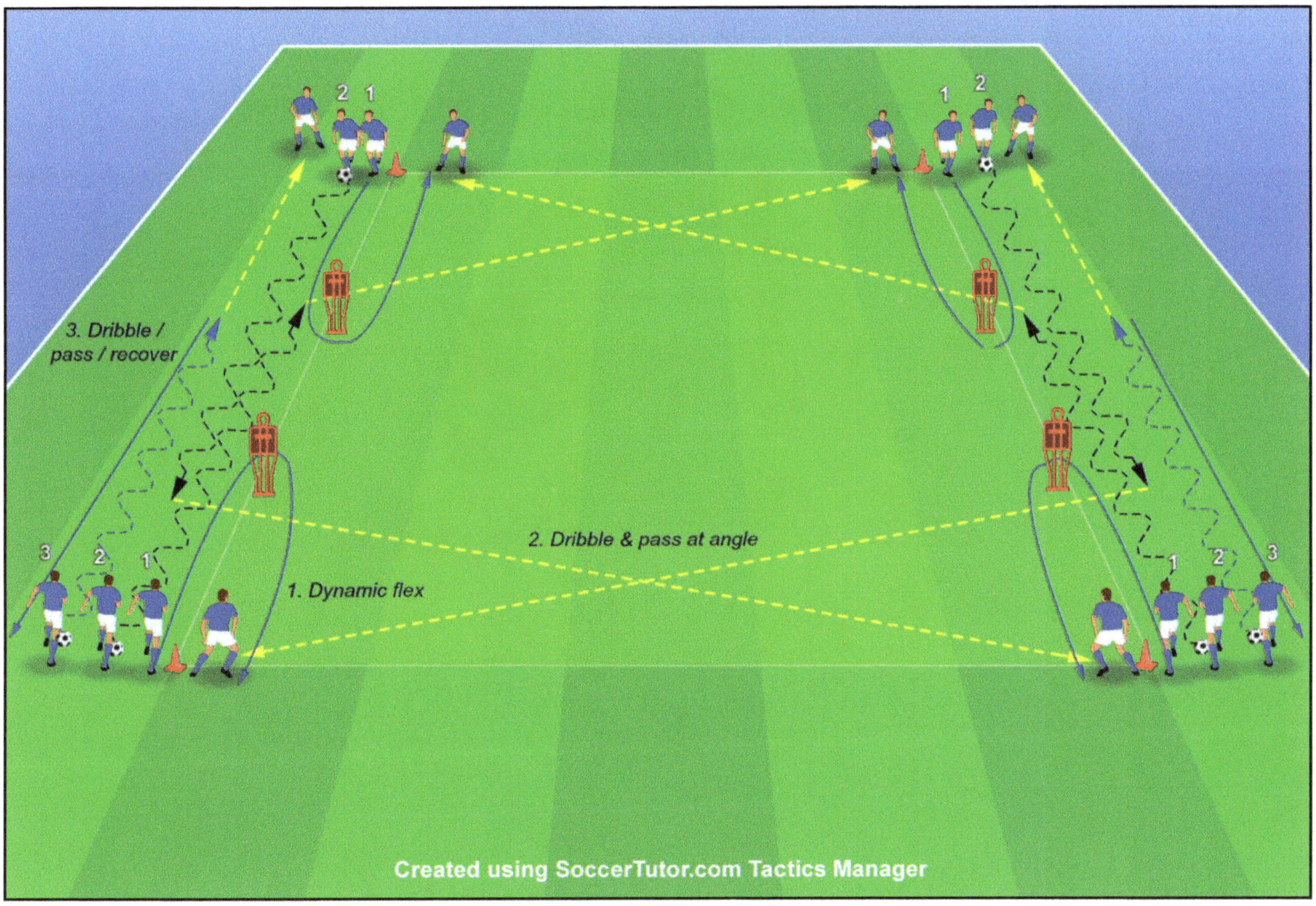

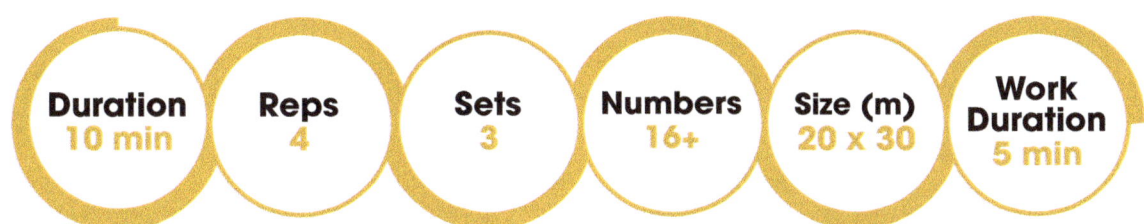

PRACTICE INFORMATION

Duration	Reps	Sets	Numbers	Size (m)	Work Duration
10 min	4	3	16+	20 x 30	5 min

OBJECTIVE: Physically and mentally prepare the players for the training session (with the ball)

Volume Metrics	Practice Total	Per Min. of Work
Total Distance (km)	0.909	0.18
High Speed Running (m)	12.76	2.55
Sprint Distance (m)	-	-
Work Ratio (%)	26.38	
Power Plays (HiActs)	8.45	1.69

Intensity Metrics	Practice Total	Per Min. of Work
Max Speed (m/s)	5.94	
Intensity (m/min)		63.56
Power Score (w/kg)	5.18	
No. of Max Accels >4m²	11.08	2.2
No. of Max Decels >4m²	7.8	1.56

* The data shows the physical output per player based on research from elite level teams - see **pages 81-83** for details

Football Periodization to Maximise Performance

WEDNESDAY Practices: Speed Endurance - 3 Days Until Match (MD +4/-3)

WEDNESDAY - 3 DAYS UNTIL MATCH (MD +4/-3):
Extensive Technical Practices

INTENSITY: All practices are performed at full intensity

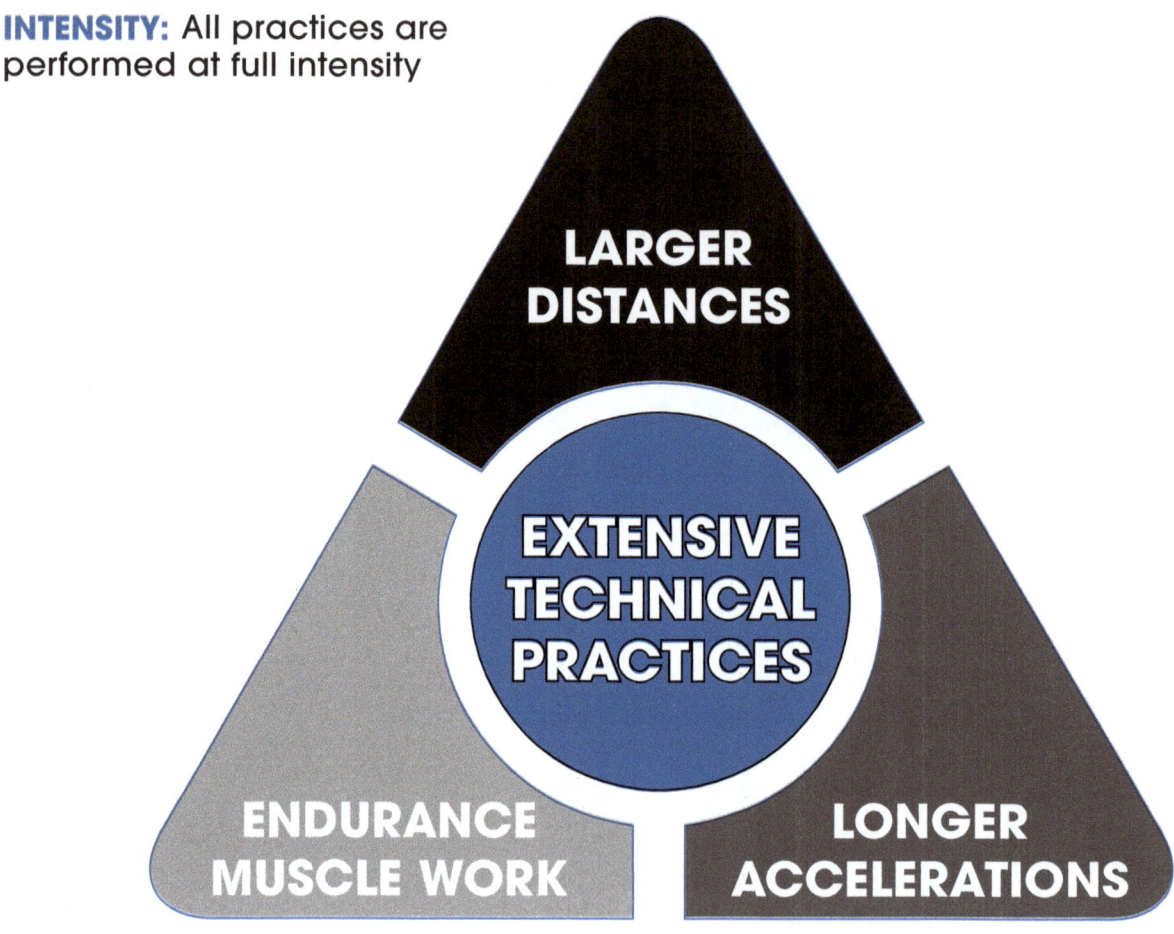

What are Extensive Technical Practices?

- Larger surface areas with longer passing ranges included within them (20+ metres).

- Larger surface areas to engage the key muscle groups required for the training session to follow.

- Longer acceleration and decelerations in larger spaces and training areas.

- They should be focused on keeping with the flow of the training day and working muscle groups on this particular day.

Why are they used on this day of the training week (MD +4/-3)?

- To prepare the players for the larger surface area type work developed through the course of the session.

How does this help to maximise performance?

- As a way of preparing the players muscles used for covering larger distances, longer acceleration and deceleration efforts.

- Generally readying the body for the session ahead in the larger spaces (large sided games).

WEDNESDAY Practices: Speed Endurance - 3 Days Until Match (MD +4/-3)

Extensive Technical 1: Timing of Movement to Receive in a "Y" Shape (One-Two + Give & Go)

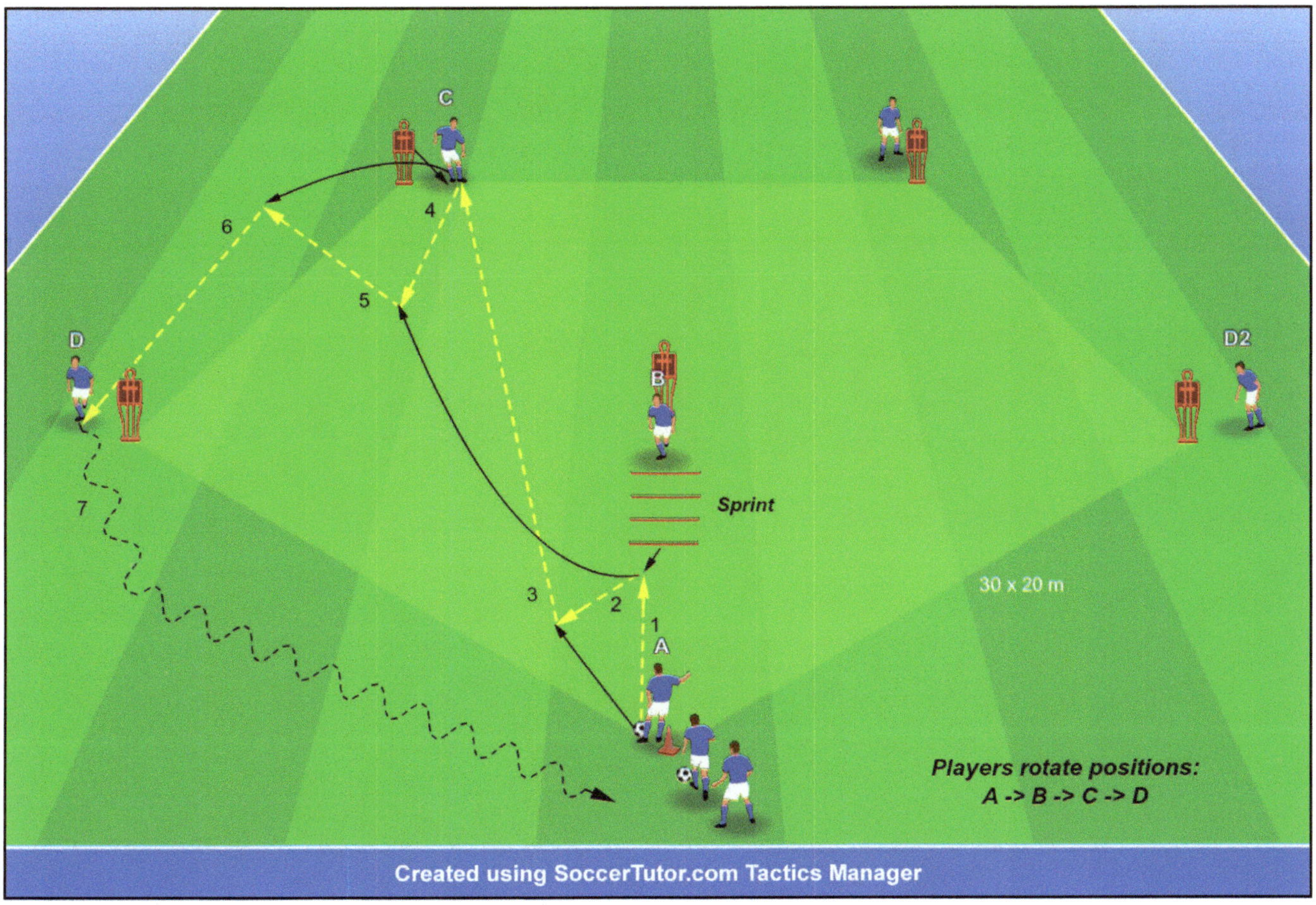

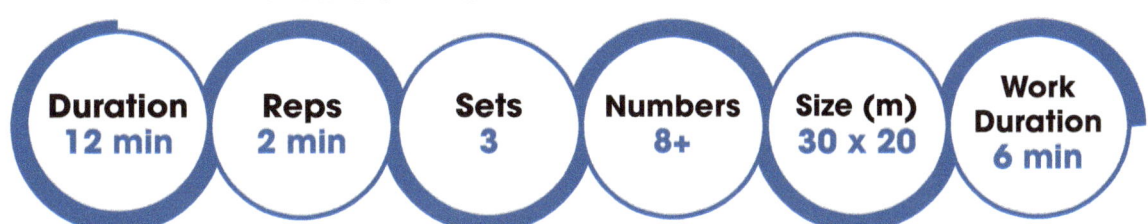

PRACTICE INFORMATION

Duration	Reps	Sets	Numbers	Size (m)	Work Duration
12 min	2 min	3	8+	30 x 20	6 min

PRACTICE OBJECTIVES: Ball speed (correct weight), timing of run, pass placement

Volume Metrics	Practice Total	Per Min. of Work
Total Distance (km)	0.631	0.105
High Speed Running (m)	-	-
Sprint Distance (m)	-	-
Work Ratio (%)	33.78	
Power Plays (HiActs)	0.13	0.02

Intensity Metrics	Practice Total	Per Min. of Work
Max Speed (m/s)	4.33	
Intensity (m/min)		73.35
Power Score (w/kg)	6.02	
No. of Max Accels >4m²	5.98	1
No. of Max Decels >4m²	1.31	0.22

* The data shows the physical output per player based on research from elite level teams - see **pages 81-83** for details

WEDNESDAY Practices: Speed Endurance - 3 Days Until Match (MD +4/-3)

Extensive Technical 2: Quick Feet and Lay-offs in a Technical Pass and Move Drill

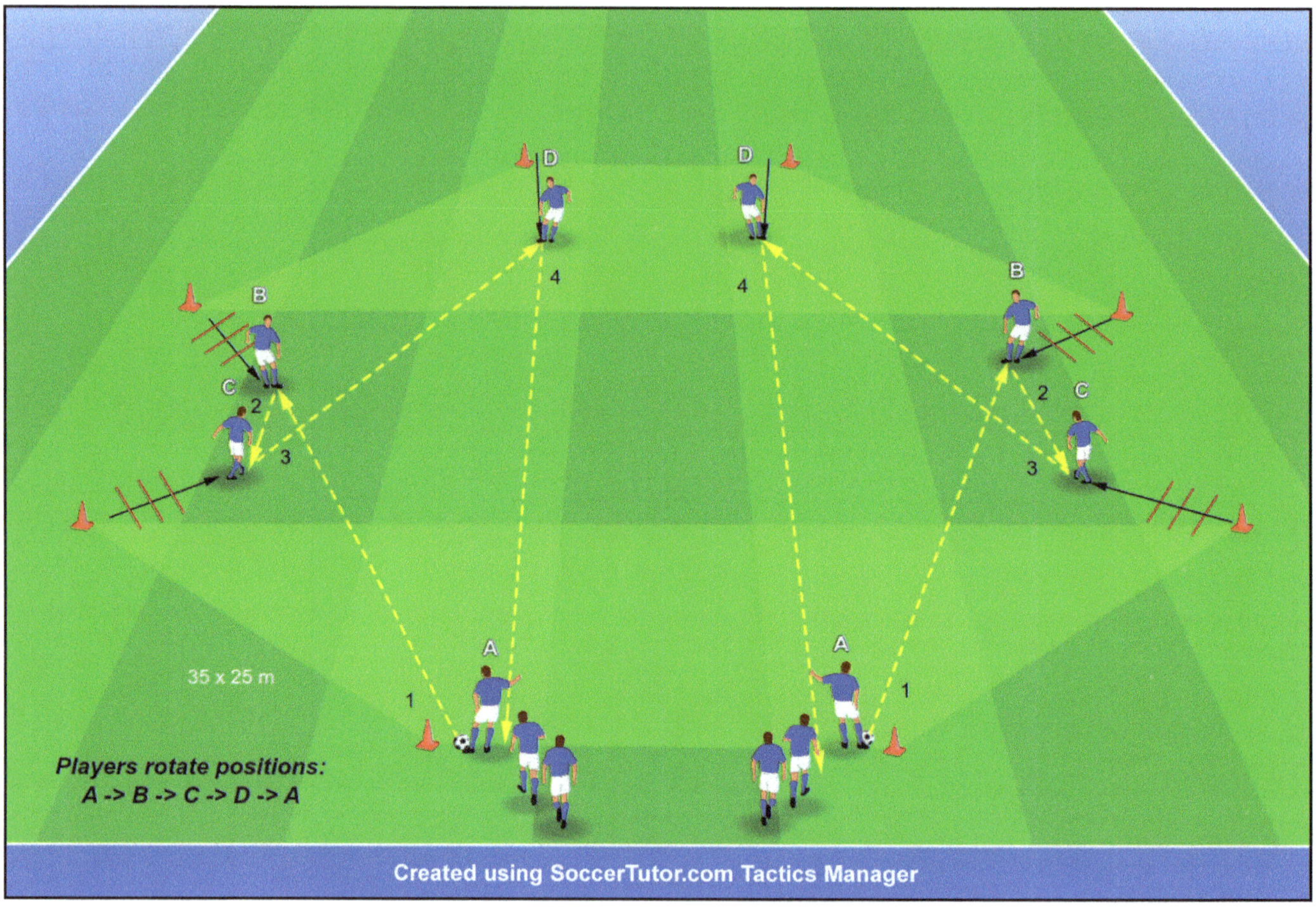

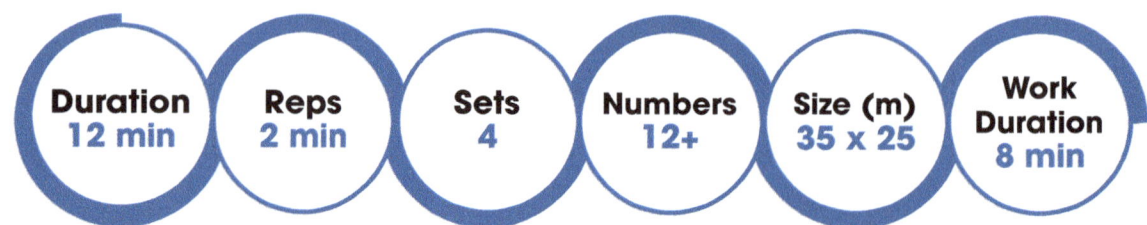

35 x 25 m

Players rotate positions:
A -> B -> C -> D -> A

Created using SoccerTutor.com Tactics Manager

PRACTICE INFORMATION

Duration	Reps	Sets	Numbers	Size (m)	Work Duration
12 min	2 min	4	12+	35 x 25	8 min

PRACTICE OBJECTIVES (2 BALLS): Ball speed (correct weight), timing of run, pass placement

Volume Metrics	Practice Total	Per Min. of Work
Total Distance (km)	0.869	0.11
High Speed Running (m)	5.42	0.68
Sprint Distance (m)	-	-
Work Ratio (%)	32.29	
Power Plays (HiActs)	4.71	0.59

Intensity Metrics	Practice Total	Per Min. of Work
Max Speed (m/s)	5.47	
Intensity (m/min)		75.94
Power Score (w/kg)	6.19	
No. of Max Accels >4m²	11.55	1.44
No. of Max Decels >4m²	3.08	0.39

* The data shows the physical output per player based on research from elite level teams - see **pages 81-83** for details

Football Periodization to Maximise Performance

WEDNESDAY Practices: Speed Endurance - 3 Days Until Match (MD +4/-3)

Extensive Technical 3: Pass Inside to Outside at Speed in a Practice with Middle Players

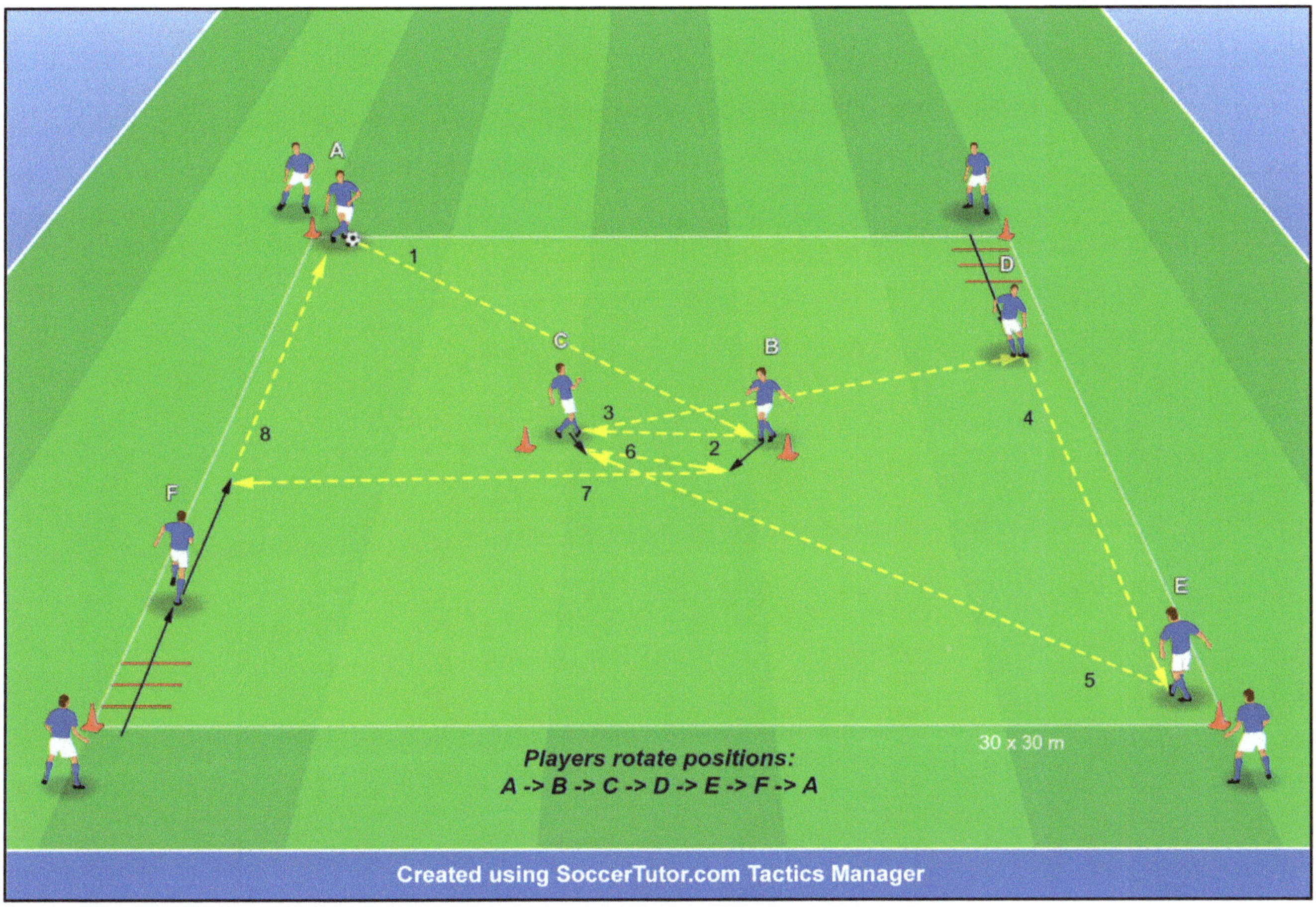

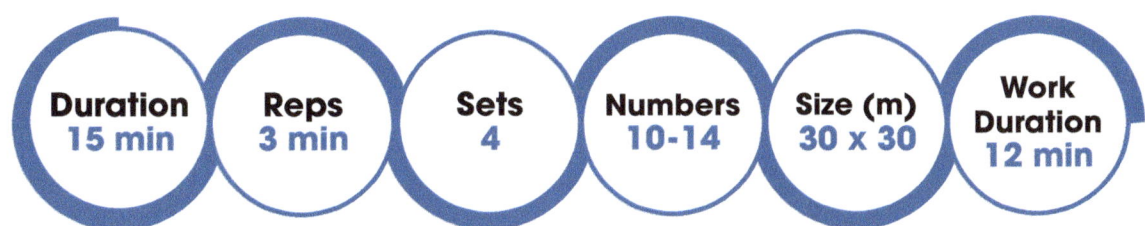

Players rotate positions:
A -> B -> C -> D -> E -> F -> A

30 x 30 m

PRACTICE INFORMATION

Duration	Reps	Sets	Numbers	Size (m)	Work Duration
15 min	3 min	4	10-14	30 x 30	12 min

PRACTICE OBJECTIVES: Ball speed (correct weight), timing of run, pass placement

Volume Metrics	Practice Total	Per Min. of Work
Total Distance (km)	1.144	0.095
High Speed Running (m)	0.98	0.08
Sprint Distance (m)	-	-
Work Ratio (%)	16.92	
Power Plays (HiActs)	20.34	1.7

Intensity Metrics	Practice Total	Per Min. of Work
Max Speed (m/s)	5.04	
Intensity (m/min)		74.61
Power Score (w/kg)	6.24	
No. of Max Accels >4m²	15.81	1.32
No. of Max Decels >4m²	4.14	0.35

* The data shows the physical output per player based on research from elite level teams - see pages 81-83 for details

WEDNESDAY Practices: Speed Endurance - 3 Days Until Match (MD +4/-3)

Extensive Technical 4: Fast Combination Play in a Pass & Move Drill with Final "Give & Go"

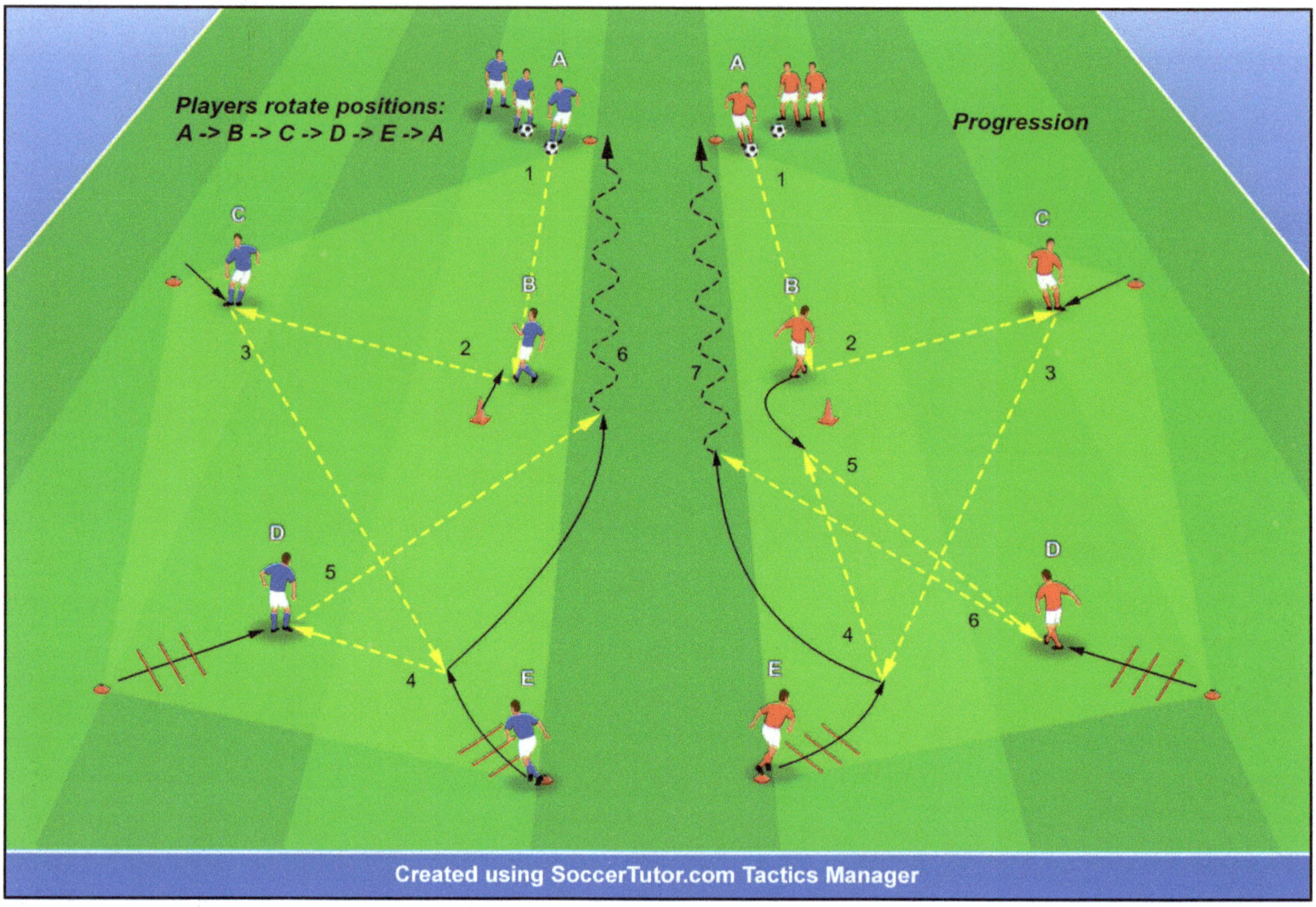

[Diagram: Players rotate positions: A -> B -> C -> D -> E -> A. Progression shown on right side.]

PRACTICE INFORMATION

Duration	Reps	Sets	Numbers	Size (m)	Work Duration
15 min	3 min	4	14-20	40 x 30	12 min

PRACTICE OBJECTIVES (2 BALLS): Ball speed (correct weight), timing of run, pass placement

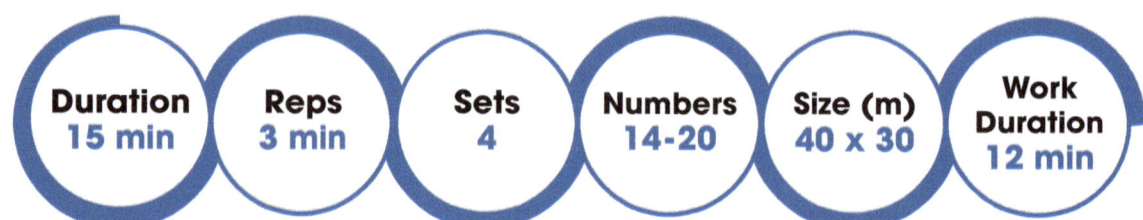

Volume Metrics	Practice Total	Per Min. of Work
Total Distance (km)	1.41	0.12
High Speed Running (m)	57.82	4.82
Sprint Distance (m)	4.08	0.34
Work Ratio (%)	43.55	
Power Plays (HiActs)	12.44	1.04

Intensity Metrics	Practice Total	Per Min. of Work
Max Speed (m/s)	6.66	
Intensity (m/min)		94.39
Power Score (w/kg)	7.98	
No. of Max Accels >4m²	20.96	1.75
No. of Max Decels >4m²	6.84	0.57

* The data shows the physical output per player based on research from elite level teams - see **pages 81-83** for details

WEDNESDAY Practices: Speed Endurance - 3 Days Until Match (MD +4/-3)

Extensive Technical 5: Quick Feet and Timing of Movement to Receive in a Passing Circuit

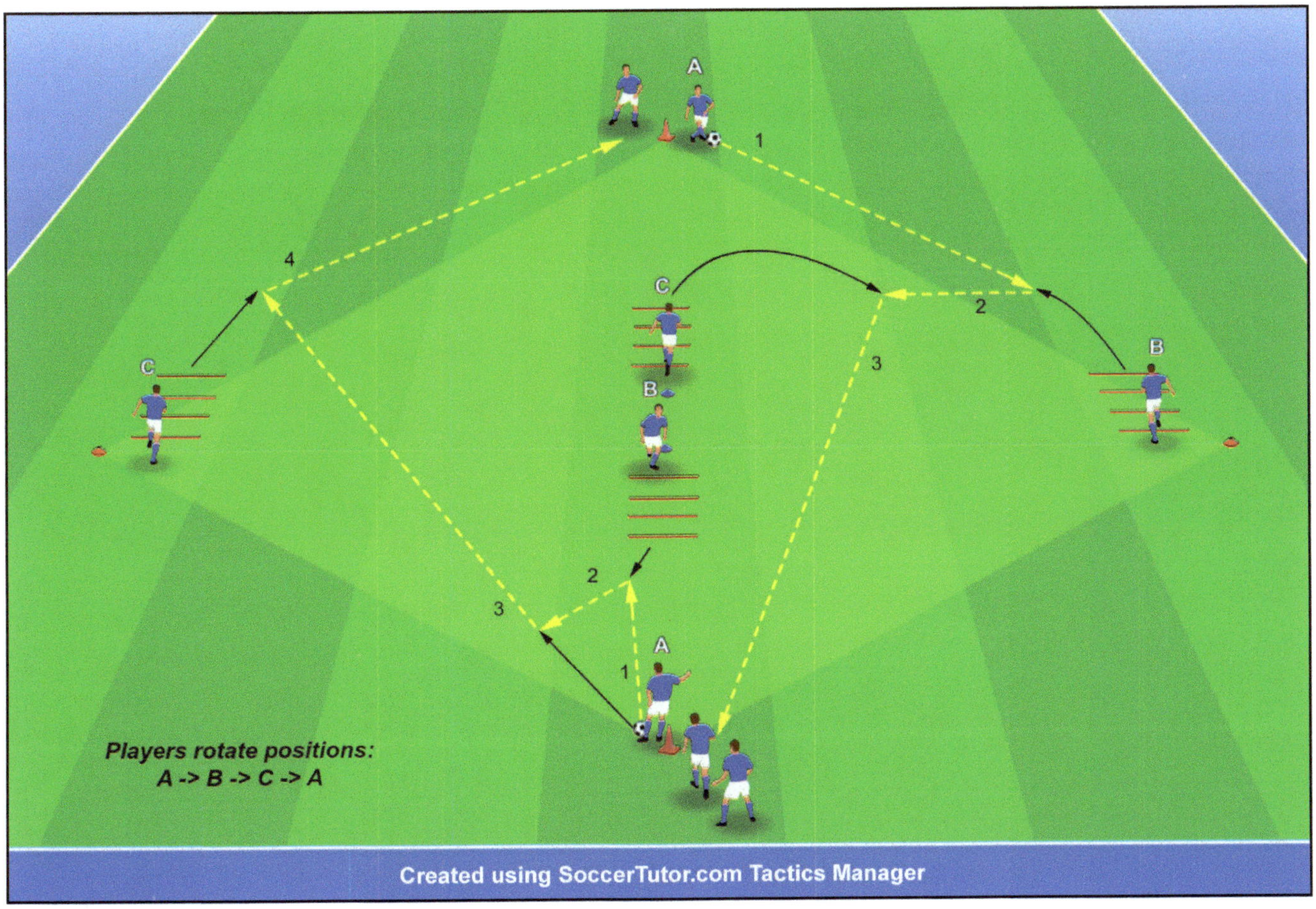

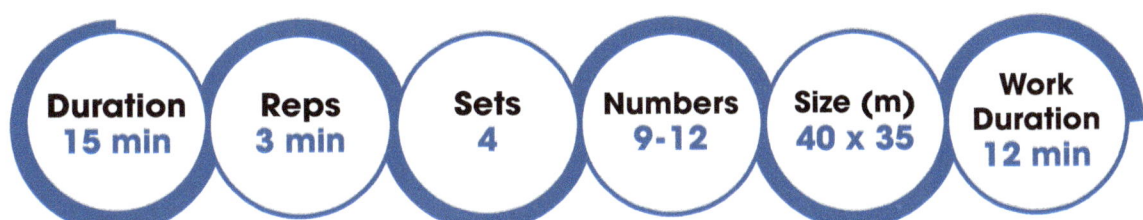

Players rotate positions: A -> B -> C -> A

Created using SoccerTutor.com Tactics Manager

PRACTICE INFORMATION

Duration	Reps	Sets	Numbers	Size (m)	Work Duration
15 min	3 min	4	9-12	40 x 35	12 min

PRACTICE OBJECTIVES (2 BALLS): Ball speed (correct weight), timing of run, pass placement

Volume Metrics	Practice Total	Per Min. of Work
Total Distance (km)	1.256	0.1
High Speed Running (m)	2.42	0.2
Sprint Distance (m)	-	-
Work Ratio (%)	45.99	
Power Plays (HiActs)	2.12	0.18

Intensity Metrics	Practice Total	Per Min. of Work
Max Speed (m/s)	5.21	
Intensity (m/min)		92.44
Power Score (w/kg)	7.46	
No. of Max Accels >4m²	7.6	0.63
No. of Max Decels >4m²	3	0.25

* The data shows the physical output per player based on research from elite level teams - see **pages 81-83** for details

WEDNESDAY Practices: Speed Endurance - 3 Days Until Match (MD +4/-3)

Extensive Technical 6: Switching Play Through Centre in a Square Drill with Middle Players

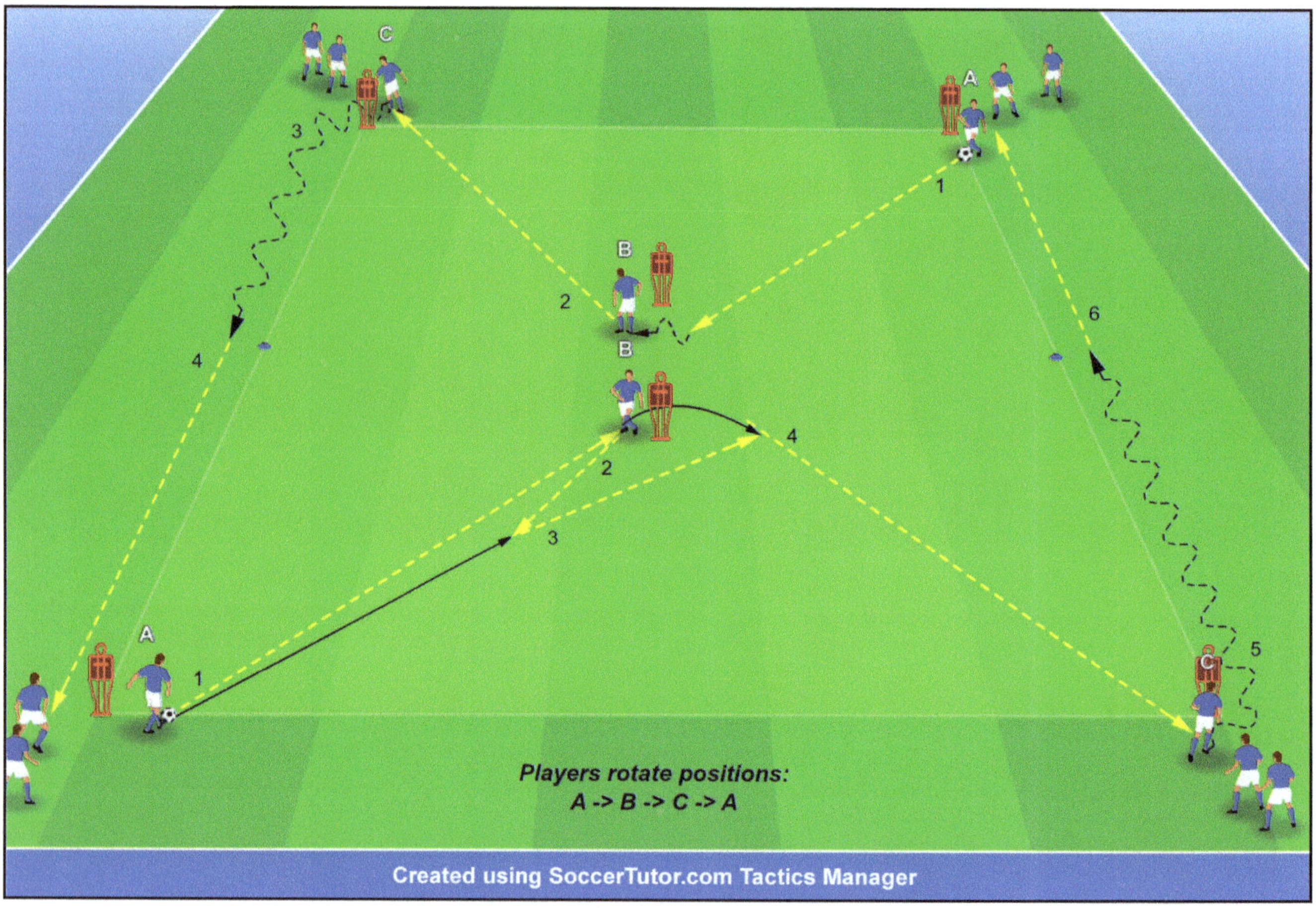

Players rotate positions:
A -> B -> C -> A

PRACTICE INFORMATION

Duration	Reps	Sets	Numbers	Size (m)	Work Duration
15 min	2.5 min	4	10-14	50 x 70	10 min

PRACTICE OBJECTIVE: Progression to play one-two combinations (working left and right)

Volume Metrics	Practice Total	Per Min. of Work
Total Distance (km)	0.764	0.076
High Speed Running (m)	5	0.5
Sprint Distance (m)	-	-
Work Ratio (%)	48.76	
Power Plays (HiActs)	3.32	0.33

Intensity Metrics	Practice Total	Per Min. of Work
Max Speed (m/s)	4.44	
Intensity (m/min)		91
Power Score (w/kg)	4.44	
No. of Max Accels >4m²	1	0.1
No. of Max Decels >4m²	-	-

* The data shows the physical output per player based on research from elite level teams - see **pages 81-83** for details

Football Periodization to Maximise Performance

WEDNESDAY Practices: Speed Endurance - 3 Days Until Match (MD +4/-3)

Extensive Technical 7: Progressive Passing with Lay-offs in a Positional Passing Practice

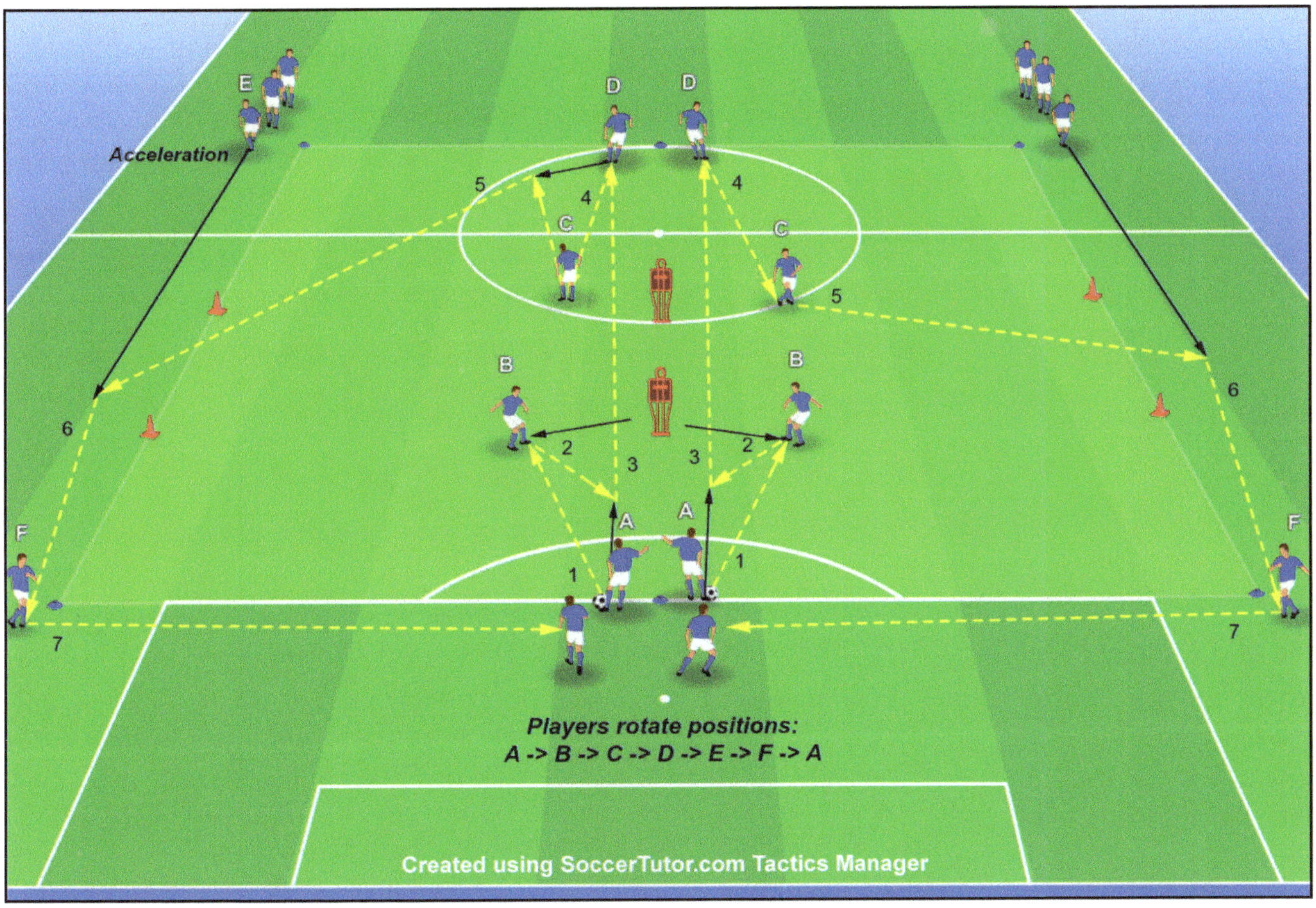

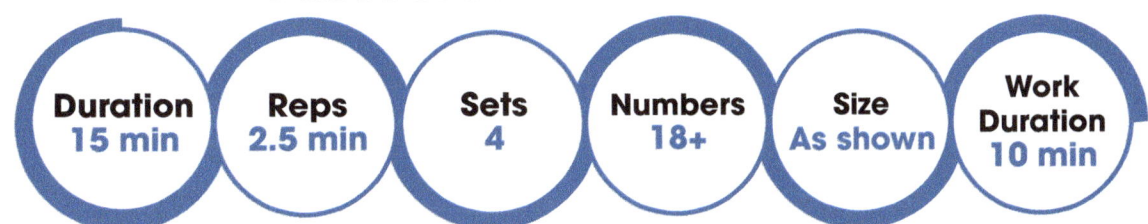

Players rotate positions:
A -> B -> C -> D -> E -> F -> A

PRACTICE INFORMATION

Duration	Reps	Sets	Numbers	Size	Work Duration
15 min	2.5 min	4	18+	As shown	10 min

PRACTICE OBJECTIVE: Technical extensive passing pattern with a tactical focus

Volume Metrics	Practice Total	Per Min. of Work
Total Distance (km)	0.825	0.08
High Speed Running (m)	61.07	6.1
Sprint Distance (m)	9	0.9
Work Ratio (%)	65.44	
Power Plays (HiActs)	5.31	0.53

Intensity Metrics	Practice Total	Per Min. of Work
Max Speed (m/s)	3.61	
Intensity (m/min)		53.17
Power Score (w/kg)	4.49	
No. of Max Accels >4m²	6.31	0.63
No. of Max Decels >4m²	0.79	0.08

* The data shows the physical output per player based on research from elite level teams - see pages 81-83 for details

Football Periodization to Maximise Performance

WEDNESDAY Practices: Speed Endurance - 3 Days Until Match (MD +4/-3)

Extensive Technical 8: Speed Exercises and Patterns of Play in a Tactical Rotational Drill

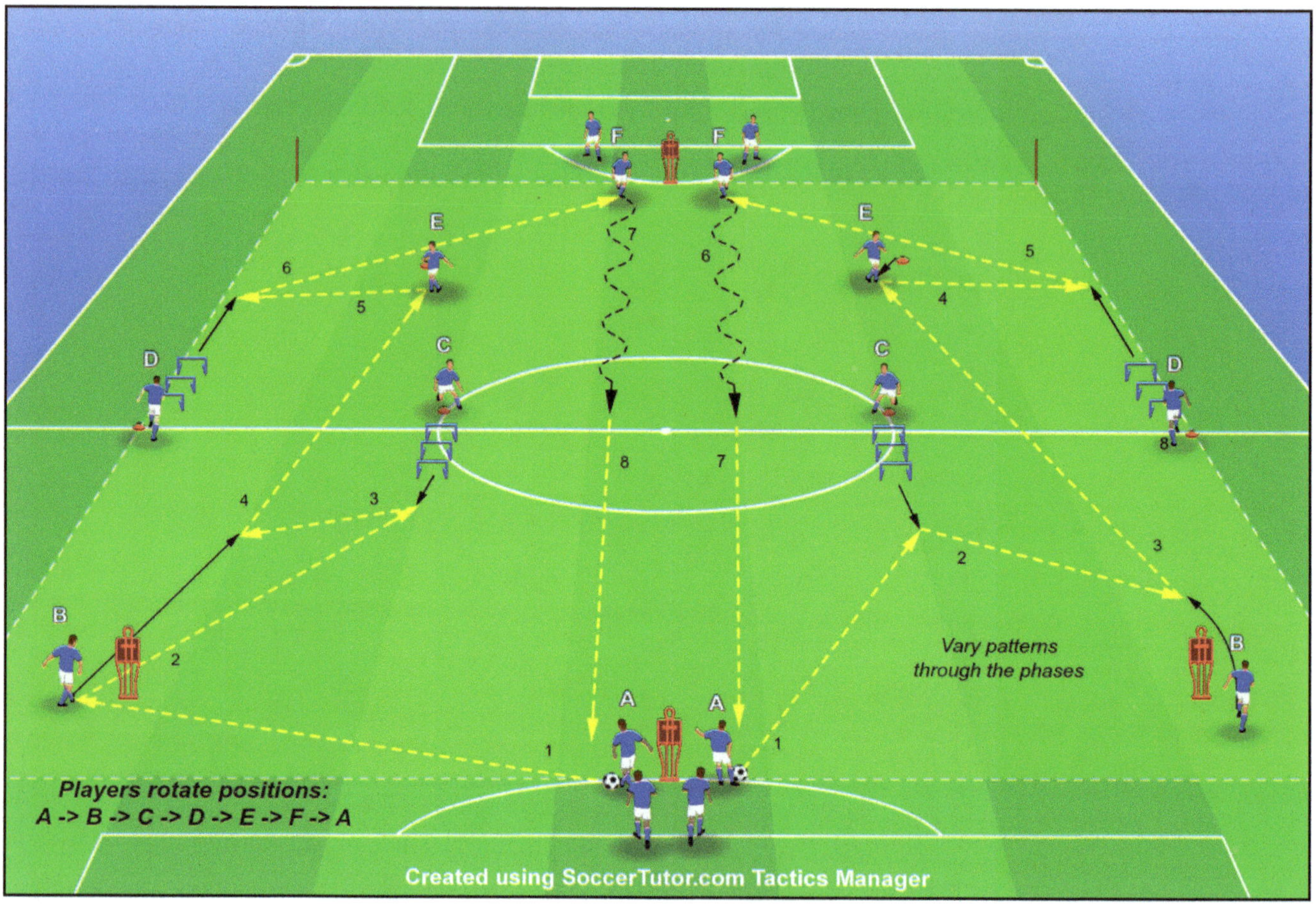

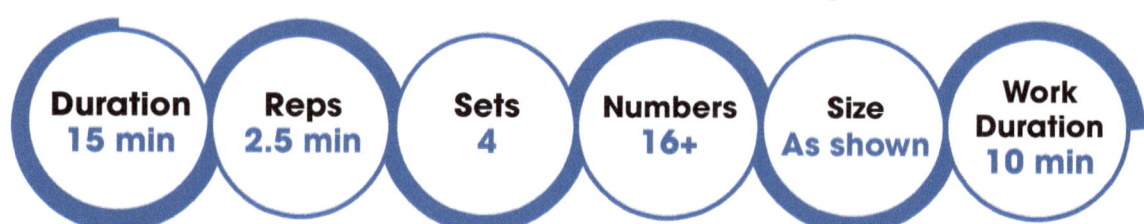

Players rotate positions:
A -> B -> C -> D -> E -> F -> A

Vary patterns through the phases

PRACTICE INFORMATION

Duration	Reps	Sets	Numbers	Size	Work Duration
15 min	2.5 min	4	16+	As shown	10 min

PRACTICE OBJECTIVE: Technical extensive passing pattern drill with a tactical focus

Volume Metrics	Practice Total	Per Min. of Work
Total Distance (km)	1.04	0.1
High Speed Running (m)	23.37	2.34
Sprint Distance (m)	-	-
Work Ratio (%)	89.15	
Power Plays (HiActs)	8.11	0.81

Intensity Metrics	Practice Total	Per Min. of Work
Max Speed (m/s)	6.01	
Intensity (m/min)		74.35
Power Score (w/kg)	6.08	
No. of Max Accels >4m²	5.6	0.56
No. of Max Decels >4m²	1.1	0.11

* The data shows the physical output per player based on research from elite level teams - see **pages 81-83** for details

WEDNESDAY Practices: Speed Endurance - 3 Days Until Match (MD +4/-3)

WEDNESDAY - 3 DAYS UNTIL MATCH (MD +4/-3):
Speed Endurance Conditioning Practices

INTENSITY: All practices are performed at full intensity

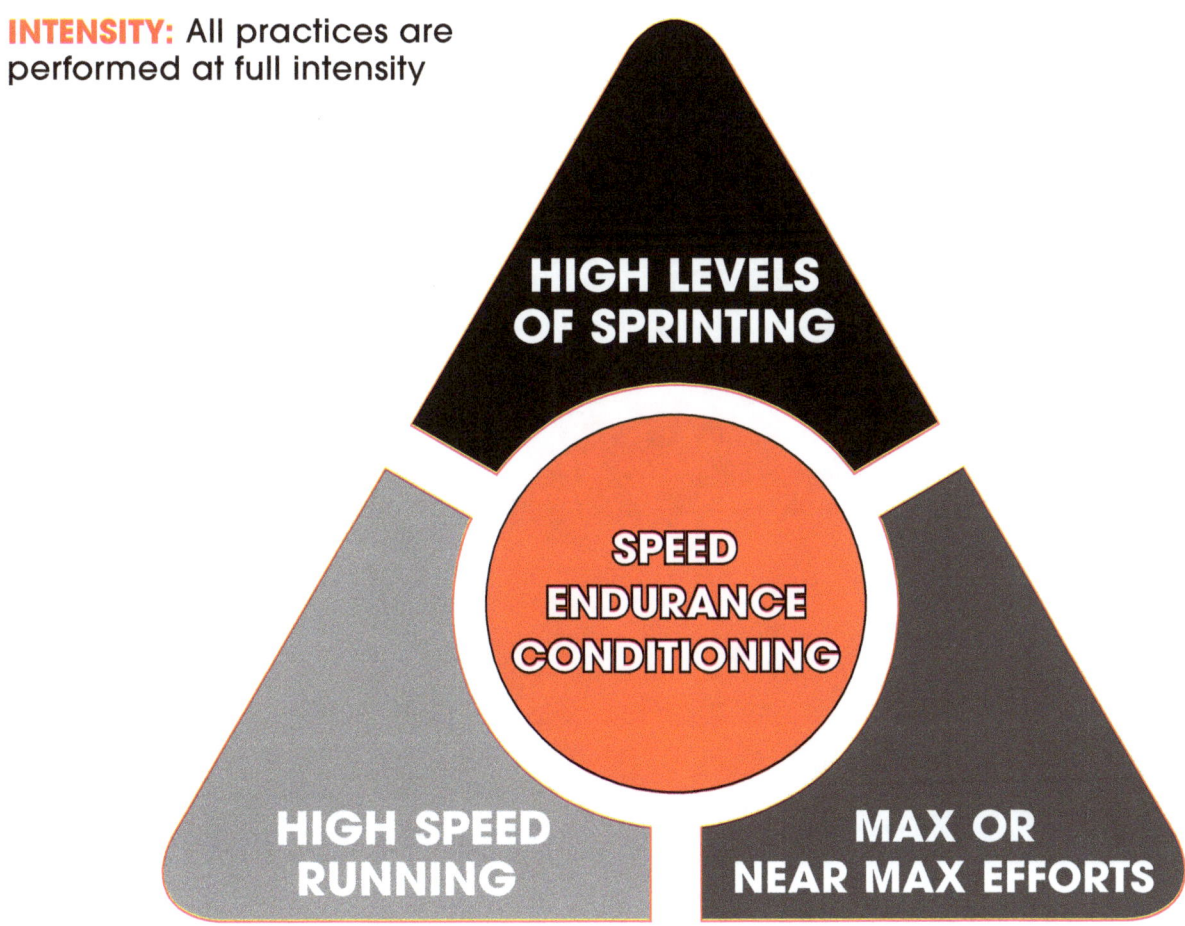

What are Speed Endurance Conditioning Practices?

- These physical conditioning exercises are classed as 'speed endurance' as they expose players to high levels of sprinting and high-speed running metrics.
- They include larger surface areas with maximum or near maximum efforts to run or sprint.

Why are they used on this day of the training week (MD +4/-3)?

- To overload the key muscle groups required on a day that is far enough away from the match day to recover but still elicit a stimulus in order to progress the players' capability to improve their conditioning.

How does this help to maximise performance?

- These high speed and sprint based practices are used on this day as a way of preparing and developing the players' muscles and capacity to perform this type of work in matches.

FOOTBALL SPECIFIC CONDITIONING

SPEED ENDURANCE: Based on 2 x 4 minute repetitions

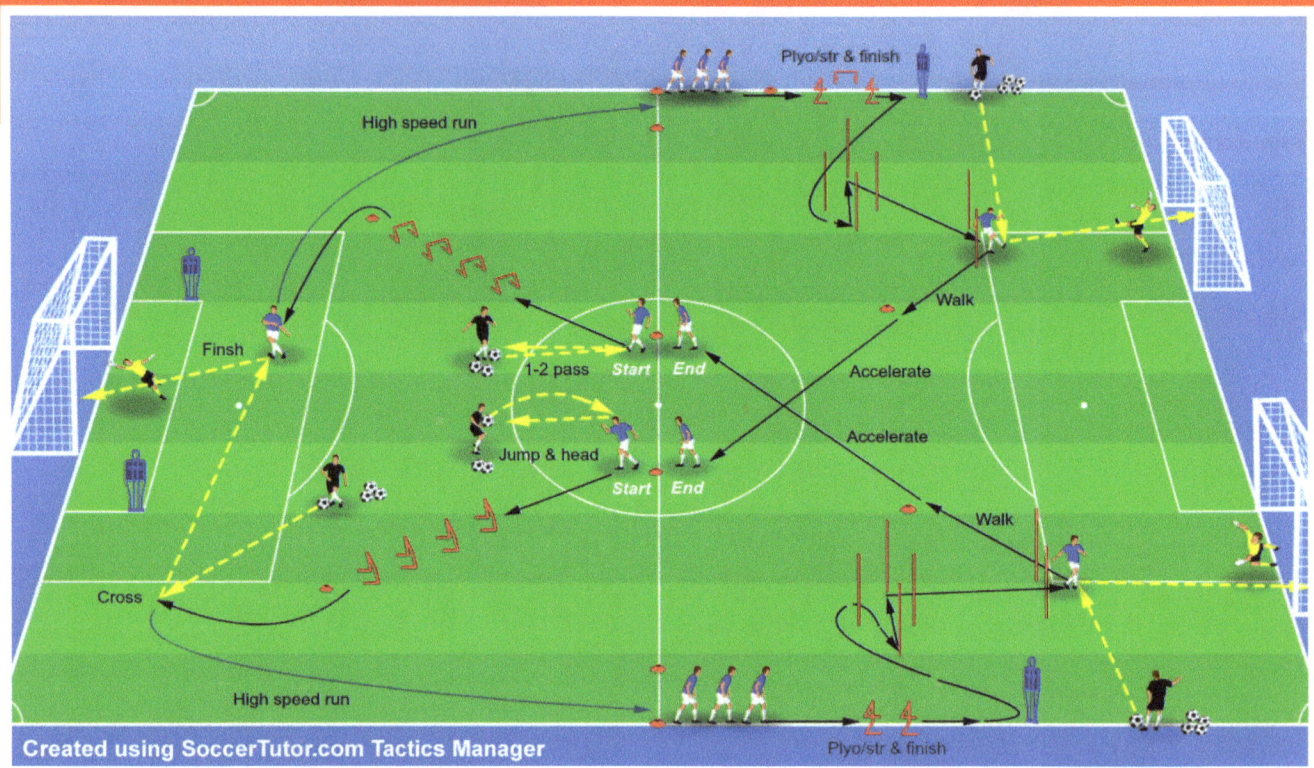

Benefits of this Speed Endurance Practice?

- Stimulation of football specific muscles
- High speed demands
- Injury prevention aspect

- ↑ Technical involvement - quality under physical stress
- ↑ Recovery between High Speed Efforts (improved recovery)
- ↑ Motivation of players due to technical focus
- ↑ Speed of play

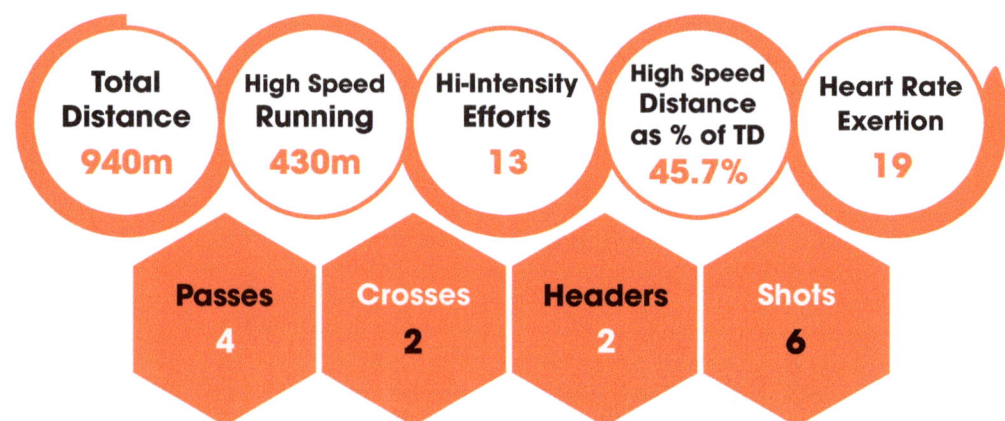

@adamowen1980

@SoccerTutor.com | 150 | Football Periodization to Maximise Performance

REFERENCE Rogan, S. (2015) Asian J Sports Med. Jun; 6(2). | Owen, AL. et al (2015). J Strength Cond Res. Jun; 29(6): 1705-12.

TECHNICAL / TACTICAL CONDITIONING

SPEED ENDURANCE: Based on 1 Set of 4 x reps (45s recovery)

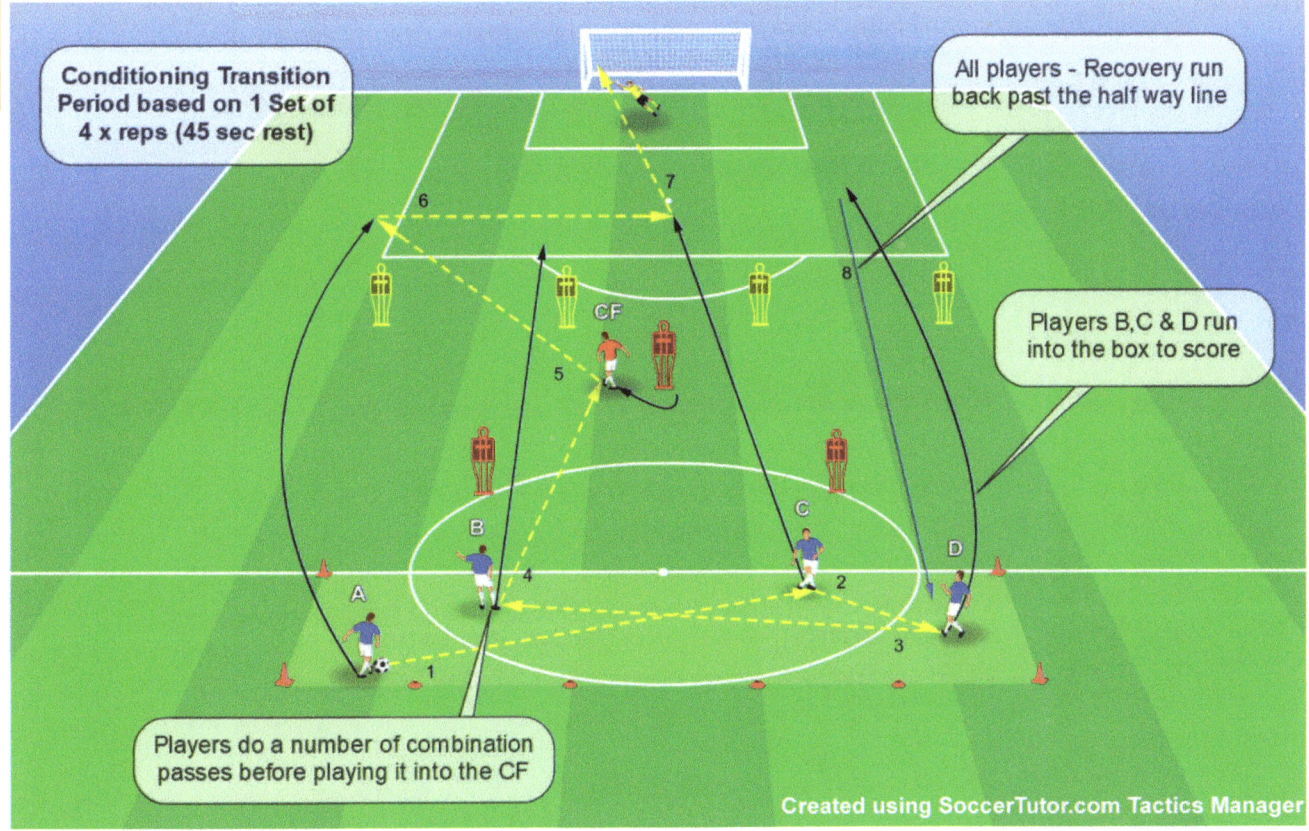

Conditioning Transition Period based on 1 Set of 4 x reps (45 sec rest)

All players - Recovery run back past the half way line

Players B, C & D run into the box to score

Players do a number of combination passes before playing it into the CF

Benefits of this Speed Endurance Practice?

- Balance between work and recovery
- High specific muscle overload
- Increase number of sets and reps as players become conditioned
- Allows players to improve playing intensity and recovery within game situations
- Improve players capacity to work and recover within the practice
- Technical and tactical focus
- Technical focus and quality is maintained throughout
- Improved motivation of players due to inclusion of technical element
- Ensure quality of movement and speed throughout!
- Direct link between the outcome of the practice/session and performance in a match

Total Distance	Hi-Intensity Efforts	Hi-Speed Running	Heart Rate Exertion	Time Above 85%
490m	14	279m	10	2.3 min

@adamowen1980

WEDNESDAY Practices: Speed Endurance - 3 Days Until Match (MD +4/-3)

THE EFFECT OF TWO SPEED ENDURANCE TRAINING REGIMES ON THE PERFORMANCE OF FOOTBALL PLAYERS

Designed by @YLMSportScience

During the last 3 weeks of the competitive season, 13 young male professional football players reduced their training volume by -20% and replaced their regular conditioning work with the following:

Speed Endurance Production	OR	Speed Endurance Maintenance
6-8 x 20 second all-out running bouts followed by 2 minutes of passive recovery		6-8 x 20 second all-out efforts interspersed with 40 seconds of passive recovery
3 times per week		3 times per week

Speed Endurance Production	Test	Speed Endurance Maintenance
-2.5%	Total Time in a Repeated Sprint Ability Test	+1.0%
+9.3%	Percentage Change on Score of the Repeated Sprint Ability Test	-2.7%
-1.2%	200m Sprint Time	-2.1%
+10.1%	Yo-Yo Intermittent Recovery Test Level 2	+3.8%
No changes	20m and 40m Sprint Performance	No changes

Improved repeated sprint and high-intensity intermittent exercise performance

Increased muscle ability to maximise fatigue tolerance and maintain speed development during repeated all-out and continuous short-duration maximal exercises

Reference: by Iaia, Fiorenzo, Perri, Alberti, GP Millet & Bangsbo, PloS ONE, 2015

Images provided by PresenterMedia

@SoccerTutor.com — Football Periodization to Maximise Performance

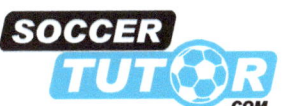

Speed Endurance Conditioning 1: Explosive Sprinting, Jogging and High Speed Running

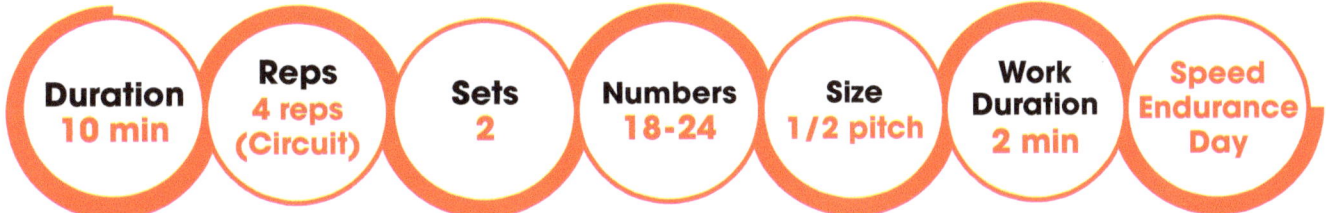

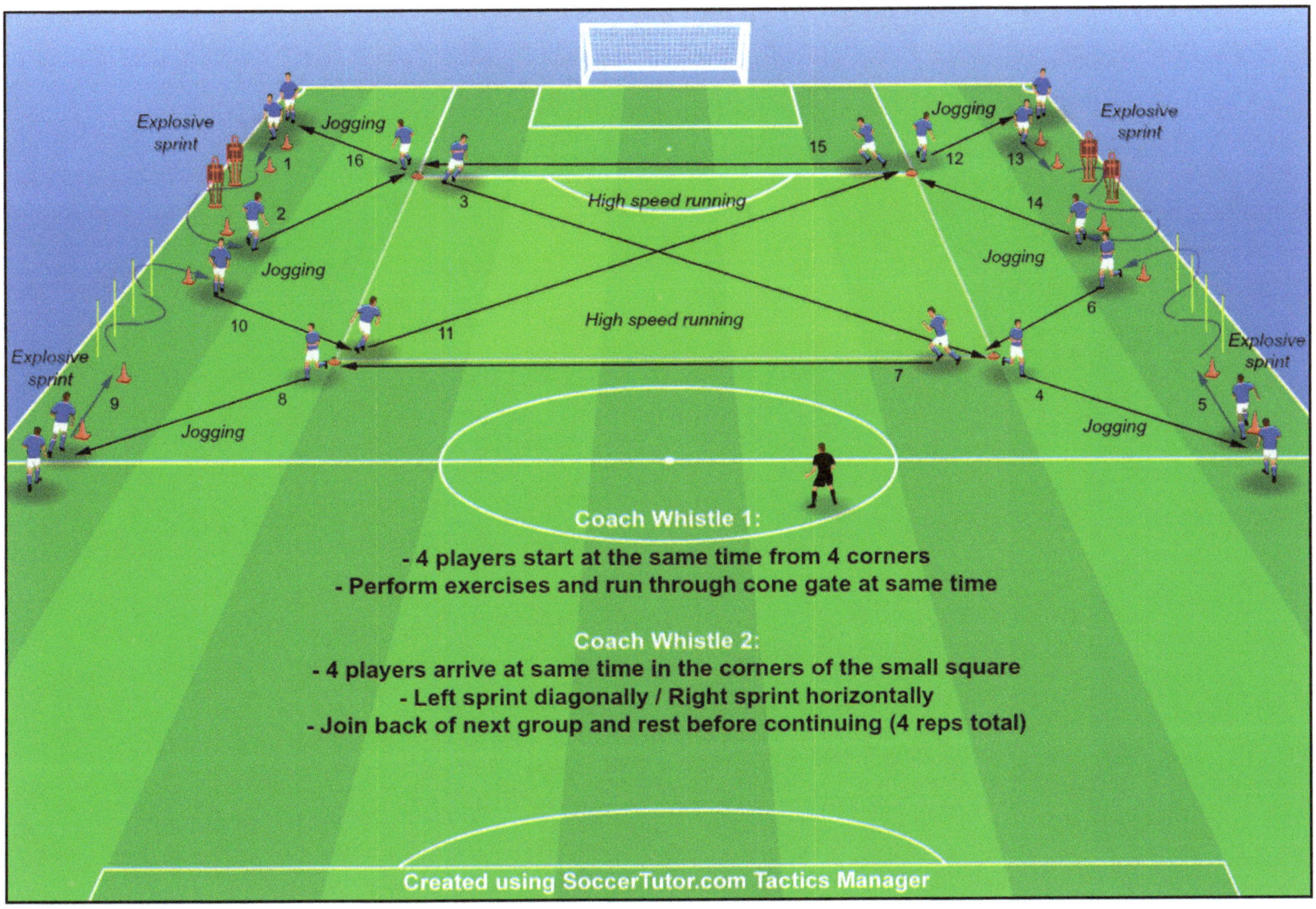
Explosive sprint
Jogging
Jogging
High speed running
High speed running
Explosive sprint
Jogging
Explosive sprint
Jogging
Jogging
Explosive sprint
Jogging
1
2
3
4
5
6
7
8
9
10
11
12
13
14
15
16
Coach Whistle 1:
- 4 players start at the same time from 4 corners
- Perform exercises and run through cone gate at same time
Coach Whistle 2:
- 4 players arrive at same time in the corners of the small square
- Left sprint diagonally / Right sprint horizontally
- Join back of next group and rest before continuing (4 reps total)
Created using SoccerTutor.com Tactics Manager

PRACTICE INFORMATION

Duration	Reps	Sets	Numbers	Size	Work Duration	Speed Endurance Day
10 min	4 reps (Circuit)	2	18-24	1/2 pitch	2 min	

OBJECTIVES: Physical stimulation - high-speed and sprints to develop the capacity to run fast

Volume Metrics	Practice Total	Per Min. of Work
Total Distance (km)	0.734	0.37
High Speed Running (m)	245.62	122.81
Sprint Distance (m)	38.48	19.24
Work Ratio (%)	21.6	
Power Plays (HiActs)	7.4	0.93

Intensity Metrics	Practice Total	Per Min. of Work
Max Speed (m/s)	7.95	
Intensity (m/min)		73.77
Power Score (w/kg)	6.13	
Max Accel. Distance (m)	7	3.5
Max Decel. Distance (m)	4.61	2.3

* The data shows the physical output per player based on research from elite level teams - see pages 81-83 for details

WEDNESDAY Practices: Speed Endurance - 3 Days Until Match (MD +4/-3)

Speed Endurance Conditioning 2: Slalom Run or Dribble and Pass + 45m Sprints

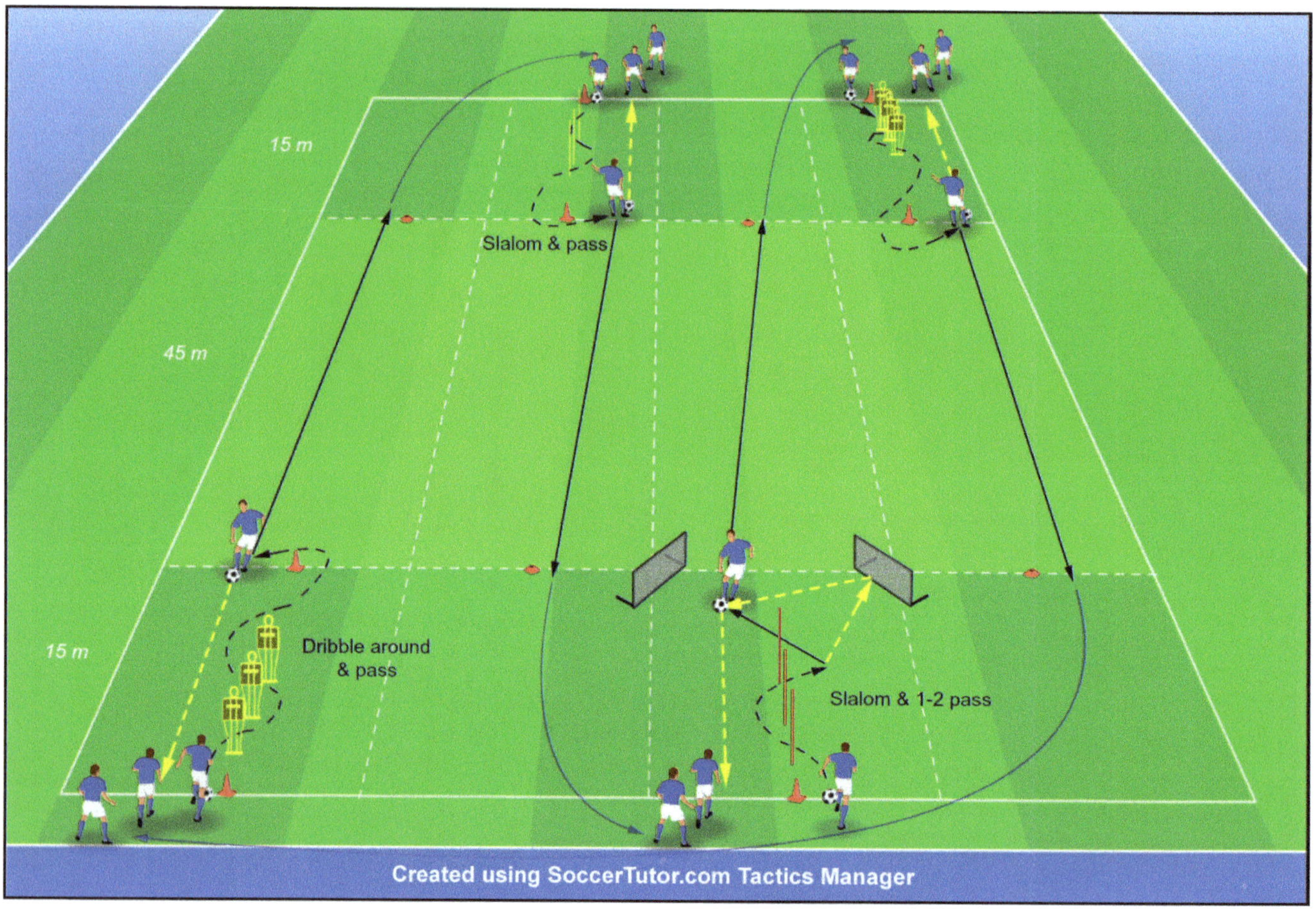

[Diagram: 30 x 75 field showing four channels with Slalom & pass, Dribble around & pass, Slalom & 1-2 pass practices; 45m sprint lanes; 15m widths marked]

PRACTICE INFORMATION

Duration	Reps	Sets	Numbers	Size (m)	Work Duration	
10 min	All 4 Channels	3	16+	30 x 75	2 min	Explosive Actions Throughout

OBJECTIVES: Physical stimulation - high-speed and sprints to develop the capacity to run fast

Volume Metrics	Practice Total	Per Min. of Work
Total Distance (km)	0.68	0.34
High Speed Running (m)	288	144
Sprint Distance (m)	40	20
Work Ratio (%)	23.55	
Power Plays (HiActs)	8	4

Intensity Metrics	Practice Total	Per Min. of Work
Max Speed (m/s)	7.6	
Intensity (m/min)		93
Power Score (w/kg)	5.55	
No. of Max Accels >4m²	2	1
No. of Max Decels >4m²	-	-

* The data shows the physical output per player based on research from elite level teams - see **pages 81-83** for details

Football Periodization to Maximise Performance

WEDNESDAY Practices: Speed Endurance - 3 Days Until Match (MD +4/-3)

Speed Endurance Conditioning 3: Dribble and Pass, High Speed Run, and Recover

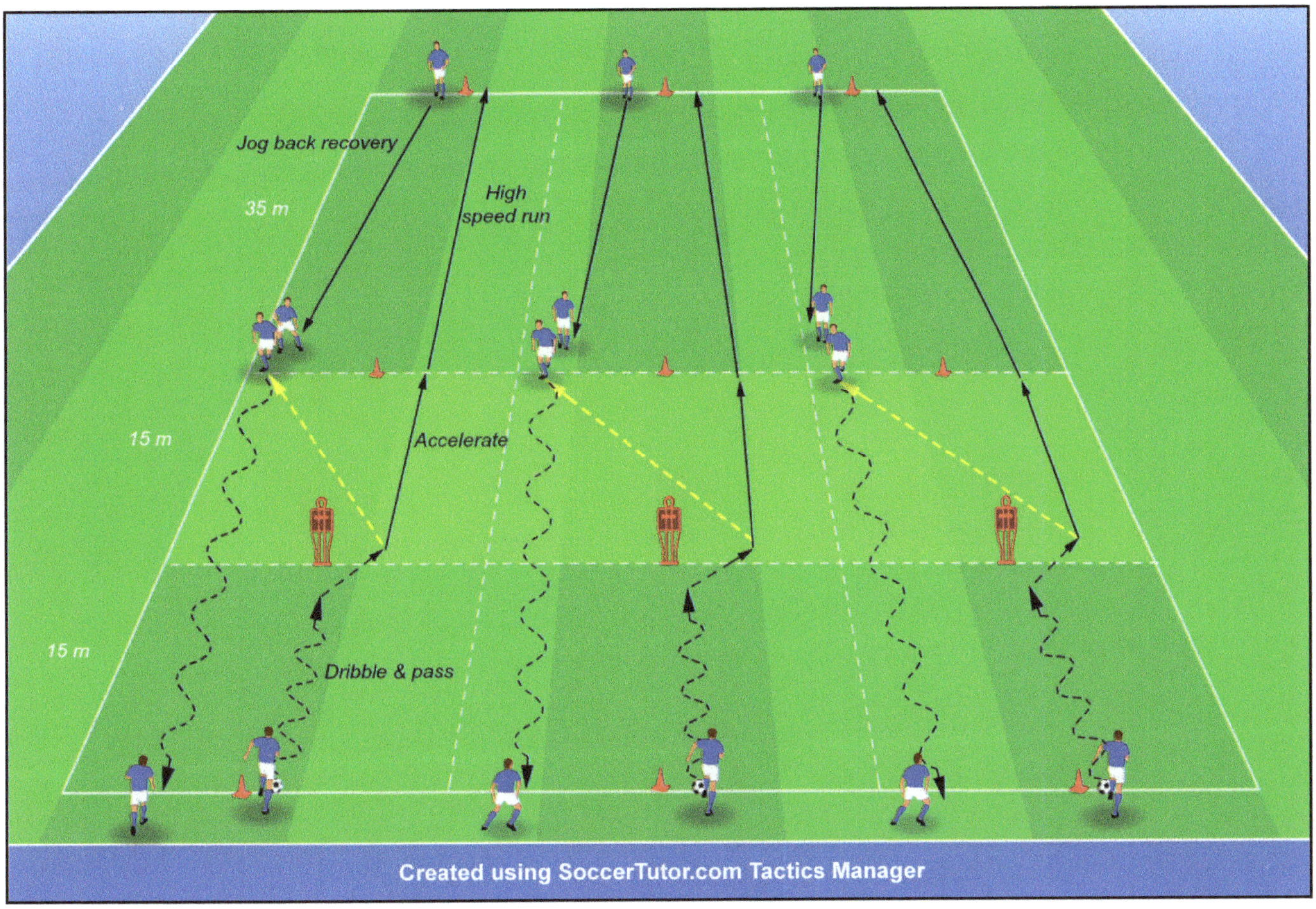

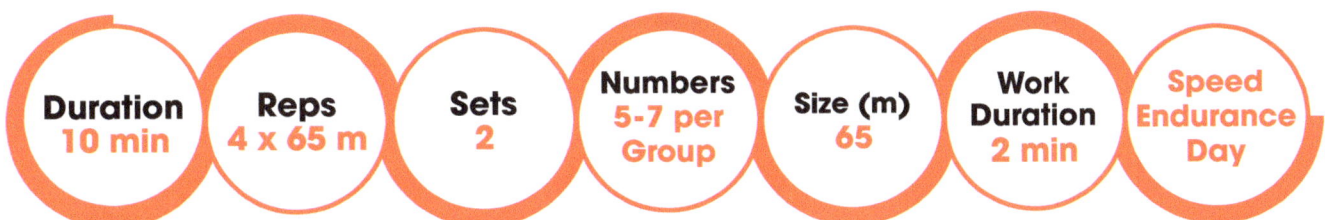

PRACTICE INFORMATION

Duration	Reps	Sets	Numbers	Size (m)	Work Duration	
10 min	4 x 65 m	2	5-7 per Group	65	2 min	Speed Endurance Day

OBJECTIVES: Physical stimulation - high-speed and sprints to develop the capacity to run fast

Volume Metrics	Practice Total	Per Min. of Work
Total Distance (km)	1.15	0.58
High Speed Running (m)	339	169.5
Sprint Distance (m)	201	100.5
Work Ratio (%)	36.54	
Power Plays (HiActs)	8.4	4.2

Intensity Metrics	Practice Total	Per Min. of Work
Max Speed (m/s)	8.43	
Intensity (m/min)		97.21
Power Score (w/kg)	7.81	
No. of Max Accels >4m²	3.43	1.72
No. of Max Decels >4m²	0.42	0.21

* The data shows the physical output per player based on research from elite level teams - see **pages 81-83** for details

155

@SoccerTutor.com Football Periodization to Maximise Performance

REFERENCE @adamowen1980

WEDNESDAY Practices: Speed Endurance - 3 Days Until Match (MD +4/-3)

Speed Endurance Conditioning 4: Crossing and Finishing + Dribble and Shoot

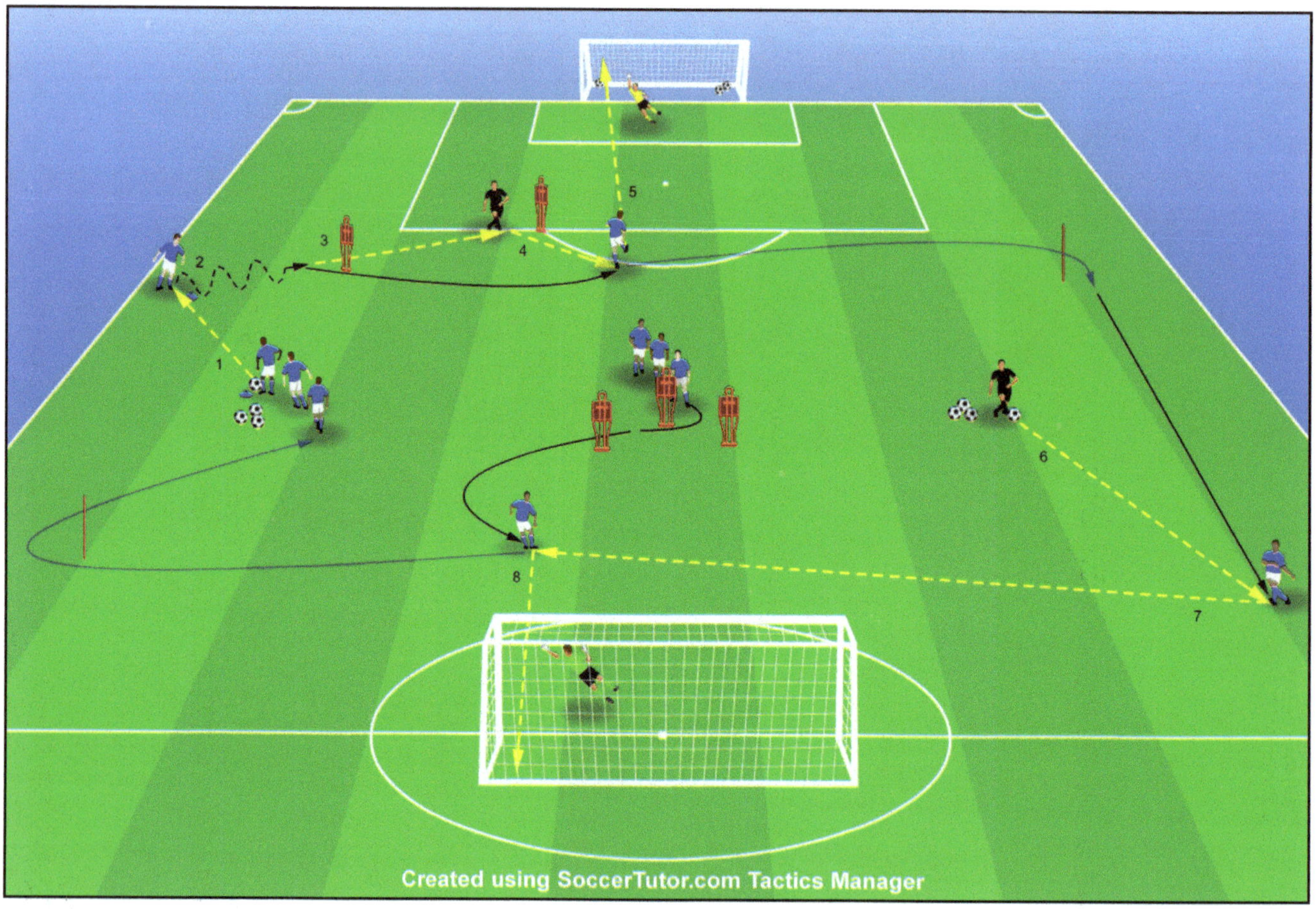

[Diagram: half-pitch practice setup with players, cones and ball movement arrows]

PRACTICE INFORMATION

Duration	Reps	Sets	Numbers	Size	Work Duration	
15 min	4	2	10+ (+GKs)	1/2 pitch	2 min	Speed Endurance Day

OBJECTIVES: Physical stimulation - high-speed and sprints to develop the capacity to run fast

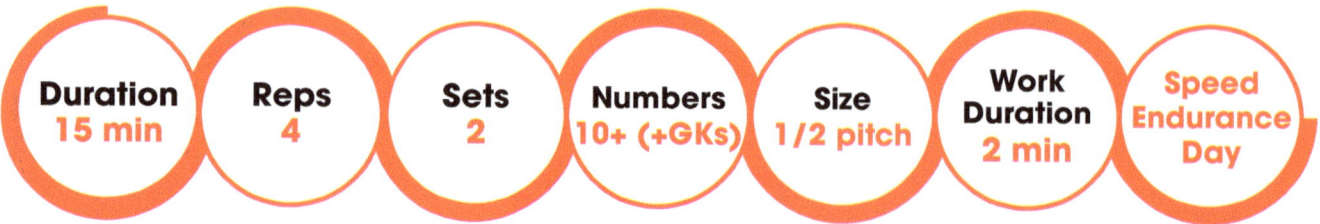

Volume Metrics	Practice Total	Per Min. of Work
Total Distance (km)	1.4	0.7
High Speed Running (m)	301	150.5
Sprint Distance (m)	90.65	45.33
Work Ratio (%)	21.79	
Power Plays (HiActs)	21.9	10.95

Intensity Metrics	Practice Total	Per Min. of Work
Max Speed (m/s)	7.73	
Intensity (m/min)		85.49
Power Score (w/kg)	7.2	
Max Accel. Distance (m)	15.33	7.67
Max Decel. Distance (m)	9.21	4.6

* The data shows the physical output per player based on research from elite level teams - **see pages 81-83** for details

WEDNESDAY Practices: Speed Endurance - 3 Days Until Match (MD +4/-3)

Speed Endurance Conditioning 5: Agility, Running with Ball, Finish, Jog, and Final Sprint

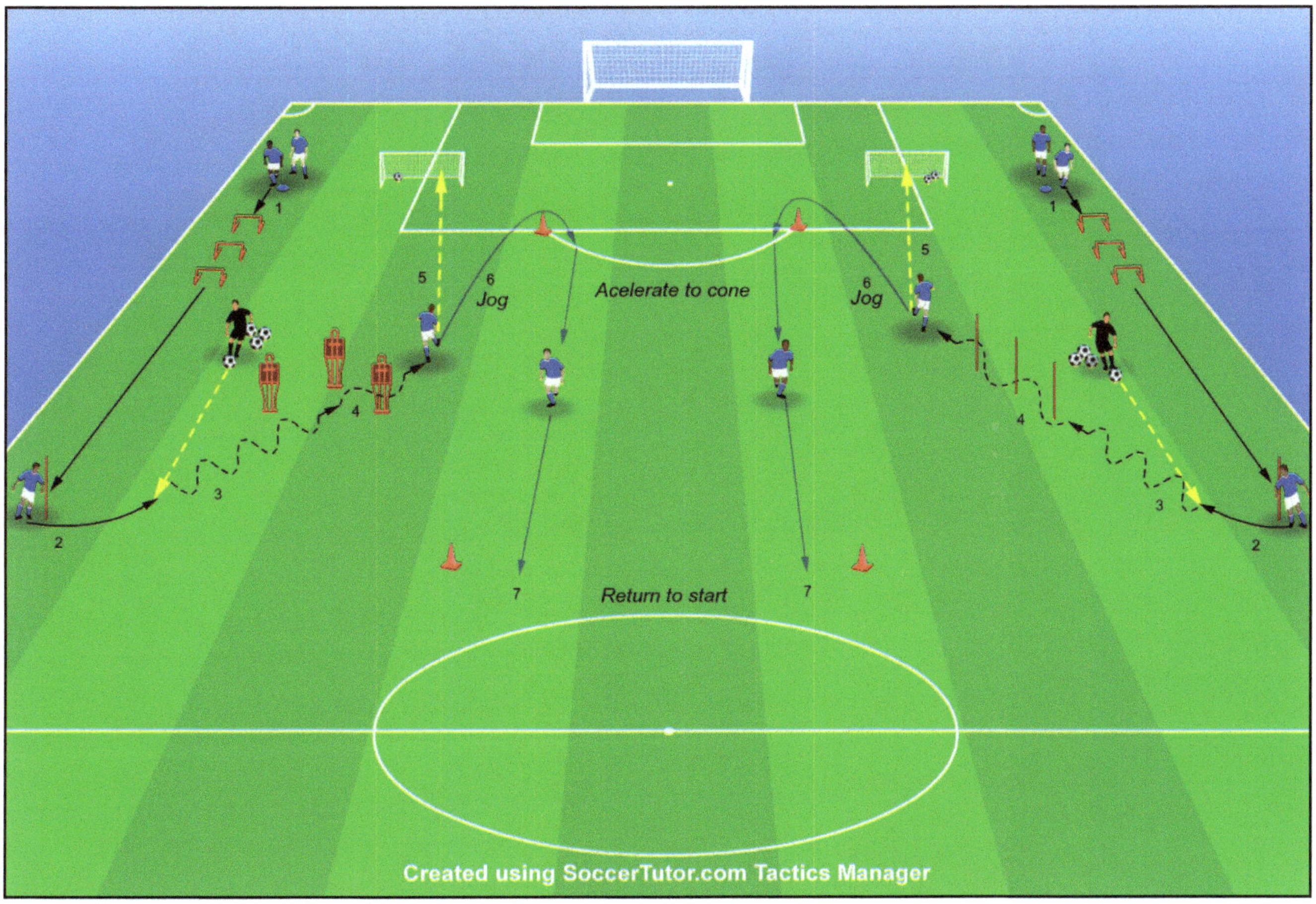

PRACTICE INFORMATION

Duration	Reps	Sets	Numbers	Size (m)	Work Duration	Explosive Actions
10 min	3	2	10-20	75 x 40	2 min	Throughout

OBJECTIVES: Physical stimulation - high-speed and sprints to develop the capacity to run fast

Volume Metrics	Practice Total	Per Min. of Work
Total Distance (km)	0.753	0.38
High Speed Running (m)	94	47
Sprint Distance (m)	12	6
Work Ratio (%)	22.3	
Power Plays (HiActs)	6	3

Intensity Metrics	Practice Total	Per Min. of Work
Max Speed (m/s)	7.3	
Intensity (m/min)		93
Power Score (w/kg)	4.44	
No. of Max Accels >4m²	-	-
No. of Max Decels >4m²	1	0.5

* The data shows the physical output per player based on research from elite level teams - see **pages 81-83** for details

Football Periodization to Maximise Performance

WEDNESDAY Practices: Speed Endurance - 3 Days Until Match (MD +4/-3)

Speed Endurance Conditioning 6: Dribbling, Passing, and Finishing in a Sprinting Circuit

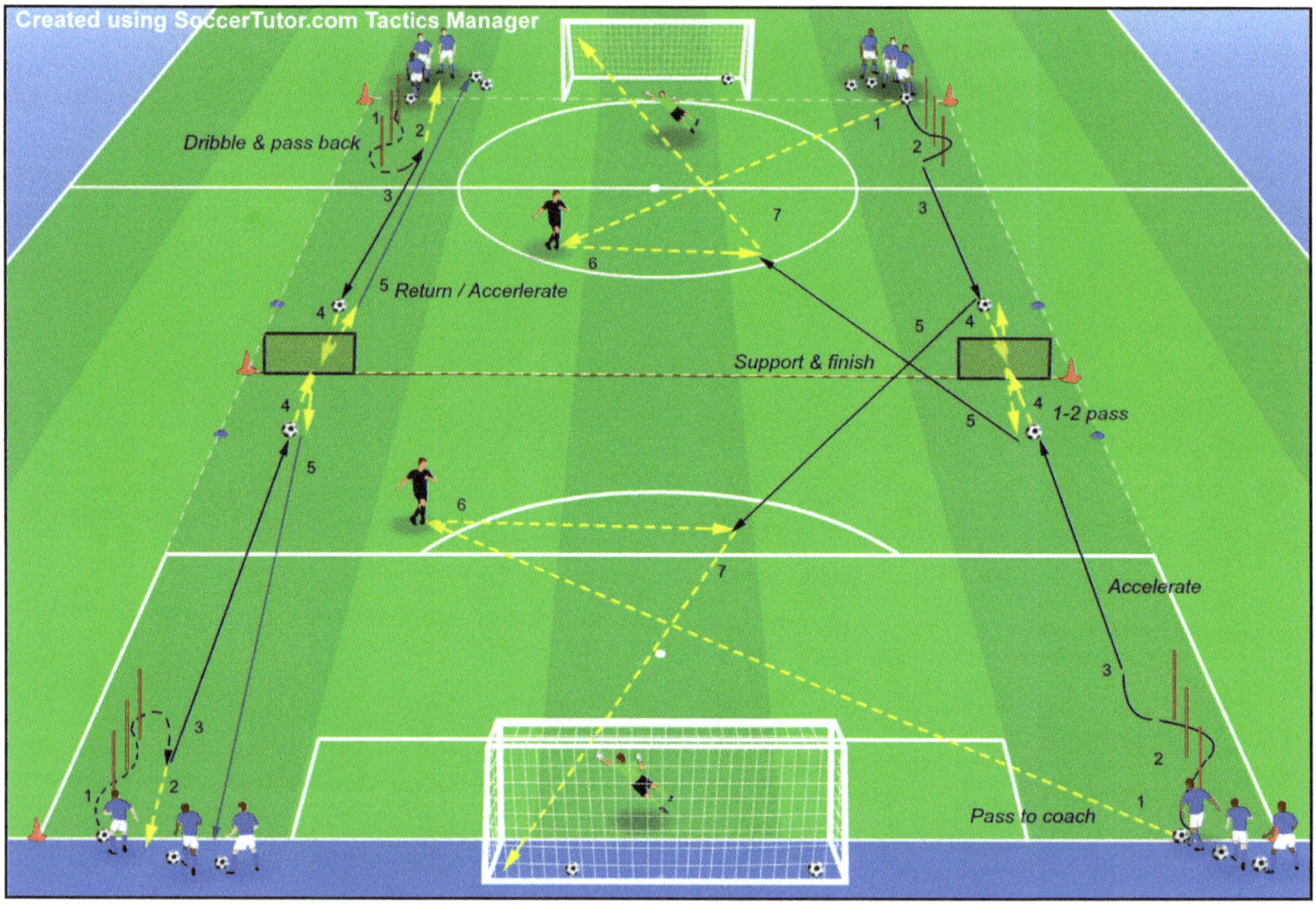

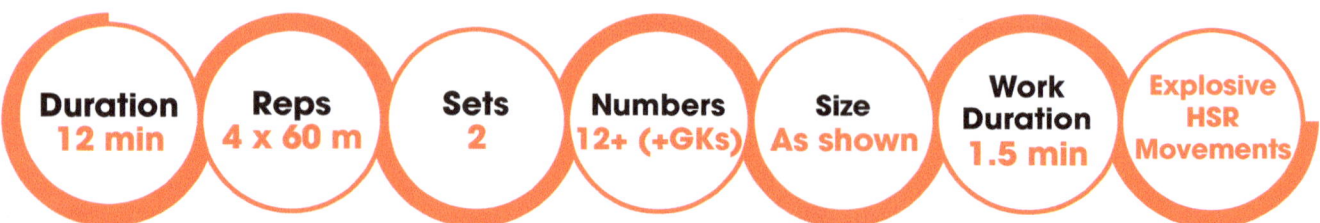

PRACTICE INFORMATION

Duration	Reps	Sets	Numbers	Size	Work Duration	
12 min	4 x 60 m	2	12+ (+GKs)	As shown	1.5 min	Explosive HSR Movements

OBJECTIVES: Physical stimulation - high-speed and sprints to develop the capacity to run fast

Volume Metrics	Practice Total	Per Min. of Work
Total Distance (km)	1.04	0.69
High Speed Running (m)	304	202.67
Sprint Distance (m)	50	33.33
Work Ratio (%)	37.8	
Power Plays (HiActs)	8	5.33

Intensity Metrics	Practice Total	Per Min. of Work
Max Speed (m/s)	7.44	
Intensity (m/min)		89
Power Score (w/kg)	4.45	
No. of Max Accels >4m²	2	1.33
No. of Max Decels >4m²	5	3.33

* The data shows the physical output per player based on research from elite level teams - **see pages 81-83** for details

@SoccerTutor.com Football Periodization to Maximise Performance

WEDNESDAY Practices: Speed Endurance - 3 Days Until Match (MD +4/-3)

Speed Endurance Conditioning 7: Attacking Wave in Pairs on a Full Pitch

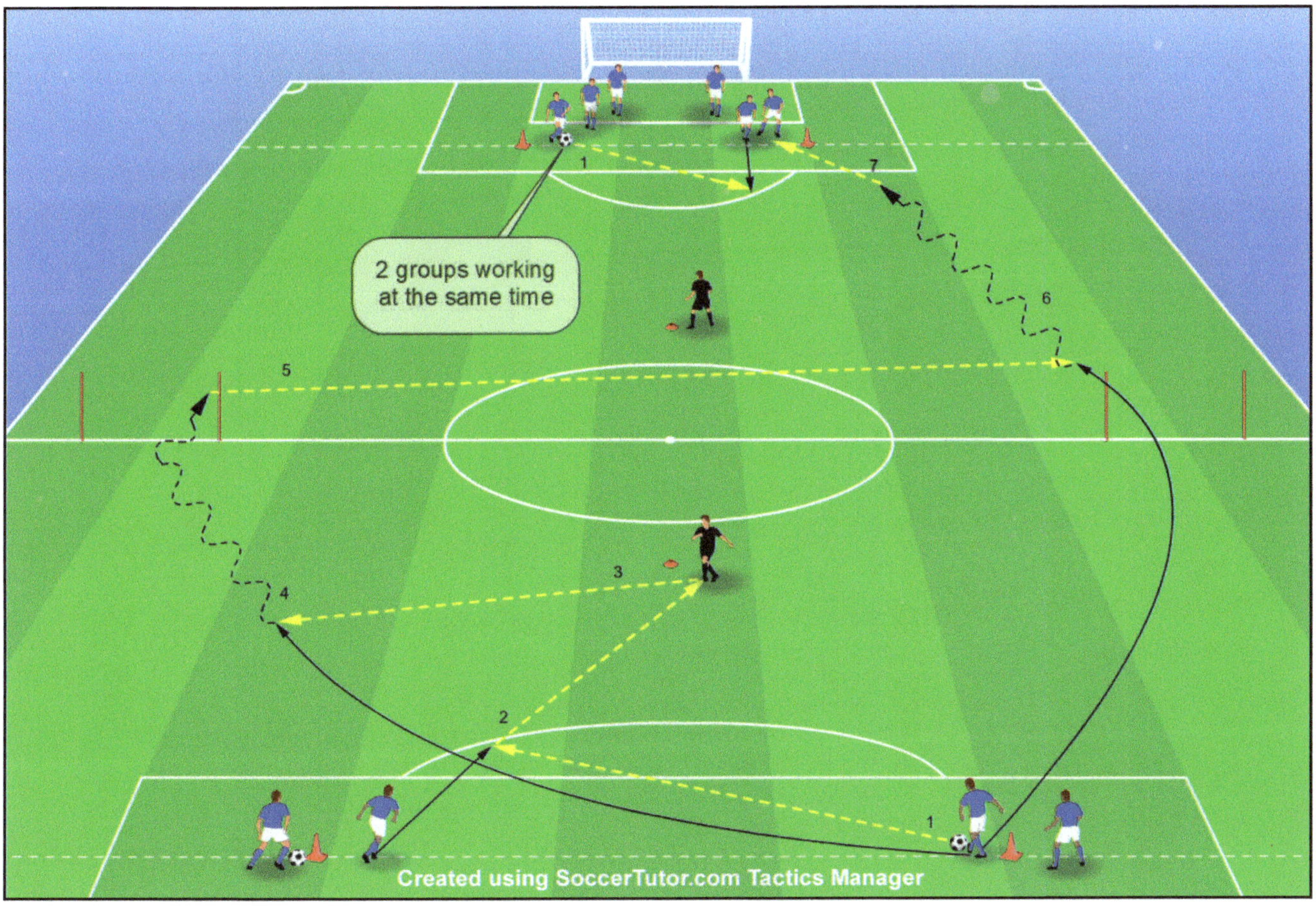

[Diagram: 2 groups working at the same time]

PRACTICE INFORMATION

Duration	Reps	Sets	Numbers	Size	Work Duration	
5 min	2 x 40 m	4	10+	As shown	80 sec	Speed Endurance Day

OBJECTIVES: Physical stimulation - high-speed and sprints to develop the capacity to run fast

Volume Metrics	Practice Total	Per Min. of Work
Total Distance (km)	1.055	0.79
High Speed Running (m)	482.22	361.7
Sprint Distance (m)	171.48	128.61
Work Ratio (%)	17.27	
Power Plays (HiActs)	8.93	6.7

Intensity Metrics	Practice Total	Per Min. of Work
Max Speed (m/s)	7.85	
Intensity (m/min)		73.38
Power Score (w/kg)	5.98	
Max Accel. Distance (m)	8.85	6.64
Max Decel. Distance (m)	3.49	2.62

* The data shows the physical output per player based on research from elite level teams - see **pages 81-83** for details

WEDNESDAY Practices: Speed Endurance - 3 Days Until Match (MD +4/-3)

Speed Endurance Conditioning 8: 3-Player Passing Combination, Run in Behind & Finish

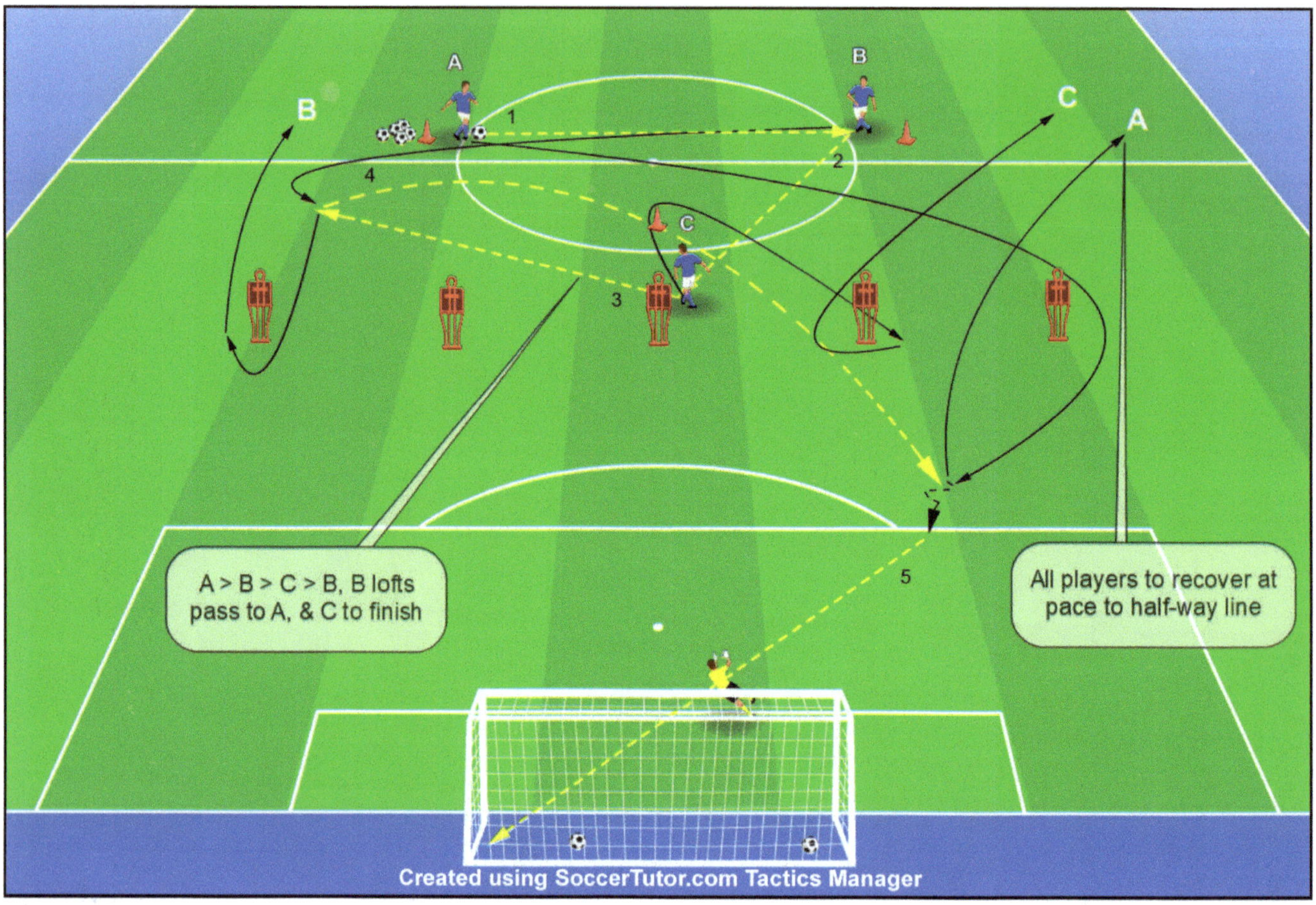

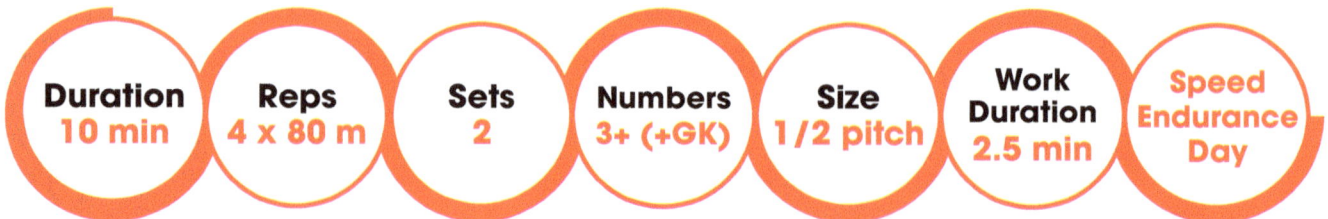

A > B > C > B, B lofts pass to A, & C to finish

All players to recover at pace to half-way line

PRACTICE INFORMATION

- **Duration:** 10 min
- **Reps:** 4 x 80 m
- **Sets:** 2
- **Numbers:** 3+ (+GK)
- **Size:** 1/2 pitch
- **Work Duration:** 2.5 min
- **Speed Endurance Day**

OBJECTIVES: Physical stimulation - high-speed and sprints to develop the capacity to run fast

Volume Metrics	Practice Total	Per Min. of Work
Total Distance (km)	1.08	0.43
High Speed Running (m)	397	158.8
Sprint Distance (m)	97.75	39.1
Work Ratio (%)	21.35	
Power Plays (HiActs)	15.19	6.08

Intensity Metrics	Practice Total	Per Min. of Work
Max Speed (m/s)	8.04	
Intensity (m/min)		80.66
Power Score (w/kg)	6.93	
Max Accel. Distance (m)	16.09	6.44
Max Decel. Distance (m)	10.38	4.15

* The data shows the physical output per player based on research from elite level teams - see **pages 81-83** for details

WEDNESDAY Practices: Speed Endurance - 3 Days Until Match (MD +4/-3)

Speed Endurance Conditioning 9: Continuous Sprints in a 2v2 Duel Transition Cycle

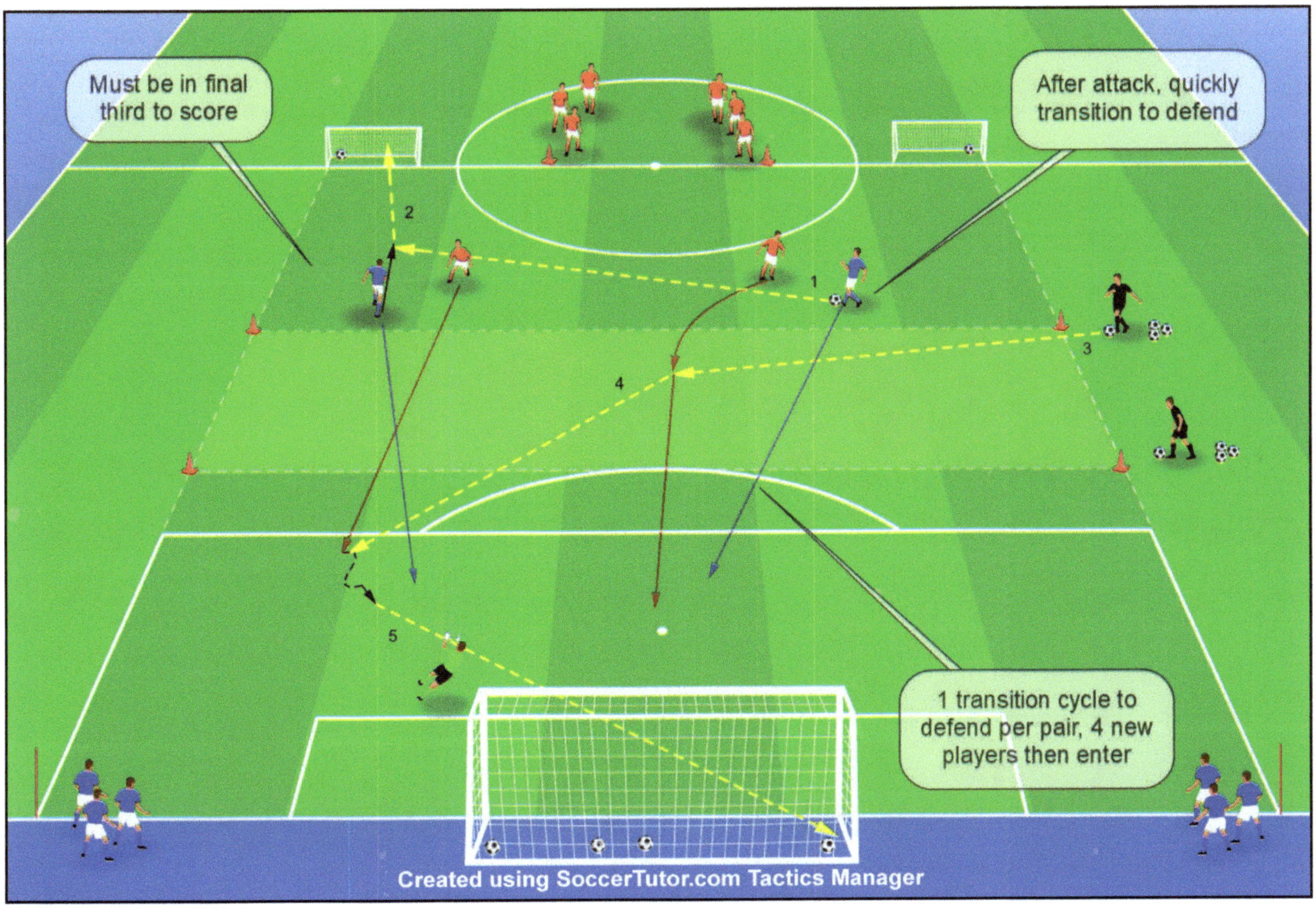

- Must be in final third to score
- After attack, quickly transition to defend
- 1 transition cycle to defend per pair, 4 new players then enter

PRACTICE INFORMATION

- **Duration:** 10 min
- **Reps:** 4 x 80 m
- **Sets:** 2
- **Numbers:** 16 + GK
- **Size:** 1/2 pitch
- **Work Duration:** 2.5 min
- **Speed Endurance Day**

OBJECTIVES: Physical stimulation - high-speed and sprints to develop the capacity to run fast

Volume Metrics	Practice Total	Per Min. of Work
Total Distance (km)	0.876	0.35
High Speed Running (m)	202.7	81.08
Sprint Distance (m)	58.53	23.41
Work Ratio (%)	16.13	
Power Plays (HiActs)	11.5	4.6

Intensity Metrics	Practice Total	Per Min. of Work
Max Speed (m/s)	7.9	
Intensity (m/min)		57.36
Power Score (w/kg)	5.13	
Max Accel. Distance (m)	18.96	7.58
Max Decel. Distance (m)	24.11	9.64

* The data shows the physical output per player based on research from elite level teams - see **pages 81-83** for details

WEDNESDAY Practices: Speed Endurance - 3 Days Until Match (MD +4/-3)

Speed Endurance Conditioning 10: Pressing in Tactical Shape + 6-Second Counter Attack

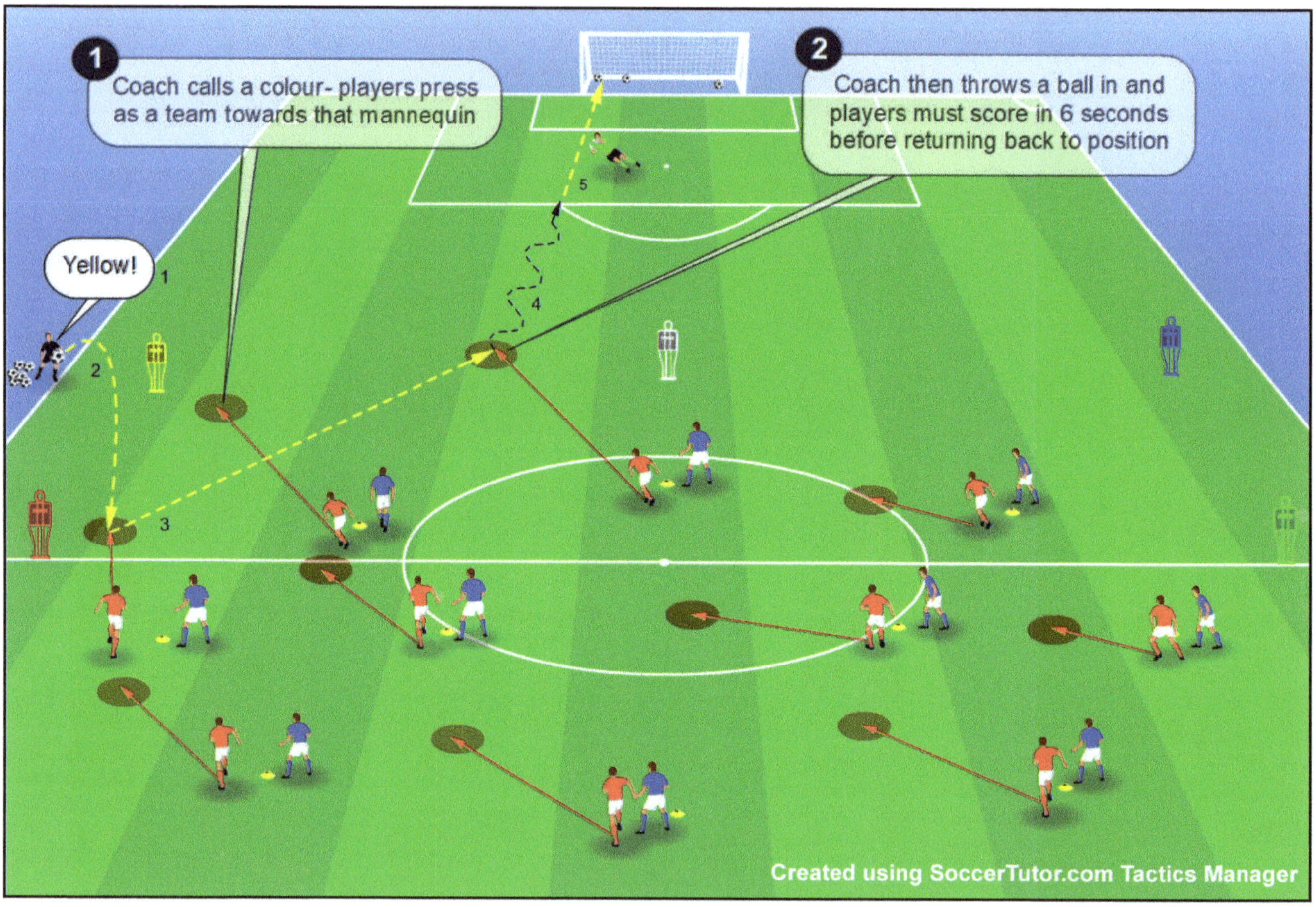

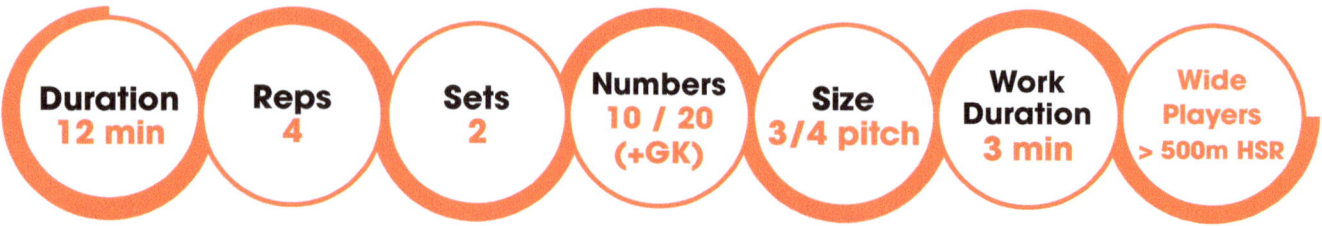

1. Coach calls a colour - players press as a team towards that mannequin
2. Coach then throws a ball in and players must score in 6 seconds before returning back to position

PRACTICE INFORMATION

Duration	Reps	Sets	Numbers	Size	Work Duration	Wide Players
12 min	4	2	10 / 20 (+GK)	3/4 pitch	3 min	> 500m HSR

OBJECTIVES: Physical stimulation - high-speed and sprints to develop the capacity to run fast

Volume Metrics	Practice Total	Per Min. of Work
Total Distance (km)	1.149	0.38
High Speed Running (m)	283.21	94.4
Sprint Distance (m)	52	17.3
Work Ratio (%)	32.14	
Power Plays (HiActs)	19	6.3

Intensity Metrics	Practice Total	Per Min. of Work
Max Speed (m/s)	7.51	
Intensity (m/min)		61.89
Power Score (w/kg)	5.49	
No. of Max Accels >4m²	12.95	4.32
No. of Max Decels >4m²	2.11	0.7

* The data shows the physical output per player based on research from elite level teams - see **pages 81-83** for details

WEDNESDAY Practices: Speed Endurance - 3 Days Until Match (MD +4/-3)

WEDNESDAY - 3 DAYS UNTIL MATCH (MD +4/-3):
Large Sided Possession Practices

INTENSITY: All practices are performed at full intensity

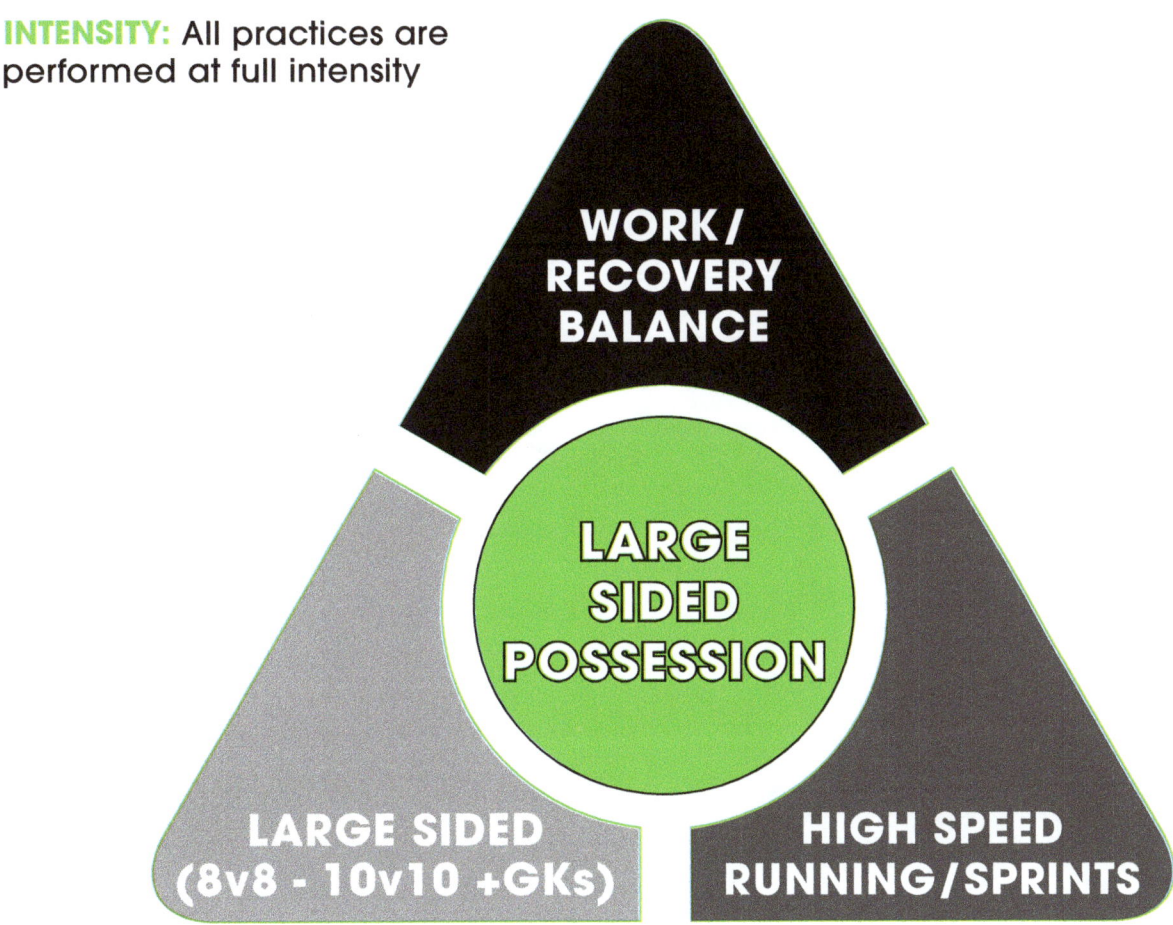

What are Large Sided Possession Practices?
- Large sided possession games are defined as including at least 8 outfield players per side = 8v8 - 10v10 (+GKs).

Why are they used on this day of the training week (MD +4/-3)?
- They can be used in different periods of the training week but within this framework, they are focused around the MD +4/-3 training day with larger playing areas to train the collective team tactical principles and provide a match simulation focus.
- They are also performed on this training day to ensure specific muscle groups have a good balance between work and recovery.

How does this help to maximise performance?
- These game types result in more high-speed running and or higher running speeds versus other game types.
- They also enable more position specific technical qualities to be performed and trained.

WEDNESDAY Practices: Speed Endurance - 3 Days Until Match (MD +4/-3)

Large Sided Possession 1: Positional Shape Game with Mannequin Gates (9v9 +2)

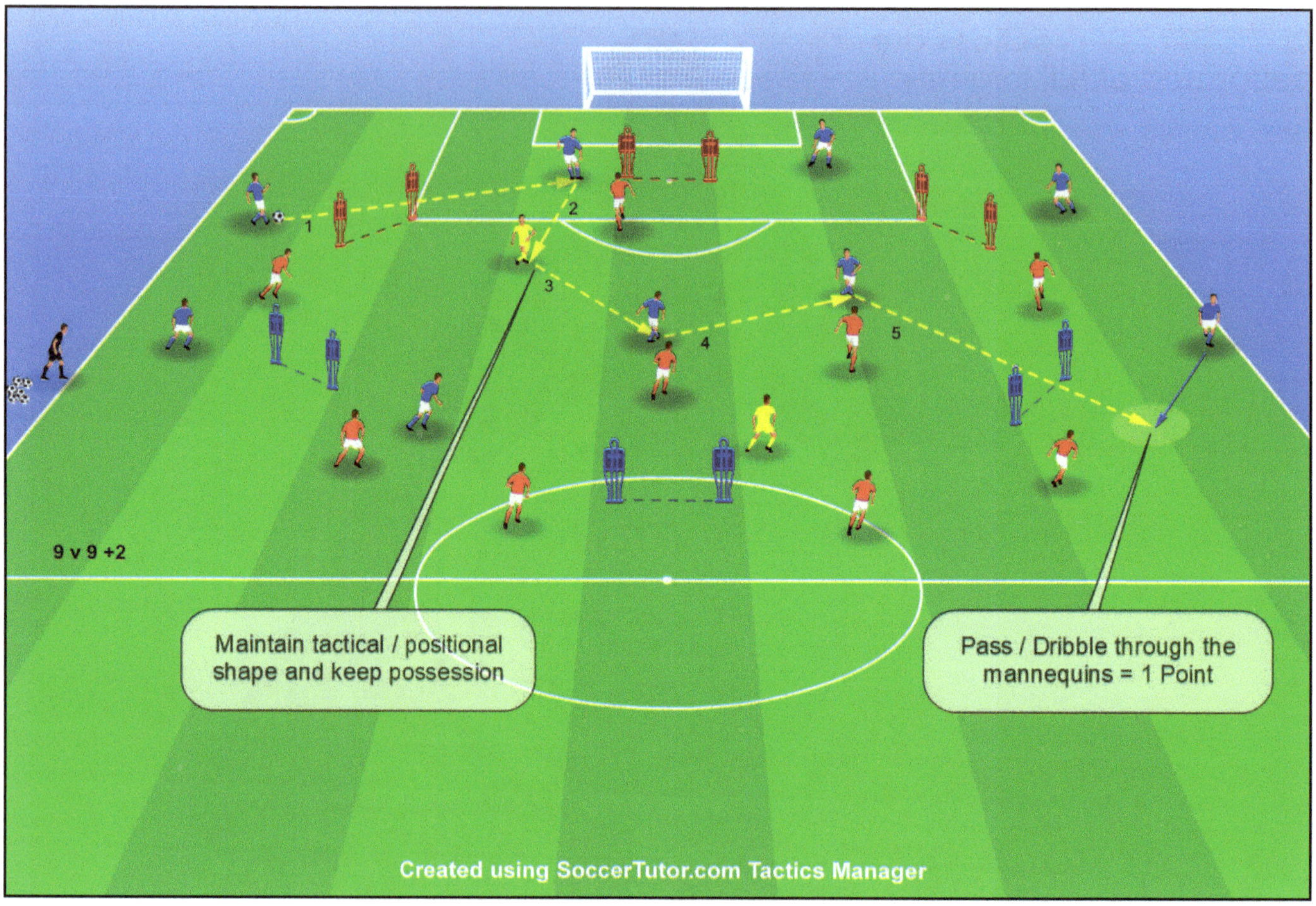

PRACTICE INFORMATION

Duration	Reps	Sets	Numbers	Size	Work Duration	Player Density
14 min	6 min	2	20	1/2 Pitch	12 min	218 m²

OBJECTIVE: Positional shape and directional possession within a tactical possession game

Volume Metrics	Practice Total	Per Min. of Work
Total Distance (km)	1.778	0.15
High Speed Running (m)	56.88	4.74
Sprint Distance (m)	6.6	0.55
HML Distance (m)	199.95	16.7
Power Plays (HiActs)	12	1

Intensity Metrics	Practice Total	Per Min. of Work
Max Speed (m/s)	6.86	
Intensity (m/min)		95.36
Power Score (w/kg)	7.92	
Max Accel Distance (m)	16	1.3
Max Decel Distance (m)	27	2.25

* The data shows the physical output per player based on research from elite level teams - see **pages 81-83** for details

164

@SoccerTutor.com | Football Periodization to Maximise Performance

REFERENCE | @adamowen1980

WEDNESDAY Practices: Speed Endurance - 3 Days Until Match (MD +4/-3)

Large Sided Possession 2: Tactical 9v9 (+2) Directional Theme Game with 4 Progressive Zones

[Diagram: Field set-up with 4 progressive zones. Annotations: "Dribble past end-line = 1 Goal"; "In possession, create overloads by advancing into next zone"; zones labelled "3 v 2", "2 v 2 +1", "2 v 2 +1", "3 v 2"; End Line markers.]

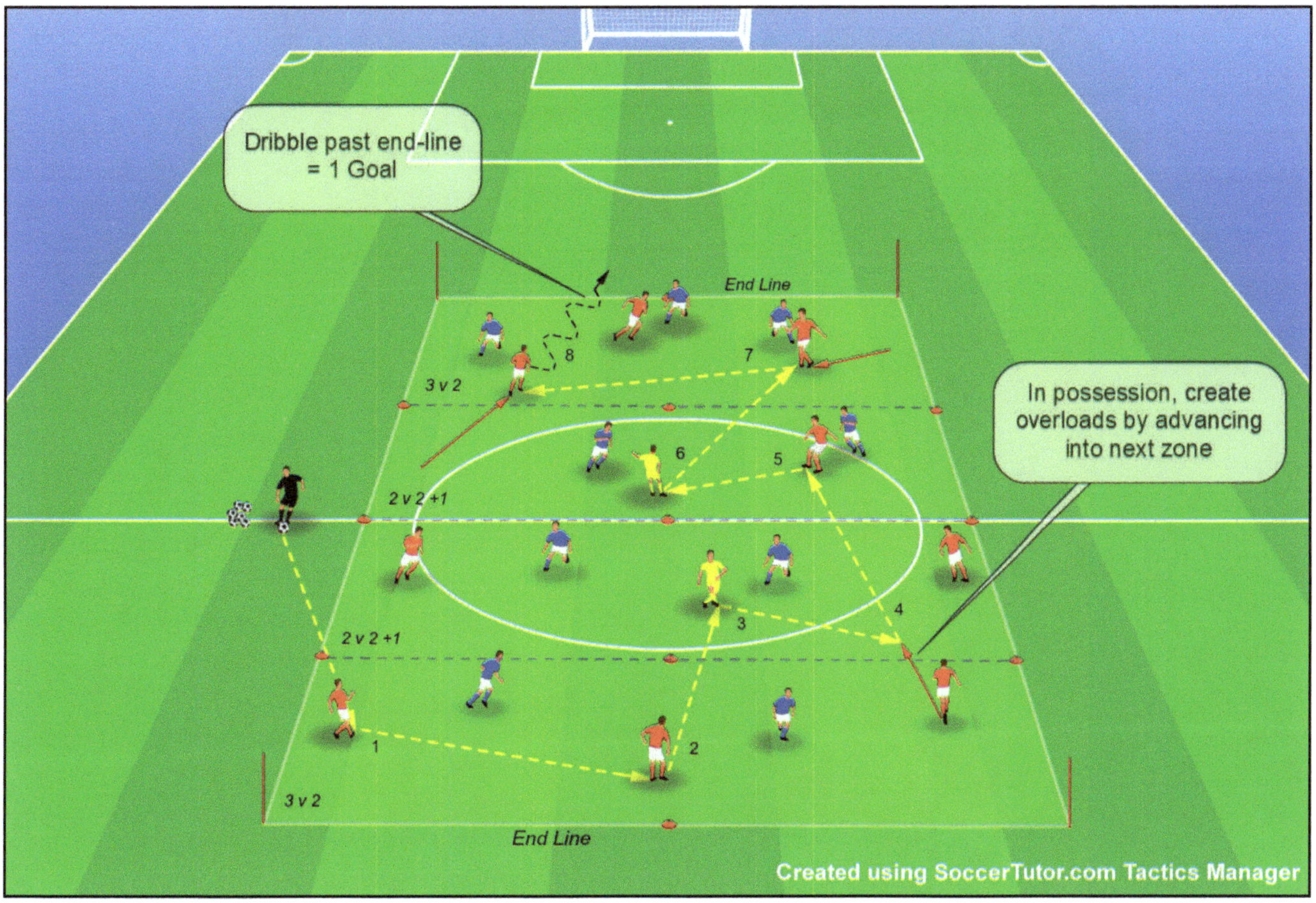

PRACTICE INFORMATION

Duration	Reps	Sets	Numbers	Size (m)	Work Duration	Player Density
15 min	4 min	3	20	25 x 40	12 min	48 m²

OBJECTIVE: Creating overloads and stepping forward in possession to break defensive lines

Volume Metrics	Practice Total	Per Min. of Work
Total Distance (km)	1.115	0.09
High Speed Running (m)	12.16	1.01
Sprint Distance (m)	2	0.17
HML Distance (m)	147.19	12.27
Power Plays (HiActs)	3.26	0.27

Intensity Metrics	Practice Total	Per Min. of Work
Max Speed (m/s)	5.91	
Intensity (m/min)		59.2
Power Score (w/kg)	5.11	
No. of Max Accels >4m²	9.89	0.82
No. of Max Decels >4m²	10.26	0.86

* The data shows the physical output per player based on research from elite level teams - see **pages 81-83** for details

Football Periodization to Maximise Performance

WEDNESDAY Practices: Speed Endurance - 3 Days Until Match (MD +4/-3)

Large Sided Possession 3: Positional and Directional Build-up Practice with Receiving GKs

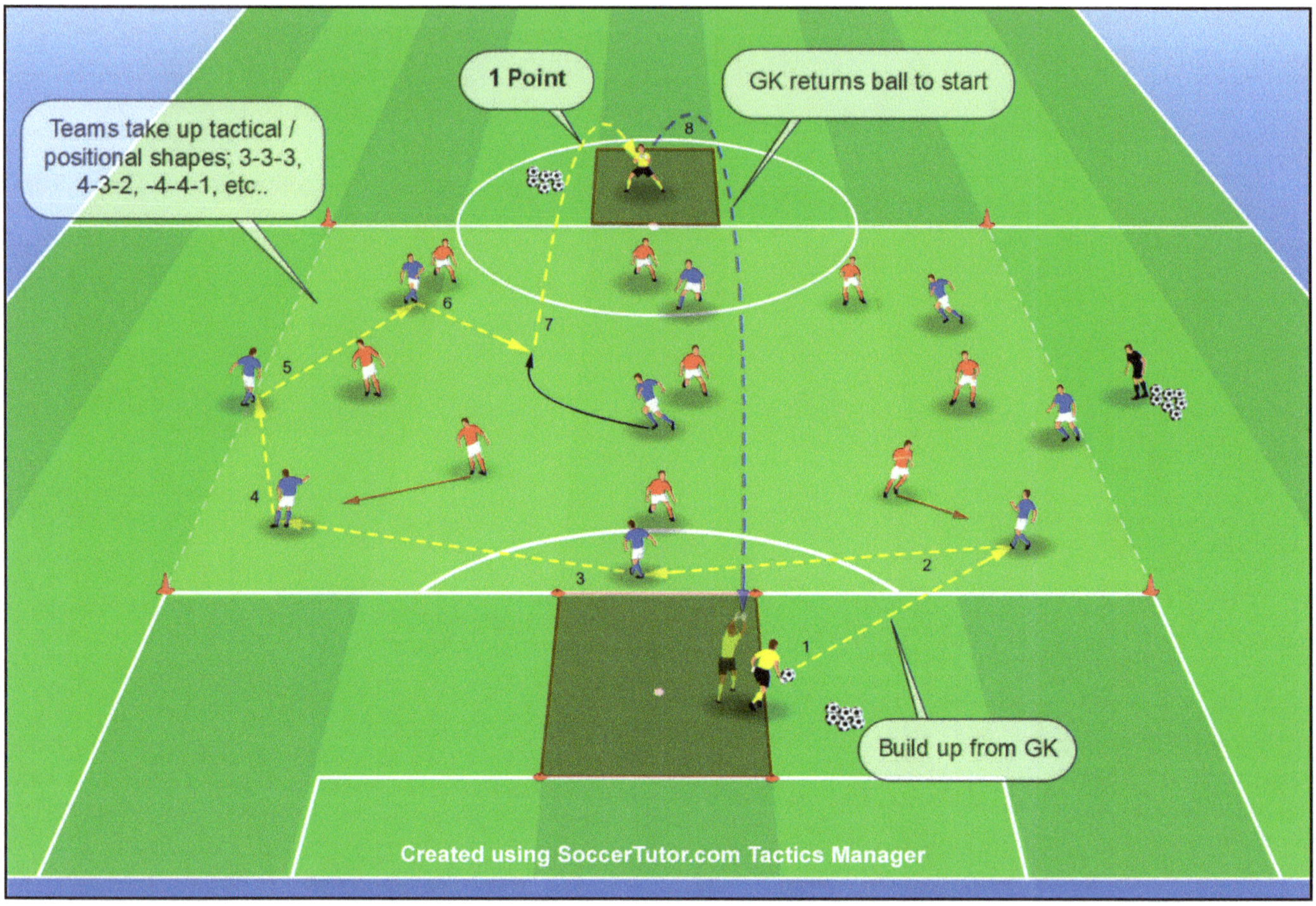

[Diagram: Teams take up tactical / positional shapes; 3-3-3, 4-3-2, -4-4-1, etc.. — 1 Point — GK returns ball to start — Build up from GK]

PRACTICE INFORMATION

Duration	Reps	Sets	Numbers	Size	Work Duration	Player Density
15 min	4 min	3	18 + GKs	As shown	12 min	100 m²

OBJECTIVE: Build-up play from back to front with positional play - tactical shape

Volume Metrics	Practice Total	Per Min. of Work
Total Distance (km)	1.295	0.1
High Speed Running (m)	6	0.5
Sprint Distance (m)	-	-
HML Distance (m)	194	16.17
Power Plays (HiActs)	4	0.33

Intensity Metrics	Practice Total	Per Min. of Work
Max Speed (m/s)	4.88	
Intensity (m/min)		87
Power Score (w/kg)	4.22	
No. of Max Accels >4m²	3	0.25
No. of Max Decels >4m²	4	0.33

* The data shows the physical output per player based on research from elite level teams - see **pages 81-83** for details

WEDNESDAY Practices: Speed Endurance - 3 Days Until Match (MD +4/-3)

Large Sided Possession 4: Switch After Winning the Ball in a 10v10 Game with Split Halves

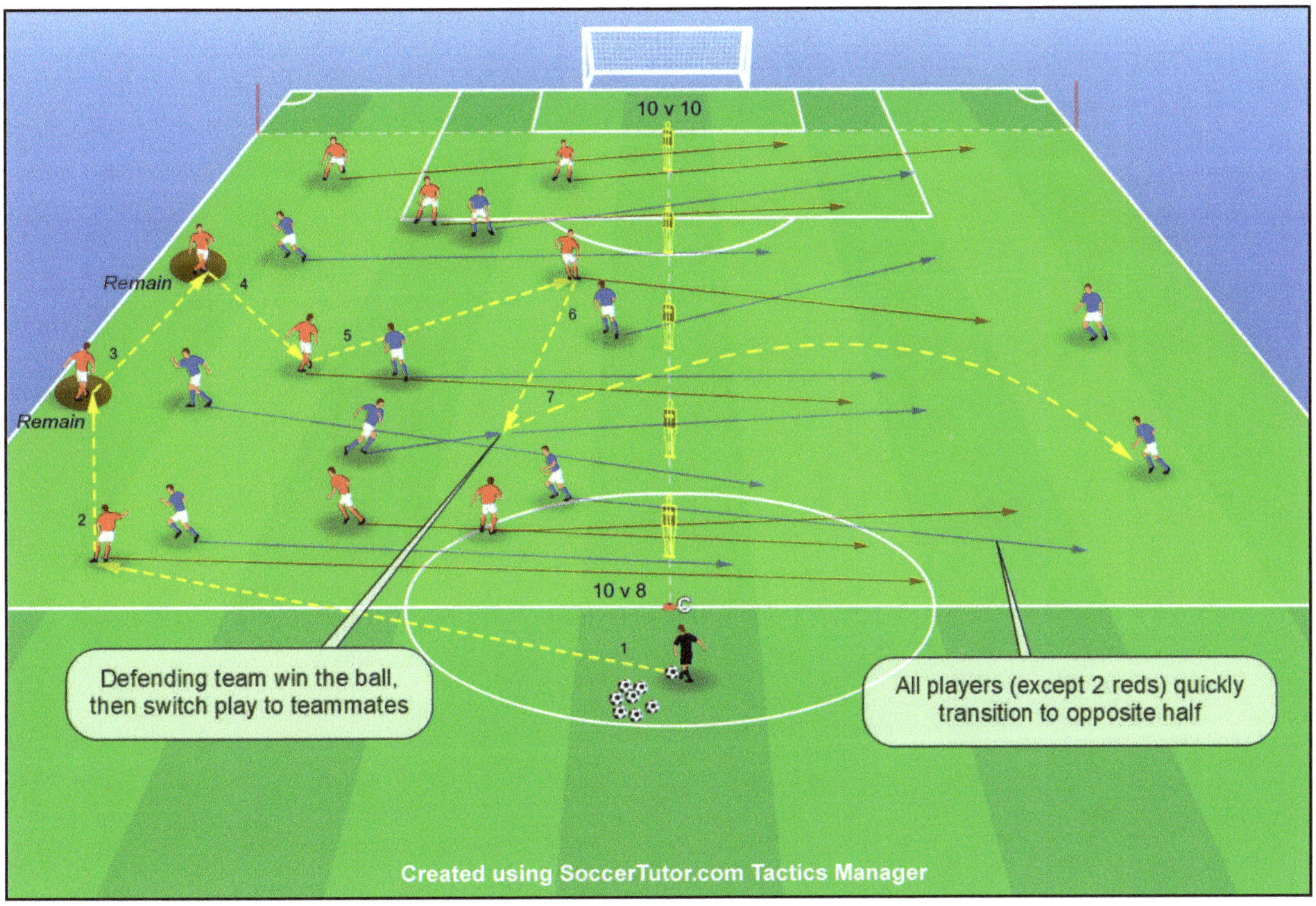

PRACTICE INFORMATION

Duration	Reps	Sets	Numbers	Size	Work Duration	Player Density
10 min	4 min	2	20	As shown	8 min	195 m²

OBJECTIVE: Possession with an advantage + high intensity transition with focus on switching play

Volume Metrics	Practice Total	Per Min. of Work
Total Distance (km)	1.2	0.15
High Speed Running (m)	49.19	6.15
Sprint Distance (m)	1	0.13
HML Distance (m)	155	19.38
Power Plays (HiActs)	10.18	1.27

Intensity Metrics	Practice Total	Per Min. of Work
Max Speed (m/s)	6.4	
Intensity (m/min)		100.72
Power Score (w/kg)	8.55	
No. of Max Accels >4m²	4.3	0.54
No. of Max Decels >4m²	5.38	0.67

* The data shows the physical output per player based on research from elite level teams - see pages 81-83 for details

@SoccerTutor.com — Football Periodization to Maximise Performance

WEDNESDAY Practices: Speed Endurance - 3 Days Until Match (MD +4/-3)

Large Sided Possession 5: Build-up Play from Back to Front in an End to End Game with GKs

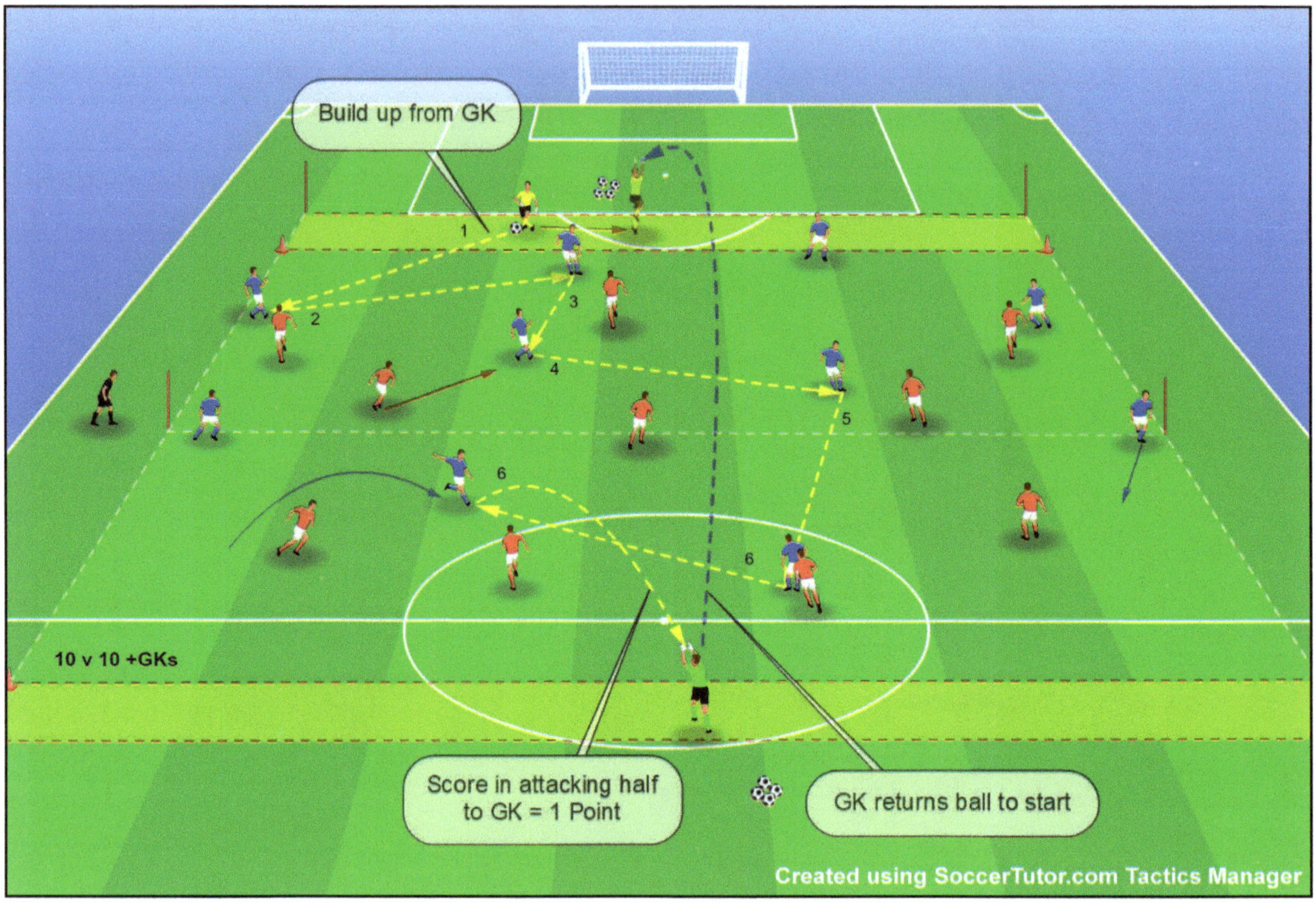

PRACTICE INFORMATION

Duration	Reps	Sets	Numbers	Size	Work Duration	Player Density
12 min	5 min	2	20 + GKs	As shown	10 min	138 m²

OBJECTIVE: Directional and positional possession play to build-up play from back to front

Volume Metrics	Practice Total	Per Min. of Work
Total Distance (km)	1.264	0.13
High Speed Running (m)	23	2.3
Sprint Distance (m)	1	0.1
HML Distance (m)	-	-
Power Plays (HiActs)	8	0.8

Intensity Metrics	Practice Total	Per Min. of Work
Max Speed (m/s)	6.77	
Intensity (m/min)		105
Power Score (w/kg)	6.5	
No. of Max Accels >4m²	2	0.2
No. of Max Decels >4m²	3	0.3

* The data shows the physical output per player based on research from elite level teams - see **pages 81-83** for details

WEDNESDAY Practices: Speed Endurance - 3 Days Until Match (MD +4/-3)

Large Sided Possession 6: Tactical Three Zone Themed Game with Two Phases

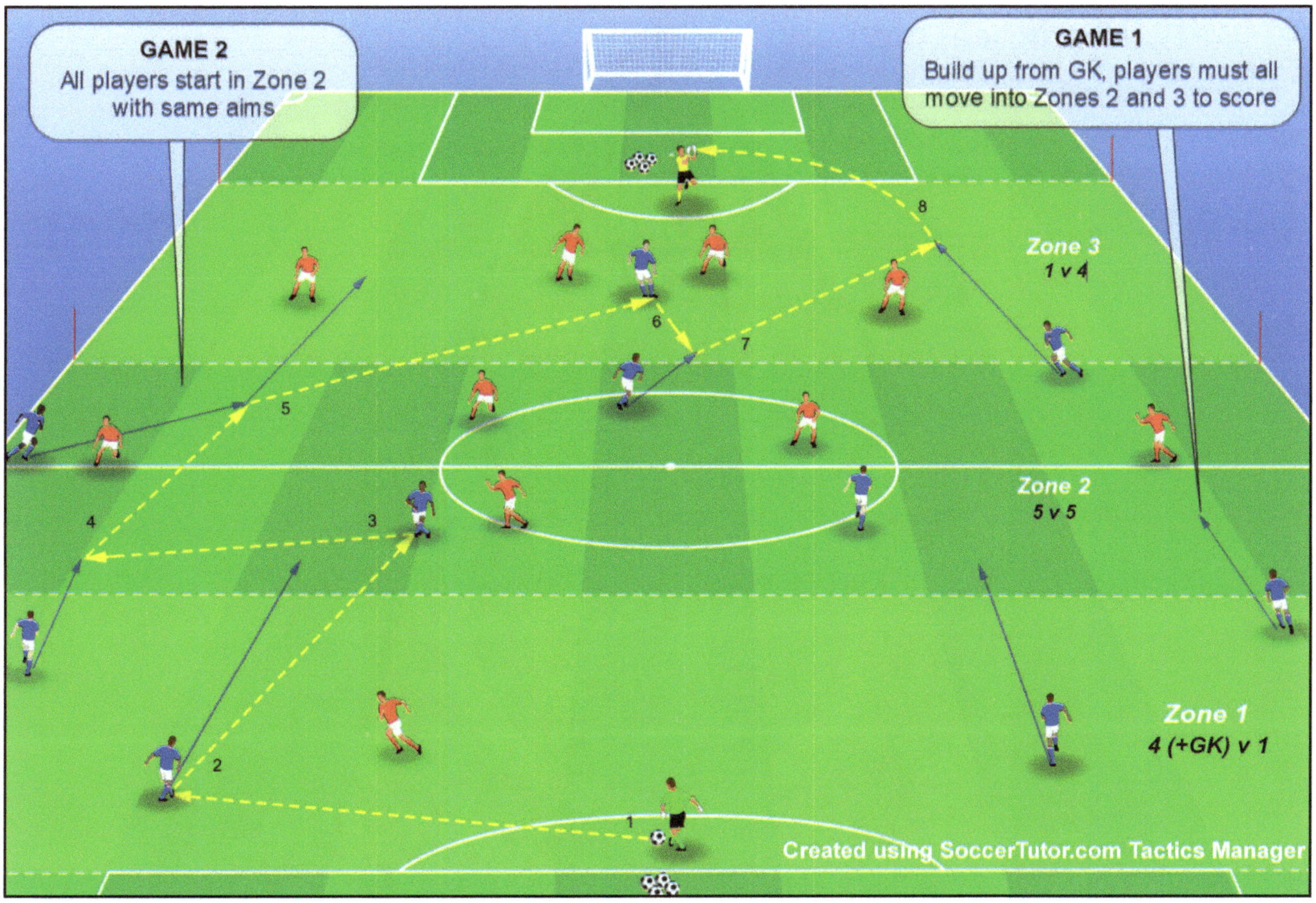

GAME 2: All players start in Zone 2 with same aims.

GAME 1: Build up from GK, players must all move into Zones 2 and 3 to score

Zone 3 — 1 v 4
Zone 2 — 5 v 5
Zone 1 — 4 (+GK) v 1

PRACTICE INFORMATION

Duration	Reps	Sets	Numbers	Size	Work Duration	Player Density
10 min	4 min	2	20 + GKs	As shown	8 min	273 m²

OBJECTIVE: Directional and positional possession play to build-up play from back to front

Volume Metrics	Practice Total	Per Min. of Work
Total Distance (km)	1.2	0.15
High Speed Running (m)	36.75	4.6
Sprint Distance (m)	2.7	0.34
HML Distance (m)	128.12	16
Power Plays (HiActs)	8.95	1.12

Intensity Metrics	Practice Total	Per Min. of Work
Max Speed (m/s)	6.62	
Intensity (m/min)		101.52
Power Score (w/kg)	8.39	
No. of Max Accels >4m²	4.26	0.53
No. of Max Decels >4m²	4.47	0.56

* The data shows the physical output per player based on research from elite level teams - see **pages 81-83** for details

@SoccerTutor.com — Football Periodization to Maximise Performance

REFERENCE @adamowen1980

WEDNESDAY Practices: Speed Endurance - 3 Days Until Match (MD +4/-3)

WEDNESDAY - 3 DAYS UNTIL MATCH (MD +4/-3):
Large Sided Games in Large Area

INTENSITY: All practices are performed at full intensity

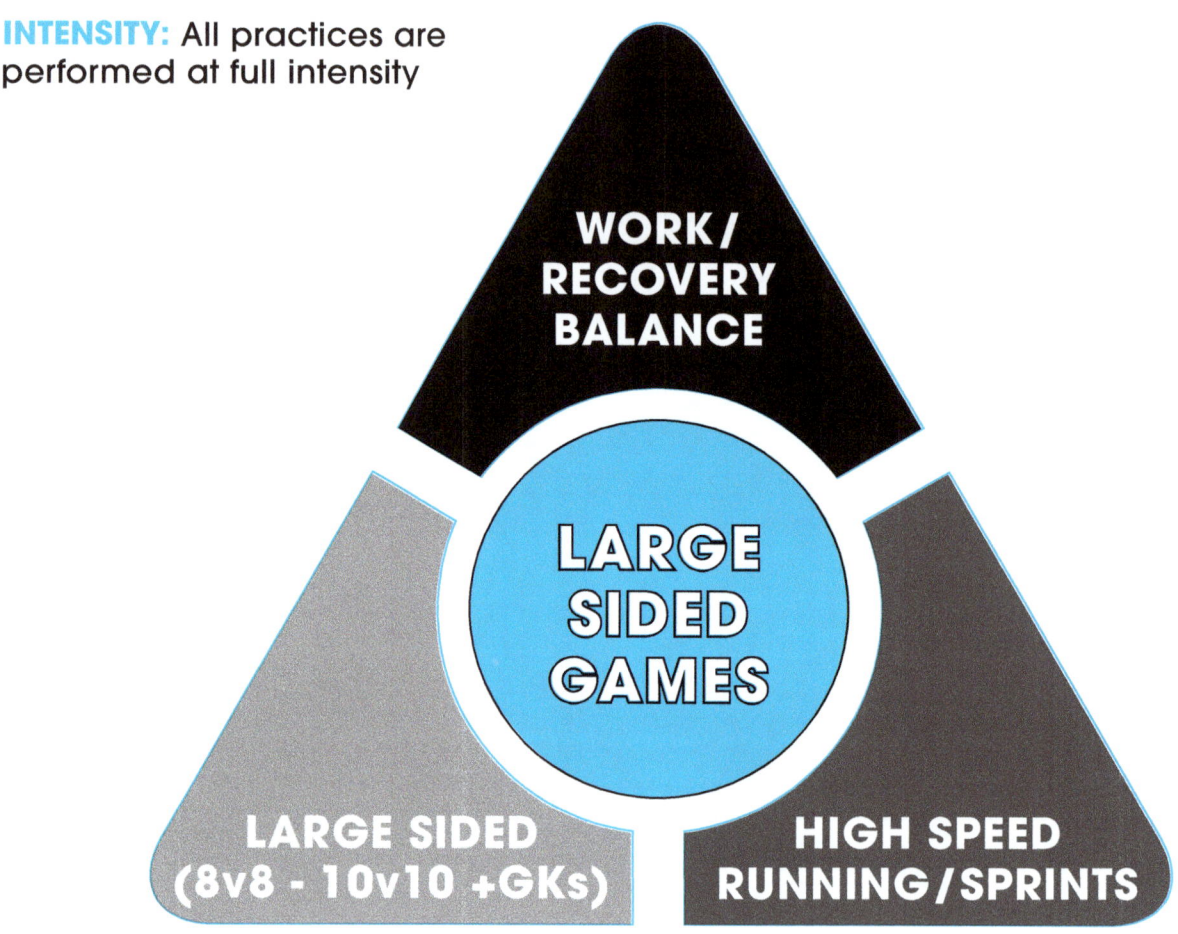

What are Large Sided Games?

- Large sided games are defined as including at least 8 outfield players per side = 8v8 - 10v10 (+GKs).

Why are they used on this day of the training week (MD +4/-3)?

- They can be used in different periods of the training week but within this framework, they are focused around the MD +4/-3 training day with larger playing areas to train the collective team tactical principles and provide a match simulation focus.

- They are also performed on this training day to ensure specific muscle groups have a good balance between work and recovery.

How does this help to maximise performance?

- Large sided games in larger playing areas result in more high-speed running and sprint distance vs. other game types.

- They also enable more position specific technical qualities to be performed and trained.

WEDNESDAY Practices: Speed Endurance - 3 Days Until Match (MD +4/-3)

LSG (Large Area) 1: Fast Decision Making in a 9v9 (+GKs) Game within a Narrow Pitch

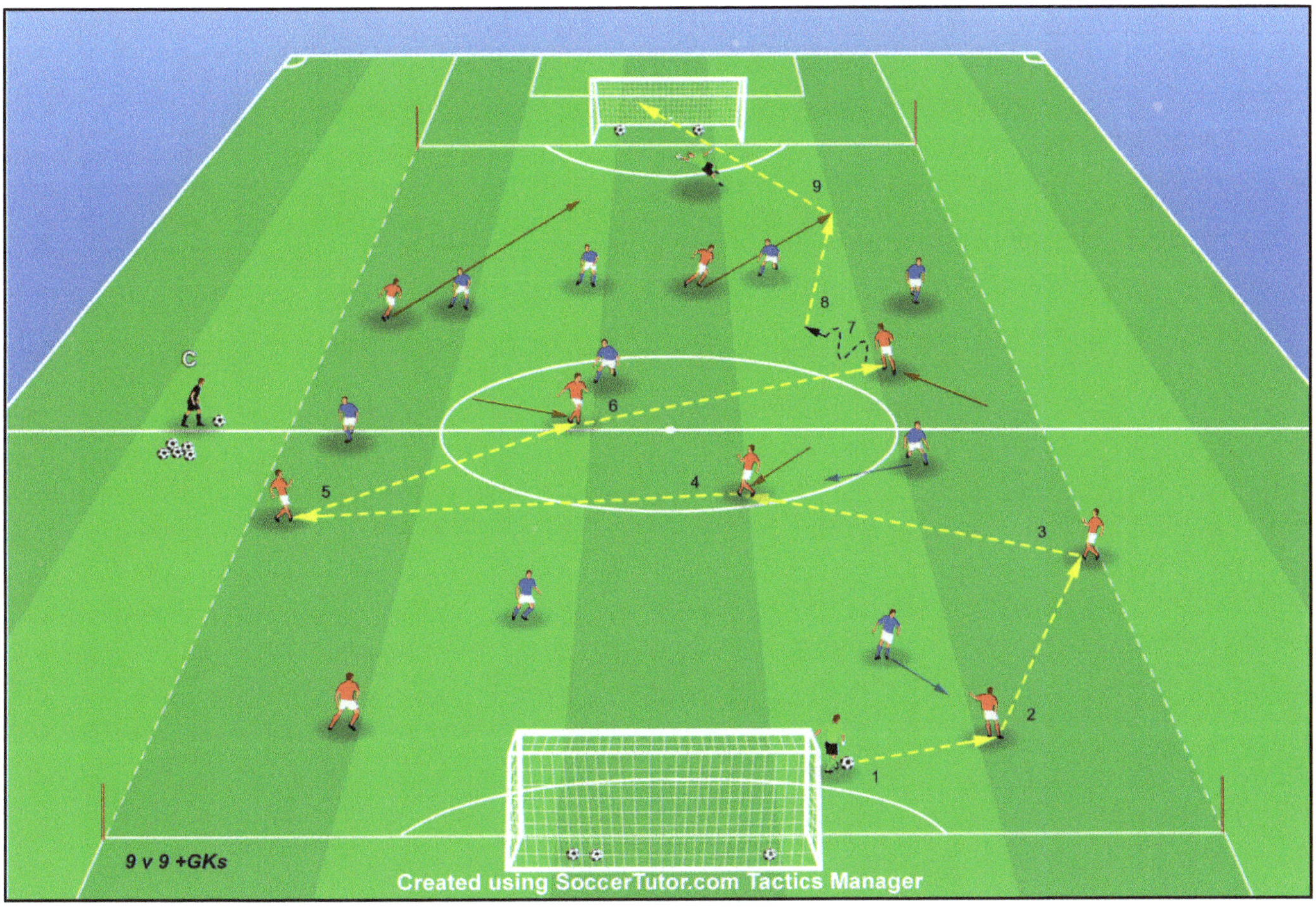

PRACTICE INFORMATION

Duration	Reps	Sets	Numbers	Size	Work Duration	Player Density
18 min	8 min	2	18 + GKs	As Shown	16 min	160 m²

OBJECTIVE: Force players to create repetitive fast thinking and execution within a narrow area

Volume Metrics	Practice Total	Per Min. of Work
Total Distance (km)	1.856	0.12
High Speed Running (m)	71.54	4.47
Sprint Distance (m)	8.69	0.54
Work Ratio (%)	38.62	
Power Plays (HiActs)	12.33	0.77

Intensity Metrics	Practice Total	Per Min. of Work
Max Speed (m/s)	7.04	
Intensity (m/min)		92.69
Power Score (w/kg)	7.74	
Max Accel. Distance (m)	18.39	1.15
Max Decel. Distance (m)	27.48	1.72

* The data shows the physical output per player based on research from elite level teams - see pages 81-83 for details

Football Periodization to Maximise Performance

WEDNESDAY Practices: Speed Endurance - 3 Days Until Match (MD +4/-3)

LSG (Large Area) 2: Tactical Three Zone Game with "Pushing Up" Rule

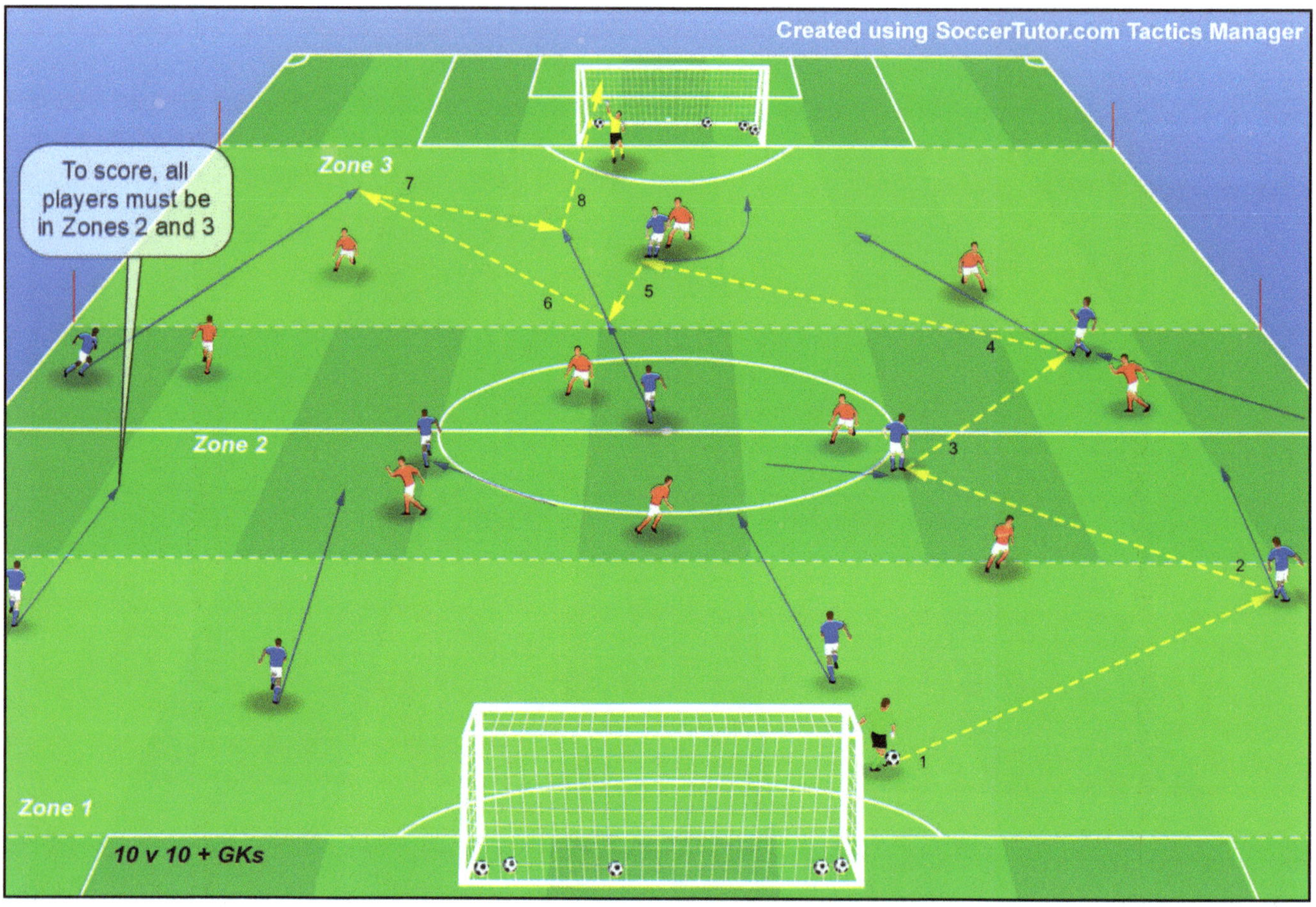

![Diagram showing 10v10 + GKs tactical three zone game. Text on diagram: "To score, all players must be in Zones 2 and 3". Zones labelled Zone 1, Zone 2, Zone 3. 10 v 10 + GKs]

PRACTICE INFORMATION

Duration	Reps	Sets	Numbers	Size	Work Duration	Player Density
16 min	7 min	2	20 + GKs	As Shown	14 min	272 m²

OBJECTIVE: Build-up play, securing possession, and creating overloads to progress the ball

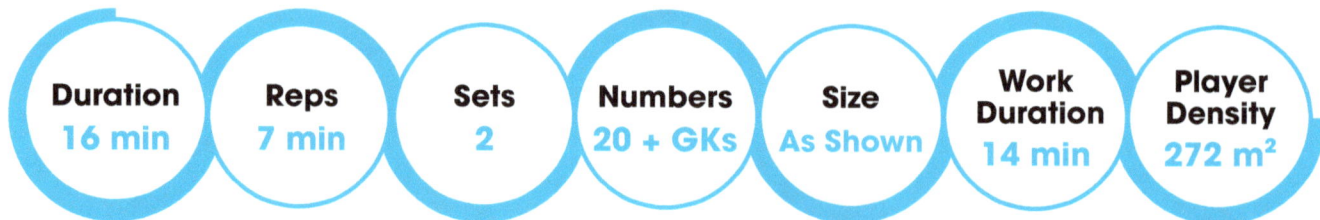

Volume Metrics	Practice Total	Per Min. of Work
Total Distance (km)	1.845	0.13
High Speed Running (m)	89.95	6.43
Sprint Distance (m)	9	0.64
HML Distance (m)	248.7	17.76
Power Plays (HiActs)	14	1

Intensity Metrics	Practice Total	Per Min. of Work
Max Speed (m/s)	7.22	
Intensity (m/min)		99.45
Power Score (w/kg)	8.26	
No. of Max Accels >4m²	8	0.57
No. of Max Decels >4m²	8.38	0.6

* The data shows the physical output per player based on research from elite level teams - see **pages 81-83** for details

@SoccerTutor.com   Football Periodization to Maximise Performance

WEDNESDAY Practices: Speed Endurance - 3 Days Until Match (MD +4/-3)

LSG (Large Area) 3: Box to Box Area Tactical Game

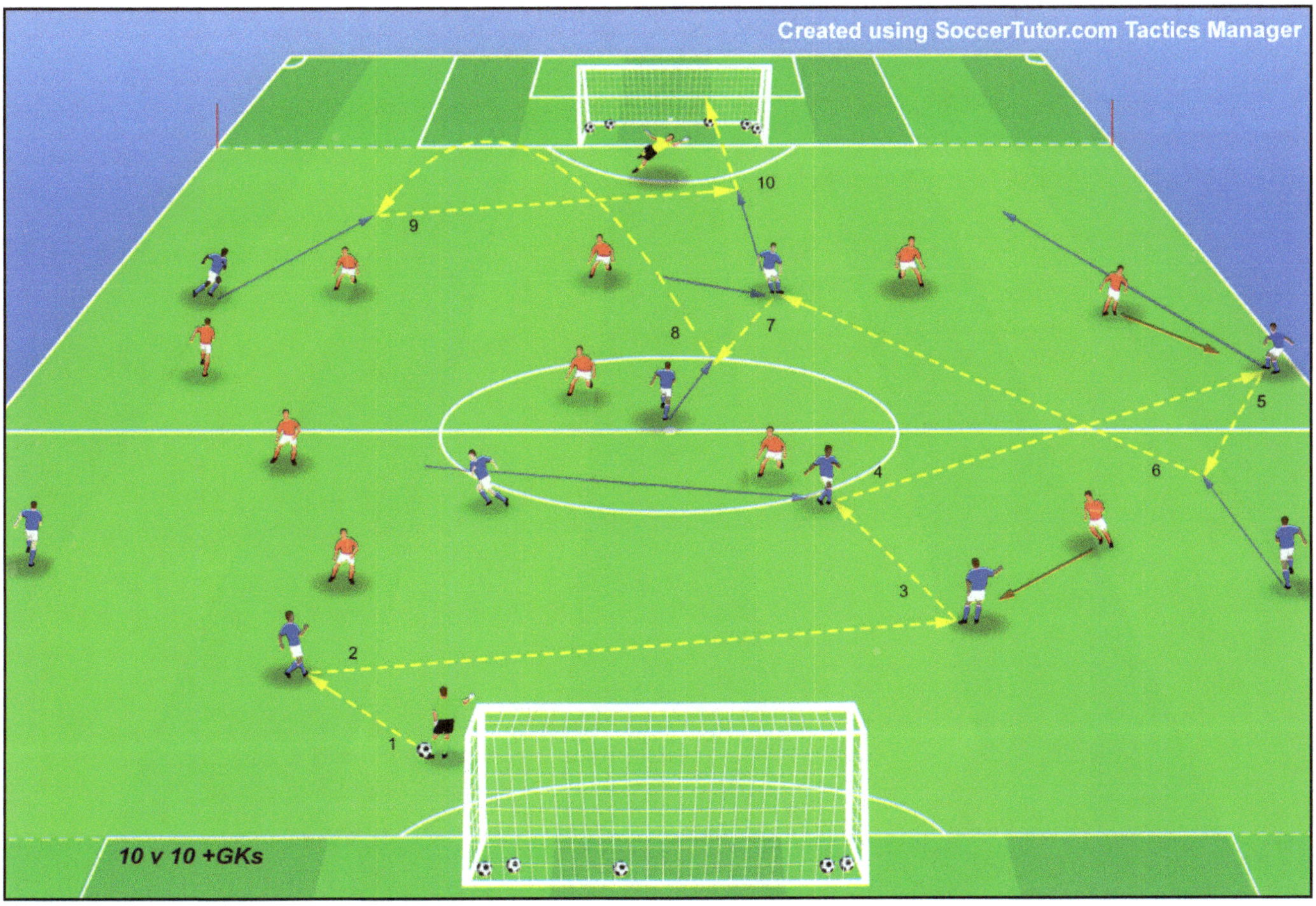

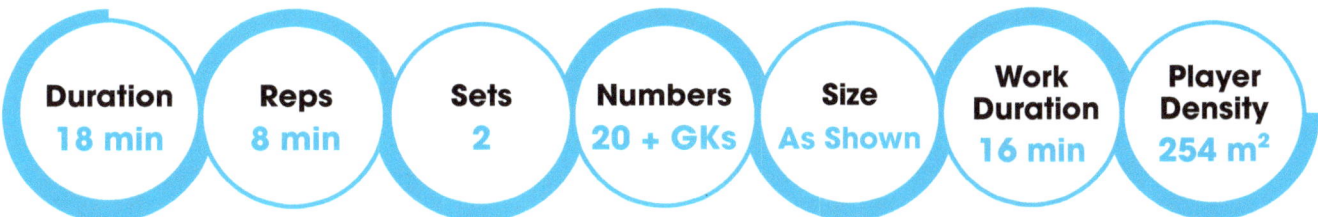

10 v 10 +GKs

PRACTICE INFORMATION

Duration	Reps	Sets	Numbers	Size	Work Duration	Player Density
18 min	8 min	2	20 + GKs	As Shown	16 min	254 m²

OBJECTIVE: Implement the game model and coaching strategy within 11v11 phase of training

Volume Metrics	Practice Total	Per Min. of Work
Total Distance (km)	2.384	0.15
High Speed Running (m)	141.6	8.85
Sprint Distance (m)	24.36	1.52
HML Distance (m)	352.62	22
Power Plays (HiActs)	17.42	1.09

Intensity Metrics	Practice Total	Per Min. of Work
Max Speed (m/s)	7.55	
Intensity (m/min)		109.62
Power Score (w/kg)	9.2	
No. of Max Accels >4m²	11.47	0.72
No. of Max Decels >4m²	10	0.63

* The data shows the physical output per player based on research from elite level teams - see **pages 81-83** for details

WEDNESDAY Practices: Speed Endurance - 3 Days Until Match (MD +4/-3)

LSG (Large Area) 4: Tactical Game Focus on a Full Pitch

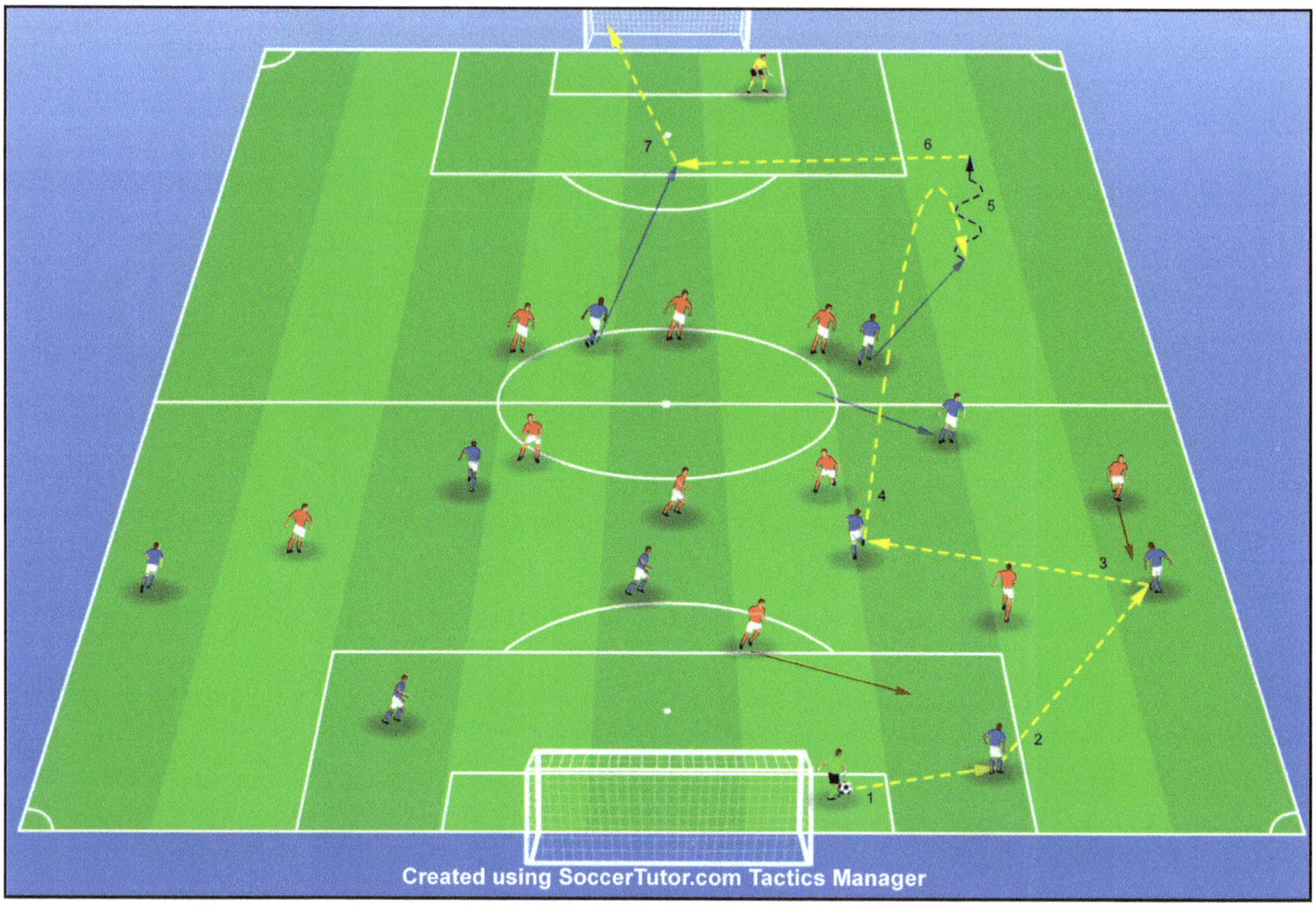

PRACTICE INFORMATION

Duration	Reps	Sets	Numbers	Size	Work Duration	Player Density
50 min	10 min	4	20 + GKs	Full Pitch	40 min	378 m²

OBJECTIVE: Implement the game model and coaching strategy within 11v11 phase of training

Volume Metrics	Practice Total	Per Min. of Work
Total Distance (km)	5.27	0.13
High Speed Running (m)	413.7	10.34
Sprint Distance (m)	100	2.5
HML Distance (m)	814.21	20.36
Power Plays (HiActs)	40.27	1

Intensity Metrics	Practice Total	Per Min. of Work
Max Speed (m/s)	8.18	
Intensity (m/min)		105.1
Power Score (w/kg)	8.66	
No. of Max Accels >4m²	16.7	0.42
No. of Max Decels >4m²	19.5	0.49

*The data shows the physical output per player based on research from elite level teams - see pages 81-83 for details

THURSDAY TRAINING DAY: REACTION SPEED

2 DAYS UNTIL MATCH (MD +5/-2)

THURSDAY Training Day: Reaction Speed - 2 Days Until Match (MD +5/-2)

2 DAYS UNTIL THE MATCH (MD +5/-2):
Unit Principle Training and Reaction Speed Development

Duration	45 min	70-75 min	85-95 min	60-70 min	45-60 min	90 min
Daily Theme	Recovery	Resistance	Speed Endurance	Reaction Speed	Activation	Match
Preparation	Match Day (MD) +2/-5	Match Day (MD) +3/-4	Match Day (MD) +4/-3	Match Day (MD) +5/-2	Match Day (MD) +6/-1	Match Day
		Positional Principles	Collective Principles	Unit Principles		
Game Type Focus	-	SSGs 1v1-4v4 (+GKs) Small Area	LSGs 8v8-10v10 (+GKs) Large Area	MSGs 5v5-7v7 (+GKs) Medium Area	LSGs 8v8-10v10 (+GKs) Small/Med Area	Match Day 11v11
Bout Durations	-	1-3 min	5-10 min	3-5 min	4 min	2 x 45 min
	Mon: Recovery	Tue-Wed: Conditioning		Thu-Fri: Preparation		Perform

* **Training Week based on Professional Microcycle Example** - see pages 74-75.

Key Focus on:
- **Unit Based Principles**
- **Near Maximum Acceleration Efforts**
- **Agility Based Content**

THURSDAY (MD +5/-2) TRAINING DAY:
Physical and Physiological Focus

This **Thursday (MD +5/-2) Training Day** is the first day of the "preparation" or "tapering" phase of the training week (microcycle) within this coaching philosophy. It is focused around the positional units (defence, midfield, attack) which engage players with short acceleration and agility based efforts.

The creation of practices situated around the **defence-midfield-attack units with acceleration based tactical repetitions is the main emphasis** placed on this training day within the microcycle. These **very short duration exercises will allow fast-cognitive reactive movements with large recovery periods** to ensure the opportunity for quality information and enhanced coaching blocks within the natural breaks of the practices. By ensuring the recovery is substantial in relation to the working periods, **coaches can maximise the learning whilst reducing the further risk of the build up of fatigue**.

Fatigue and Recovery

With respect to this training day within the weekly plan, it is vitally important to consider the recovery and restoration elements across all facets of player performance. As the competitive game is now within 48 hours and **this session is only 24 hours after two very physically and psychologically demanding training sessions** (Tuesday MD-4 and Wednesday MD-3 sessions), **accumulative fatigue** levels will have increased.

As a result of some in-house based monitoring and assessment, players reported significantly reduced energy levels and increased fatigue related results obtained from Ratings of Perceived Exertion (RPE) and wellness assessments pre-training on MD-2 during this methodology.

As a result, **drastically reducing the training volume and speed exposures in its totality is key**.

The Tapering Strategy

Key Point: With this tapering strategy on the MD +5/-2 training session, we enable a quality balance effect between fitness vs. freshness, whist focussing on training the "brain" rather than the "physicality."

Reducing the training volume of this session on this particular training day (MD-2) is seen as the key aim of this tapering strategy.

Based on this periodized approach described by Dr. Javier Mallo, the technical staff are able to **train the Unit Principles of the game at sectoral and individual levels**.

When integrating the science behind the concept, it is also accepted that in any tapering period, **anything between 40-60% reduction in volume is seen as advantageous to generate the required performance enhancement**. Although this is true from a volume perspective, in no way should the reduction of intensity or speed of movement in performing football activities be administered.

THURSDAY Training Day: Reaction Speed - 2 Days Until Match (MD +5/-2)

Reaction Speed and Transitional Game Focus (MSGs)

Physical and cognitive - acceleration focused	Reduced time >85% HRMax
High accelerations (limit eccentrics) - 20 metres work maximum	Lots of recovery between bouts or games
Larger numbered games	Players' awareness to quickly exploit or defend transitions
Tactical emphasis Manipulation of areas Large recovery coaching blocks	**Key Coaching Themes:** Short explosive acceleration emphasis (non-fatiguing), >recovery periods between work, limited HSR opportunity, key manipulation of training areas (small areas: MSGs)
Transition based games - react, accelerate	

Thursday (MD +5/-2) Training Day practices should:

- Have little or minimal opposition
- Be executed in reduced (medium sized density) spaces
- Be configured around "Unit Principles"
- Have short bout durations

With this session being at the start of the tapering phase of the microcycle, **a greater number of recovery intervals between practices are needed to assist players to recover adequately,** which results in the maximum relative intensity when performing the unit based content. This is a vitally important coaching tool to ensure players work with minimal overload or fatigue build up. To ensure more of an active recovery period after 2 previous days of conditioning work, the use of training that enables specific football movement patterns may link directly to an on-pitch tapering phase.

Inducing **too much training load within this particular training day will be difficult to eliminate 24-48 hours pre-match and cause an accumulative fatigue response for the players on match day.**

The benefits of starting the tapering on this day results in the restoration of biochemical, physical and psychological subjective assessment. This is key to starting the freshness and regeneration of the players 48 hours pre-match in this methodology, according to the testing and monitoring protocols involved.

Clemente et al., (2018) recommends **small, half-size pitch dimensions for lower-intensity, reduced muscle tension-based training sessions** and field exploration for players in different positions.

Owen et al., (2014) revealed how **MSGs induce more technical actions per player vs. LSGs but less physical output in terms of high speed running (HSR) and sprint demands**, which ensures players are having to react more to technical and tactical situations without increased physical overloads.

Session design in this phase of the microcycle is key to ensure the correct player density within the playing area, to enable a tactical focus (Owen et al., 2014).

THURSDAY Training Day: Reaction Speed - 2 Days Until Match (MD +5/-2)

THURSDAY (MD +5/-2) TRAINING DAY:
Technical and Tactical Focus

Within this training methodology from a technical-tactical perspective, the Thursday training day **MD +5/-2 focus is centralised around "Unit" principles** of the game.

This method tries to ensure all the "principles" are highlighted within different units (defence-midfield-attack), positional roles and tactical strategy, so that each unit understands and gains clarity on the key messages.

Whilst addressing the Unit Principles through **reactive agility-based specific content**, the key coaching principles can be achieved through splitting the group and working with greater detail in the key areas of the pitch to heighten the learning process and information provided.

The agility-based content can be induced in a variety of ways post-warm up, prior to entering the actual main focus of the unit based principles (e.g. midfield rotation, attacking the opponent's weak side area, distances between units, preventing penetrating passing, etc).

Medium Sided Games (MSGs)

The game stimulus around the **Unit Principles should revolve around medium sided-games (5v5 – 7v7 +GKs) where the playing density is slightly reduced to ensure minimal high speed running (HSR) or sprint exposures**. This is as a result of the previous two training days (Tuesday and Wednesday) "overloading" these mechanical movements.

All these principles will be constructed within a Unit based structure with key references highlighted in line with the tactical strategy employed moving into the upcoming match.

THURSDAY Training Day: Reaction Speed - 2 Days Until Match (MD +5/-2)

THURSDAY (MD +5/-2) TRAINING DAY:
Game Stimulus Response for Unit Principle Game Type

UNIT TRAINING PRINCIPLES

- **Unit Principles** (defence, midfield, or attack for individual focus)
- **Tactical Unit Principles** in medium density areas
- **Positional Technical Skills** in medium sized areas
- **Fast Reactive Situations** - attacking and defensive learning

THURSDAY (MD +5/-2) TRAINING DAY: Fundamental Concepts of Unit Principle Training and Reaction Speed Development

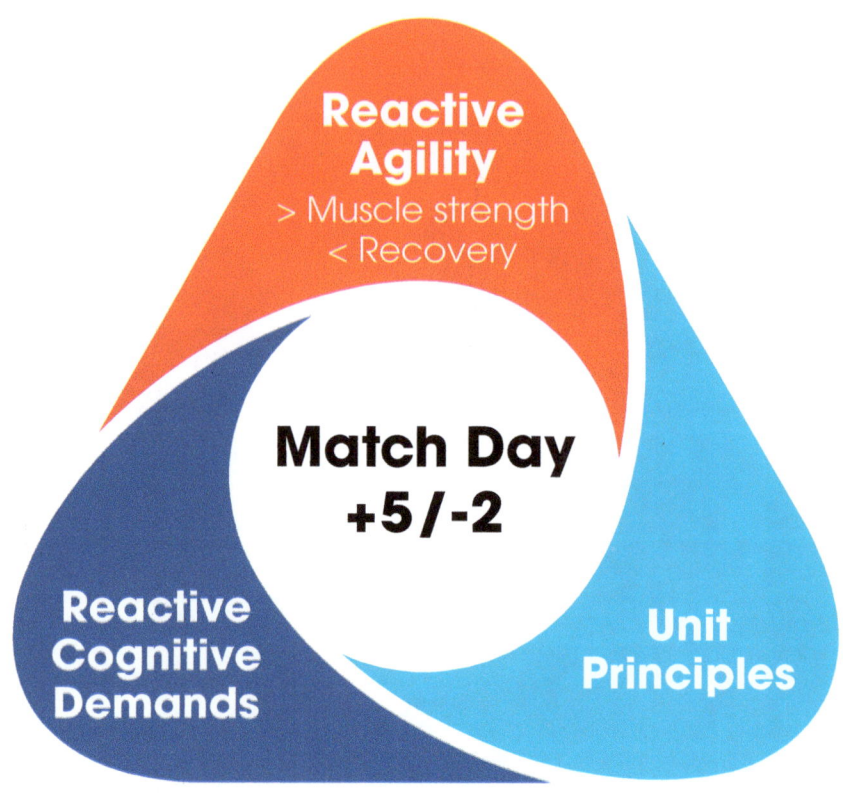

THURSDAY TRAINING DAY PRACTICES: REACTION SPEED

2 DAYS UNTIL MATCH (MD +5/-2)

THURSDAY TRAINING SESSION (60-70 min)

Unit Principle Training and Reaction Speed Development:

1. Reaction Speed Warm-up (5-7 min)
2. Intensive Technical Practice (10-15 min)
3. Reaction Speed Conditioning Practice (5-15 min)
4. Medium Sided Possession (6-15 min)
5. Medium Sided Game (10-25 min)

THURSDAY - 2 DAYS UNTIL MATCH (MD +5/-2):
Reaction Speed Warm-Up Practices

INTENSITY: All practices are performed at full intensity

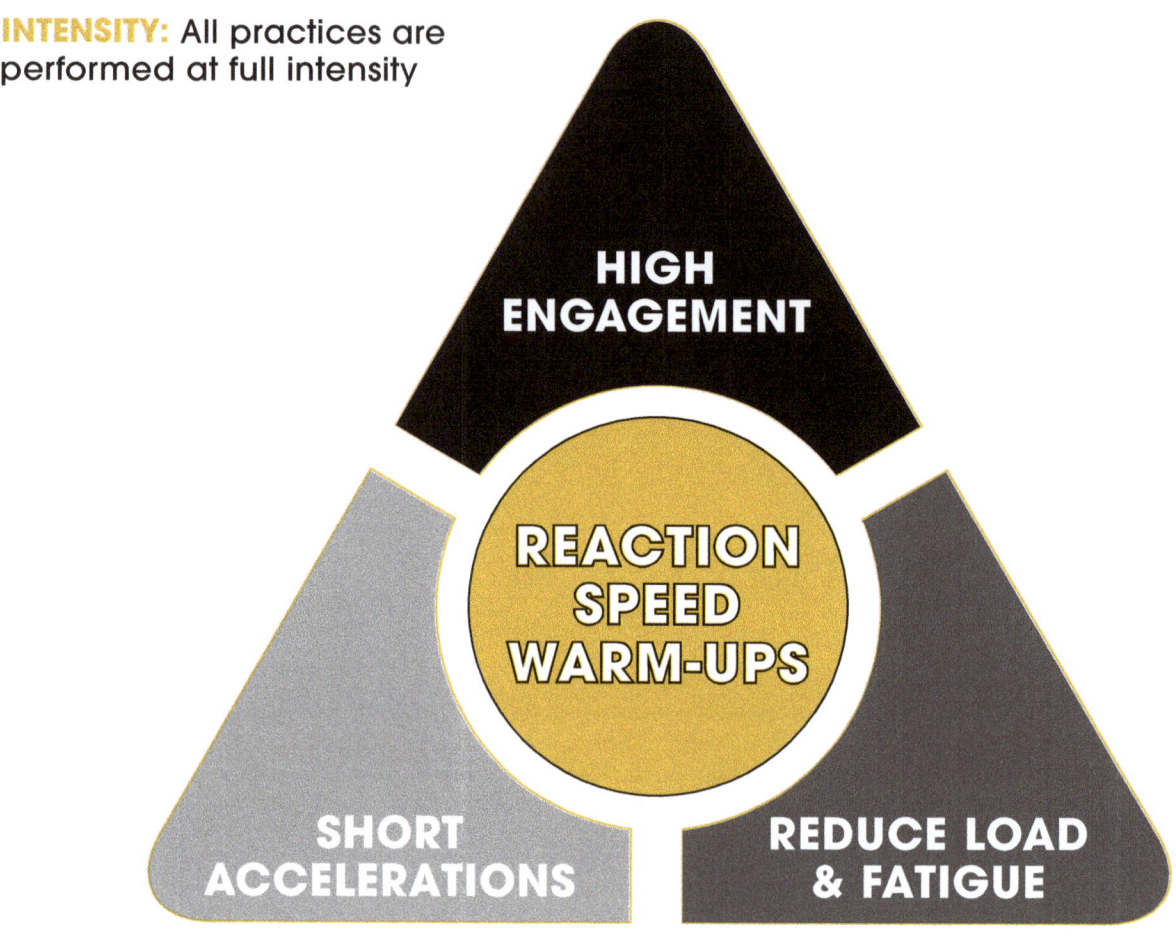

What are Reaction Speed Warm-ups?

- Inclusive of lots of reaction based work.
- The focus is to move quickly from a physical perspective but also react fast.
- Includes lots of shorter acceleration based work but reduced aggressive decelerations.

Why are they used on this day of the training week (MD +5/-2)?

- Reaction speed warm-ups are used around the MD +5/-2 training day where the key is to try and reduce fatigue in the players legs while remaining engaged to react quickly from a psychological perspective.

How does this help to maximise performance?

- Reaction speed warm-ups are used on this day as a way of reducing the load based on the previous two training days being of a higher training load volume.

THURSDAY Training Practices: Reaction Speed - 2 Days Until Match (MD +5/-2)

Reaction Speed Warm-up 1: Dead Leg & Lateral Runs, Rapid Feet, and Sprints Circuit

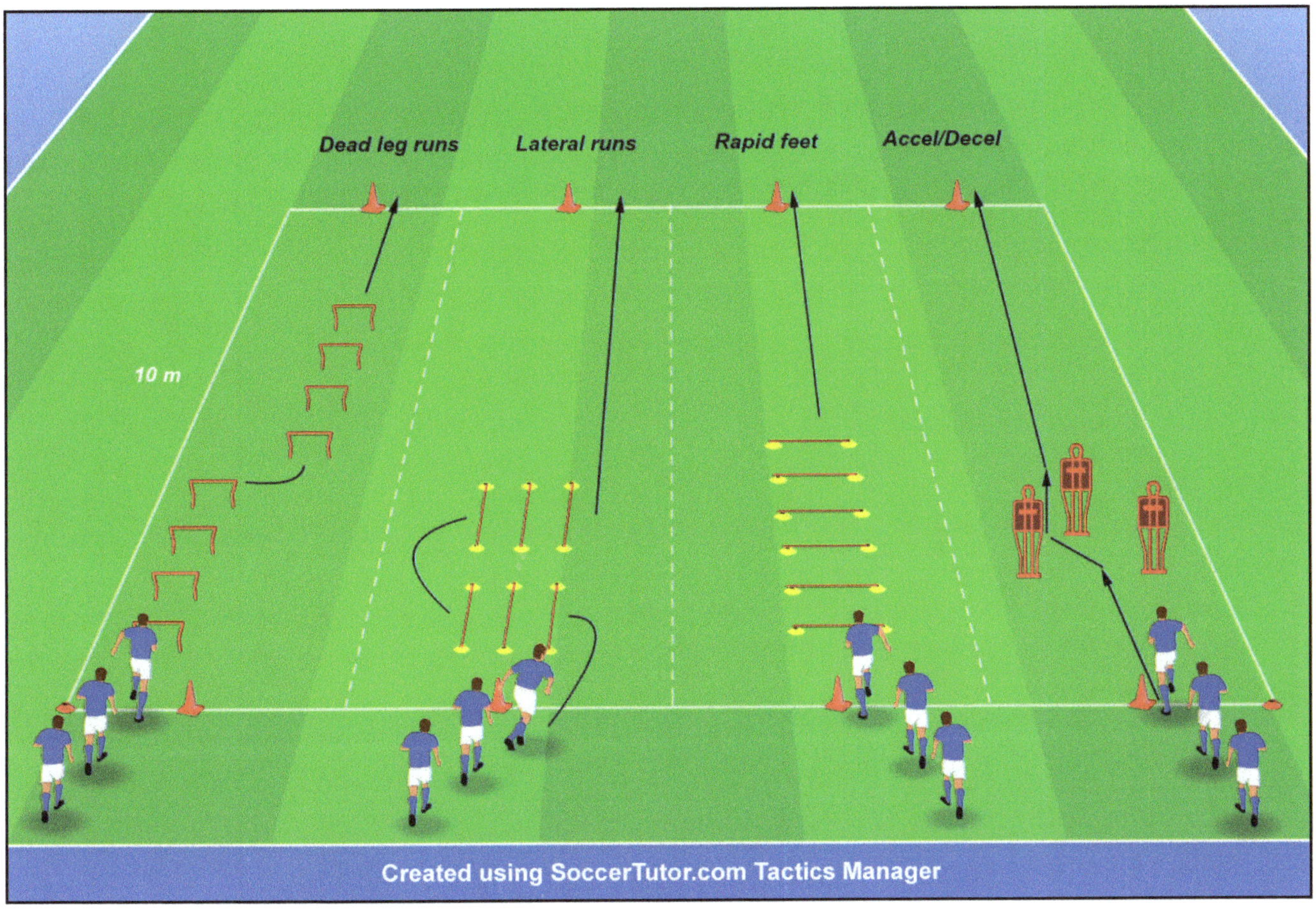

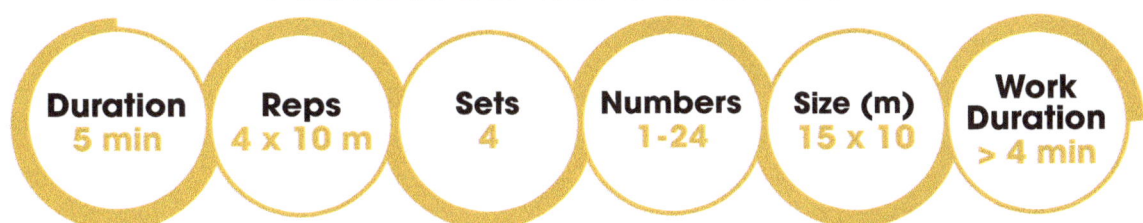

PRACTICE INFORMATION

- **Duration:** 5 min
- **Reps:** 4 x 10 m
- **Sets:** 4
- **Numbers:** 1-24
- **Size (m):** 15 x 10
- **Work Duration:** > 4 min

OBJECTIVE: Physically and mentally prepare the players for the training session (without the ball)

Volume Metrics	Practice Total	Per Min. of Work
Total Distance (km)	0.35	0.09
High Speed Running (m)	-	-
Sprint Distance (m)	-	-
Work Ratio (%)	57	
Power Plays (HiActs)	4	1

Intensity Metrics	Practice Total	Per Min. of Work
Max Speed (m/s)	5	
Intensity (m/min)		80
Power Score (w/kg)	4.44	
No. of Max Accels >4m²	4	1
No. of Max Decels >4m²	1	0.25

*The data shows the physical output per player based on research from elite level teams - see pages 81-83 for details

183

Football Periodization to Maximise Performance

THURSDAY Training Practices: Reaction Speed - 2 Days Until Match (MD +5/-2)

Reaction Speed Warm-up 2: React to Signal, Fast Feet, and Sprint in a Speed Exercise

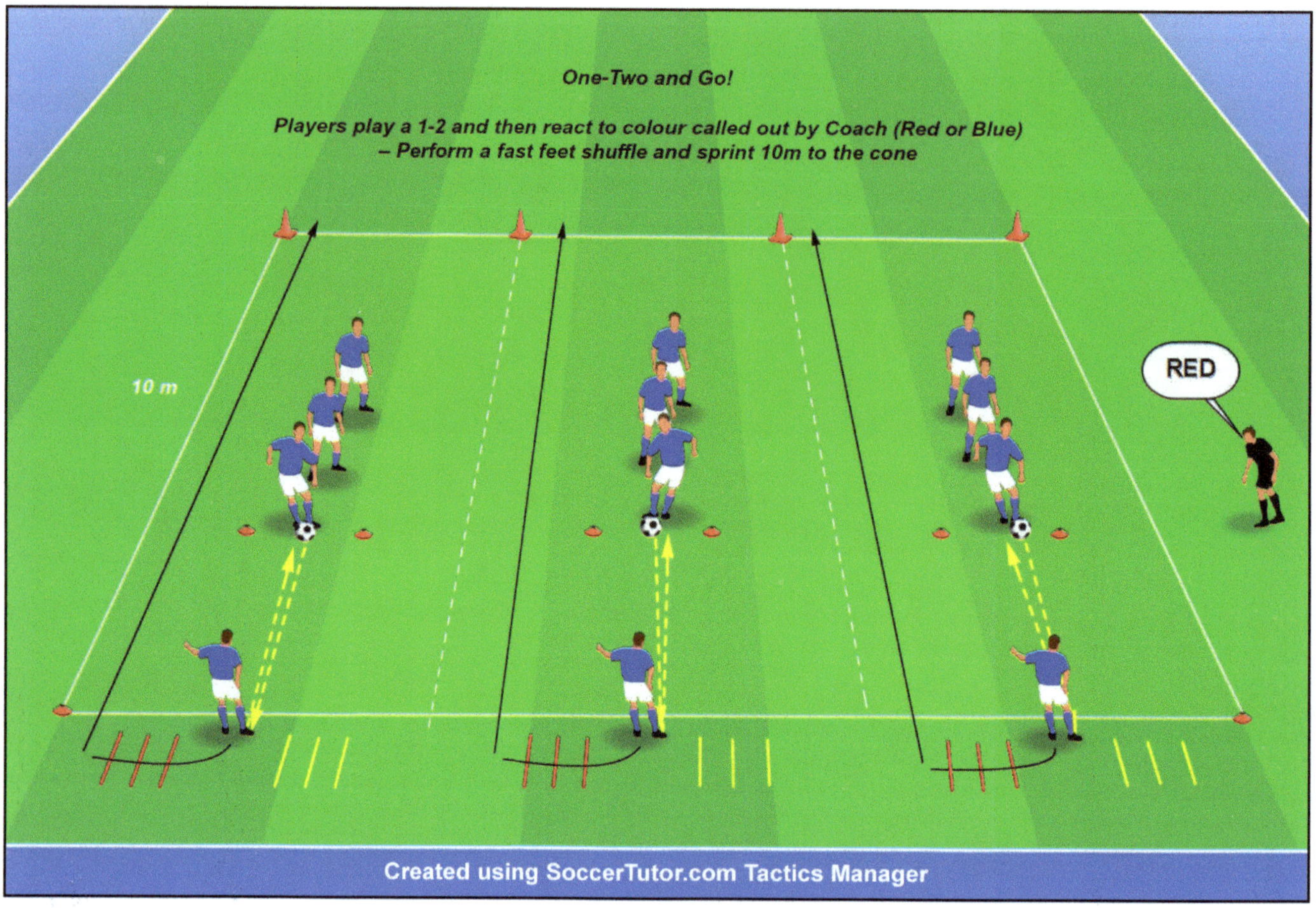

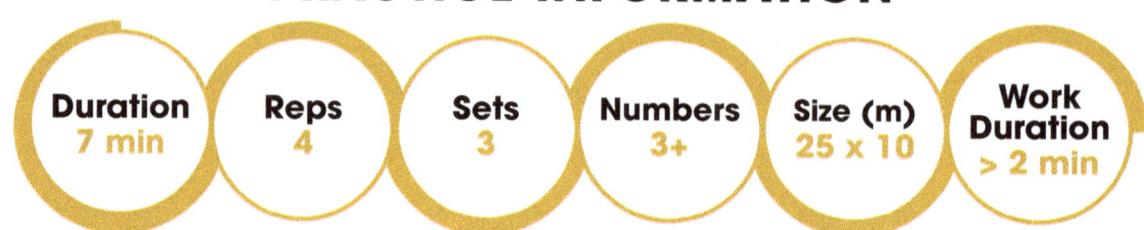

One-Two and Go!

Players play a 1-2 and then react to colour called out by Coach (Red or Blue) – Perform a fast feet shuffle and sprint 10m to the cone

PRACTICE INFORMATION

Duration	Reps	Sets	Numbers	Size (m)	Work Duration
7 min	4	3	3+	25 x 10	> 2 min

OBJECTIVE: Physically and mentally prepare the players for the training session (with the ball)

Volume Metrics	Practice Total	Per Min. of Work
Total Distance (km)	0.264	0.13
High Speed Running (m)	26	13
Sprint Distance (m)	4	2
HML Distance (m)	57	28.5
Power Plays (HiActs)	6	3

Intensity Metrics	Practice Total	Per Min. of Work
Max Speed (m/s)	6.66	
Intensity (m/min)		60
Power Score (w/kg)	4.44	
No. of Max Accels >4m²	3	1.5
No. of Max Decels >4m²	-	-

* The data shows the physical output per player based on research from elite level teams - **see pages 81-83** for details

Football Periodization to Maximise Performance

THURSDAY Training Practices: Reaction Speed - 2 Days Until Match (MD +5/-2)

THURSDAY - 2 DAYS UNTIL MATCH (MD +5/-2):
Intensive Technical Practices

INTENSITY: All practices are performed at full intensity

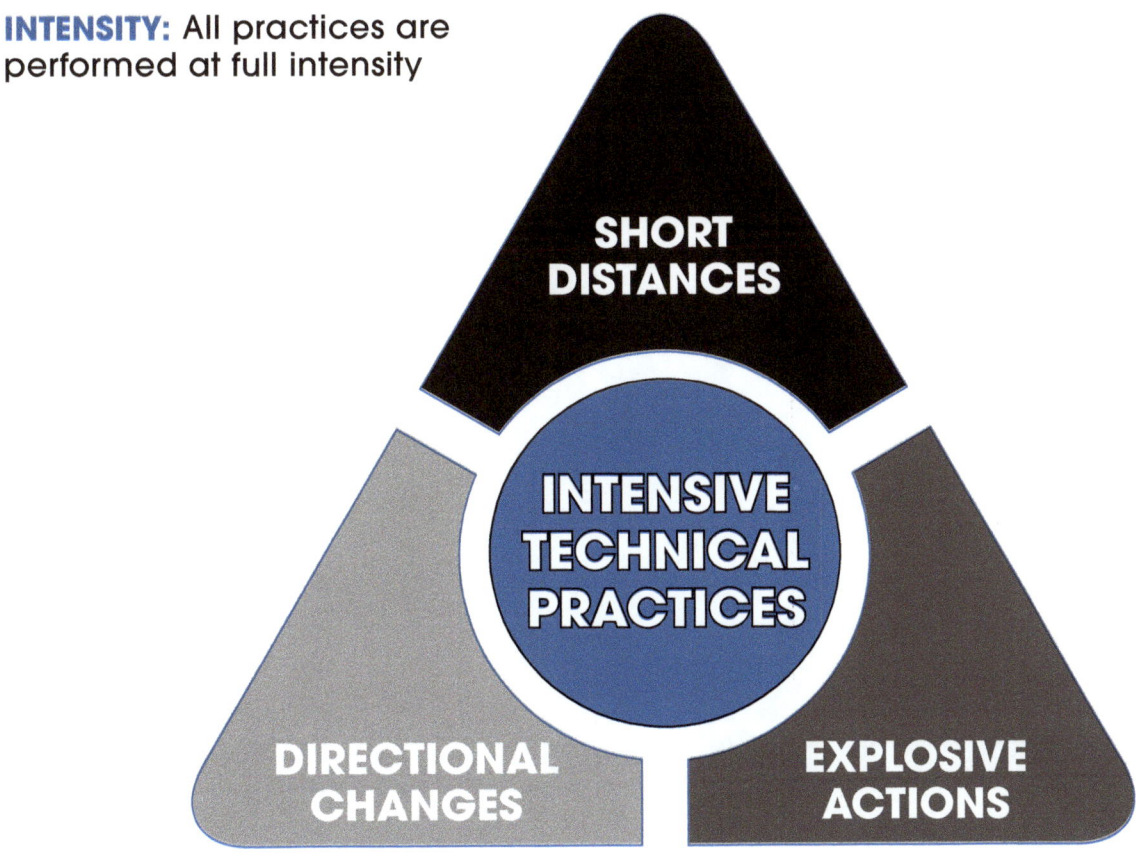

What are Intensive Technical Practices?

- Short passing distances (10-15 metres).
- These practice types include many lower level accelerations and decelerations in tight spaces to activate the muscle groups for the explosive maximum accelerations and decelerations later in the session.
- Focused and in-keeping with the flow of the session and working muscle groups on this particular training day (MD +5/-2).

Why are they used on this day of the training week (MD +5/-2)?

- To prepare the players for the smaller surface area type work developed through the course of the session.

How does this help to maximise performance?

- These intensive technical practices are used on this training day as a way of preparing the players' muscles used for changing direction, acceleration and deceleration efforts, and generally readying the body for the session ahead (small sided games).

NOTE: There are 5 more Intensive Technical Practices you can use from the **Tuesday Training Day (pages - 100-104)** - this section starts from Practice No.6...

THURSDAY Training Practices: Reaction Speed - 2 Days Until Match (MD +5/-2)

Intensive Technical 6: One-Two Combinations and Timing of Third Man Run

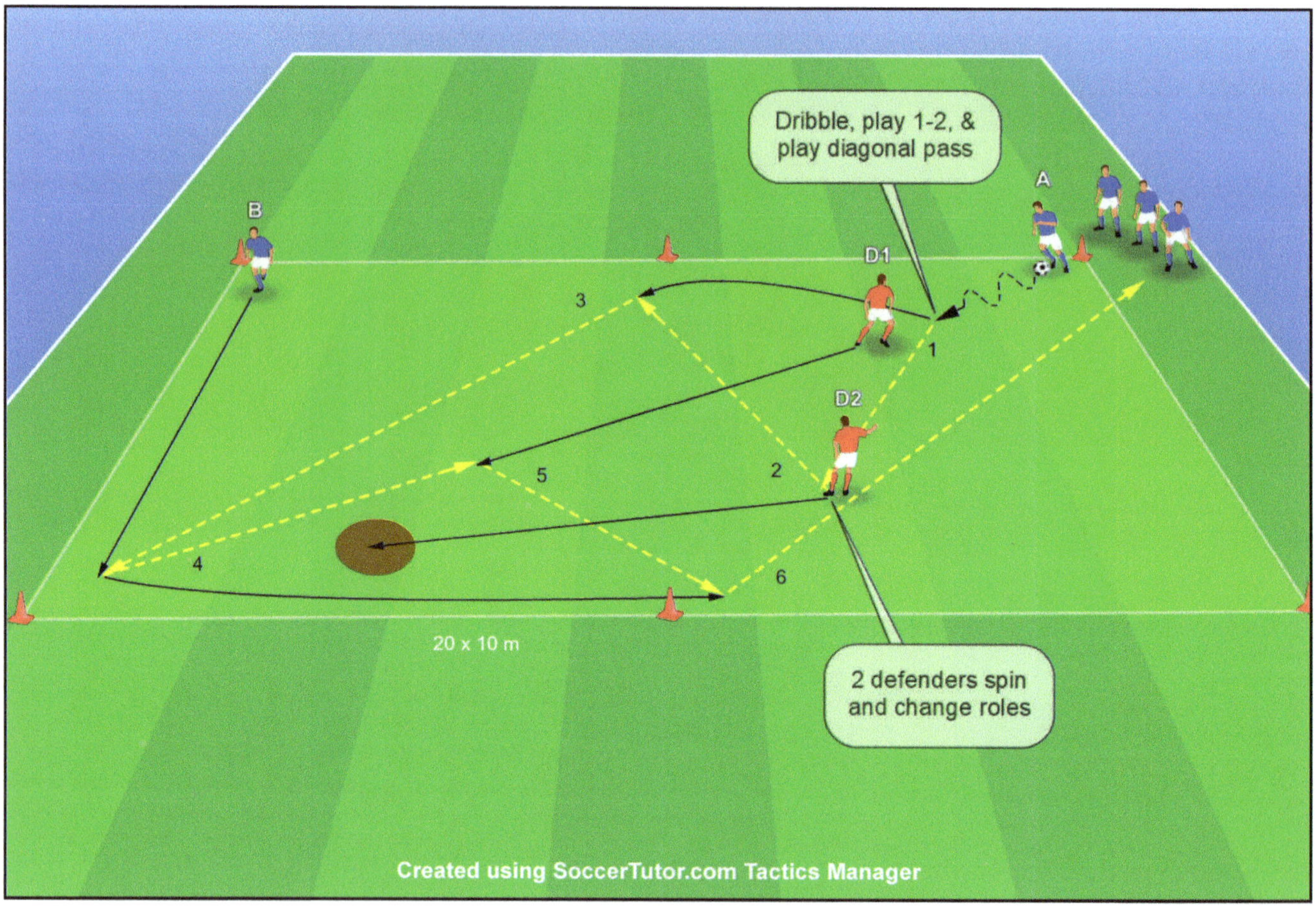

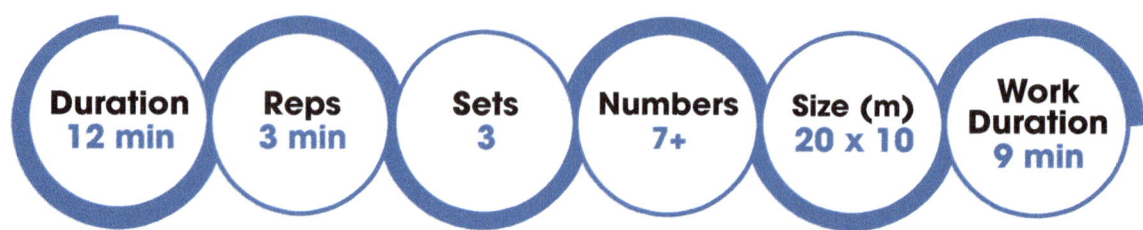

PRACTICE INFORMATION

Duration	Reps	Sets	Numbers	Size (m)	Work Duration
12 min	3 min	3	7+	20 x 10	9 min

PRACTICE OBJECTIVES: Ball speed (correct weight), timing of run, pass placement

Volume Metrics	Practice Total	Per Min. of Work
Total Distance (km)	0.24	0.027
High Speed Running (m)	22.6	2.5
Sprint Distance (m)	-	-
Work Ratio (%)	22.23	
Power Plays (HiActs)	10	1.1

Intensity Metrics	Practice Total	Per Min. of Work
Max Speed (m/s)	5.94	
Intensity (m/min)		60.63
Power Score (w/kg)	5.17	
Max Accel. Distance (m)	17.16	1.9
Max Decel. Distance (m)	12.92	1.44

* The data shows the physical output per player based on research from elite level teams - see **pages 81-83** for details

THURSDAY Training Practices: Reaction Speed - 2 Days Until Match (MD +5/-2)

Intensive Technical 7: Double "Give & Go" + Sprint Forward for Through Pass in a Diamond

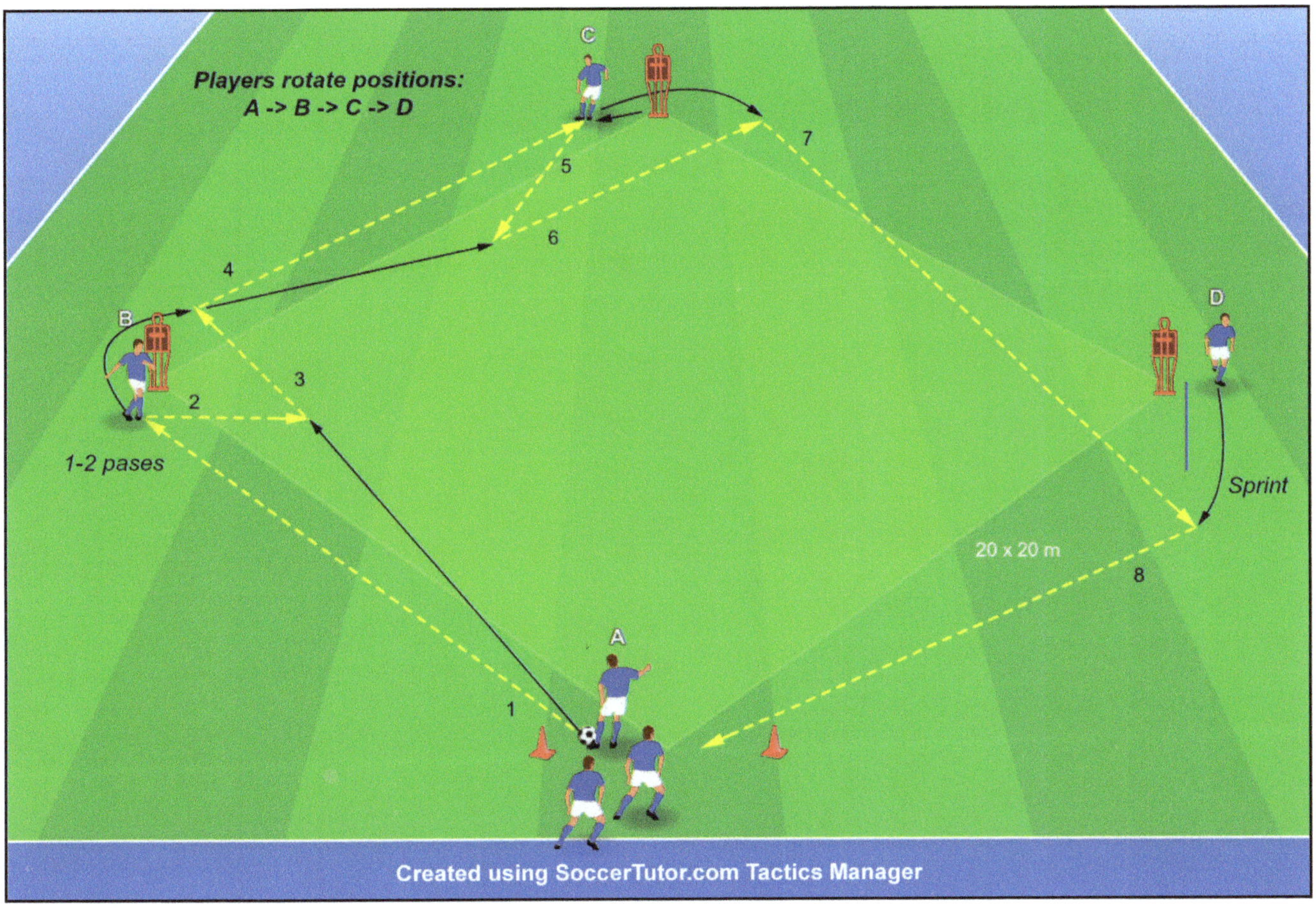

Players rotate positions: A -> B -> C -> D

1-2 pases

Sprint

20 x 20 m

Created using SoccerTutor.com Tactics Manager

PRACTICE INFORMATION

Duration	Reps	Sets	Numbers	Size (m)	Work Duration
10 min	2 min	4	6-8	20 x 20	8 min

PRACTICE OBJECTIVES: Ball speed (correct weight), timing of run, pass placement

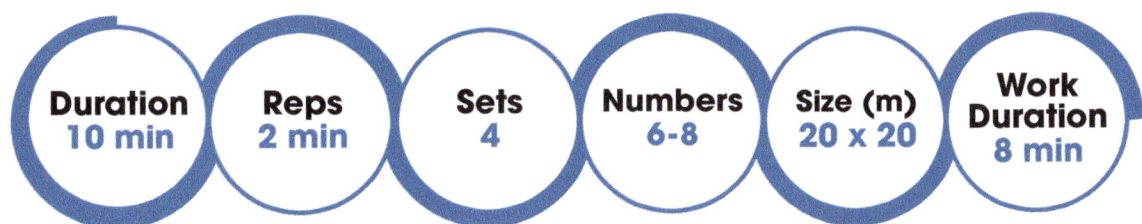

Volume Metrics	Practice Total	Per Min. of Work
Total Distance (km)	0.7	0.09
High Speed Running (m)	0.37	0.05
Sprint Distance (m)	-	-
Work Ratio (%)	45.5	
Power Plays (HiActs)	0.61	0.08

Intensity Metrics	Practice Total	Per Min. of Work
Max Speed (m/s)	4.50	
Intensity (m/min)		66.24
Power Score (w/kg)	5.48	
No. of Max Accels >4m²	3.2	0.4
No. of Max Decels >4m²	6.6	0.83

* The data shows the physical output per player based on research from elite level teams - see pages 81-83 for details

@SoccerTutor.com Football Periodization to Maximise Performance

REFERENCE   @adamowen1980

THURSDAY Training Practices: Reaction Speed - 2 Days Until Match (MD +5/-2)

Intensive Technical 8: Short Combinations with Lay-offs in an End to End Pass & Move Drill

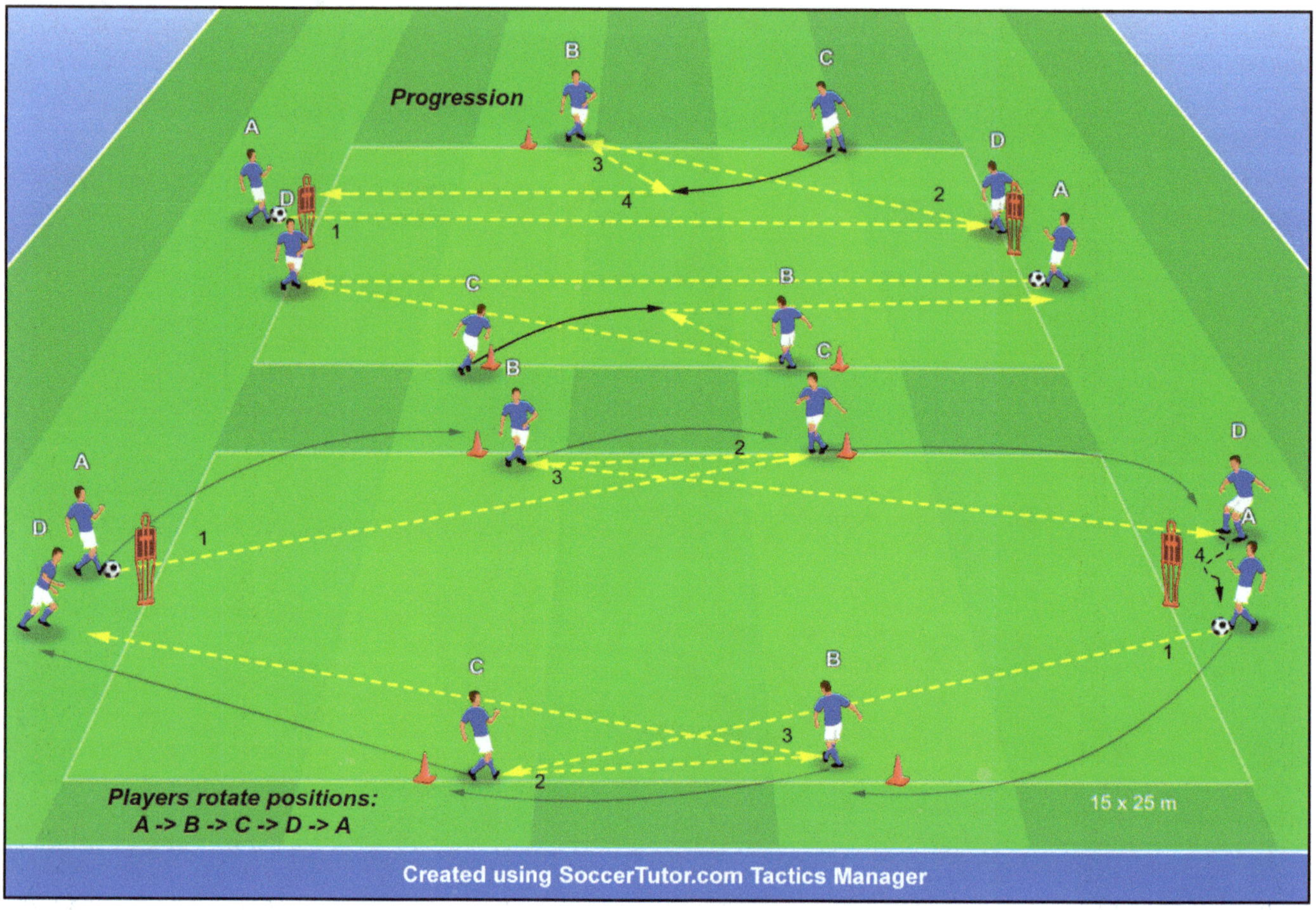

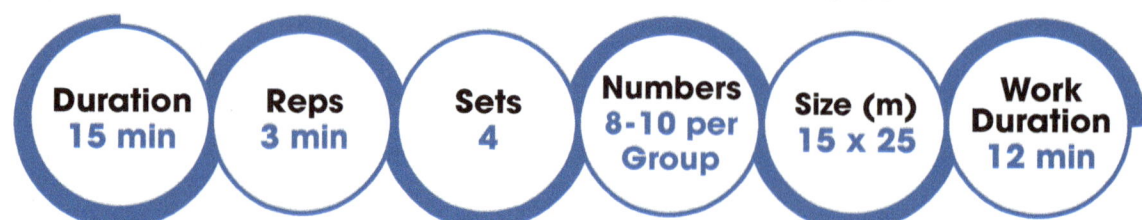

Players rotate positions:
A -> B -> C -> D -> A

15 x 25 m

PRACTICE INFORMATION

Duration	Reps	Sets	Numbers	Size (m)	Work Duration
15 min	3 min	4	8-10 per Group	15 x 25	12 min

PRACTICE OBJECTIVES (2 BALLS): Ball speed (correct weight), timing of run, pass placement

Volume Metrics	Practice Total	Per Min. of Work
Total Distance (km)	1.178	0.1
High Speed Running (m)	0.38	0.03
Sprint Distance (m)	-	-
Work Ratio (%)	34.93	
Power Plays (HiActs)	0.5	0.04

Intensity Metrics	Practice Total	Per Min. of Work
Max Speed (m/s)	4.74	
Intensity (m/min)		75.5
Power Score (w/kg)	6.05	
No. of Max Accels >4m²	8	0.67
No. of Max Decels >4m²	3	0.25

* The data shows the physical output per player based on research from elite level teams - see **pages 81-83** for details

Football Periodization to Maximise Performance

THURSDAY Training Practices: Reaction Speed - 2 Days Until Match (MD +5/-2)

Intensive Technical 9: Breaking the Lines in a Continuous End to End Pass & Move Drill

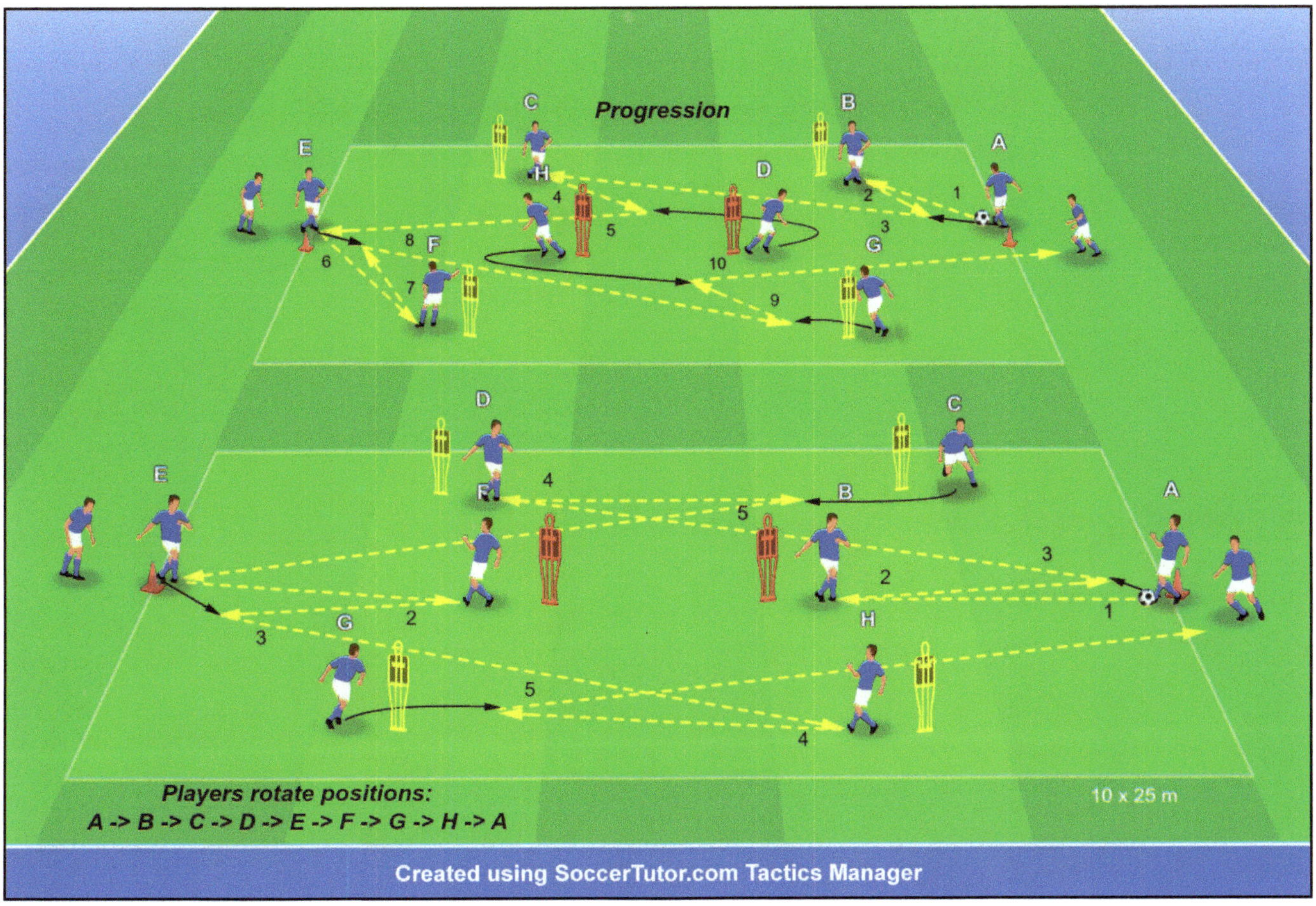

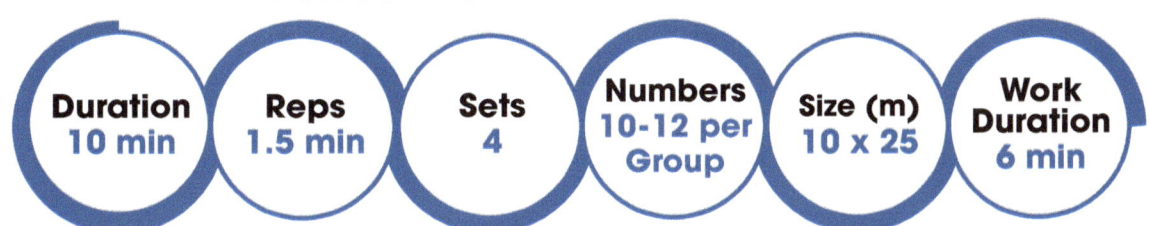

Players rotate positions:
A -> B -> C -> D -> E -> F -> G -> H -> A

10 x 25 m

Created using SoccerTutor.com Tactics Manager

PRACTICE INFORMATION

Duration	Reps	Sets	Numbers	Size (m)	Work Duration
10 min	1.5 min	4	10-12 per Group	10 x 25	6 min

PRACTICE OBJECTIVES: Ball speed (correct weight), timing of run, pass placement

Volume Metrics	Practice Total	Per Min. of Work
Total Distance (km)	0.69	0.12
High Speed Running (m)	0.03	0.005
Sprint Distance (m)	-	-
Work Ratio (%)	48.22	
Power Plays (HiActs)	-	-

Intensity Metrics	Practice Total	Per Min. of Work
Max Speed (m/s)	4.17	
Intensity (m/min)		79.46
Power Score (w/kg)	6.47	
No. of Max Accels >4m²	5.6	0.93
No. of Max Decels >4m²	2.7	0.45

* The data shows the physical output per player based on research from elite level teams - see **pages 81-83** for details

189

Football Periodization to Maximise Performance

THURSDAY Training Practices: Reaction Speed - 2 Days Until Match (MD +5/-2)

Intensive Technical 10: Incisive Diagonal Passing Circuit with Pattern Variations

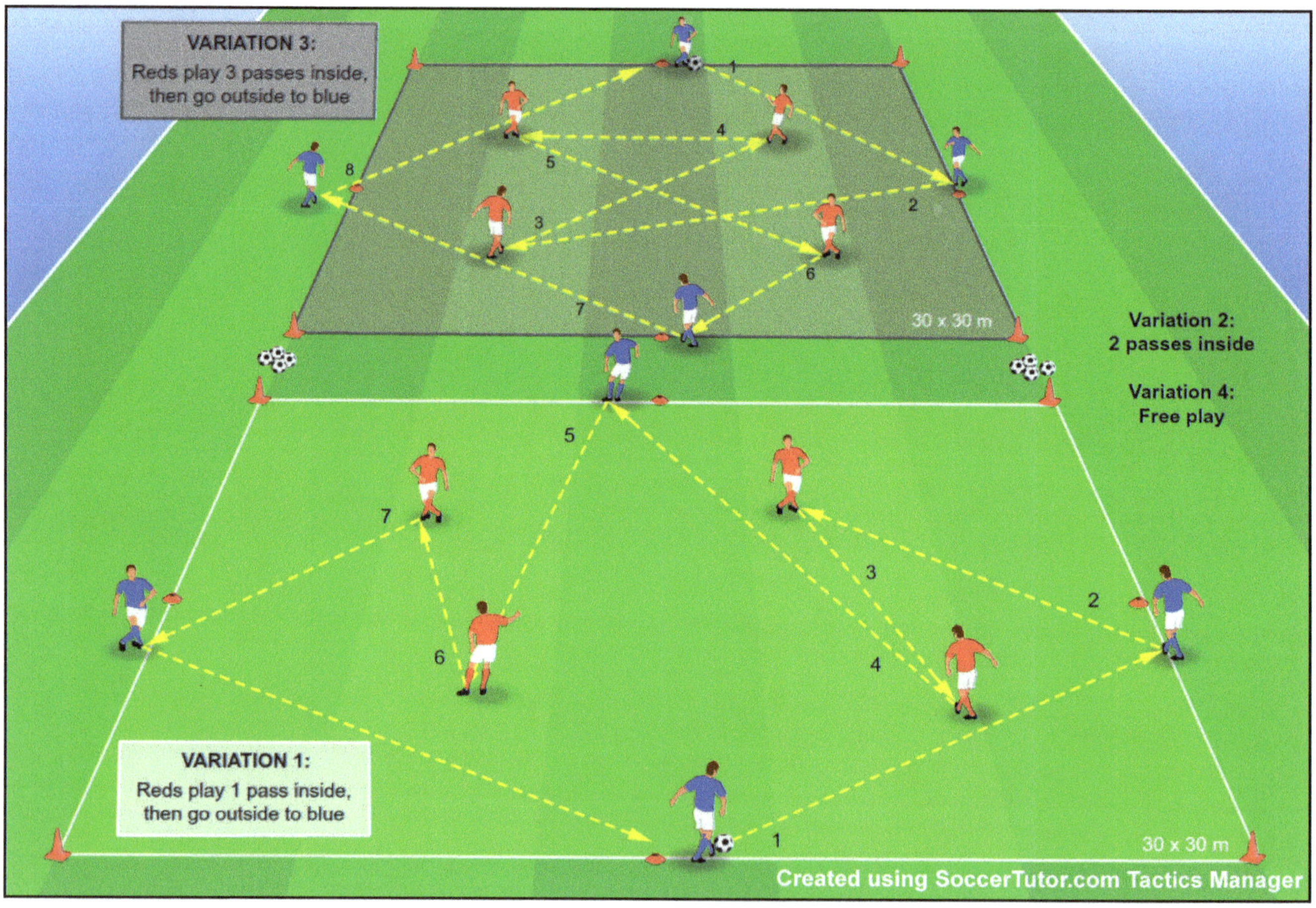

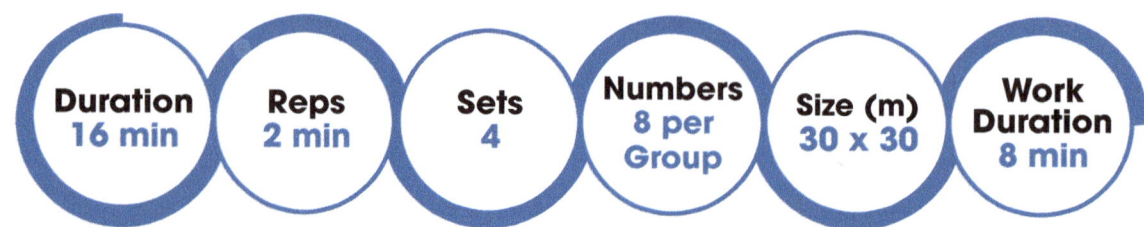

PRACTICE INFORMATION

Duration	Reps	Sets	Numbers	Size (m)	Work Duration
16 min	2 min	4	8 per Group	30 x 30	8 min

PRACTICE OBJECTIVES: Technical and tactical training, positional roles, and rotations

Volume Metrics	Practice Total	Per Min. of Work
Total Distance (km)	0.96	0.12
High Speed Running (m)	-	-
Sprint Distance (m)	-	-
Work Ratio (%)	38.6	
Power Plays (HiActs)	0.1	0.013

Intensity Metrics	Practice Total	Per Min. of Work
Max Speed (m/s)	4.25	
Intensity (m/min)		54.55
Power Score (w/kg)	4.16	
No. of Max Accels >4m²	2.2	0.28
No. of Max Decels >4m²	0.55	0.07

The data shows the physical output per player based on research from elite level teams - see pages 81-83 for details

@SoccerTutor.com — Football Periodization to Maximise Performance

THURSDAY - 2 DAYS UNTIL MATCH (MD +5/-2):
Reaction Speed Conditioning Practices

INTENSITY: All practices are performed at full intensity

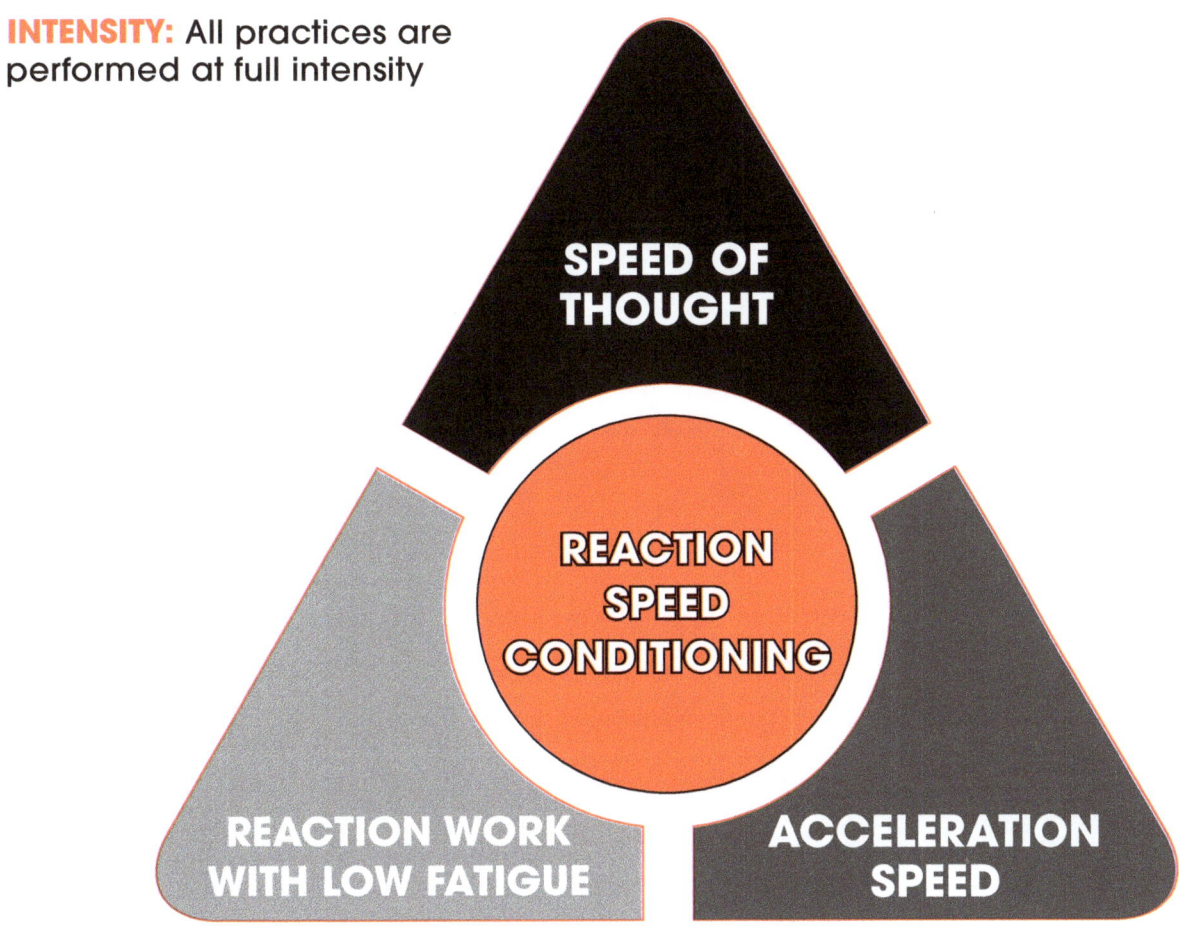

What are Reaction Speed Conditioning Practices?

- Inclusive of lots of reaction based work.
- The focus is to move quickly from a physical perspective but also react fast.
- Lots of shorter acceleration based work but reduced aggressive decelerations.

Why are they used on this day of the training week (MD +5/-2)?

- Key = reduce the fatigue in the players legs.
- Remain engaged for fast reactions from a psychological and acceleration/speed perspective.

How does this help to maximise performance?

- Reaction speed conditioning practices engage players from a cognitive perspective and stimulate fast movements without adding additional fatigue.

THURSDAY Training Practices: Reaction Speed - 2 Days Until Match (MD +5/-2)

Reaction Speed Conditioning 1: Quick Reactions to Signals + Race to the Pole

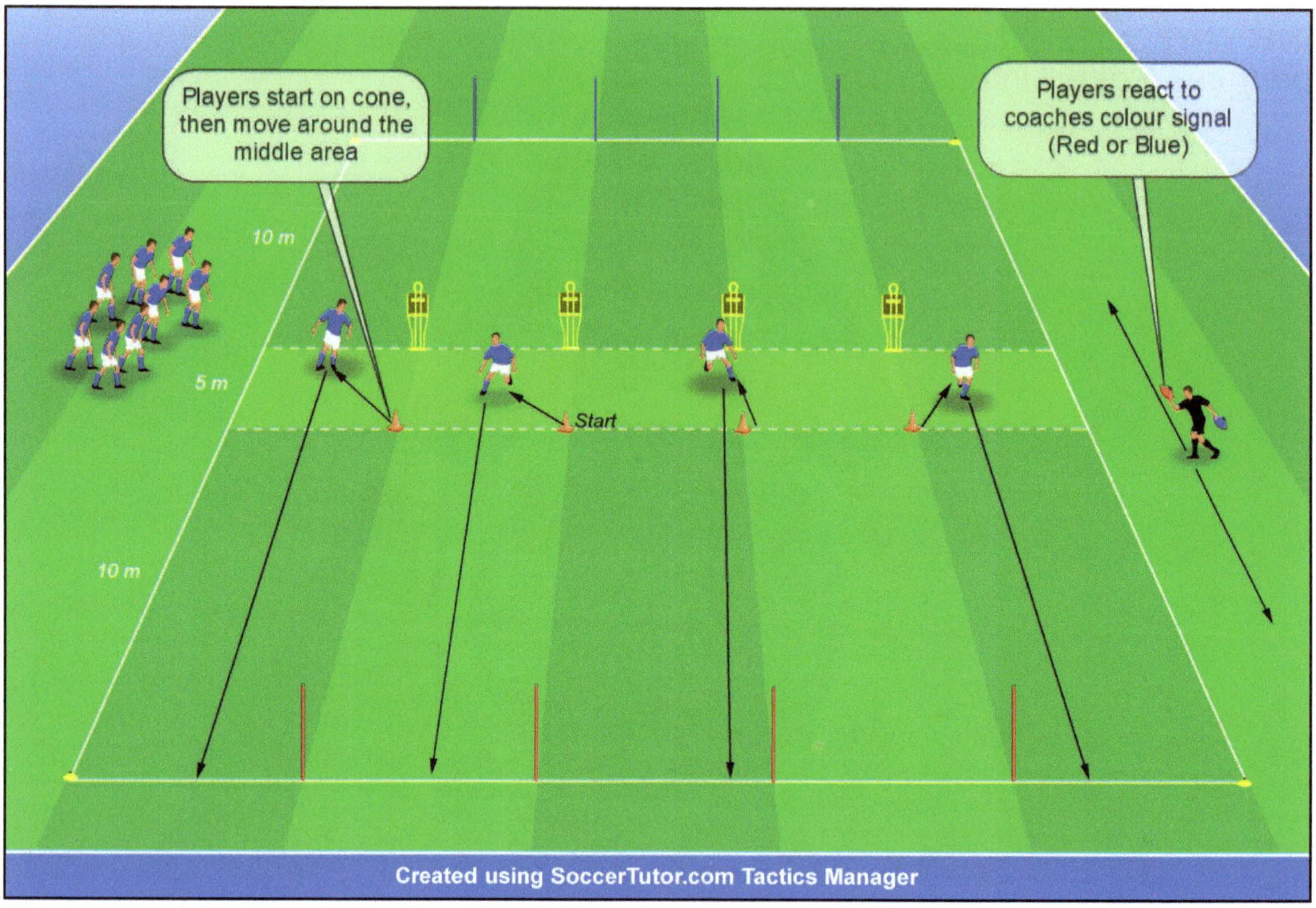

PRACTICE INFORMATION

- **Duration:** 5 min
- **Reps:** 4 x 10 m
- **Sets:** 1
- **Numbers:** 4 per Group
- **Size (m):** 15 x 25
- **Work Duration:** 10 sec
- **Reaction Day**

OBJECTIVES: Stimulate and provide players with reactive based accelerations over a short distance

Volume Metrics	Practice Total	Per Min. of Work
Total Distance (km)	0.35	2.1
High Speed Running (m)	50.57	303.4
Sprint Distance (m)	5	30
Work Ratio (%)	10.16	
Power Plays (HiActs)	5	30

Intensity Metrics	Practice Total	Per Min. of Work
Max Speed (m/s)	6.96	
Intensity (m/min)		41.75
Power Score (w/kg)	3.7	
No. of Max Accels >4m²	7.22	43.32
No. of Max Decels >4m²	1.16	6.96

* The data shows the physical output per player based on research from elite level teams - see **pages 81-83** for details

THURSDAY Training Practices: Reaction Speed - 2 Days Until Match (MD +5/-2)

Reaction Speed Conditioning 2: Agility Work with Hurdles + React and Race to the Cone

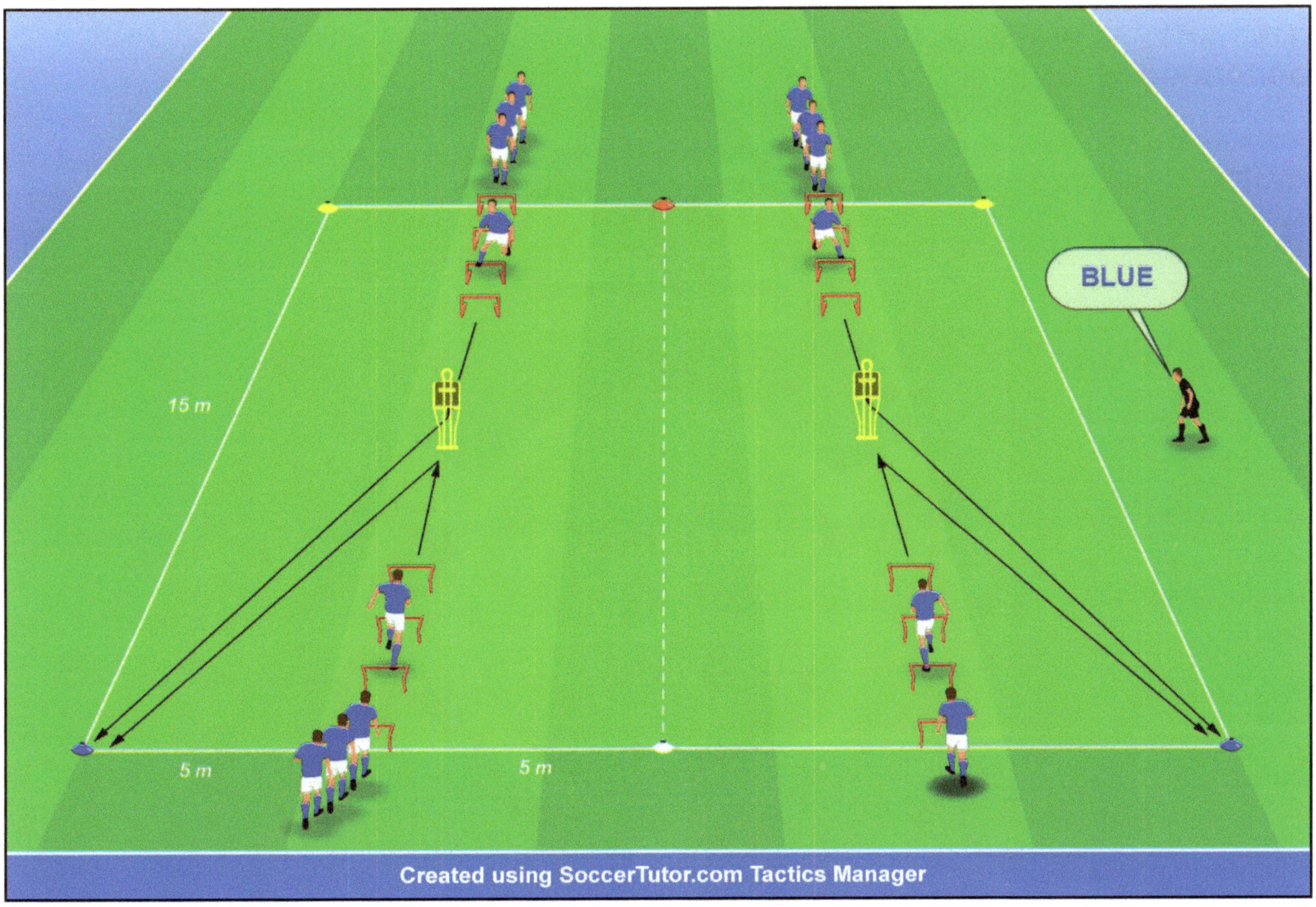

PRACTICE INFORMATION

- **Duration:** 5 min
- **Reps:** 2
- **Sets:** 4
- **Numbers:** 2-10 per Group
- **Size (m):** 20 x 15
- **Work Duration:** 40 sec
- **Reaction Day**

OBJECTIVES: Stimulate and provide players with reactive based accelerations over a short distance

Volume Metrics	Practice Total	Per Min. of Work
Total Distance (km)	0.314	0.47
High Speed Running (m)	4.78	7.17
Sprint Distance (m)	2	3
Work Ratio (%)	16.82	
Power Plays (HiActs)	1.46	2.19

Intensity Metrics	Practice Total	Per Min. of Work
Max Speed (m/s)	5.38	
Intensity (m/min)		54.98
Power Score (w/kg)	5.49	
Max Accel. Distance (m)	4	6
Max Decel. Distance (m)	4	6

* The data shows the physical output per player based on research from elite level teams - see **pages 81-83** for details

Football Periodization to Maximise Performance

THURSDAY Training Practices: Reaction Speed - 2 Days Until Match (MD +5/-2)

THURSDAY - 2 DAYS UNTIL MATCH (MD +5/-2):
Medium Sided Possession Practices

INTENSITY: All practices are performed at full intensity

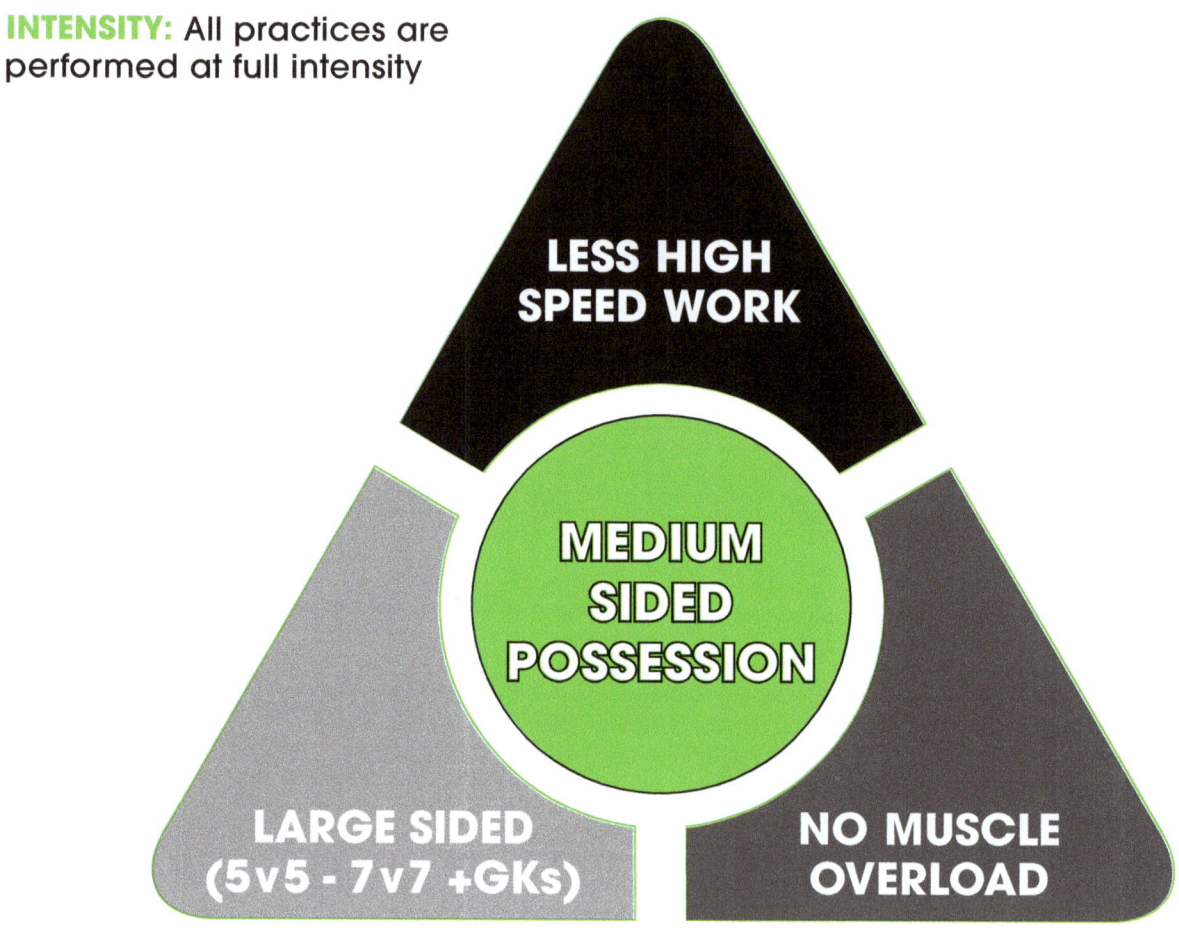

What are Medium Sided Possession Practices?

- Medium sided possession games are defined as including 5 to 7 outfield players per side = 5v5 - 7v7 (+GKs).

Why are they used on this day of the training week (MD +5/-2)?

- They can be used in different periods of the training week but within this framework, they are focused around this training days with medium sized playing areas to train the unit principles (defence-midfield-attack).

- Medium sized areas are used to focus on specific areas of the pitch.

- Medium sided possession games are performed in this part of the training week to ensure specific muscle groups are not overloaded.

How does this help to maximise performance?

- Reduced high-speed running and sprint distance vs. larger game types.

- Expose players to reduced cardiovascular loads when compared to small sided possession games, due to a reduced intensity.

SMALL VS. LARGE AREA POSSESSION COMPARISON

Small Area vs. Large Area Possession Games (based on 5 min periods)

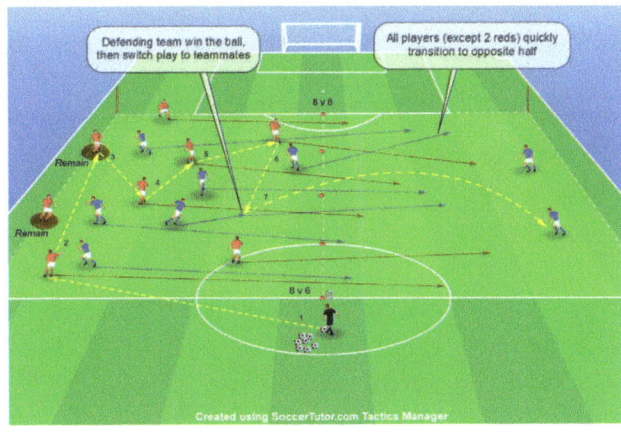

Small Area (SA)

- ⬆ **Speed of Thought** - closer pressure from opponents
- ⬆ **Cardiovascular Load** - higher heart rate response
- ⬆ **Lower Body Strength Work** - change of directions
- ⬆ **Technical Demand per Player** - touches
- ⬇ **Sprint Distance** - reduced area
- ⬇ **Tactical Focus**

Large Area (LA)

- ⬆ **Position Specific** - tactical focus of roles and responsibilities
- ⬆ **Sprint and High Speed Runs** - larger area size
- ⬇ **Cardiovascular Load** - less pressure
- ⬇ **Technical Demand per Player** - > numbers
- ● **Acts as Injury Prevention** - 'hamstring' primer

SA	Variable	LA
620m	Total Distance	720m
60	Speed of Play (m.min)	122
1.67m	High Speed Distance	20m
0m	Sprint Distance	1m
45 sec	Time @ >85% HRmax	2.15 min

SA	Variable	LA
220	Passes	97
25	Interceptions	10
0	Dribbles	9
0	Headers	2
36	Average Touches	18

Football Periodization to Maximise Performance

REFERENCE Dellal A et al (2012). Hum Mov Sci. Aug; 31 (4): 957-69. / Owen AL et al (2011). J Strength Cond. Aug; 25(8): 2104-10.

THURSDAY Training Practices: Reaction Speed - 2 Days Until Match (MD +5/-2)

Medium Possession 1: Creating Space in a 5v5 Game with "No-Go" Middle Circle

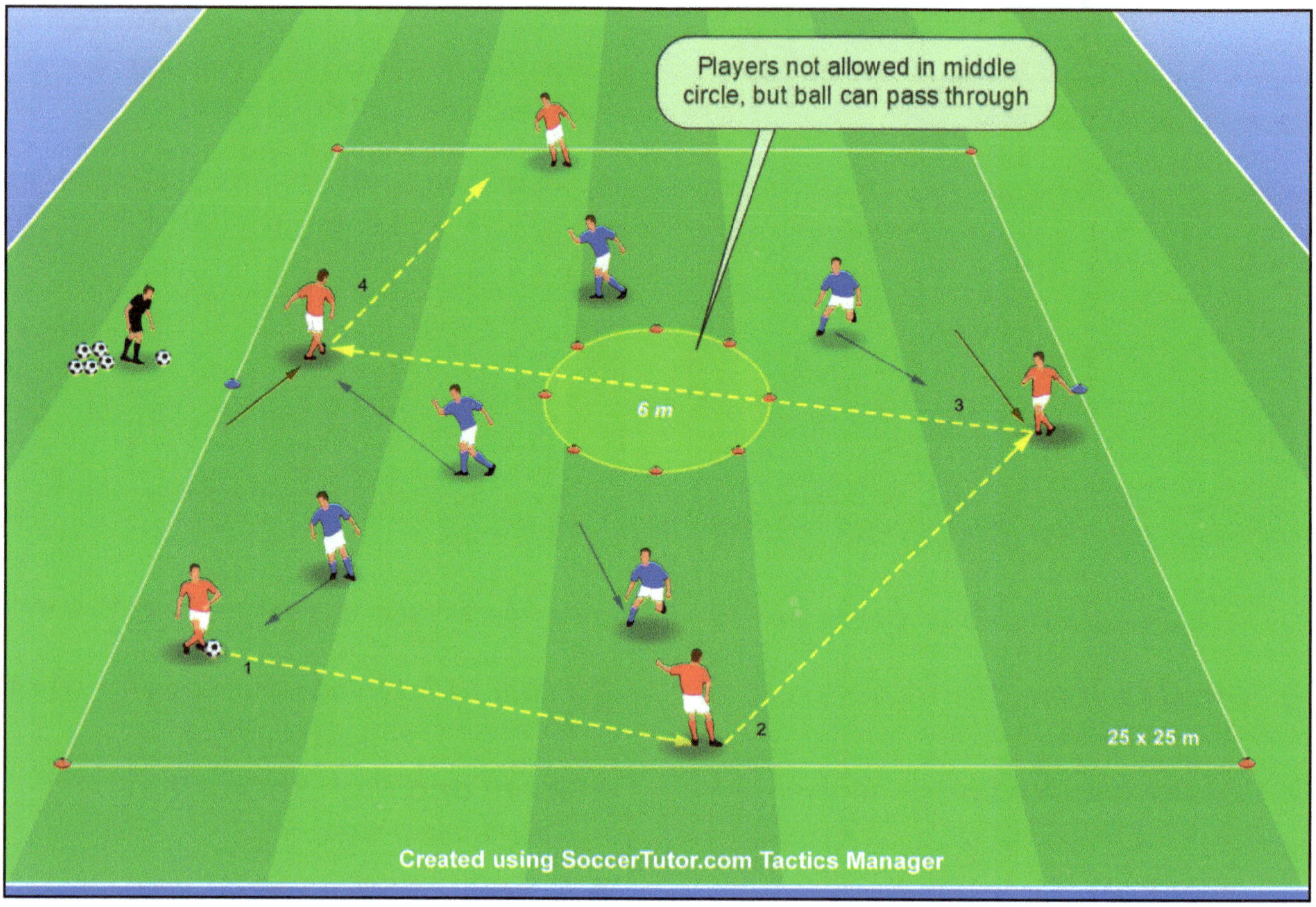

PRACTICE INFORMATION

Duration	Reps	Sets	Numbers	Size (m)	Work Duration	Player Density
12 min	3 min	3	10	25 x 25	9 min	63 m²

OBJECTIVE: Possession based practice with the focus on creating space

Volume Metrics	Practice Total	Per Min. of Work
Total Distance (km)	1.114	0.12
High Speed Running (m)	3	0.33
Sprint Distance (m)	-	-
HML Distance (m)	5	0.56
Power Plays (HiActs)	4	0.44

Intensity Metrics	Practice Total	Per Min. of Work
Max Speed (m/s)	4.55	
Intensity (m/min)		88
Power Score (w/kg)	5.55	
No. of Max Accels >4m²	2	0.22
No. of Max Decels >4m²	3	0.33

* The data shows the physical output per player based on research from elite level teams - see **pages 81-83** for details

THURSDAY Training Practices: Reaction Speed - 2 Days Until Match (MD +5/-2)

Medium Possession 2: Complete 6 Passes and Move in a Four Box Competition Game

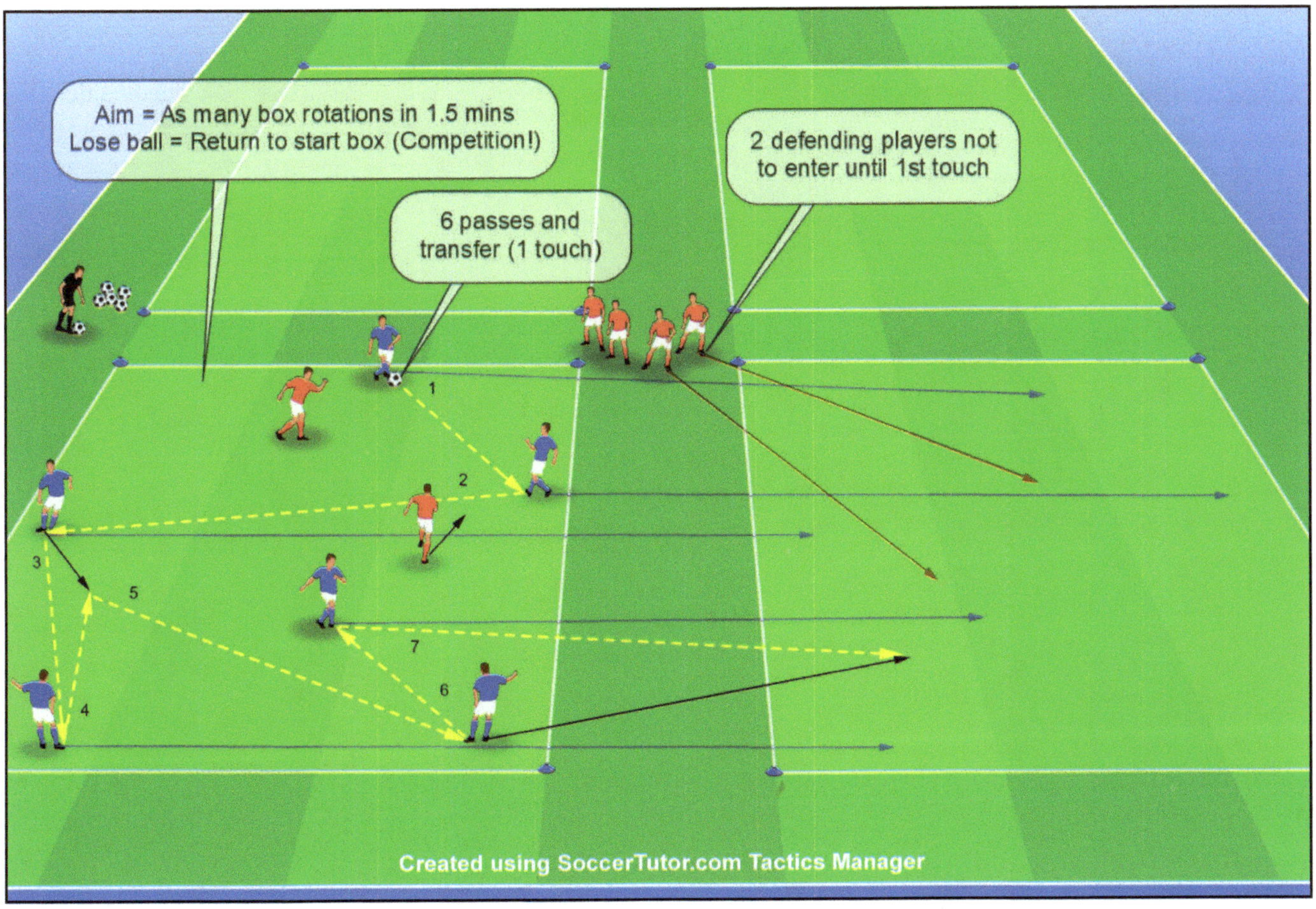

PRACTICE INFORMATION

Duration	Reps	Sets	Numbers	Size (m)	Work Duration	Player Density
10 min	1.5 min	6	12	10 x 10 Boxes	9 min	10 m²

OBJECTIVE: Progressive directional possession with focus on finding the correct passing lane

Volume Metrics	Practice Total	Per Min. of Work
Total Distance (km)	0.823	0.09
High Speed Running (m)	8.95	1
Sprint Distance (m)	-	-
Work Ratio (%)	28.28	
Power Plays (HiActs)	5.87	0.65

Intensity Metrics	Practice Total	Per Min. of Work
Max Speed (m/s)	5.66	
Intensity (m/min)		74.57
Power Score (w/kg)	6.73	
Max Accel Distance (m)	26.53	2.95
Max Decel Distance (m)	24.99	2.78

* The data shows the physical output per player based on research from elite level teams - see **pages 81-83** for details

@SoccerTutor.com | 197 | Football Periodization to Maximise Performance

REFERENCE   @adamowen1980

THURSDAY Training Practices: Reaction Speed - 2 Days Until Match (MD +5/-2)

Medium Possession 3: Play Through the Middle in a 5v5 (+2) Game with Central Zone

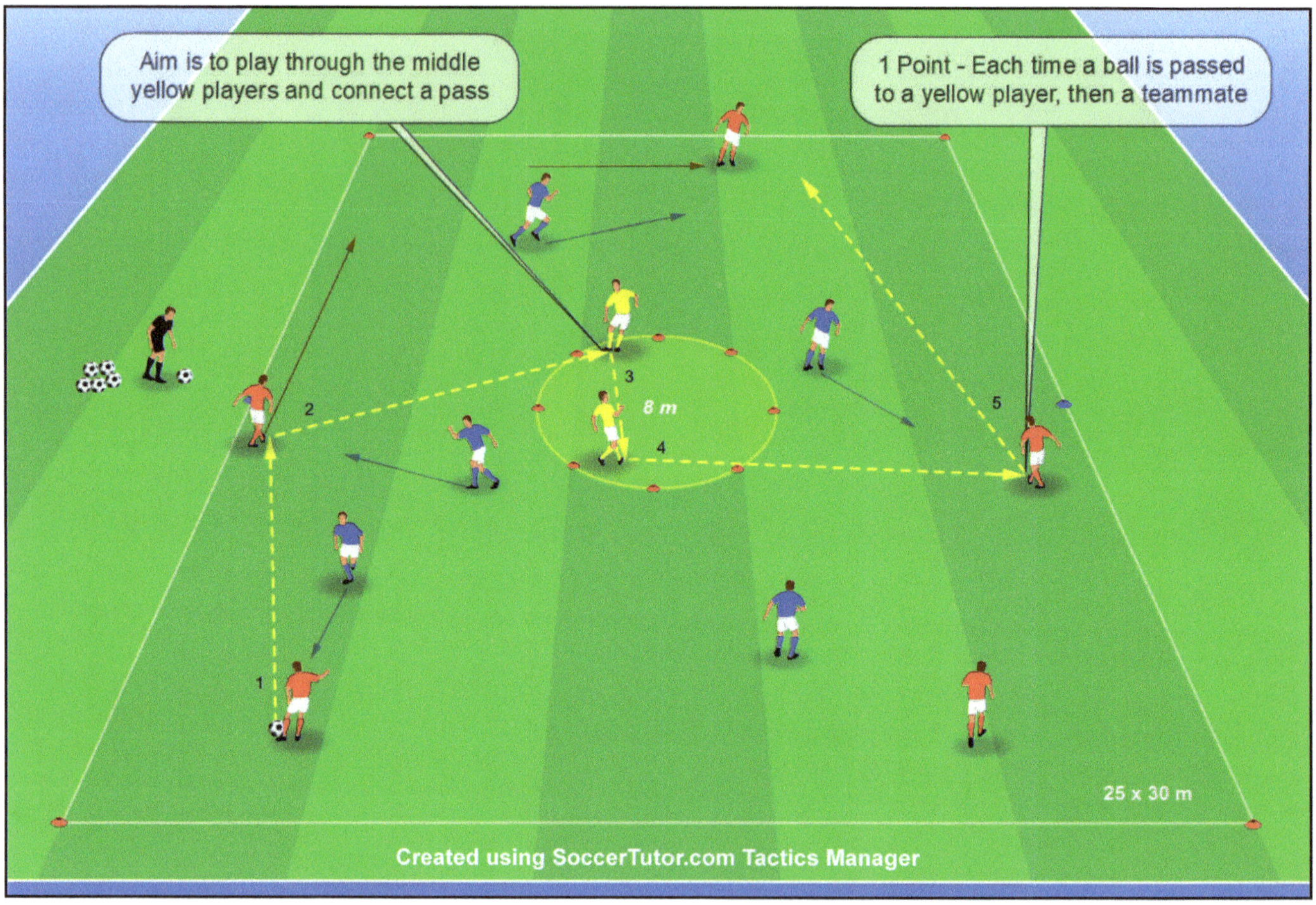

Aim is to play through the middle yellow players and connect a pass

1 Point - Each time a ball is passed to a yellow player, then a teammate

25 x 30 m

PRACTICE INFORMATION

Duration	Reps	Sets	Numbers	Size (m)	Work Duration	Player Density
15 min	4 min	3	12	25 x 30	12 min	75 m²

OBJECTIVE: Positional based possession game with focus to play through the middle

Volume Metrics	Practice Total	Per Min. of Work
Total Distance (km)	1.35	0.11
High Speed Running (m)	1.77	0.15
Sprint Distance (m)	-	-
HML Distance (m)	161.15	13.43
Power Plays (HiActs)	1.95	0.16

Intensity Metrics	Practice Total	Per Min. of Work
Max Speed (m/s)	5.20	
Intensity (m/min)		81.58
Power Score (w/kg)	7	
No. of Max Accels >4m²	11.85	1
No. of Max Decels >4m²	8.89	0.74

*The data shows the physical output per player based on research from elite level teams - see pages 81-83 for details

Football Periodization to Maximise Performance

THURSDAY Training Practices: Reaction Speed - 2 Days Until Match (MD +5/-2)

Medium Possession 4: Double 3v3 (+1) Two Zone Directional Possession Game

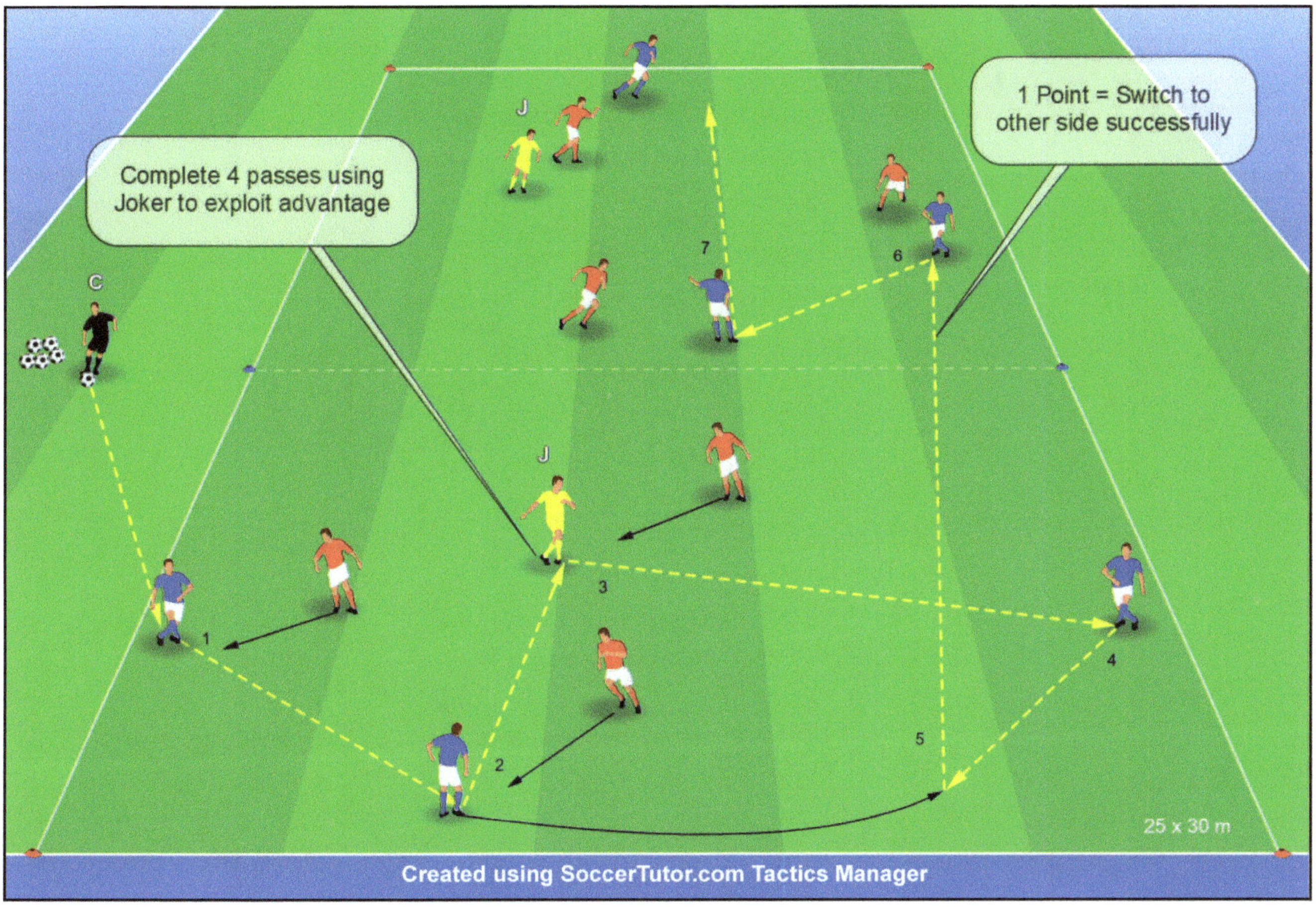

[Diagram: Complete 4 passes using Joker to exploit advantage. 1 Point = Switch to other side successfully. Field size 25 x 30 m]

PRACTICE INFORMATION

Duration	Reps	Sets	Numbers	Size (m)	Work Duration	Player Density
12 min	3 min	3	14	25 x 30	9 min	54 m²

OBJECTIVE: Small-sided possession (3v3 +1 in each square) within medium-sized format

Volume Metrics	Practice Total	Per Min. of Work
Total Distance (km)	1.014	0.11
High Speed Running (m)	2.61	0.29
Sprint Distance (m)	-	-
Work Ratio (%)	17.56	
Power Plays (HiActs)	16.99	1.89

Intensity Metrics	Practice Total	Per Min. of Work
Max Speed (m/s)	5.21	
Intensity (m/min)		78.58
Power Score (w/kg)	6.78	
Max Accel Distance (m)	16.28	1.8
Max Decel Distance (m)	22.24	2.47

* The data shows the physical output per player based on research from elite level teams - see pages 81-83 for details

Football Periodization to Maximise Performance

THURSDAY Training Practices: Reaction Speed - 2 Days Until Match (MD +5/-2)

Medium Possession 5: Secure Possession After Winning the Ball in a Transitional Game

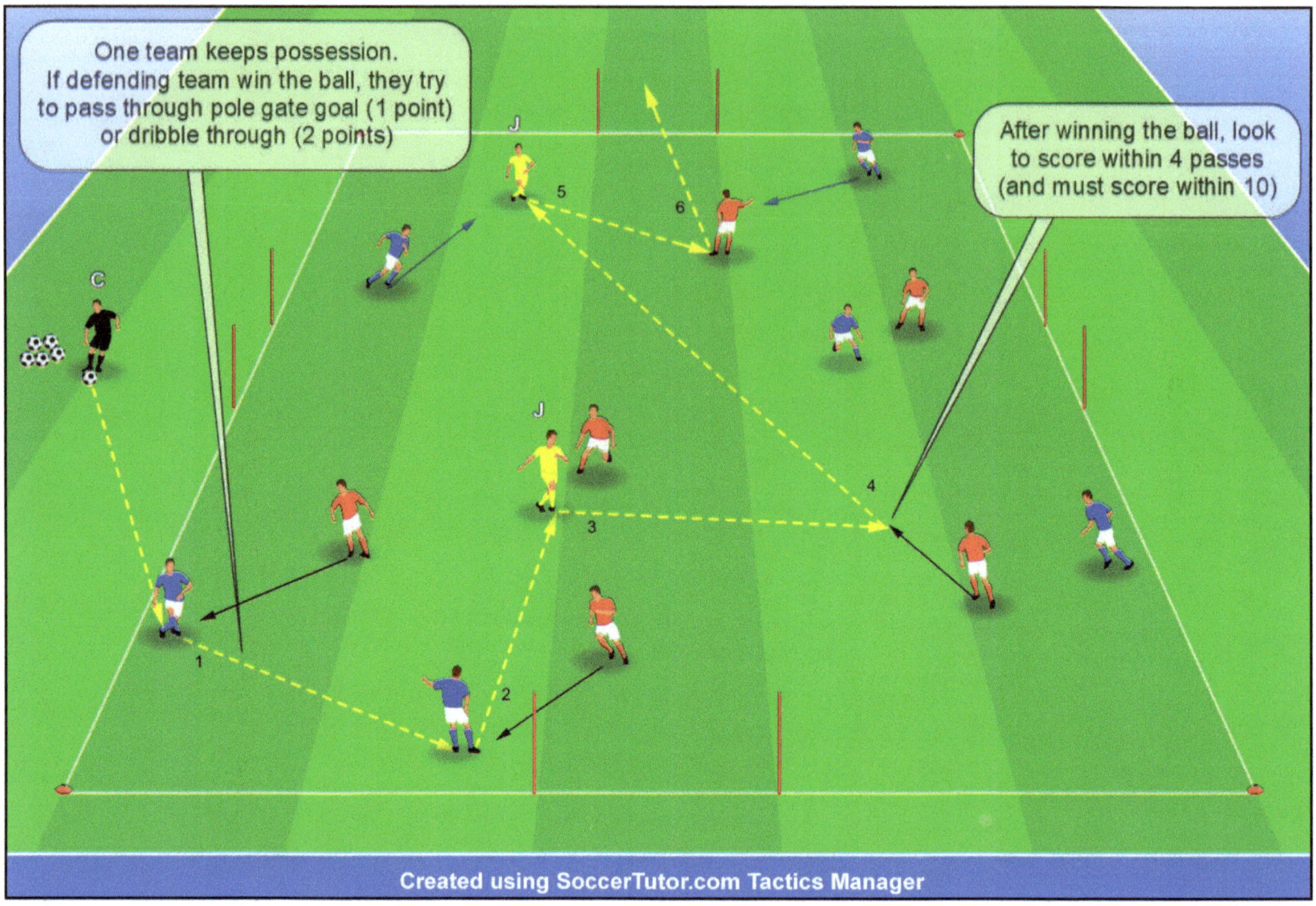

One team keeps possession. If defending team win the ball, they try to pass through pole gate goal (1 point) or dribble through (2 points)

After winning the ball, look to score within 4 passes (and must score within 10)

PRACTICE INFORMATION

Duration	Reps	Sets	Numbers	Size (m)	Work Duration	Player Density
14 min	4 min	3	14	40 x 40	12 min	114 m²

OBJECTIVE: Maintaining possession and securing possession in the transition

Volume Metrics	Practice Total	Per Min. of Work
Total Distance (km)	1.482	0.12
High Speed Running (m)	12.14	1.01
Sprint Distance (m)	-	-
Work Ratio (%)	41.52	
Power Plays (HiActs)	6.46	0.54

Intensity Metrics	Practice Total	Per Min. of Work
Max Speed (m/s)	5.75	
Intensity (m/min)		94.85
Power Score (w/kg)	8.08	
Max Accel Distance (m)	3.9	0.33
Max Decel Distance (m)	2	0.17

* The data shows the physical output per player based on research from elite level teams - see **pages 81-83** for details

THURSDAY Training Practices: Reaction Speed - 2 Days Until Match (MD +5/-2)

Medium Possession 6: Create Space and Play Through Press in a 6v6 Tactical Game

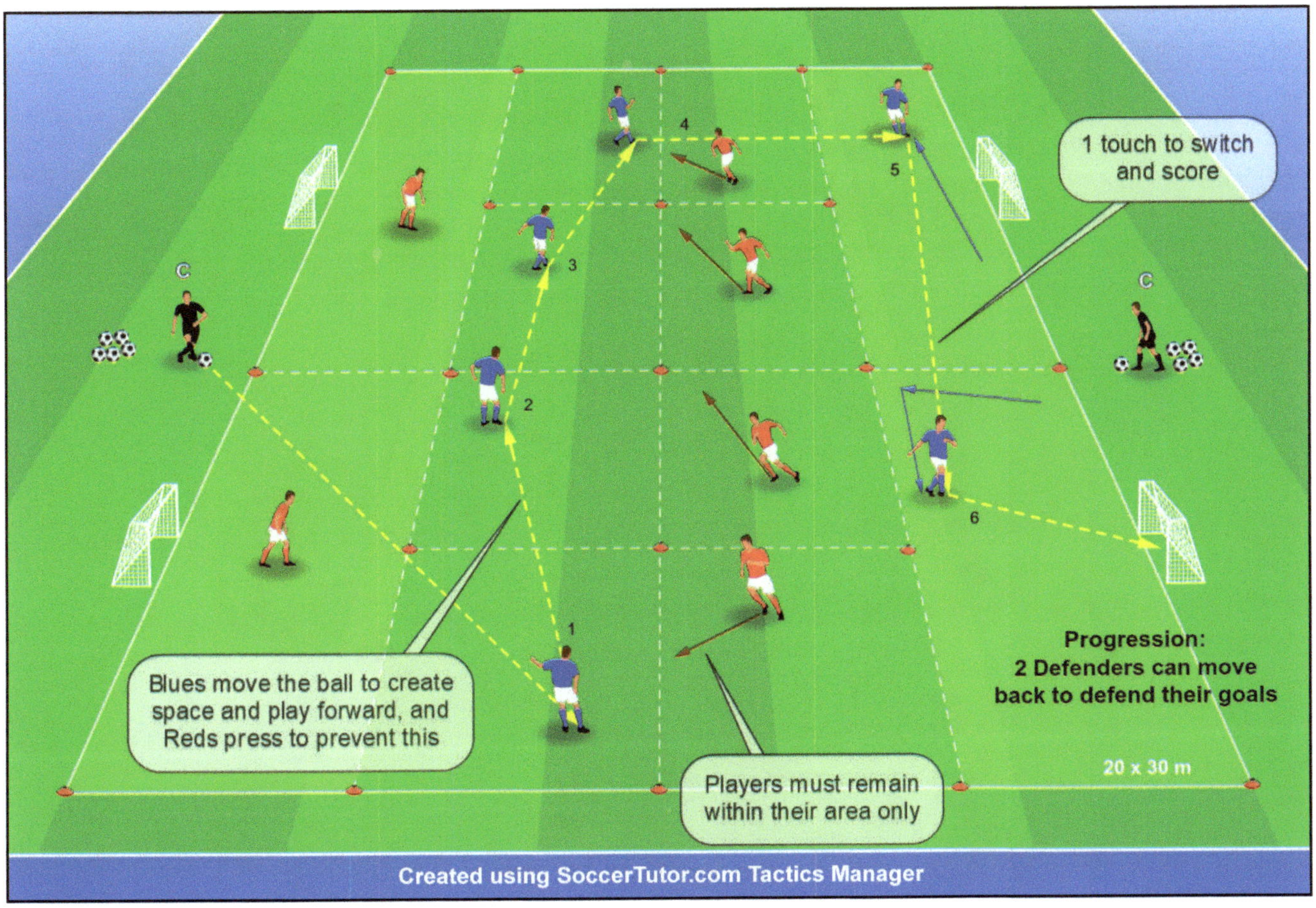

- 1 touch to switch and score
- Blues move the ball to create space and play forward, and Reds press to prevent this
- Players must remain within their area only
- Progression: 2 Defenders can move back to defend their goals
- 20 x 30 m

PRACTICE INFORMATION

Duration	Reps	Sets	Numbers	Size (m)	Work Duration	Player Density
14 min	1 min	9	12	20 x 30	9 min	50 m²

OBJECTIVE: Tactical possession - move ball, create space, play through the defensive line

Volume Metrics	Practice Total	Per Min. of Work
Total Distance (km)	1.061	0.12
High Speed Running (m)	3.98	0.44
Sprint Distance (m)	-	-
HML Distance (m)	152.72	16.97
Power Plays (HiActs)	1.33	0.15

Intensity Metrics	Practice Total	Per Min. of Work
Max Speed (m/s)	5.15	
Intensity (m/min)		51.99
Power Score (w/kg)	4.51	
No. of Max Accels >4m²	14.75	1.64
No. of Max Decels >4m²	16	1.78

* The data shows the physical output per player based on research from elite level teams - see pages 81-83 for details

Football Periodization to Maximise Performance

THURSDAY Training Practices: Reaction Speed - 2 Days Until Match (MD +5/-2)

Medium Possession 7: Breaking Lines in an End to End Two Zone Game with GKs

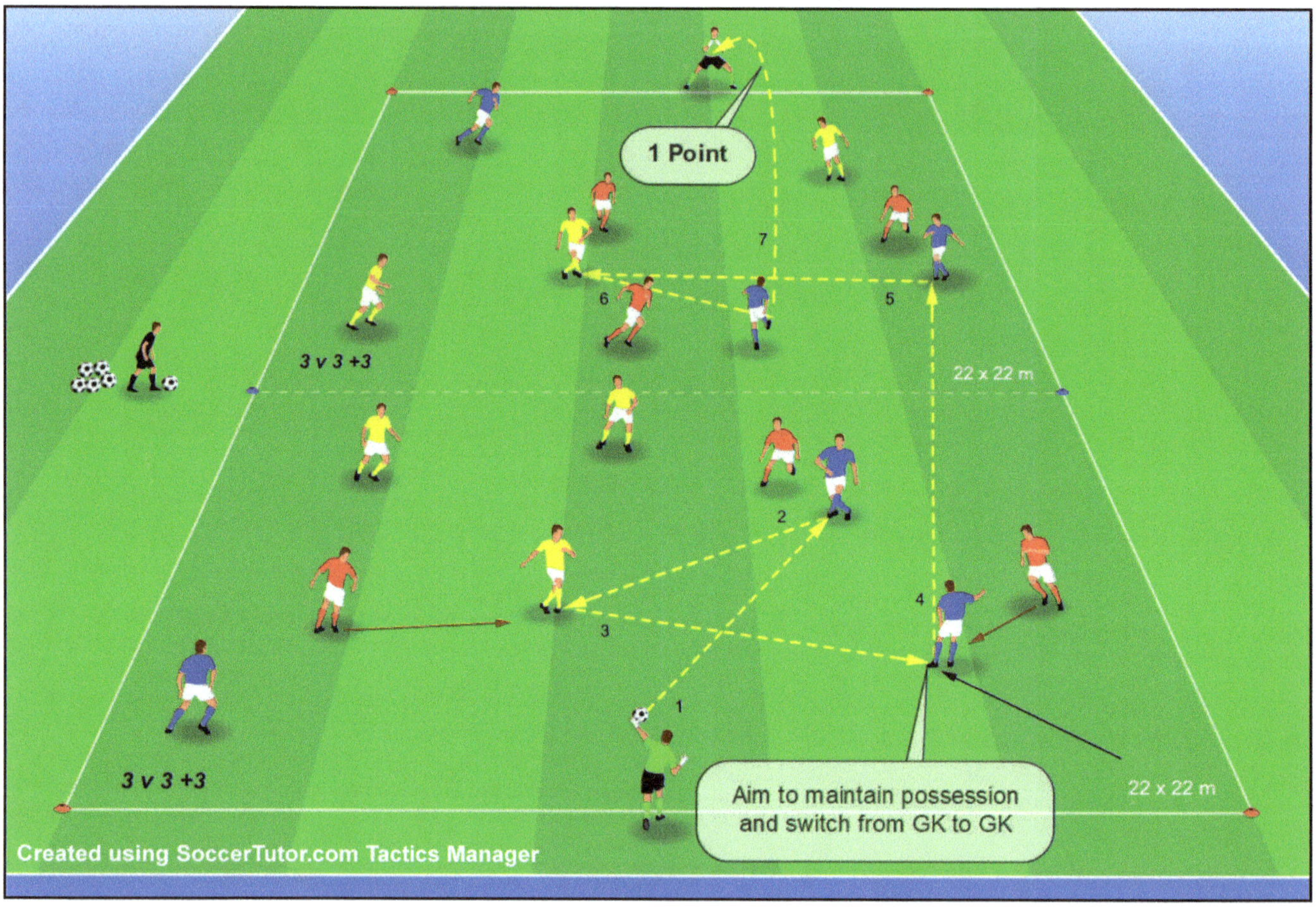

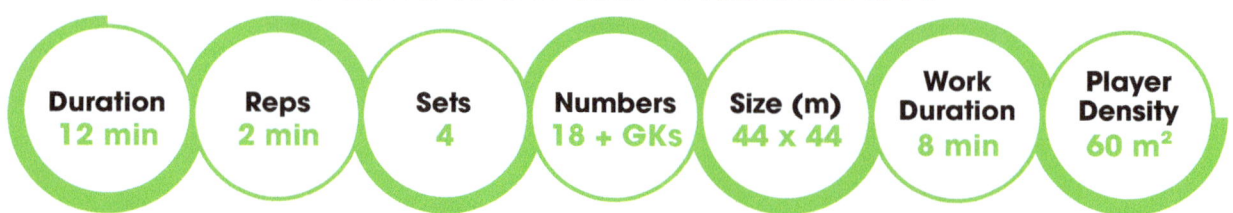

PRACTICE INFORMATION

Duration	Reps	Sets	Numbers	Size (m)	Work Duration	Player Density
12 min	2 min	4	18 + GKs	44 x 44	8 min	60 m²

OBJECTIVE: Possession play with focus on directional passing and breaking lines

Volume Metrics	Practice Total	Per Min. of Work
Total Distance (km)	1.011	0.13
High Speed Running (m)	1.4	0.18
Sprint Distance (m)	-	-
Work Ratio (%)	25.08	
Power Plays (HiActs)	1.34	0.17

Intensity Metrics	Practice Total	Per Min. of Work
Max Speed (m/s)	5.07	
Intensity (m/min)		68.31
Power Score (w/kg)	5.69	
Max Accel Distance (m)	12.29	1.54
Max Decel Distance (m)	17.98	2.25

* The data shows the physical output per player based on research from elite level teams - see **pages 81-83** for details

Football Periodization to Maximise Performance

THURSDAY Training Practices: Reaction Speed - 2 Days Until Match (MD +5/-2)

Medium Sided Possession 8: Beating the Press in a Transitional Three Team Game

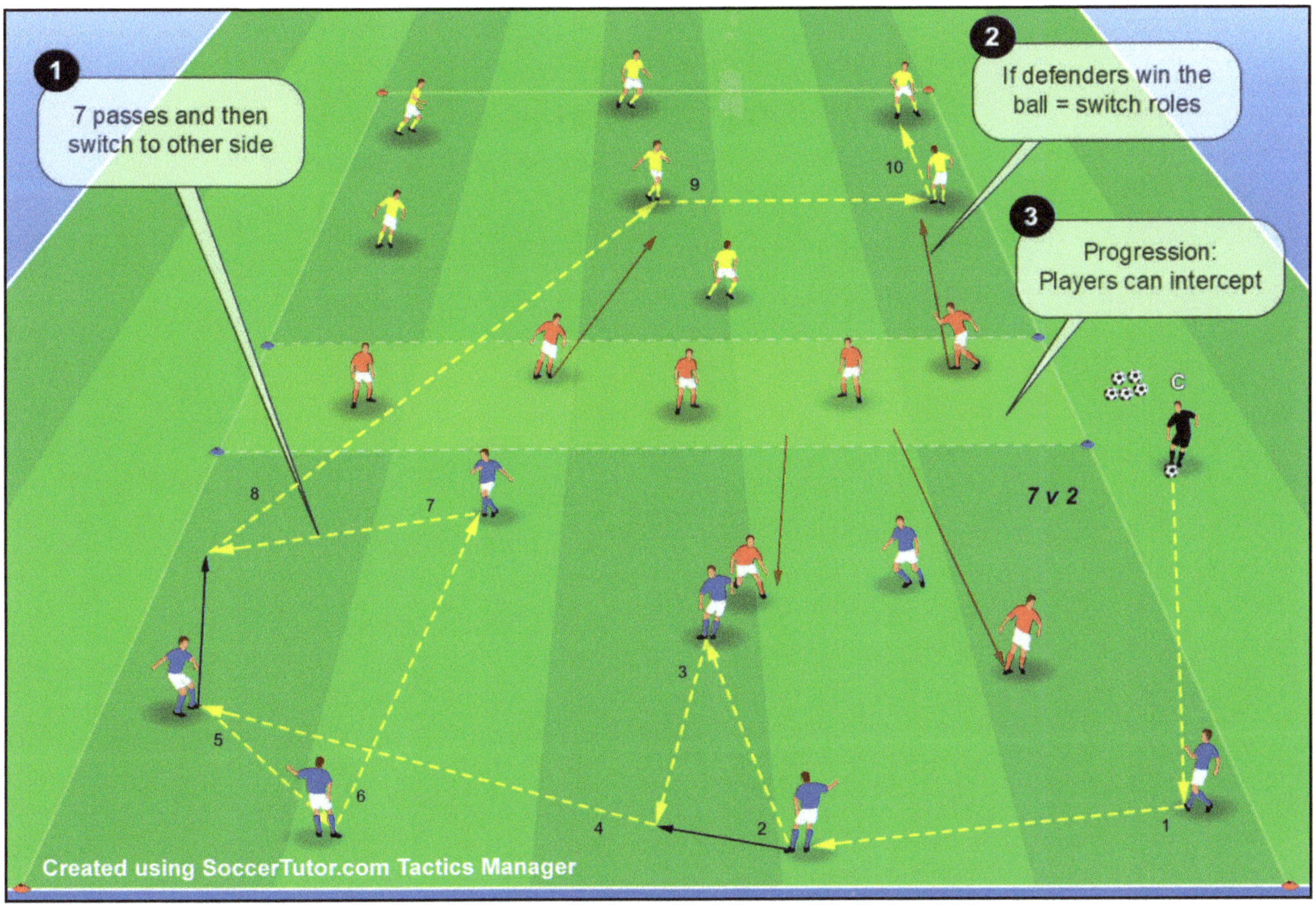

[Diagram]

1. 7 passes and then switch to other side
2. If defenders win the ball = switch roles
3. Progression: Players can intercept

7 v 2

PRACTICE INFORMATION

Duration	Reps	Sets	Numbers	Size (m)	Work Duration	Player Density
10 min	3 min	2	21	10 x 25	6 min	21 m²

OBJECTIVE: Maintaining possession, beating the press, breaking lines, and switching play

Volume Metrics	Practice Total	Per Min. of Work
Total Distance (km)	0.438	0.07
High Speed Running (m)	3.32	0.55
Sprint Distance (m)	-	-
Work Ratio (%)	13	
Power Plays (HiActs)	1.11	0.19

Intensity Metrics	Practice Total	Per Min. of Work
Max Speed (m/s)	6.74	
Intensity (m/min)		46.14
Power Score (w/kg)	3.92	
Max Accel Distance (m)	8.9	1.48
Max Decel Distance (m)	11.34	1.89

* The data shows the physical output per player based on research from elite level teams - see **pages 81-83** for details

@SoccerTutor.com   Football Periodization to Maximise Performance

THURSDAY Training Practices: Reaction Speed - 2 Days Until Match (MD +5/-2)

Medium Possession 9: Switch After Winning the Ball in an 8v8 Game with Split Halves

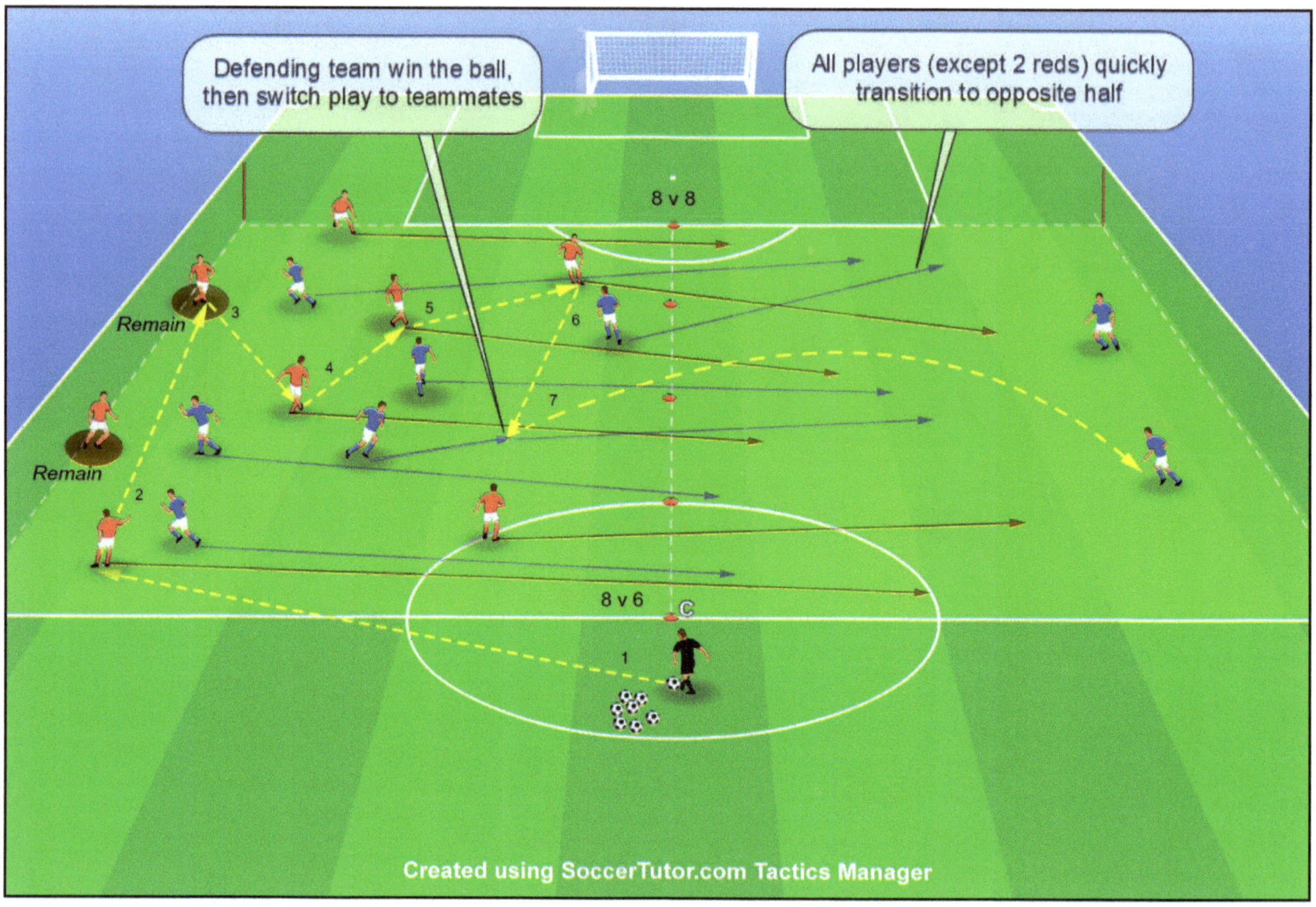

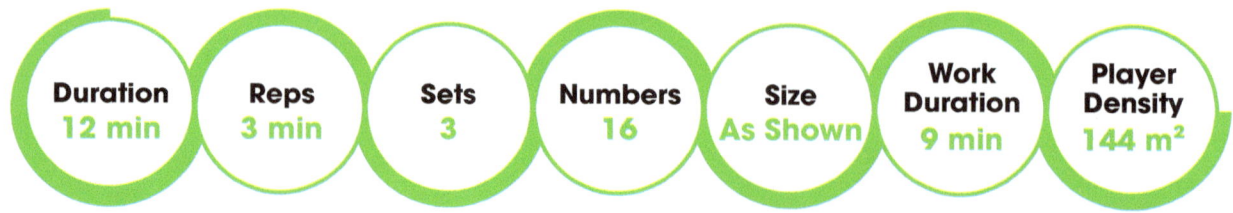

PRACTICE INFORMATION

Duration	Reps	Sets	Numbers	Size	Work Duration	Player Density
12 min	3 min	3	16	As Shown	9 min	144 m²

OBJECTIVE: High intensity transitional possession - focus on switching play after winning the ball

Volume Metrics	Practice Total	Per Min. of Work
Total Distance (km)	1.295	0.14
High Speed Running (m)	35.41	3.93
Sprint Distance (m)	1.79	0.2
Work Ratio (%)	42.67	
Power Plays (HiActs)	9.93	1.1

Intensity Metrics	Practice Total	Per Min. of Work
Max Speed (m/s)	6.48	
Intensity (m/min)		99.25
Power Score (w/kg)	8.51	
Max Accel Distance (m)	13.15	1.46
Max Decel Distance (m)	22.86	2.54

* The data shows the physical output per player based on research from elite level teams - see **pages 81-83** for details

THURSDAY Training Practices: Reaction Speed - 2 Days Until Match (MD +5/-2)

Medium Possession 10: Intensive Possession Game with Progressively Increasing Numbers

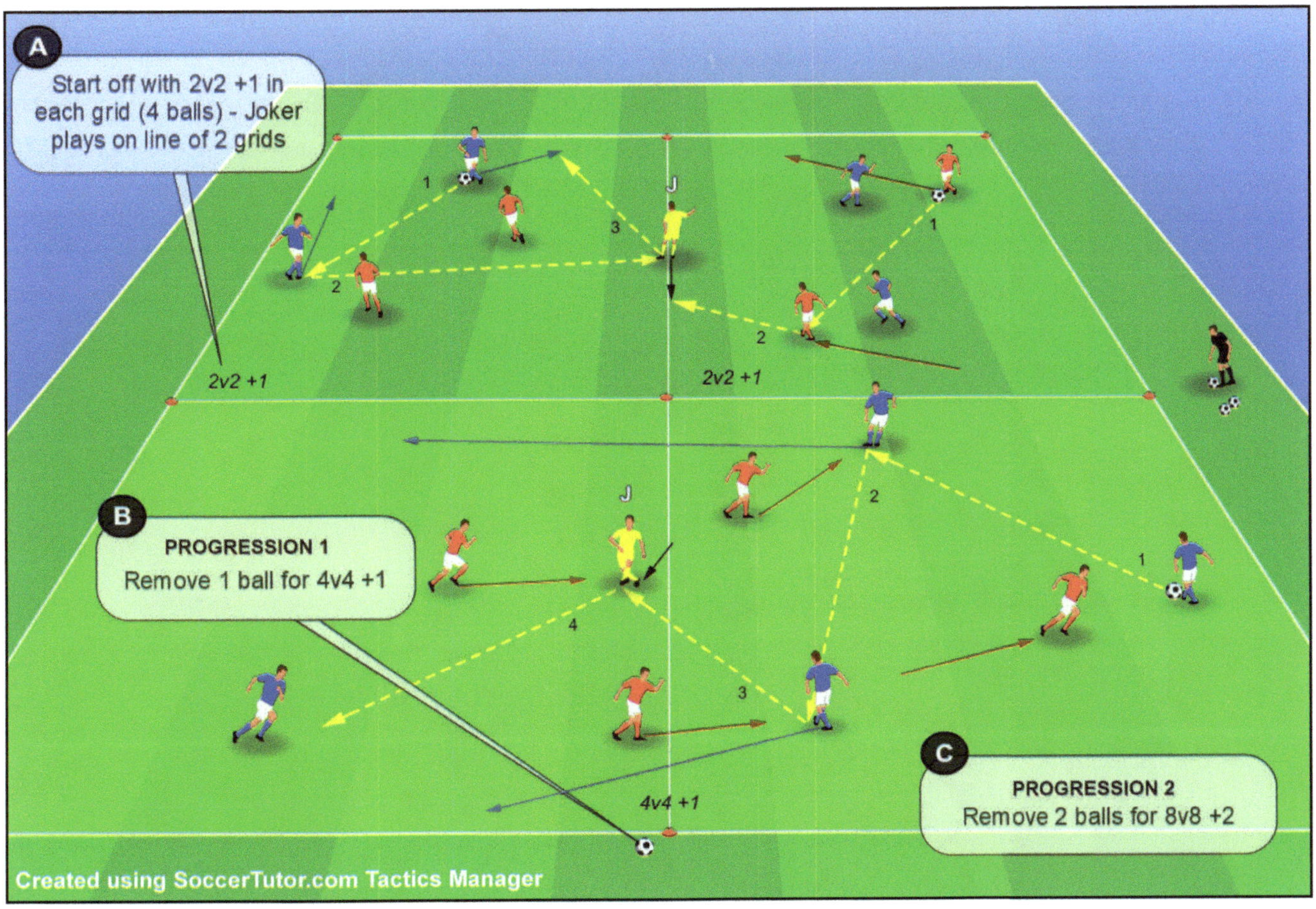

A — Start off with 2v2 +1 in each grid (4 balls) - Joker plays on line of 2 grids

B — PROGRESSION 1: Remove 1 ball for 4v4 +1

C — PROGRESSION 2: Remove 2 balls for 8v8 +2

PRACTICE INFORMATION

Duration	Reps	Sets	Numbers	Size (m)	Work Duration	Player Density
12 min	4 min	2	18	35 x 35	8 min	68 m²

OBJECTIVE: Intensive transitional game to keep possession in various different number situations

Volume Metrics	Practice Total	Per Min. of Work
Total Distance (km)	0.897	0.11
High Speed Running (m)	1.38	0.17
Sprint Distance (m)	-	-
HML Distance (m)	96.6	12
Power Plays (HiActs)	1.34	0.17

Intensity Metrics	Practice Total	Per Min. of Work
Max Speed (m/s)	5.17	
Intensity (m/min)		75.11
Power Score (w/kg)	6.44	
No. of Max Accels >4m²	7.22	0.9
No. of Max Decels >4m²	7.38	0.92

* The data shows the physical output per player based on research from elite level teams - see **pages 81-83** for details

Football Periodization to Maximise Performance

THURSDAY Training Practices: Reaction Speed - 2 Days Until Match (MD +5/-2)

Medium Possession 11: Dynamic 8v8 (+2) Possession Game with Varying Conditions

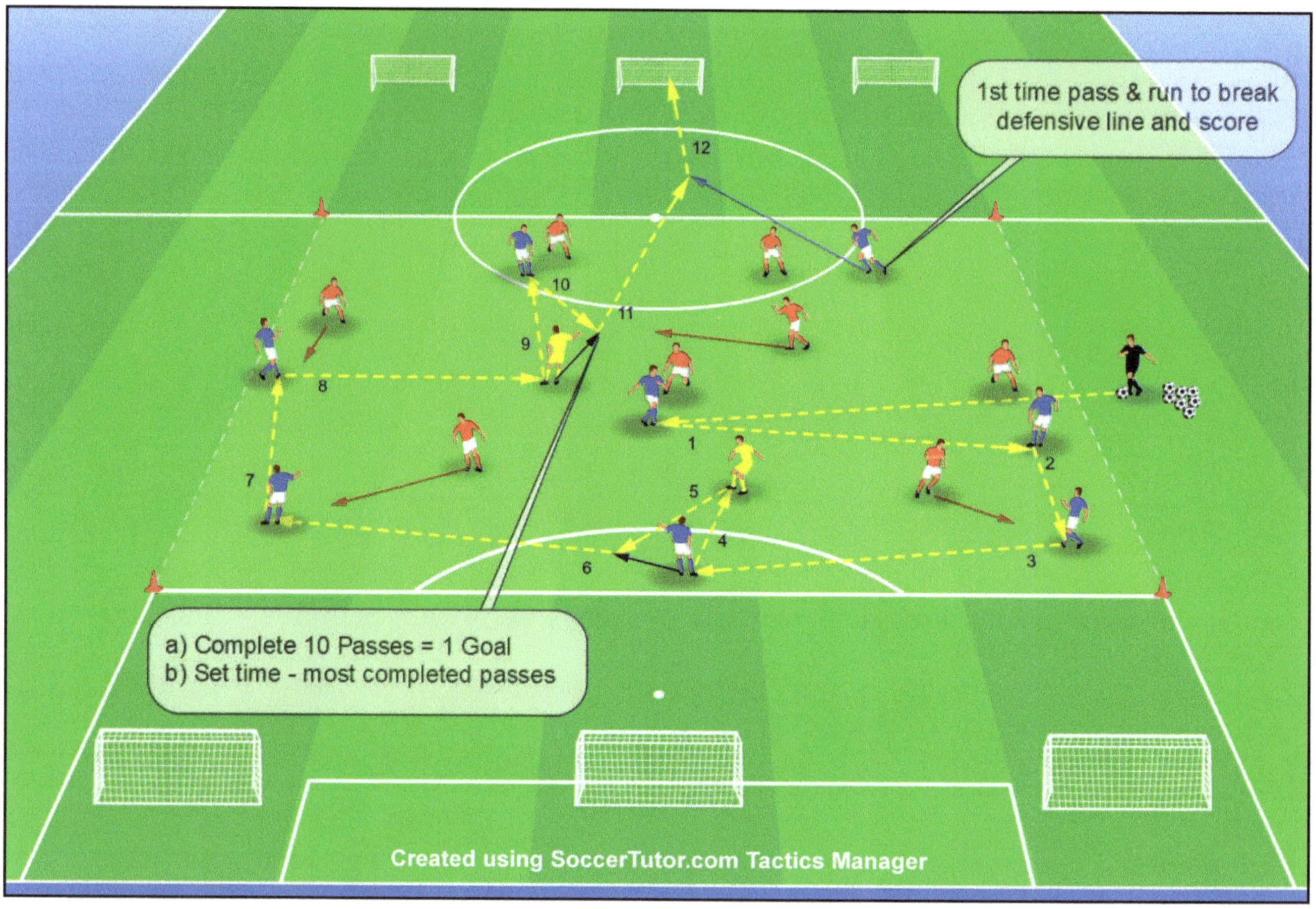

1st time pass & run to break defensive line and score

a) Complete 10 Passes = 1 Goal
b) Set time - most completed passes

Created using SoccerTutor.com Tactics Manager

PRACTICE INFORMATION

- **Duration**: 15 min
- **Reps**: 4 min
- **Sets**: 3
- **Numbers**: 18
- **Size**: As shown
- **Work Duration**: 12 min
- **Player Density**: 102 m²

OBJECTIVE: Transitional possession with varying situations + fast defensive and attacking play

Volume Metrics	Practice Total	Per Min. of Work
Total Distance (km)	1.541	0.13
High Speed Running (m)	40.6	3.38
Sprint Distance (m)	5.8	0.48
Work Ratio (%)	40.26	
Power Plays (HiActs)	8.61	0.72

Intensity Metrics	Practice Total	Per Min. of Work
Max Speed (m/s)	6.76	
Intensity (m/min)		91.6
Power Score (w/kg)	7.77	
Max Accel Distance (m)	17	1.4
Max Decel Distance (m)	29	2.4

* The data shows the physical output per player based on research from elite level teams - see **pages 81-83** for details

@SoccerTutor.com Football Periodization to Maximise Performance

REFERENCE @adamowen1980

THURSDAY Training Practices: Reaction Speed - 2 Days Until Match (MD +5/-2)

Medium Possession 12: Fast Defensive Transition to Press Ball in a Dynamic Game

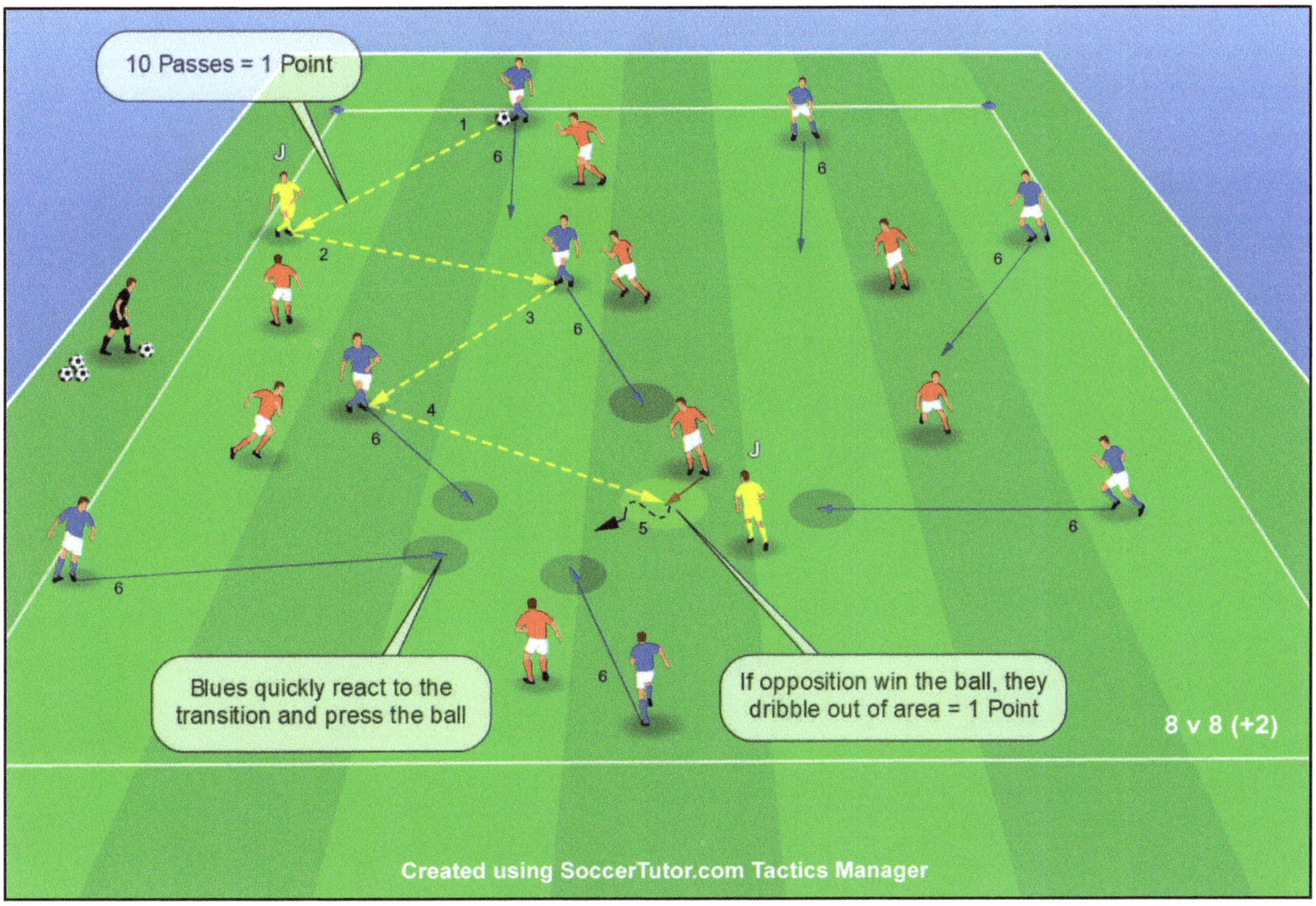

PRACTICE INFORMATION

Duration	Reps	Sets	Numbers	Size (m)	Work Duration	Player Density
6 min	2 min	2	18	35 x 35	4 min	68 m²

OBJECTIVE: Positional possession play with focus on fast defensive transition reactions

Volume Metrics	Practice Total	Per Min. of Work
Total Distance (km)	0.438	0.1
High Speed Running (m)	4.31	1.08
Sprint Distance (m)	-	-
HML Distance (m)	56.39	14.1
Power Plays (HiActs)	2.22	0.56

Intensity Metrics	Practice Total	Per Min. of Work
Max Speed (m/s)	5.29	
Intensity (m/min)		94.61
Power Score (w/kg)	8.18	
No. of Max Accels >4m²	2.5	0.63
No. of Max Decels >4m²	2.83	0.7

* The data shows the physical output per player based on research from elite level teams - see **pages 81-83** for details

@SoccerTutor.com — Football Periodization to Maximise Performance

THURSDAY Training Practices: Reaction Speed - 2 Days Until Match (MD +5/-2)

THURSDAY - 2 DAYS UNTIL MATCH (MD +5/-2):
Medium Sided Games

INTENSITY: All practices are performed at full intensity

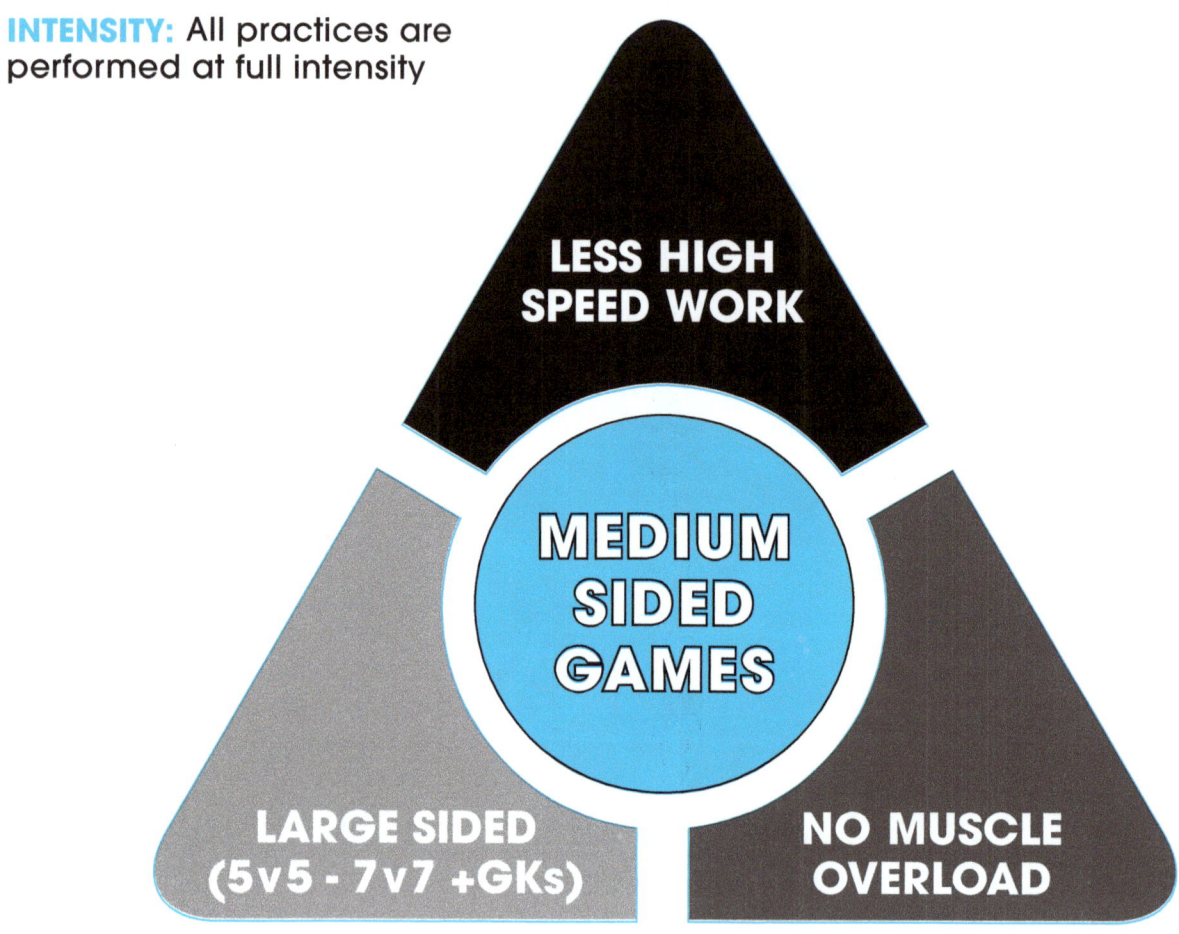

What are Medium Sided Games?
- Medium sided games (MSGs) are defined as including 5 to 7 outfield players per side = 5v5 - 7v7 (+GKs).

Why are Medium Sided Games used at this point of the training week (MD +5/-2)?
- They can be used in different periods of the training week but within this framework, they are focused around this training days with medium sized playing areas to train the unit principles (defence-midfield-attack).
- Medium sized areas are used to focus on specific areas of the pitch.
- Medium sided games are performed in this part of the training week to ensure specific muscle groups are not overloaded.

How does this help to maximise performance?
- These game types result in reduced high-speed running and sprint distance vs. larger game types.
- But expose players to reduced cardiovascular loads when compared to SSGs, due to a reduced intensity.

MEDIUM SIDED GAMES
5 (+5) v 5 (+5) + GKs - 30 x 35 m
*Data below based on 4 x 2 Minute Playing Sets per Team

Games = 2 min (outside and inside players switch roles after each one)

- ↑ Football Specific Training
- ↑ Speed of Play
- ↑ Technical Exposure
- ↑ Cardiovascular Load
- ↑ Goal Scoring Opportunities
- ↑ 1 v 1 Attacking / Defending Situations

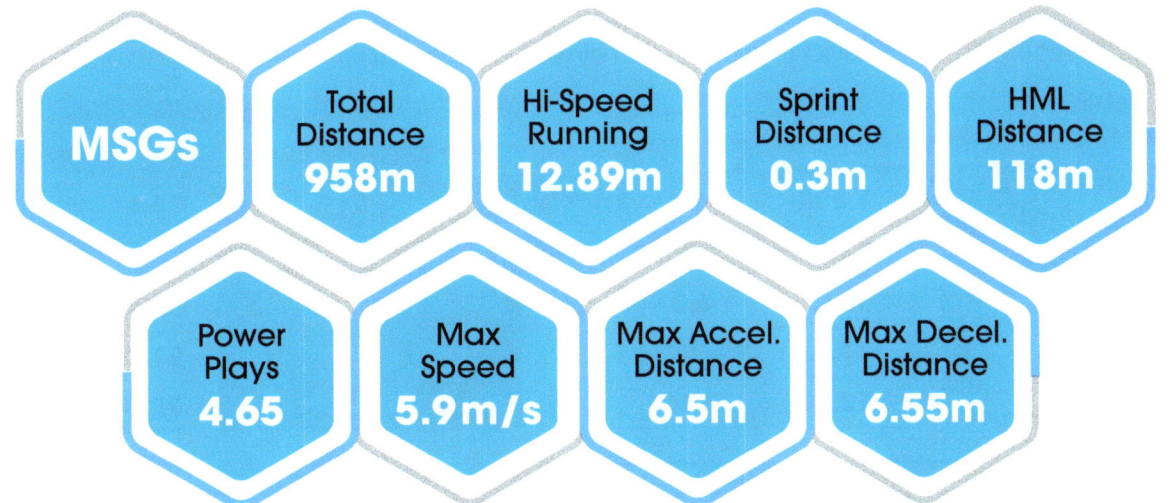

| MSGs | Total Distance 958m | Hi-Speed Running 12.89m | Sprint Distance 0.3m | HML Distance 118m |

| Power Plays 4.65 | Max Speed 5.9 m/s | Max Accel. Distance 6.5m | Max Decel. Distance 6.55m |

@adamowen1980

Football Periodization to Maximise Performance

REFERENCE: Owen Al et al., (2012). J Strength Cond Res. Oct; 26(10):27 48-54. Dellal A et al., (2012). Hum Mov Sci. Augl; 31 (4):957-69.

THURSDAY Training Practices: Reaction Speed - 2 Days Until Match (MD +5/-2)

Medium Sided Game 1: Counter Attacking in a Three Team 5v5v5 (+GKs) Game

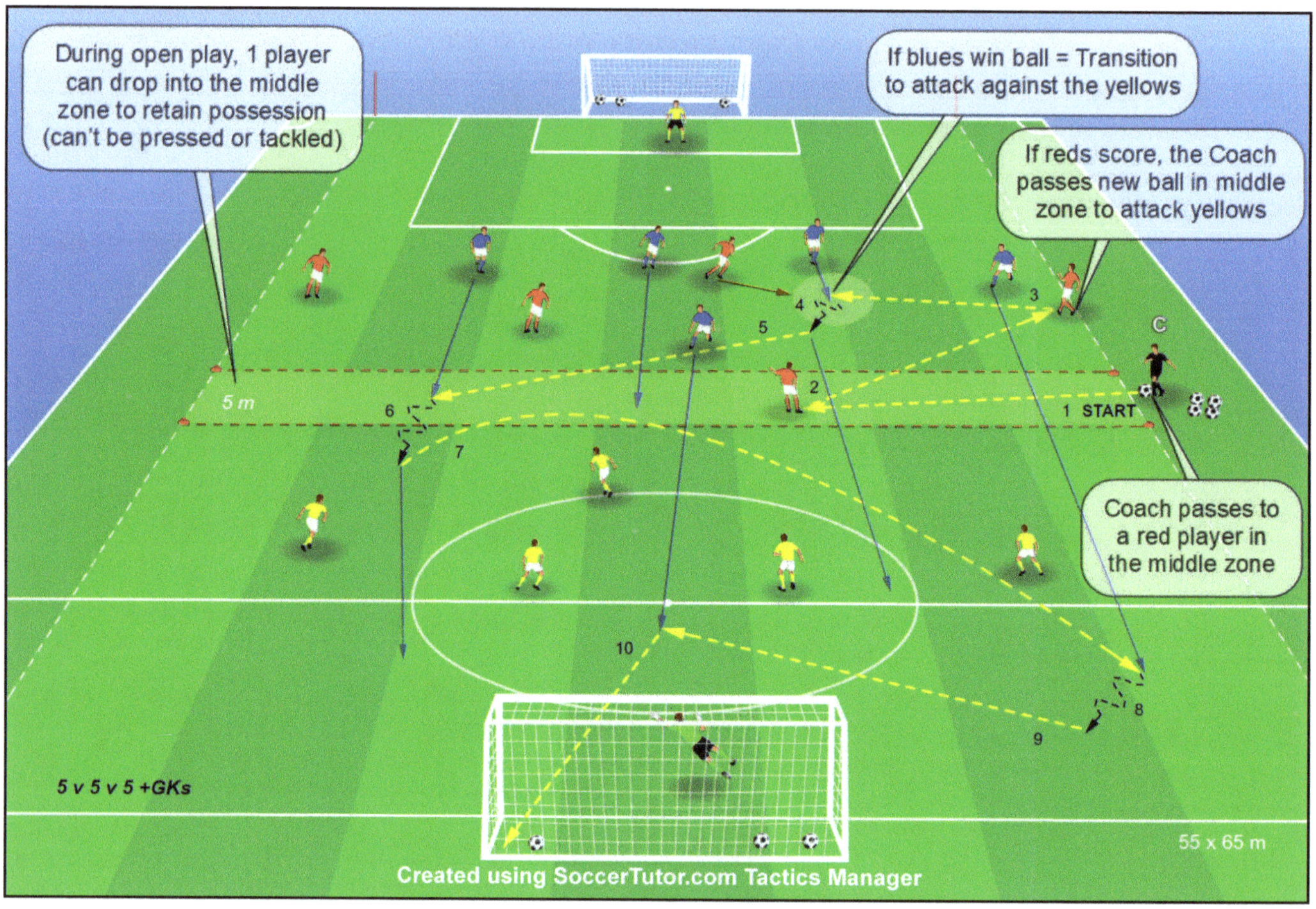

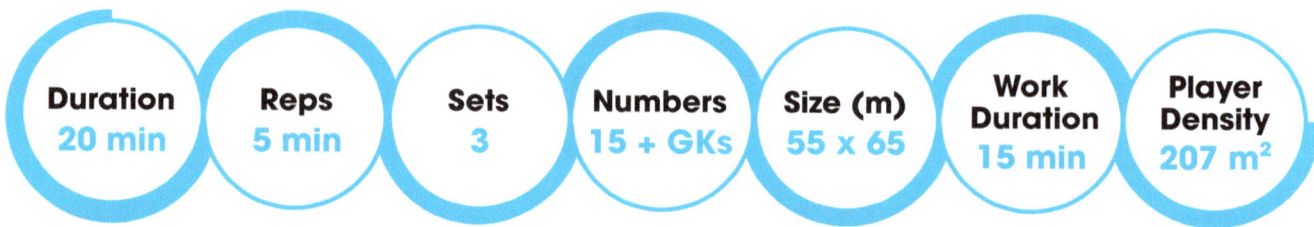

PRACTICE INFORMATION

Duration	Reps	Sets	Numbers	Size (m)	Work Duration	Player Density
20 min	5 min	3	15 + GKs	55 x 65	15 min	207 m²

OBJECTIVE: Transition based three team training game with focus on counter attacking

Volume Metrics	Practice Total	Per Min. of Work
Total Distance (km)	1.625	0.1
High Speed Running (m)	73.79	4.92
Sprint Distance (m)	4.43	0.3
Work Ratio (%)	31.36	
Power Plays (HiActs)	12.94	0.86

Intensity Metrics	Practice Total	Per Min. of Work
Max Speed (m/s)	6.8	
Intensity (m/min)		79.98
Power Score (w/kg)	6.86	
Max Accel. Distance (m)	21.58	1.44
Max Decel. Distance (m)	30.05	2

* The data shows the physical output per player based on research from elite level teams - see **pages 81-83** for details

210

Football Periodization to Maximise Performance

@SoccerTutor.com

REFERENCE @adamowen1980

THURSDAY Training Practices: Reaction Speed - 2 Days Until Match (MD +5/-2)

Medium Sided Game 2: Playing Through the Thirds in a 6v6(+2) +GKs Three Zone Game

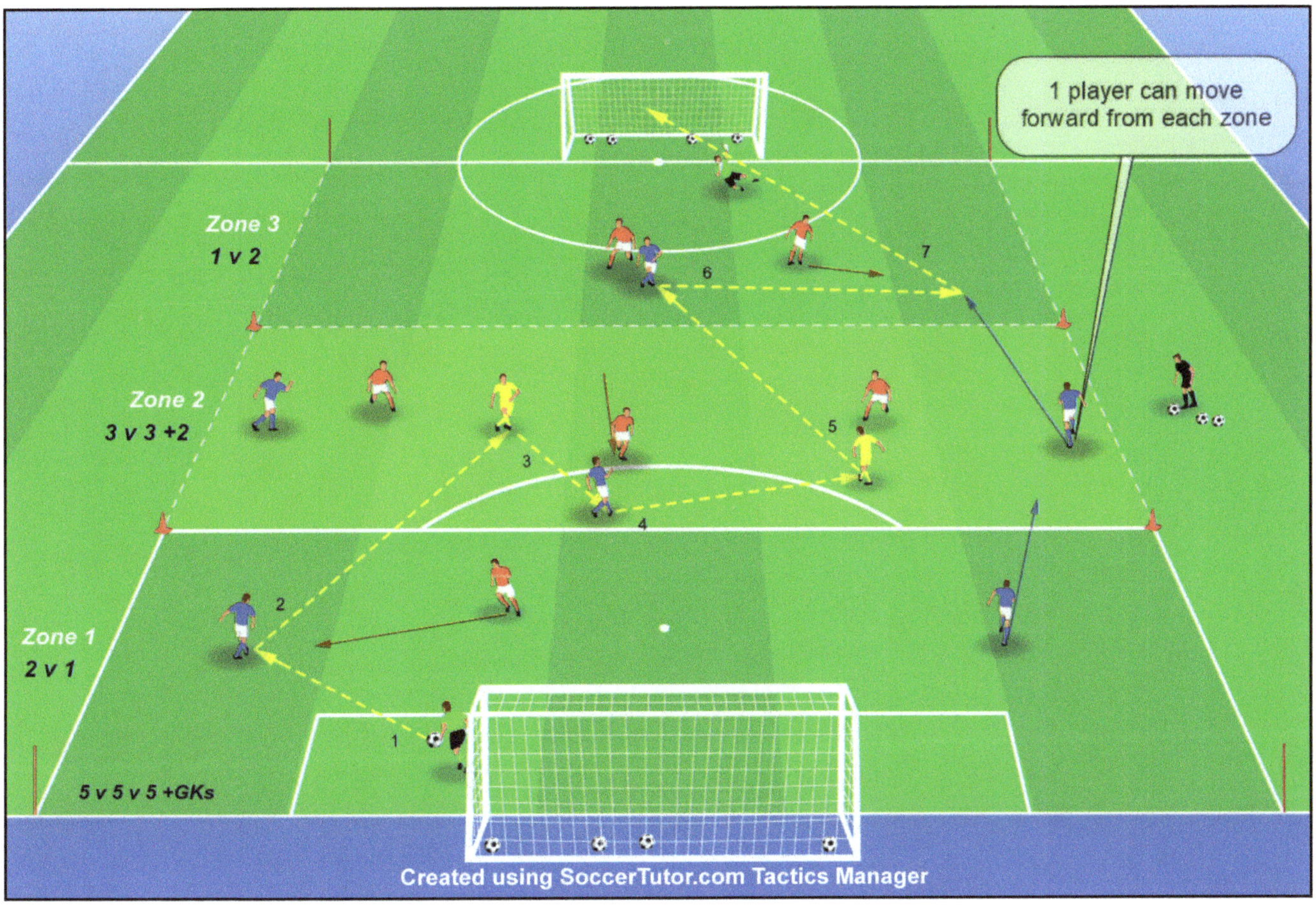

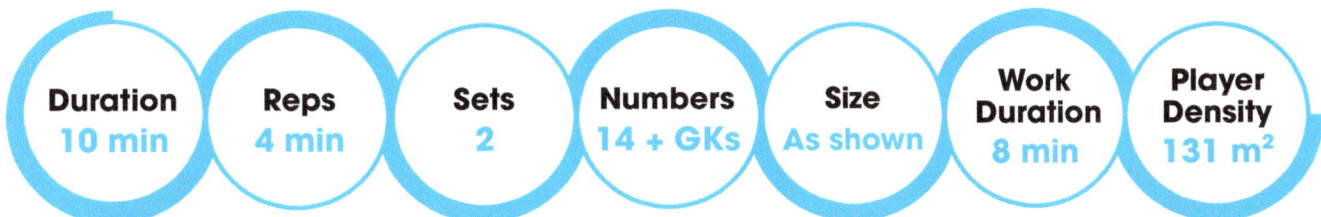

PRACTICE INFORMATION

Duration	Reps	Sets	Numbers	Size	Work Duration	Player Density
10 min	4 min	2	14 + GKs	As shown	8 min	131 m²

OBJECTIVE: Progressive build-up game with focus on playing through the thirds

Volume Metrics	Practice Total	Per Min. of Work
Total Distance (km)	0.943	0.12
High Speed Running (m)	19.55	2.44
Sprint Distance (m)	2.41	0.3
Work Ratio (%)	34.21	
Power Plays (HiActs)	4.84	0.6

Intensity Metrics	Practice Total	Per Min. of Work
Max Speed (m/s)	6.24	
Intensity (m/min)		83.03
Power Score (w/kg)	7.11	
Max Accel. Distance (m)	13.67	1.7
Max Decel. Distance (m)	19.89	2.49

* The data shows the physical output per player based on research from elite level teams - see pages 81-83 for details

THURSDAY Training Practices: Reaction Speed - 2 Days Until Match (MD +5/-2)

Medium Sided Game 3: Counter Attacking at Speed with Purpose in a 7v7v7 (+GKs) Game

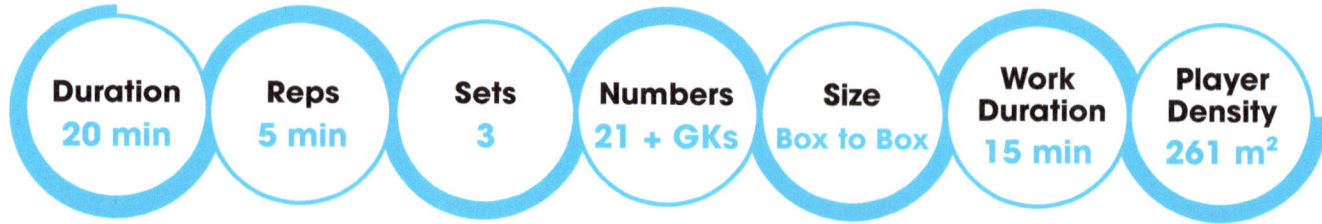

- 1 player from each team must stay in the middle zone for support
- If blues win ball = Transition to attack against the yellows
- If reds score, the Coach passes new ball in middle zone to attack yellows
- Coach passes to a red player in the middle zone

7 v 7 v 7 +GKs

PRACTICE INFORMATION

Duration	Reps	Sets	Numbers	Size	Work Duration	Player Density
20 min	5 min	3	21 + GKs	Box to Box	15 min	261 m²

OBJECTIVE: Transition game with the focus on counter attacking at speed with purpose

Volume Metrics	Practice Total	Per Min. of Work
Total Distance (km)	1.46	0.1
High Speed Running (m)	69	4.6
Sprint Distance (m)	9.9	0.66
HML Distance (m)	226.76	15.12
Power Plays (HiActs)	11.24	0.75

Intensity Metrics	Practice Total	Per Min. of Work
Max Speed (m/s)	7.04	
Intensity (m/min)		80
Power Score (w/kg)	6.85	
No. of Max Accels >4m²	8.88	0.59
No. of Max Decels >4m²	10.05	0.67

* The data shows the physical output per player based on research from elite level teams - see **pages 81-83** for details

THURSDAY Training Practices: Reaction Speed - 2 Days Until Match (MD +5/-2)

Medium Sided Game 4: Switching Play and Forward Passing with Outside Support Players

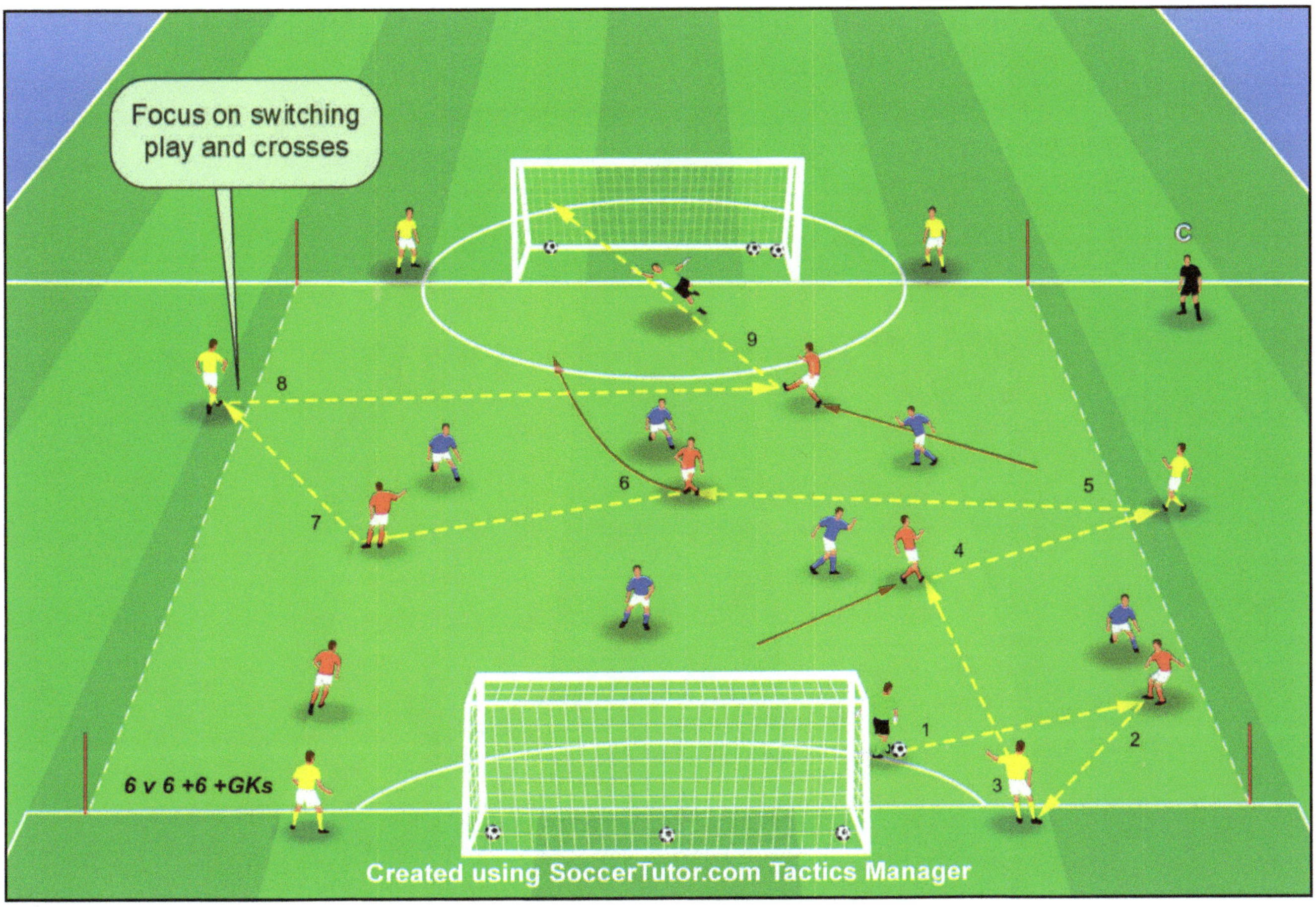

PRACTICE INFORMATION

Duration	Reps	Sets	Numbers	Size	Work Duration	Player Density
20 min	2 min	9	18 + GKs	As Shown	12 min	91 m²

OBJECTIVE: Progressive directional game with the focus on switching play using the wide players

Volume Metrics	Practice Total	Per Min. of Work
Total Distance (km)	1.3	0.1
High Speed Running (m)	17.66	1.47
Sprint Distance (m)	0.2	0.017
HML Distance (m)	167.19	13.9
Power Plays (HiActs)	5.71	0.48

Intensity Metrics	Practice Total	Per Min. of Work
Max Speed (m/s)	6.04	
Intensity (m/min)		68.28
Power Score (w/kg)	5.62	
No. of Max Accels >4m²	10.19	0.85
No. of Max Decels >4m²	9.64	0.8

* The data shows the physical output per player based on research from elite level teams - see **pages 81-83** for details

THURSDAY Training Practices: Reaction Speed - 2 Days Until Match (MD +5/-2)

Medium Sided Game 5: Maintain Possession and Fast Defensive Transition - 8v8 (+2) Game

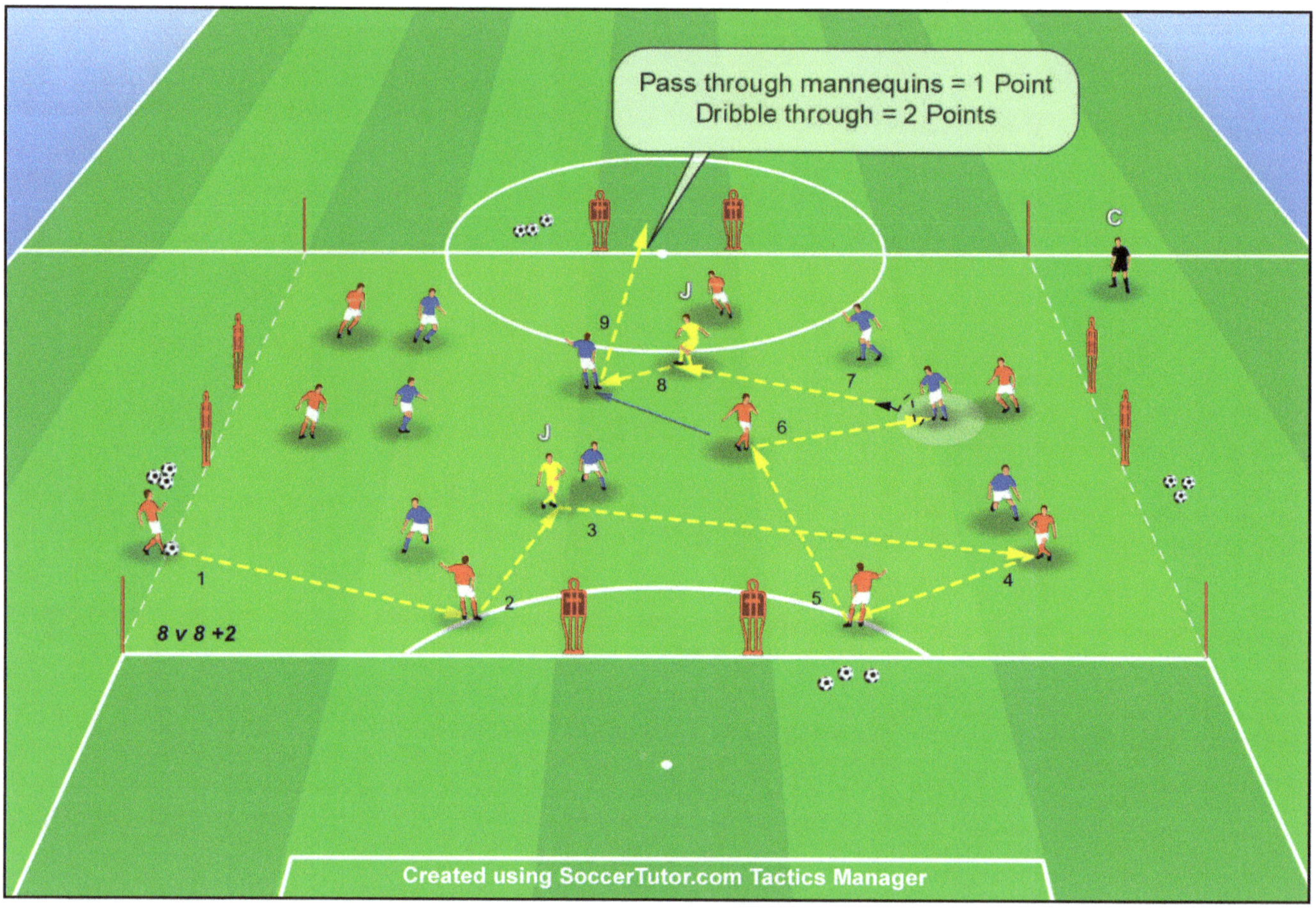

![Diagram of 8v8+2 training exercise with mannequins, showing: Pass through mannequins = 1 Point, Dribble through = 2 Points]

PRACTICE INFORMATION

Duration	Reps	Sets	Numbers	Size	Work Duration	Player Density
15 min	4 min	3	18	As Shown	12 min	92 m²

OBJECTIVE: Transition based game with the focus on possession and fast transitions

Volume Metrics	Practice Total	Per Min. of Work
Total Distance (km)	1.344	0.11
High Speed Running (m)	8.72	0.73
Sprint Distance (m)	-	-
Work Ratio (%)	33.11	
Power Plays (HiActs)	4.33	0.36

Intensity Metrics	Practice Total	Per Min. of Work
Max Speed (m/s)	5.77	
Intensity (m/min)		79.2
Power Score (w/kg)	6.52	
Max Accel. Distance (m)	10	0.83
Max Decel. Distance (m)	20	1.67

* The data shows the physical output per player based on research from elite level teams - see pages 81-83 for details

Football Periodization to Maximise Performance

THURSDAY Training Practices: Reaction Speed - 2 Days Until Match (MD +5/-2)

Medium Sided Game 6: Play Forward and Break the Lines - Narrow 7v7 (+2) +GKs Game

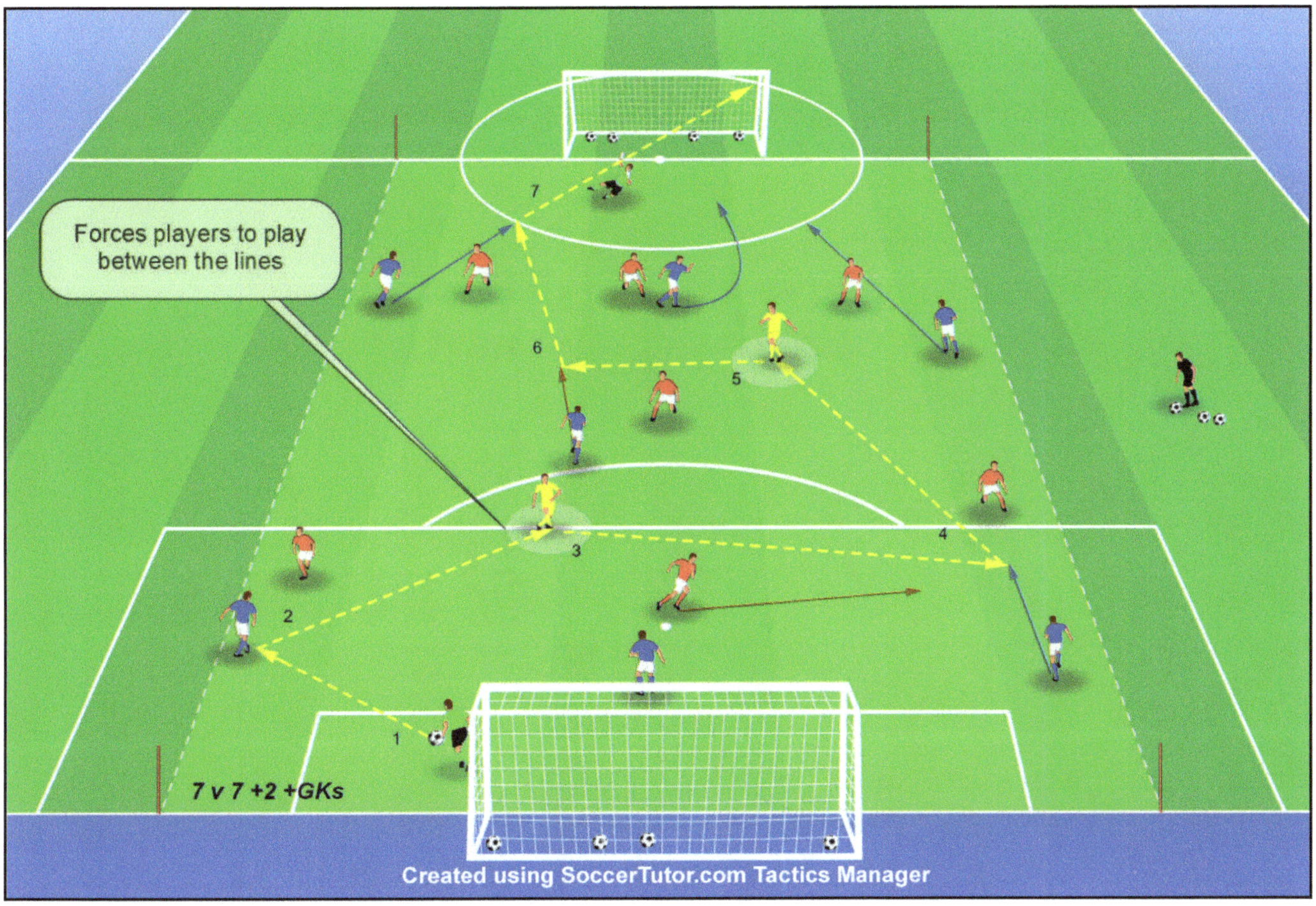

Forces players to play between the lines

7 v 7 +2 +GKs

Created using SoccerTutor.com Tactics Manager

PRACTICE INFORMATION

Duration	Reps	Sets	Numbers	Size (m)	Work Duration	Player Density
10 min	2 min	4	16 + GKs	30 x 50	8 min	102 m²

OBJECTIVE: Directional based game with focus on forcing players to play forward (narrow pitch)

Volume Metrics	Practice Total	Per Min. of Work
Total Distance (km)	1.069	0.13
High Speed Running (m)	21.47	2.68
Sprint Distance (m)	1.06	0.13
Work Ratio (%)	32.79	
Power Plays (HiActs)	4.65	0.58

Intensity Metrics	Practice Total	Per Min. of Work
Max Speed (m/s)	6.1	
Intensity (m/min)		81.94
Power Score (w/kg)	6.96	
Max Accel. Distance (m)	14.17	1.77
Max Decel. Distance (m)	19.32	2.42

* The data shows the physical output per player based on research from elite level teams - see **pages 81-83** for details

THURSDAY Training Practices: Reaction Speed - 2 Days Until Match (MD +5/-2)

Medium Sided Game 7: Play Through the Thirds in a Progressive Three Zone Game

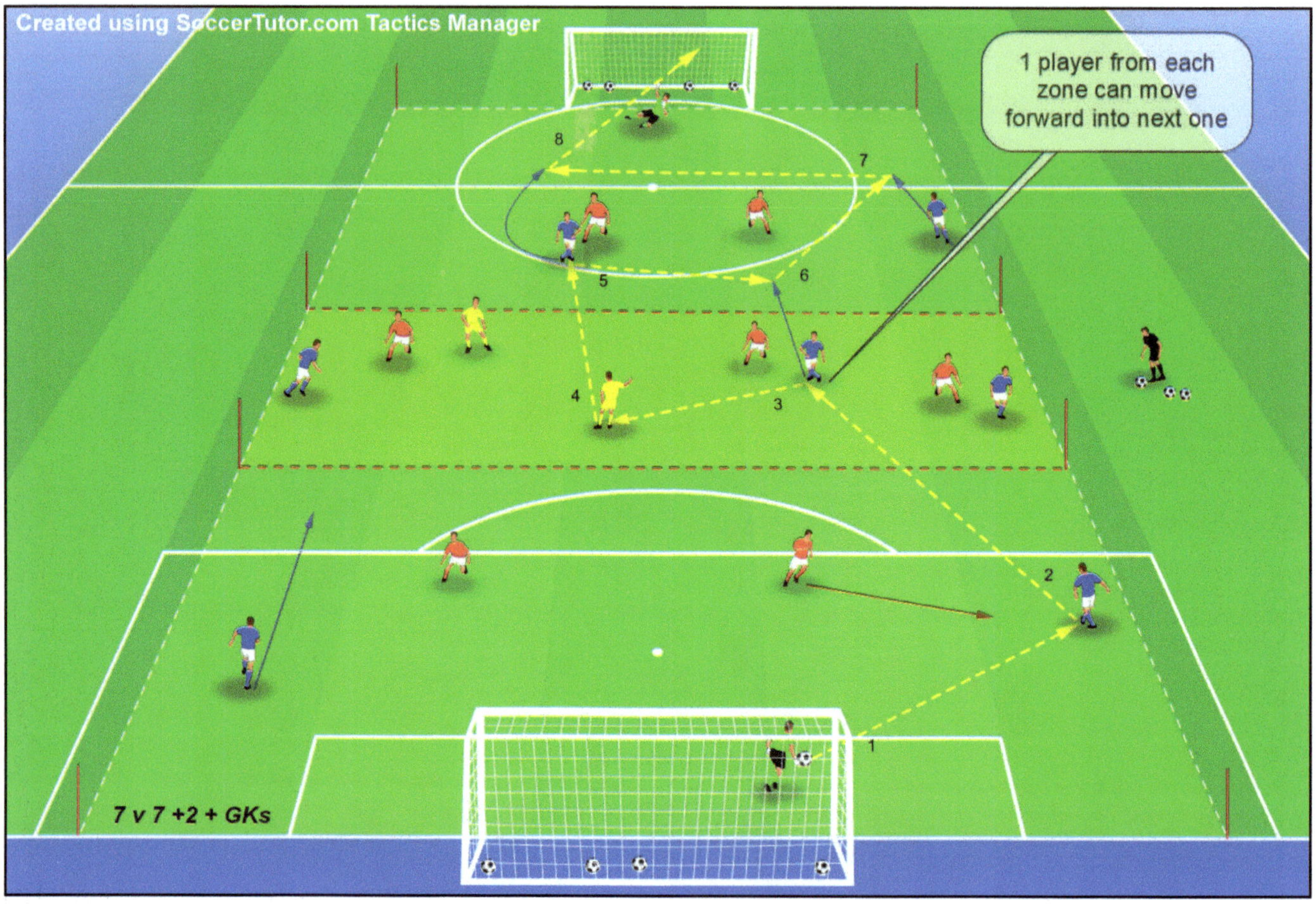

1 player from each zone can move forward into next one

7 v 7 +2 + GKs

PRACTICE INFORMATION

Duration	Reps	Sets	Numbers	Size (m)	Work Duration	Player Density
20 min	6.5 min	3 x 6.5 min	16 + GKs	40 x 60	19.5 min	145 m²

OBJECTIVE: Progressive build-up game with the focus on playing through the thirds

Volume Metrics	Practice Total	Per Min. of Work
Total Distance (km)	2.326	0.12
High Speed Running (m)	87.6	4.49
Sprint Distance (m)	7.87	0.4
Work Ratio (%)	38.99	
Power Plays (HiActs)	15.81	0.81

Intensity Metrics	Practice Total	Per Min. of Work
Max Speed (m/s)	7.03	
Intensity (m/min)		93.09
Power Score (w/kg)	7.98	
Max Accel. Distance (m)	31.68	1.62
Max Decel. Distance (m)	46.75	2.4

* The data shows the physical output per player based on research from elite level teams - see **pages 81-83** for details

THURSDAY Training Practices: Reaction Speed - 2 Days Until Match (MD +5/-2)

Medium Sided Game 8: Create Space and Overloads for Crossing on a Wide Pitch

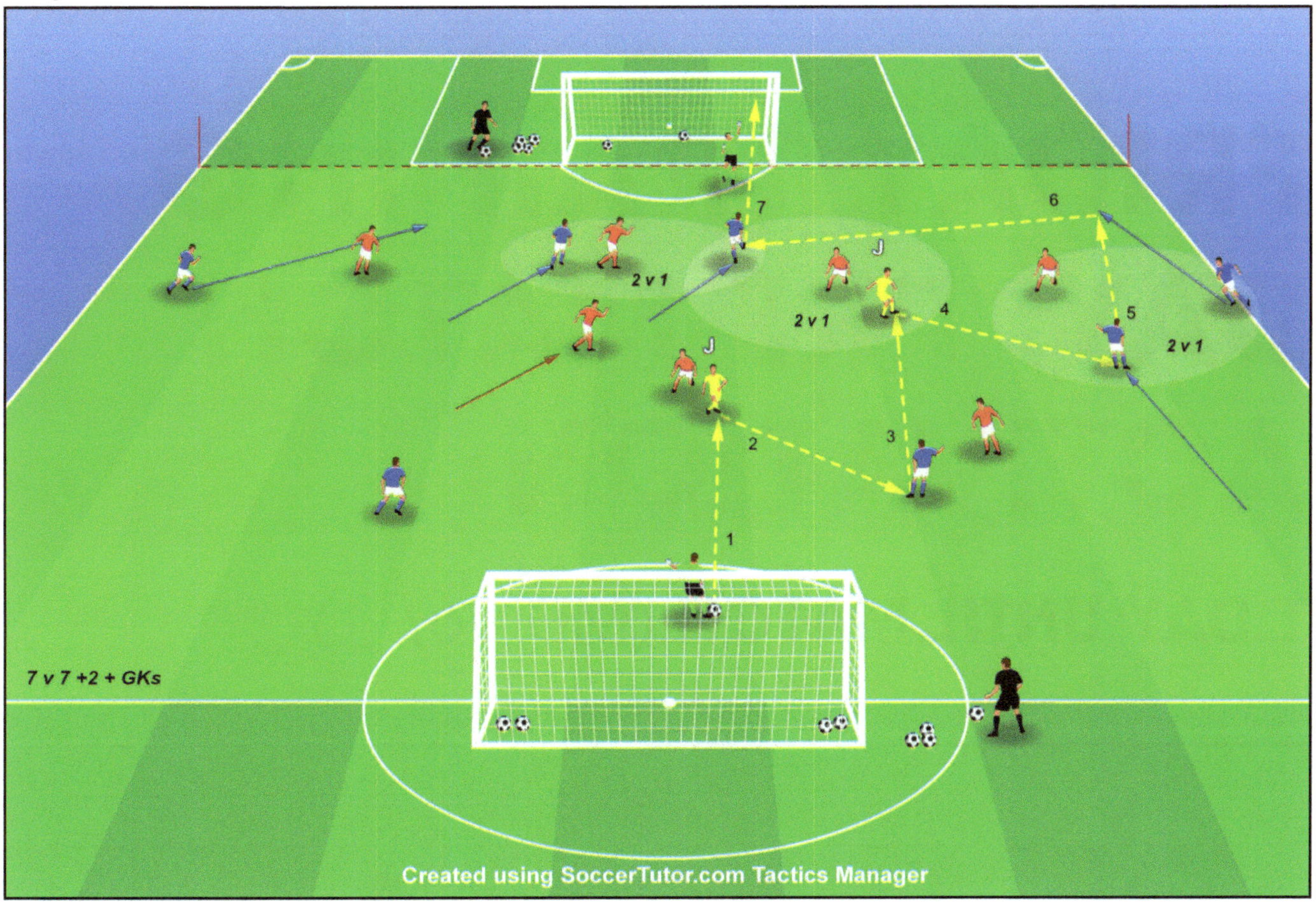

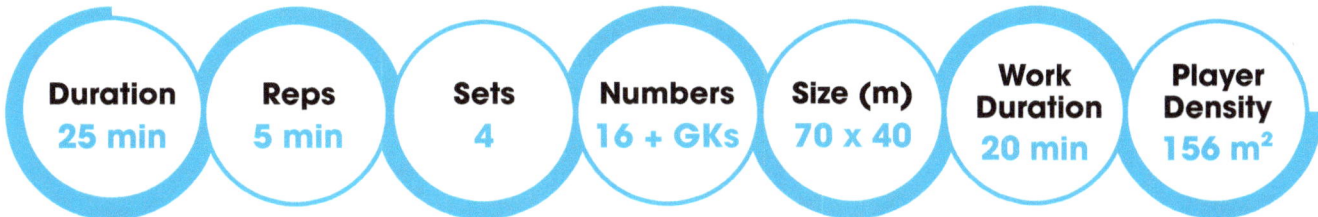

PRACTICE INFORMATION

Duration	Reps	Sets	Numbers	Size (m)	Work Duration	Player Density
25 min	5 min	4	16 + GKs	70 x 40	20 min	156 m²

OBJECTIVE: Utilising a numerical advantage and wide area to create overloads and deliver crosses

Volume Metrics	Practice Total	Per Min. of Work
Total Distance (km)	2.397	0.12
High Speed Running (m)	48.29	2.41
Sprint Distance (m)	3	0.15
HML Distance (m)	280.9	14
Power Plays (HiActs)	12.25	0.6

Intensity Metrics	Practice Total	Per Min. of Work
Max Speed (m/s)	6.51	
Intensity (m/min)		90.1
Power Score (w/kg)	7.57	
Max Accel. Distance (m)	27	1.35
Max Decel. Distance (m)	37	1.85

* The data shows the physical output per player based on research from elite level teams - see **pages 81-83** for details

217

Football Periodization to Maximise Performance

FRIDAY TRAINING DAY: PRE-MATCH ACTIVATION

1 DAY UNTIL MATCH (MD +6/-1)

FRIDAY Training Day: Pre-Match Activation - 1 Day Until Match (MD +6/-1)

1 DAY UNTIL THE MATCH (MD +6/-1):
Pre-Match Activation Training Day

Duration	45 min	70-75 min	85-95 min	60-70 min	45-60 min	90 min
Daily Theme	Recovery	Resistance	Speed Endurance	Reaction Speed	Activation	Match
Preparation	Match Day (MD) +2/-5	Match Day (MD) +3/-4	Match Day (MD) +4/-3	Match Day (MD) +5/-2	Match Day (MD) +6/-1	Match Day
		Positional Principles	Collective Principles	Unit Principles		
Game Type Focus	-	SSGs 1v1-4v4 (+GKs) Small Area	LSGs 8v8-10v10 (+GKs) Large Area	MSGs 5v5-7v7 (+GKs) Medium Area	LSGs 8v8-10v10 (+GKs) Small / Med Area	Match Day 11v11
Bout Durations	-	1-3 min	5-10 min	3-5 min	4 min	2 x 45 min
	Mon: Recovery	Tue-Wed: Conditioning		Thu-Fri: Preparation		Perform

* **Training Week based on Professional Microcycle Example** - see pages 74-75.

Key Focus on:
- **Review in Recovery** of the key principles covered across the microcycle (training week)
- Stimulating the **Neural Firing Responses**
- Stimulating **Fast Cognitive Processes**
- Reduced player density ensuring **Minimal Fatigue**

FRIDAY (MD +6/-1) TRAINING DAY:
Pre-Match Activation

This **Friday (MD +6/-1) Training Day:** is the second day of the "preparation" or "tapering" phase of the training week and is the day before the match. There is an urgent need to significantly reduce the training load further and ensure players fully recover pre-match (Malone et al., 2015).

In the key research surrounding tapering, it has been suggested that anywhere between 50-60% decrease in training loads (TL) on MD-1 is sufficient based on current published models of elite football (van Winkle et al., 2014; Owen et al., 2017; Owen et al., 2020). However, according to more recent published work in this area, ensuring a TL decrease of approximately 40% has corresponded with reduced biochemical, physical and subjective assessment from elite level players in preparation of competitive match play. This information provided is based on a conjunctive approach using the data with personal experience to manage the reduction of TLs close to matches.

My own practical assessment highlights the **benefits of the tapering continuing through this day with biochemical and physical restoration**, which is key to aiding the freshness and regeneration of the players pre-match using this approach.

Relative to this MD-1 training and preparation day, the muscle system should be stimulated by quick reactional and neuromuscular activations situated around a reduced playing area and player density.

The **psychological focus and overload should also be reduced** in order to maximise freshness going into the match-day.

The practices on this day are generally based around the lowest developmental demands and involve a **more informal approach to training due to the need to recover psychologically and reduce the potential to accumulate fatigue**. The MD-1 training content presents game-like situations on a smaller scale to elicit fast cognitive responses but reduced high speed running (HSR) and sprint demands.

Even within the game-like scenarios, the tactical strategy and key coaching points of the game model should be highlighted, reviewed and refreshed for the following match-day.

Main Objective of Training Day: Trigger some of the reactive, subconscious technical and decision making processes required by the coaching team and refresh the key aspects across the training microcycle.

Pre-Match Activation Focus (LSGs in Small Areas)

Neural firing/stimulation focus	Minimal cardio overload due to reduced bout durations
Small/medium areas, large numbers, with reduced thinking time	Acceleration focus of 10-15 metre distances
Focused on reactive elements of the game (referee, players, ball)	-25% normal pitch sizes = No high speed running (HSR) or sprint distance
LSGs with reduced pitch sizes	**Key Coaching Themes:**
Small pitch + large numbers: = Reduced physical cost + > Reactive demands	Minimise fatigue + maximise freshness, short game durations, large numbers in small/medium areas (no HSR or sprint distance), reactive nature

FRIDAY Training Day: Pre-Match Activation - 1 Day Until Match (MD +6/-1)

FRIDAY (MD +6/-1) TRAINING DAY:
Fundamental Concepts of Pre-Match Activation Training

Recent research findings across many different tapering strategies in professional football have resulted in the MD +6/-1 reduction in training duration and total load (TL) in its entirety (Owen et al., 2020; Malone et al., 2015; Owen et al., 2017).

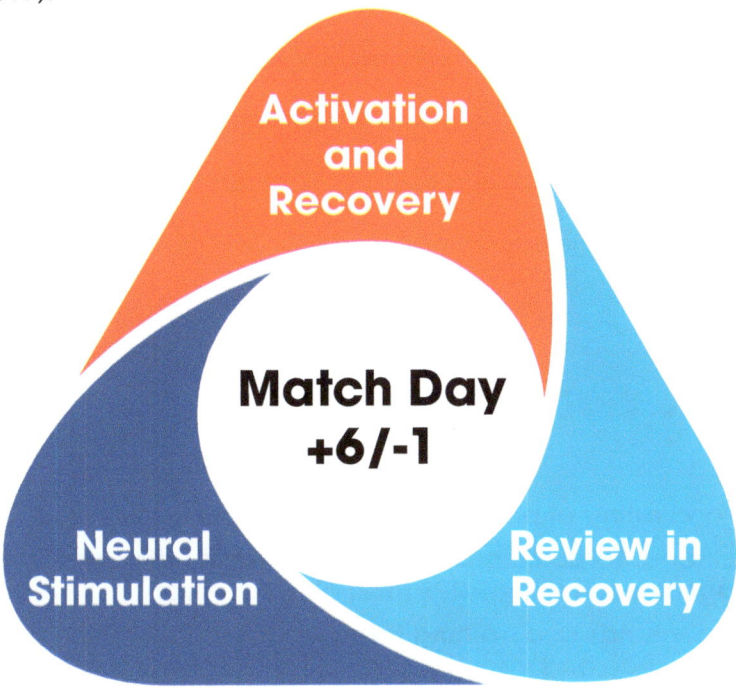

FRIDAY Training Day: Pre-Match Activation - 1 Day Until Match (MD +6/-1)

Analysis of a 6-Week Training Mesocycle and Positional Quantification in Elite European Football Players

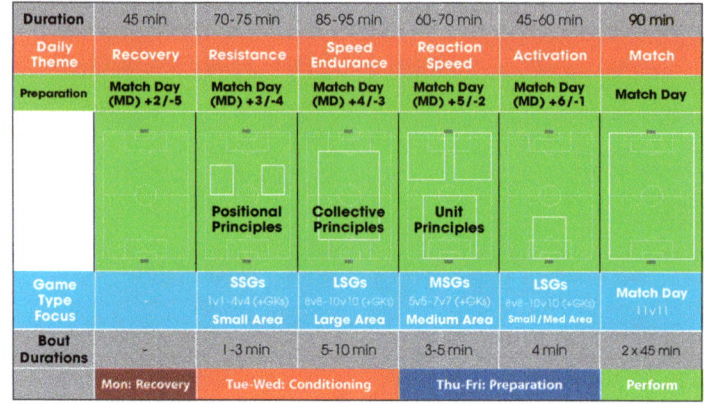

What?
Analyse a training mesocycle whilst quantifying positional demands imposed on elite European football players.

When?
Data recorded from players across a 6-week in-season training mesocycle period.

How?
- Daily **GPS** and **rating of perceived exertion (RPE)** load recorded.
- Metrics included: **Total distance** (m), **high-intensity distance** (m), **sprint distance** (m), **average speed** (m.min), **RPE load** (RPE x duration).
- **Positional demands** and **training loads** analysed in addition with match conditions (i.e. match location and match score), as well as player's age.

Who?
16 elite male European football players participated in the study.

Results?
- **Training Loads:** Typical daily training loads did not differ throughout each week of the in-season mesocycle. Total Load (TL) significantly reduced on MD-1 vs. TLs on MD-2, MD-3 and MD-4 preceding a match.
- Physical output differences found between MD-2, MD-3, and MD-4 revealed a structured, tapering approach to microcycle.
- **Positional:** **WFs =>** Total distance and Very High Intensity Running (VHIR) distance vs. other positions; **CBs** = significantly less < Total Distance (TD) and VHIR vs. other positions.
- Reduced average speeds (metres per min) reported in training sessions post-successful matches vs. post-defeats (p<0.05).
- Reduced average speeds (metres per min) also reported post-away fixtures vs. home fixtures within the microcycle.

Practical Application?
- Coaches can maintain a uniformed and structured training load mesocycle whilst inducing variation of the physical outputs during the microcycle phase.
- Additionally, the investigation also provides a tapering approach that may induce significant variation of the positional demands.

Full Scientific Reference
Owen AL., Lago-Penas C., Gomez AM., Mendes B., Dellal A. (2017).
Analysis of a Training Mesocycle & Positional Quantification in Elite European Soccer Players | International Journal of Sport Science & Coaching, DOI: 10.1177/1747954117727851

FRIDAY TRAINING DAY PRACTICES:
PRE-MATCH ACTIVATION

1 DAY UNTIL MATCH (MD +6/-1)

FRIDAY TRAINING SESSION (45-60 min)

Pre-Match Activation Training Day:

1. Resistance Warm-up (10-12 min)
2. Reaction Speed Conditioning Practice (5-15 min)
3. Large Sided Game in Small/Medium Area (10-50 min)

FRIDAY Training Practices: Pre-Match Activation - 1 Day Until Match (MD +6/-1)

FRIDAY - 1 DAY UNTIL MATCH (MD +6/-1):
Resistance Warm-Up Practices

INTENSITY: All practices are performed at full intensity

What are Resistance Warm-ups?
- Include many stop and start actions, and directional changes.
- Include many lower level accelerations and decelerations in tight spaces.
- Activate the muscle groups for the explosive maximum accelerations and decelerations later in the session.
- Provide more resistance to the working muscles through explosive actions in small spaces.

Why are they used on this day of the training week (MD +3/-4)?
- To prepare the players for the smaller surface area type work developed through the course of the session.

How does this help to maximise performance?
- Resistance warm-ups are used on this day as a way of preparing the players muscles used for changing directions, acceleration and deceleration efforts.
- Resistance warm-ups also generally ready the body for the session ahead (small sided games).

NOTE: There are 2 more Resistance Warm-up Practices you can use from the **Tuesday Training Day (pages 97-98)** - this section starts from Practice No.3...

FRIDAY Training Practices: Pre-Match Activation - 1 Day Until Match (MD +6/-1)

Resistance Warm-up 3: Lateral Hurdles, One-Two, In-and-Out Movements + Sprint Circuit

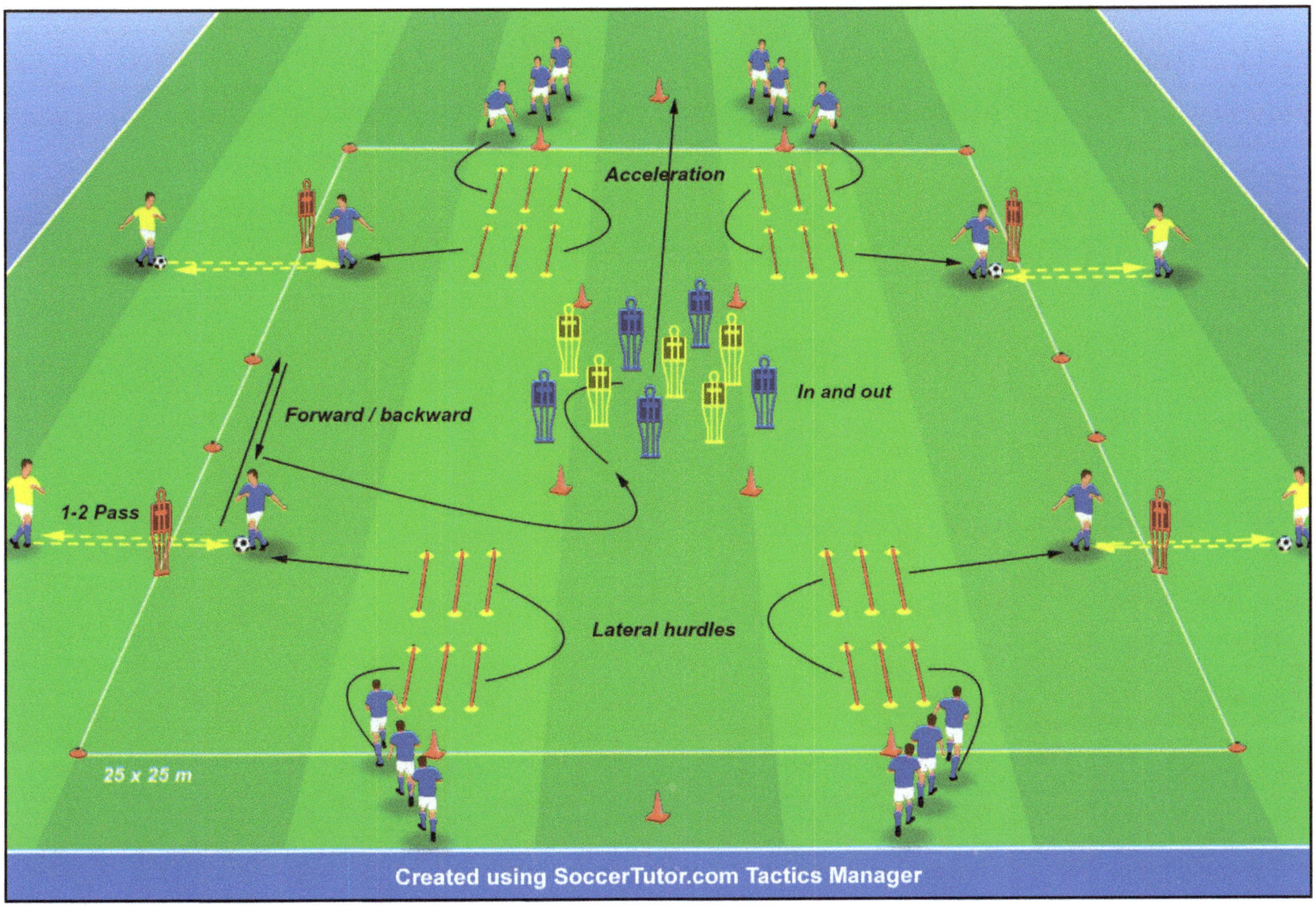

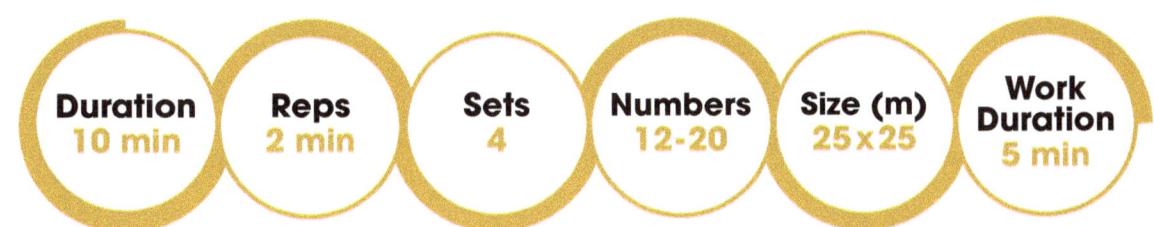

PRACTICE INFORMATION

Duration	Reps	Sets	Numbers	Size (m)	Work Duration
10 min	2 min	4	12-20	25 x 25	5 min

OBJECTIVE: Physically and mentally prepare the players for the training session (with the ball)

Volume Metrics	Practice Total	Per Min. of Work
Total Distance (km)	0.91	0.18
High Speed Running (m)	0.18	0.036
Sprint Distance (m)	-	-
Work Ratio (%)	27.3	
Power Plays (HiActs)	1.89	0.38

Intensity Metrics	Practice Total	Per Min. of Work
Max Speed (m/s)	4.78	
Intensity (m/min)		111.32
Power Score (w/kg)	5.41	
No. of Max Accels >4m²	12.59	2.52
No. of Max Decels >4m²	9.61	1.92

* The data shows the physical output per player based on research from elite level teams - see pages 81-83 for details

FRIDAY Training Practices: Pre-Match Activation - 1 Day Until Match (MD +6/-1)

Resistance Warm-up 4: Hurdles, Slalom Runs, and Side-Shuffles in a Dynamic Circuit

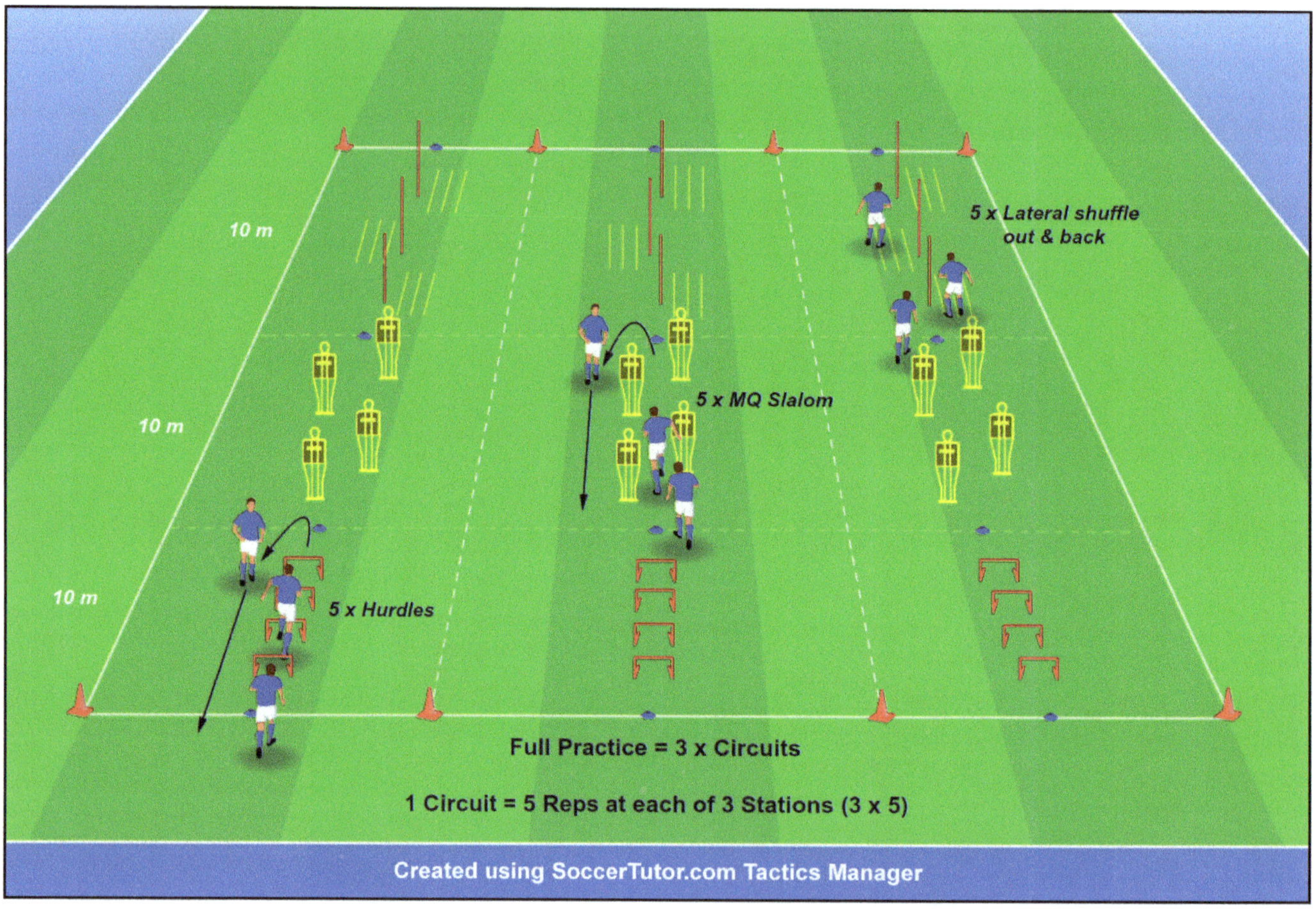

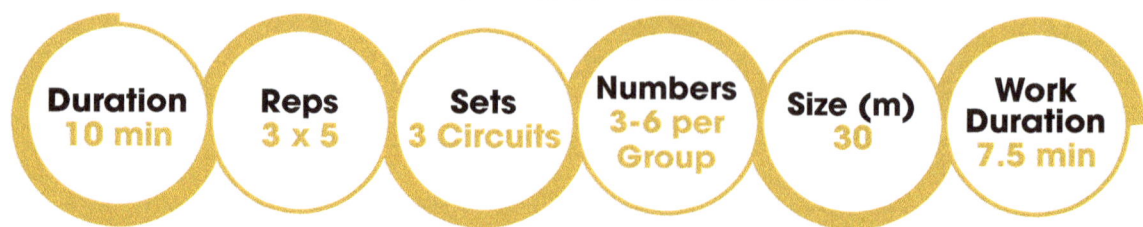

Full Practice = 3 x Circuits
1 Circuit = 5 Reps at each of 3 Stations (3 x 5)

PRACTICE INFORMATION

Duration	Reps	Sets	Numbers	Size (m)	Work Duration
10 min	3 x 5	3 Circuits	3-6 per Group	30	7.5 min

OBJECTIVE: Physically and mentally prepare the players for the training session (with the ball)

Volume Metrics	Practice Total	Per Min. of Work
Total Distance (km)	0.819	0.1
High Speed Running (m)	2	0.27
Sprint Distance (m)	-	-
Work Ratio (%)	25.4	
Power Plays (HiActs)	2.1	0.28

Intensity Metrics	Practice Total	Per Min. of Work
Max Speed (m/s)	4.55	
Intensity (m/min)		114.2
Power Score (w/kg)	5.78	
No. of Max Accels >4m²	9.24	1.23
No. of Max Decels >4m²	6.3	0.84

* The data shows the physical output per player based on research from elite level teams - see **pages 81-83** for details

FRIDAY Training Practices: Pre-Match Activation - 1 Day Until Match (MD +6/-1)

FRIDAY - 1 DAY UNTIL MATCH (MD +6/-1):
Reaction Speed Conditioning Practices

INTENSITY: All practices are performed at full intensity

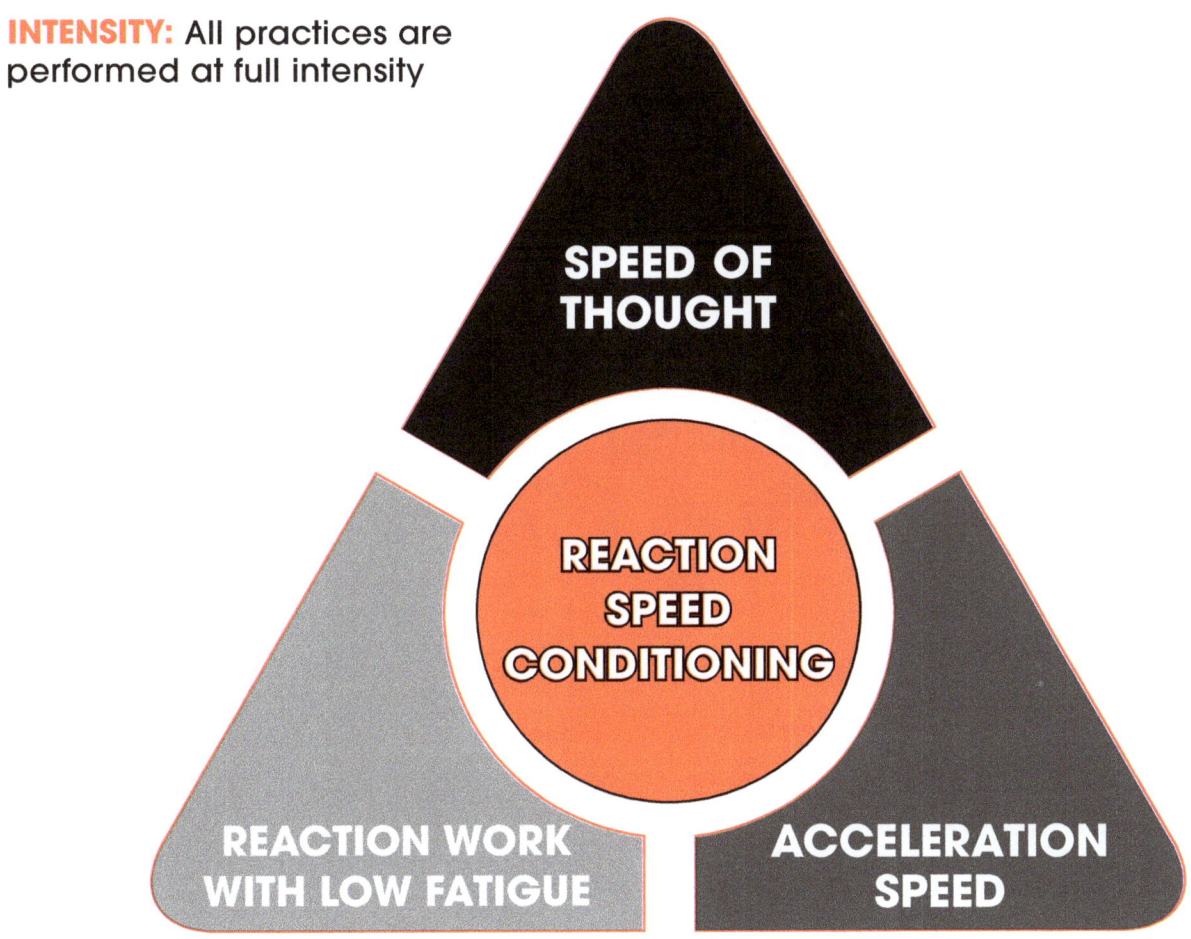

What are Reaction Speed Conditioning Practices?

- Lots of reaction based work.
- Focus to move quickly from a physical perspective but also react fast.
- Lots of shorter acceleration based work but reduced aggressive decelerations.

Why are they used on this day of the training week (MD +6/-1)?

- Reduce fatigue in the players legs.
- Remain engaged for fast reactions from a psychological and acceleration/speed perspective.

How does this help to maximise performance?

- Reaction speed conditioning practices are used on this day to engage players from a cognitive perspective and stimulate fast movements without adding additional fatigue.

NOTE: There are 2 more Reaction Speed Conditioning Practices you can use from the **Thursday Training Day (pages 192-193)** - this section starts from Practice No.3...

FRIDAY Training Practices: Pre-Match Activation - 1 Day Until Match (MD +6/-1)

Reaction Speed Conditioning 3: Rebound Pass, Lateral Foot Speed + Sprint to Cone

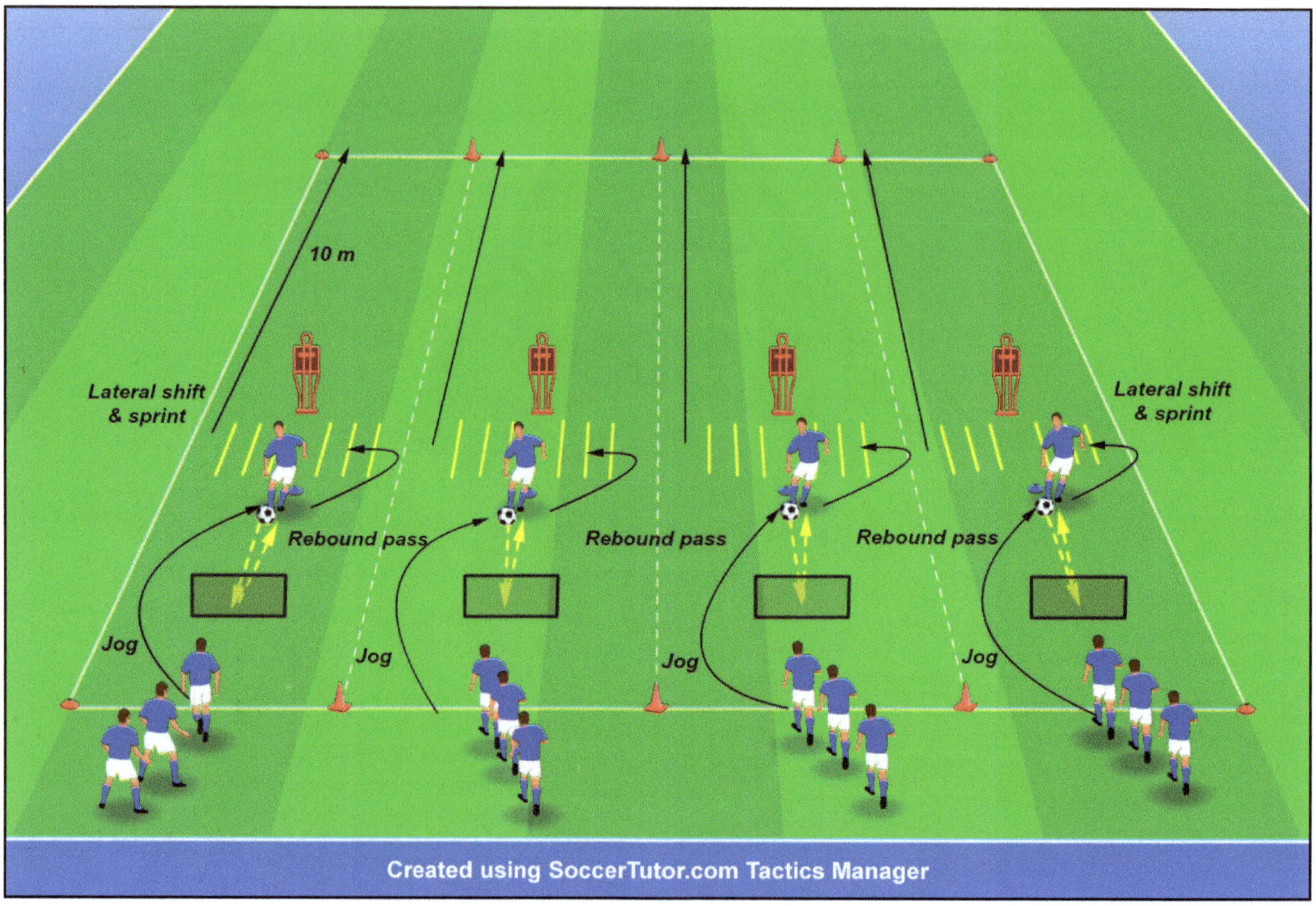

[Diagram showing four parallel lanes (10 x 35m) with players performing jog, rebound pass off rebound boards, lateral shift & sprint past mannequins, then 10m sprint to cone.]

PRACTICE INFORMATION

Duration	Reps	Sets	Numbers	Size (m)	Work Duration	
5 min	3	2	4-5 per Group	10 x 35	0.5 min	React / Activate

OBJECTIVES: Stimulate and provide players with reactive based accelerations over short distance

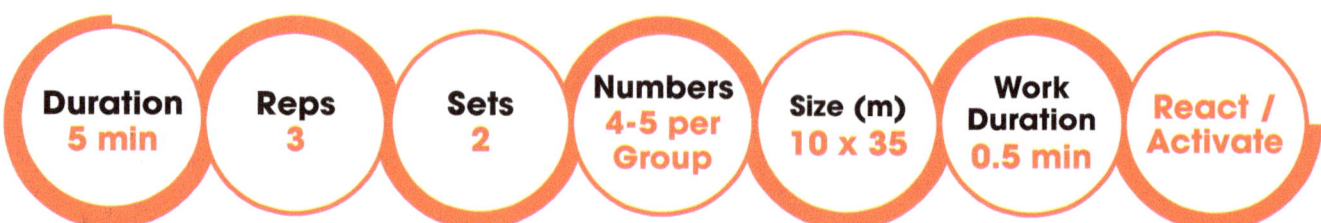

Volume Metrics	Practice Total	Per Min. of Work
Total Distance (km)	0.164	0.33
High Speed Running (m)	-	-
Sprint Distance (m)	-	-
Work Ratio (%)	30	
Power Plays (HiActs)	2	4

Intensity Metrics	Practice Total	Per Min. of Work
Max Speed (m/s)	4.88	
Intensity (m/min)		29
Power Score (w/kg)	2.33	
No. of Max Accels >4m²	2	4
No. of Max Decels >4m²	-	-

* The data shows the physical output per player based on research from elite level teams - see **pages 81-83** for details

FRIDAY Training Practices: Pre-Match Activation - 1 Day Until Match (MD +6/-1)

Reaction Speed Conditioning 4:
Agility and 4-Player Reactive Speed Square

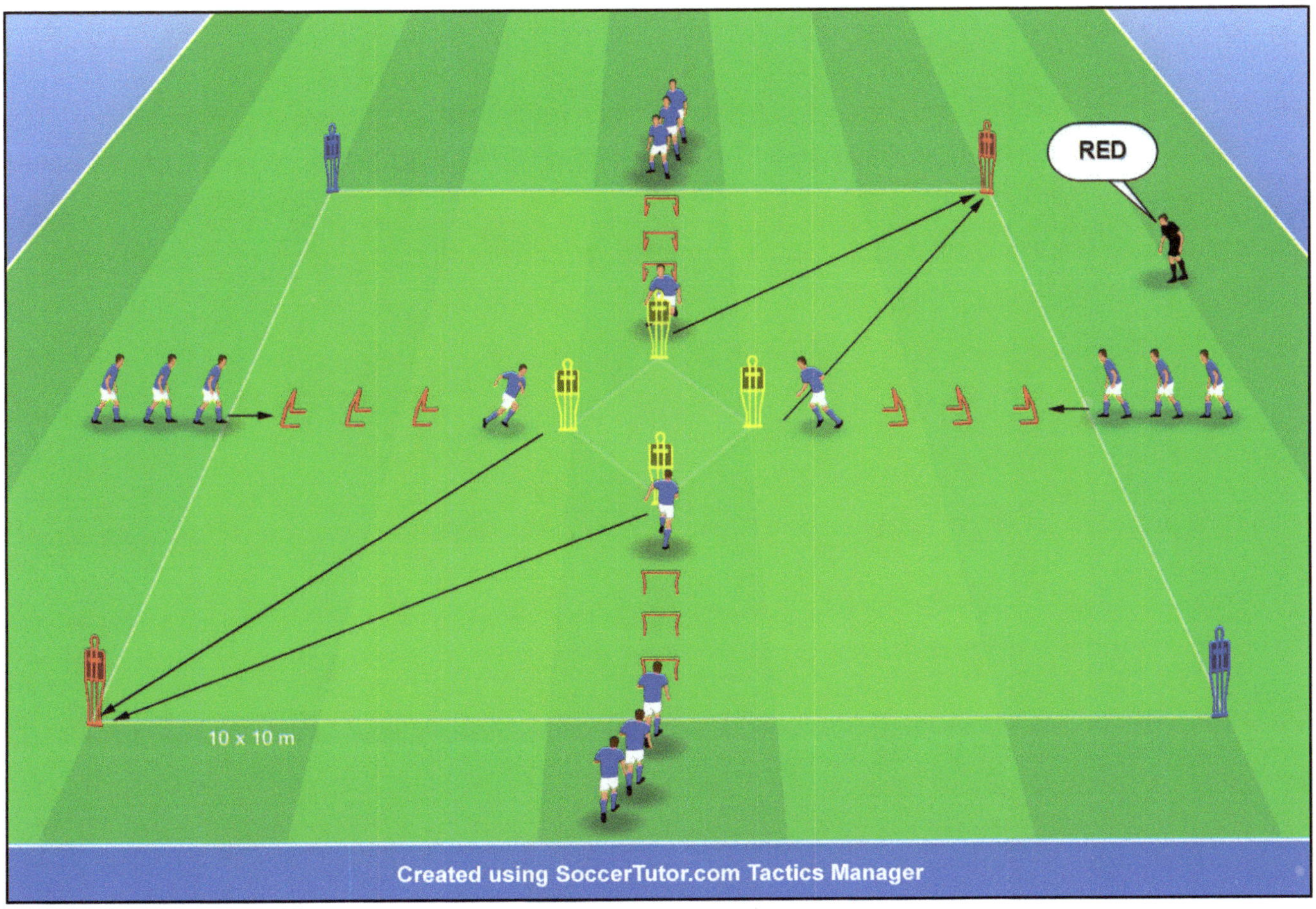

PRACTICE INFORMATION

- **Duration**: 5 min
- **Reps**: 2
- **Sets**: 4
- **Numbers**: 16-20
- **Size (m)**: 10 x 10
- **Work Duration**: 40 sec
- **React / Activate**

OBJECTIVES: Stimulate and provide players with reactive based accelerations over a short distance

Volume Metrics	Practice Total	Per Min. of Work
Total Distance (km)	0.117	0.18
High Speed Running (m)	0.8	1.2
Sprint Distance (m)	-	-
Work Ratio (%)	21.23	
Power Plays (HiActs)	4	6

Intensity Metrics	Practice Total	Per Min. of Work
Max Speed (m/s)	4.45	
Intensity (m/min)		57.6
Power Score (w/kg)	4.7	
No. of Max Accels >4m²	6.6	9.9
No. of Max Decels >4m²	2.9	4.35

* The data shows the physical output per player based on research from elite level teams - see **pages 81-83** for details

FRIDAY Training Practices: Pre-Match Activation - 1 Day Until Match (MD +6/-1)

Reaction Speed Conditioning 5:
Reactive Sprints on the Coach's Signal

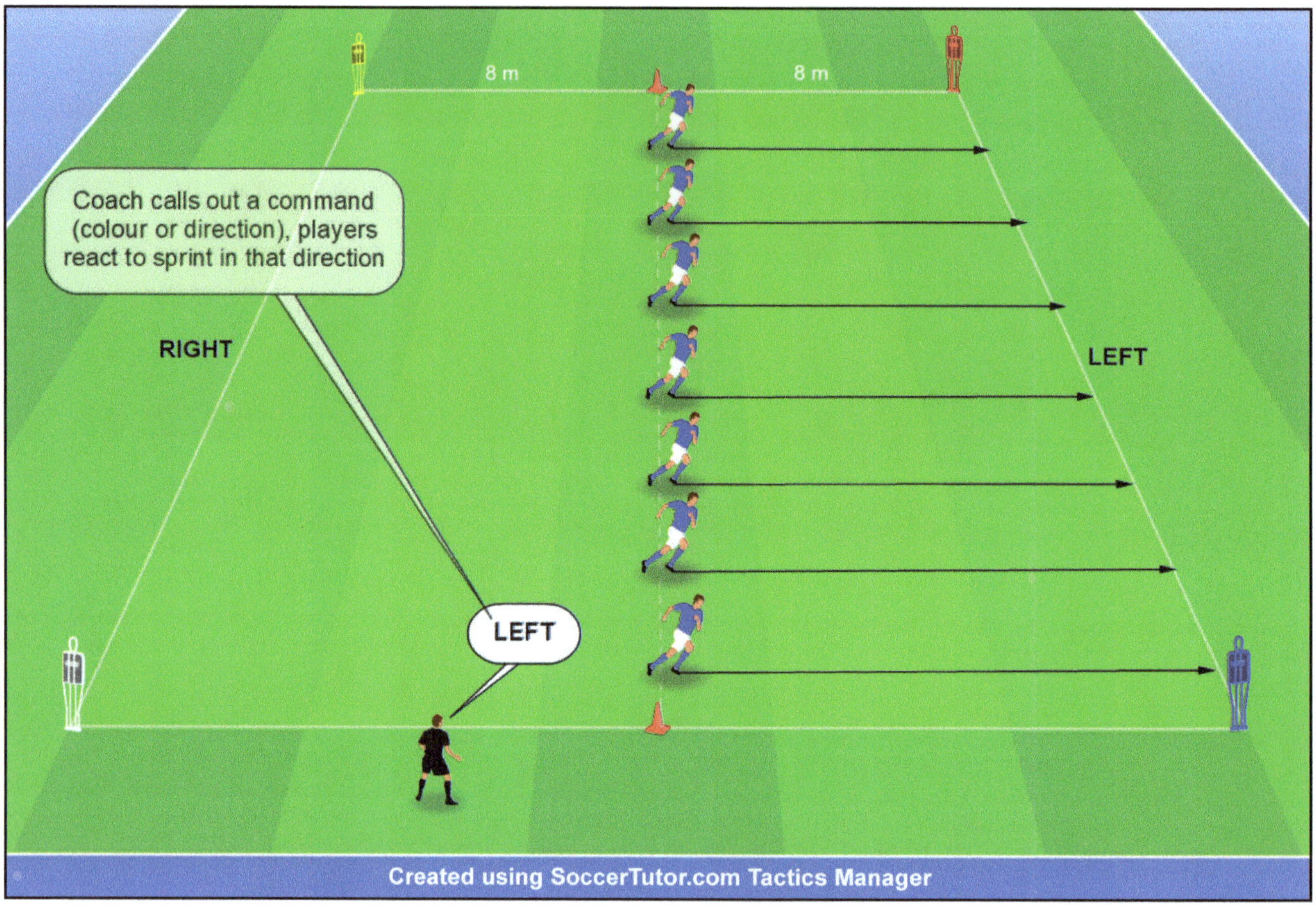

PRACTICE INFORMATION

- **Duration:** 5 min
- **Reps:** 5
- **Sets:** 1
- **Numbers:** 7 per group
- **Size (m):** 16 m
- **Work Duration:** 10 sec
- **React / Activate**

OBJECTIVES: Stimulate and provide players with reactive based accelerations over a short distance

Volume Metrics	Practice Total	Per Min. of Work
Total Distance (km)	0.14	0.84
High Speed Running (m)	10.3	61.8
Sprint Distance (m)	0.1	0.6
Work Ratio (%)	26.78	
Power Plays (HiActs)	2	12

Intensity Metrics	Practice Total	Per Min. of Work
Max Speed (m/s)	5.01	
Intensity (m/min)		34.5
Power Score (w/kg)	5.1	
No. of Max Accels >4m²	1.8	10.8
No. of Max Decels >4m²	0.9	5.4

* The data shows the physical output per player based on research from elite level teams - see **pages 81-83** for details

FRIDAY Training Practices: Pre-Match Activation - 1 Day Until Match (MD +6/-1)

WEDNESDAY - 3 DAYS UNTIL MATCH (MD +6/-1):
Large Sided Games in Small/Medium Area

INTENSITY: All practices are performed at full intensity

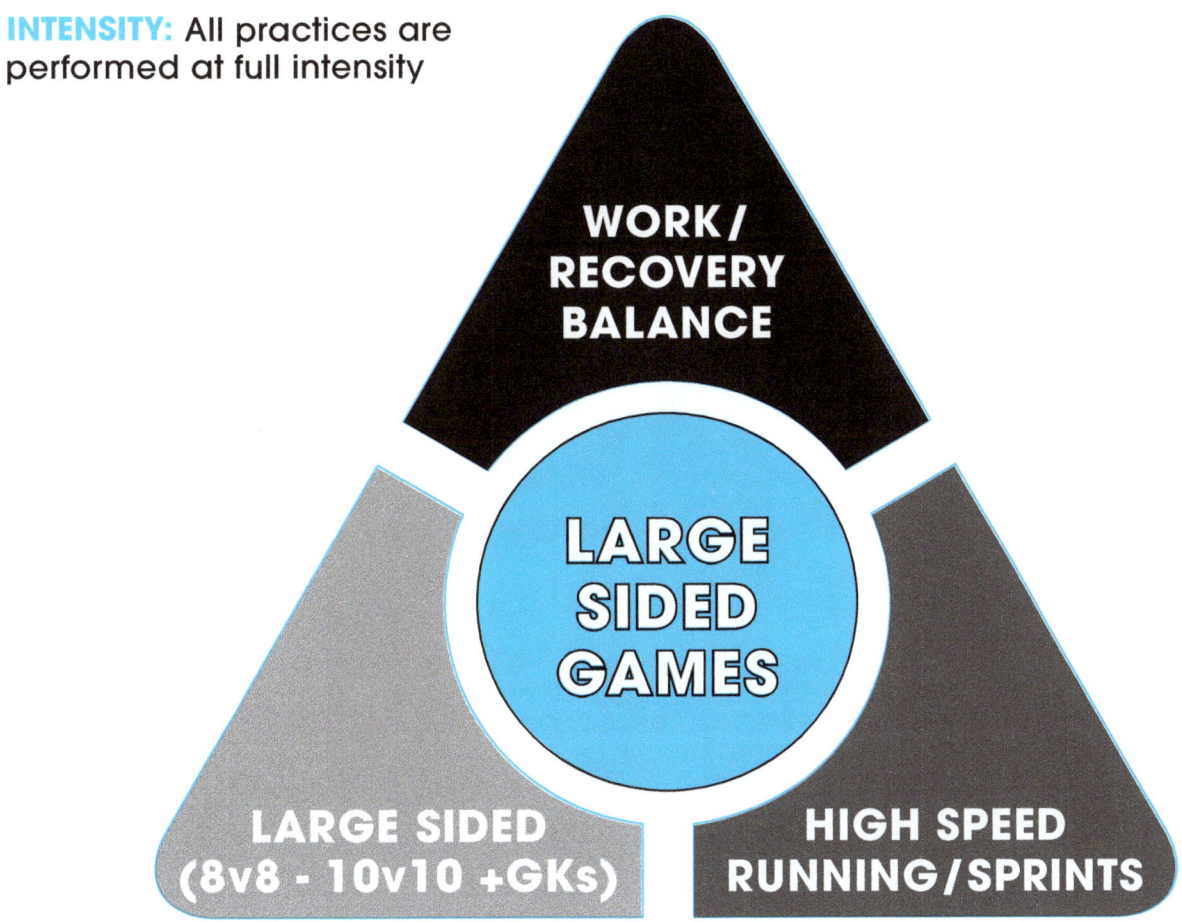

What are Large Sided Games?

- Large sided games (LSGs) are defined as including at least 8 outfield players per side = 8v8 - 10v10 (+GKs).

Why are they used on this day of the training week (MD +6/-1)?

- They can be used on different days but within this framework, they are focused around the MD +6/-1 training day with smaller playing areas to train the collective team tactical principles and provide a match simulation focus.

- There is less intensity due to the large number of players, meaning more recovery between technical actions.

How does this help to maximise performance?

- Large sided games (LSGs) performed in small/medium areas will not achieve the same high-speed running and sprint distances as the larger area games played on MD +4/-3, as they are more focused on resistance based physical developments or activities

- They also enable more position specific technical qualities to be trained.

FRIDAY Training Practices: Pre-Match Activation - 1 Day Until Match (MD +6/-1)

LSG (Small Area) 1: Fast Decision Making in an 8v8 (+GKs) Game within a Narrow Pitch

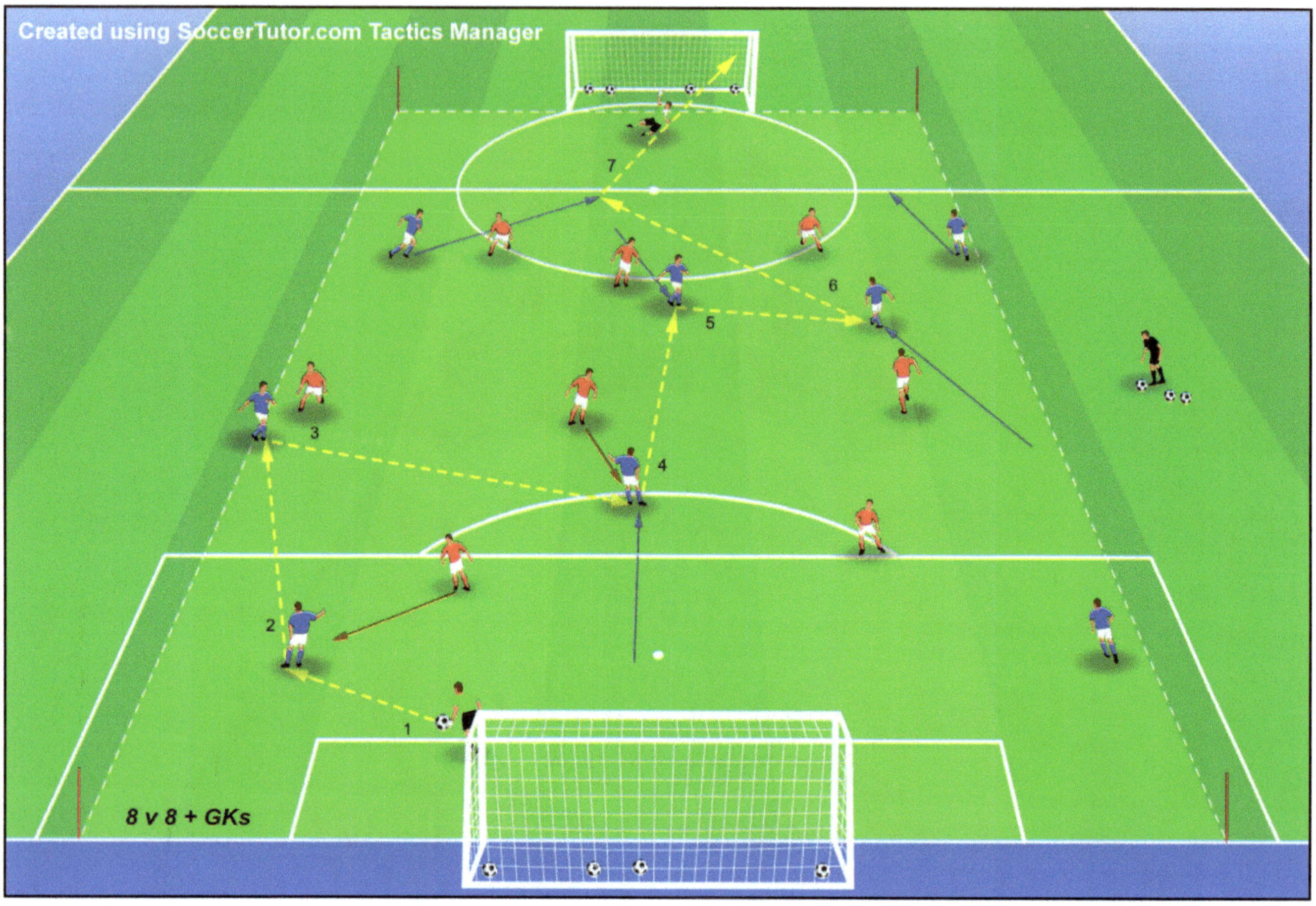

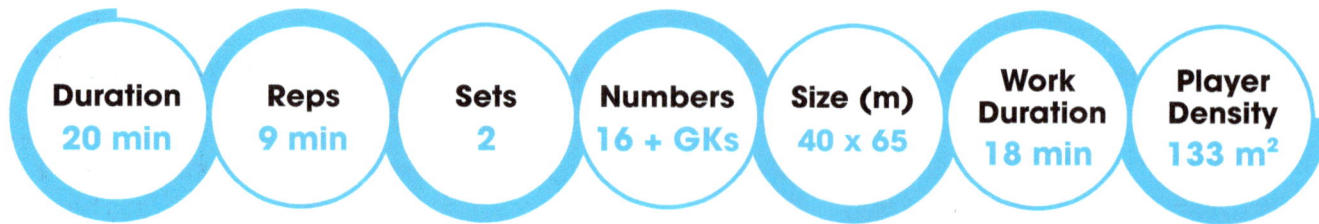

PRACTICE INFORMATION

Duration	Reps	Sets	Numbers	Size (m)	Work Duration	Player Density
20 min	9 min	2	16 + GKs	40 x 65	18 min	133 m²

OBJECTIVE: Force players to create repetitive fast thinking and execution within a small game area

Volume Metrics	Practice Total	Per Min. of Work
Total Distance (km)	2.358	0.13
High Speed Running (m)	108.51	6.03
Sprint Distance (m)	8.34	0.46
Work Ratio (%)	45.92	
Power Plays (HiActs)	18.87	1.05

Intensity Metrics	Practice Total	Per Min. of Work
Max Speed (m/s)	7.05	
Intensity (m/min)		105.96
Power Score (w/kg)	8.97	
Max Accel. Distance (m)	24.52	1.36
Max Decel. Distance (m)	40.51	2.25

*The data shows the physical output per player based on research from elite level teams - see pages 81-83 for details

FRIDAY Training Practices: Pre-Match Activation - 1 Day Until Match (MD +6/-1)

LSG (Small Area) 2: Positional Possession and Transitions in a 9v9 (+2) Tactical Game

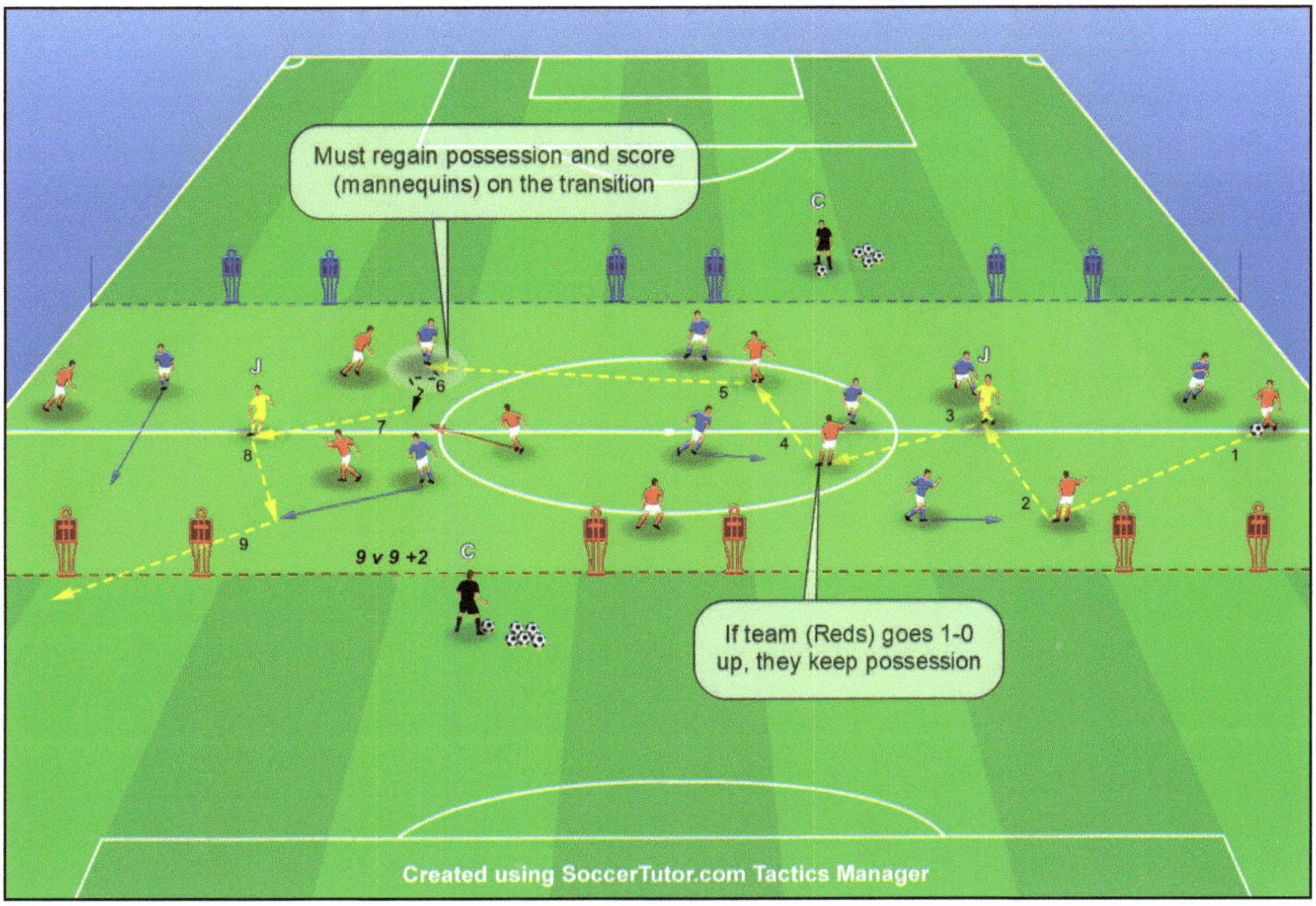

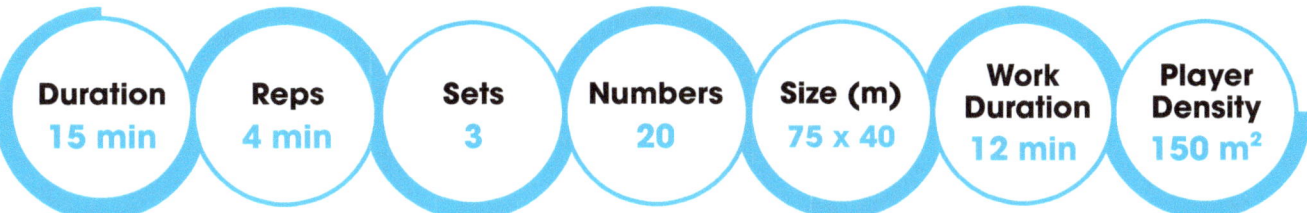

PRACTICE INFORMATION

Duration	Reps	Sets	Numbers	Size (m)	Work Duration	Player Density
15 min	4 min	3	20	75 x 40	12 min	150 m²

OBJECTIVE: Tactical focus - positional play, possession, transition play, match scenarios

Volume Metrics	Practice Total	Per Min. of Work
Total Distance (km)	1.58	0.13
High Speed Running (m)	56	4.67
Sprint Distance (m)	5	0.42
HML Distance (m)	199.5	16.63
Power Plays (HiActs)	11.63	0.97

Intensity Metrics	Practice Total	Per Min. of Work
Max Speed (m/s)	6.86	
Intensity (m/min)		93.89
Power Score (w/kg)	7.84	
No. of Max Accels >4m²	6.63	0.55
No. of Max Decels >4m²	6.47	0.54

* The data shows the physical output per player based on research from elite level teams - see **pages 81-83** for details

FRIDAY Training Practices: Pre-Match Activation - 1 Day Until Match (MD +6/-1)

LSG (Small Area) 3: Fast Decision Making in a 9v9 (+1) +GKs Game within a Small Area

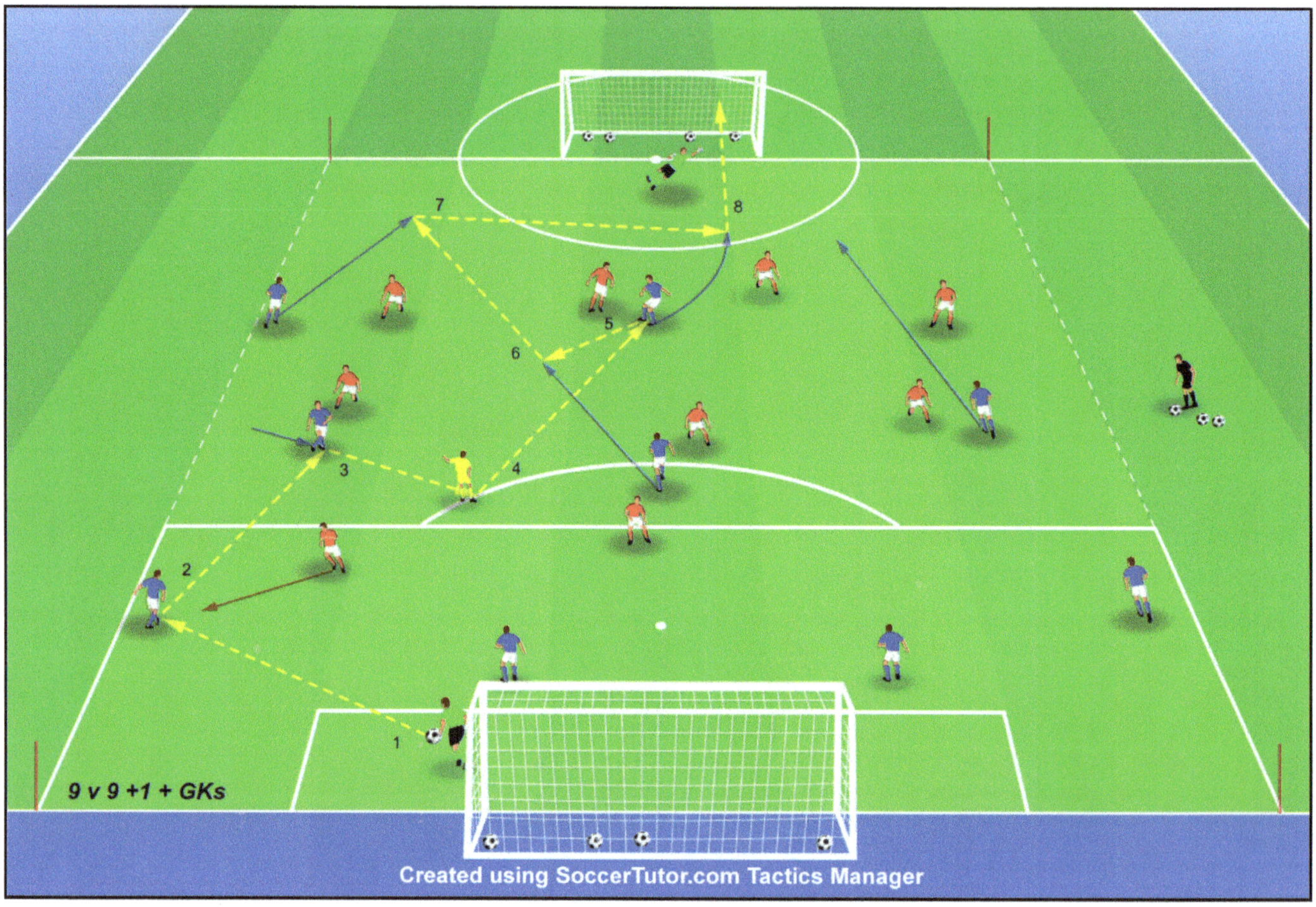

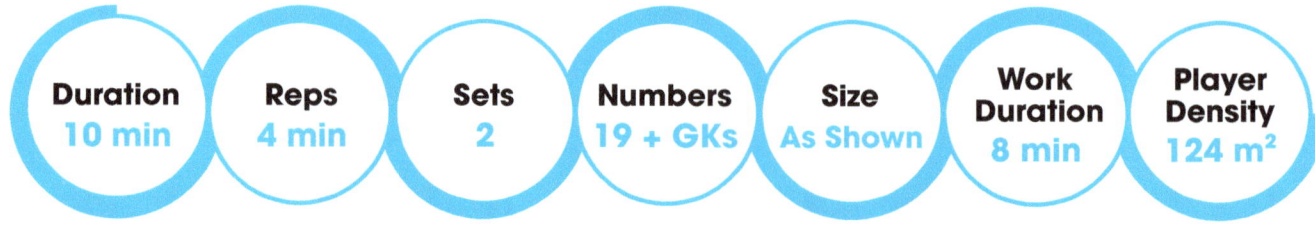

Created using SoccerTutor.com Tactics Manager

PRACTICE INFORMATION

Duration	Reps	Sets	Numbers	Size	Work Duration	Player Density
10 min	4 min	2	19 + GKs	As Shown	8 min	124 m²

OBJECTIVE: Force players to create repetitive fast thinking and execution within a small game area

Volume Metrics	Practice Total	Per Min. of Work
Total Distance (km)	0.997	0.12
High Speed Running (m)	26.31	3.3
Sprint Distance (m)	1.6	0.2
HML Distance (m)	136.21	17
Power Plays (HiActs)	5.68	0.71

Intensity Metrics	Practice Total	Per Min. of Work
Max Speed (m/s)	6.36	
Intensity (m/min)		95.98
Power Score (w/kg)	8.16	
No. of Max Accels >4m²	5.65	0.7
No. of Max Decels >4m²	6.08	0.76

* The data shows the physical output per player based on research from elite level teams - see <u>pages 81-83</u> for details

@SoccerTutor.com Football Periodization to Maximise Performance

FRIDAY Training Practices: **Pre-Match Activation** - 1 Day Until Match (MD +6/-1)

LSG (Medium Area) 1: Build-up from Back to Front in a Four Zone 8v8 (+2) +GKs Game

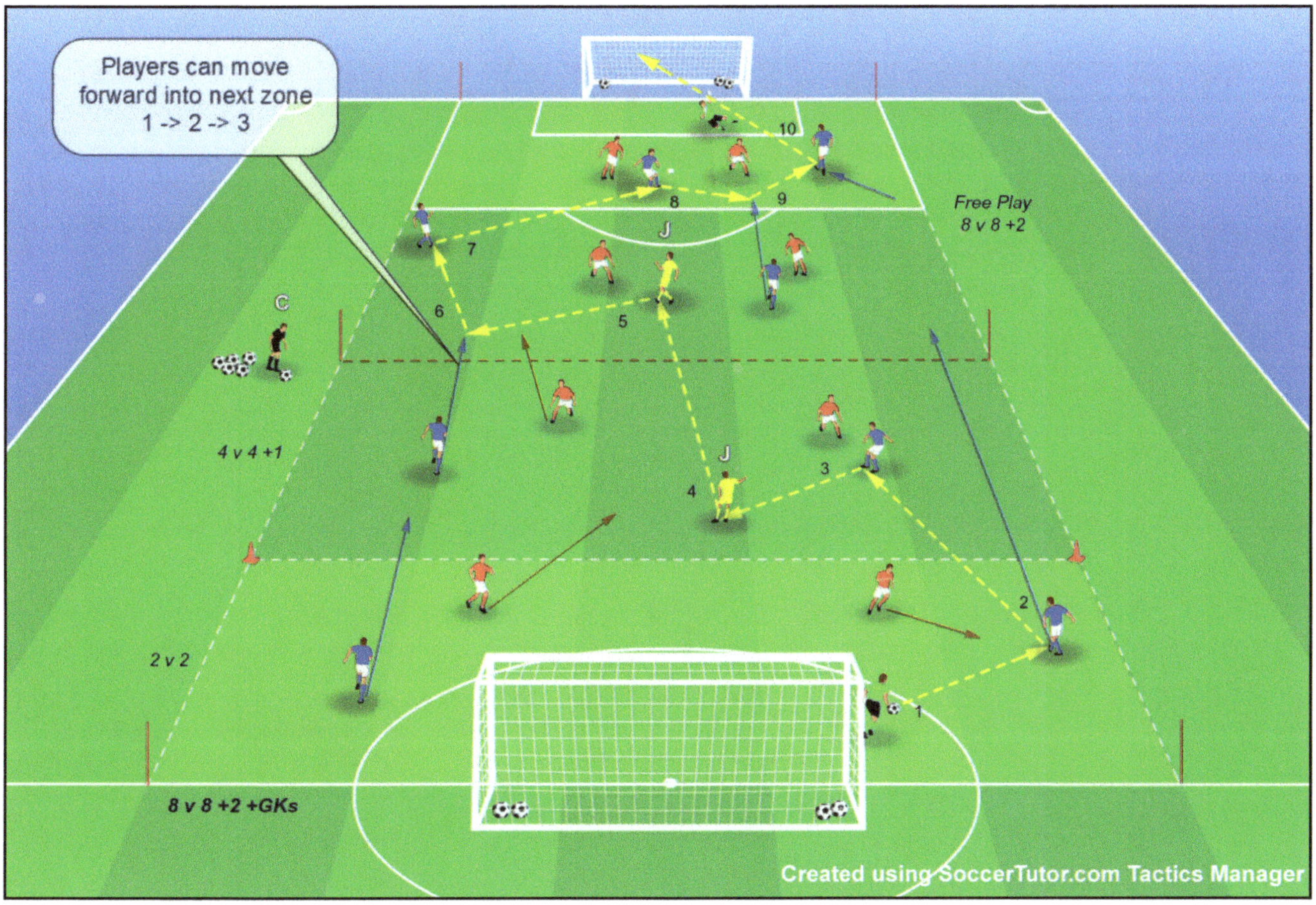

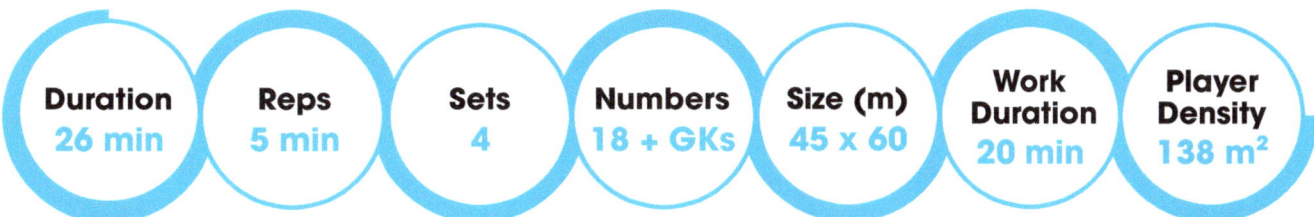

PRACTICE INFORMATION

Duration	Reps	Sets	Numbers	Size (m)	Work Duration	Player Density
26 min	5 min	4	18 + GKs	45 x 60	20 min	138 m²

OBJECTIVE: Build-up play, securing possession, and creating overloads to progress the ball

Volume Metrics	Practice Total	Per Min. of Work
Total Distance (km)	2.165	0.1
High Speed Running (m)	40.4	2.02
Sprint Distance (m)	3	0.15
Work Ratio (%)	31.48	
Power Plays (HiActs)	9.78	0.49

Intensity Metrics	Practice Total	Per Min. of Work
Max Speed (m/s)	6.67	
Intensity (m/min)		81.59
Power Score (w/kg)	6.78	
Max Accel. Distance (m)	30	1.5
Max Decel. Distance (m)	40	2

* The data shows the physical output per player based on research from elite level teams - see **pages 81-83** for details

Football Periodization to Maximise Performance

FRIDAY Training Practices: Pre-Match Activation - 1 Day Until Match (MD +6/-1)

LSG (Medium Area) 2: Positional Six Goal 9v9 (+2) Game with a Tactical Focus

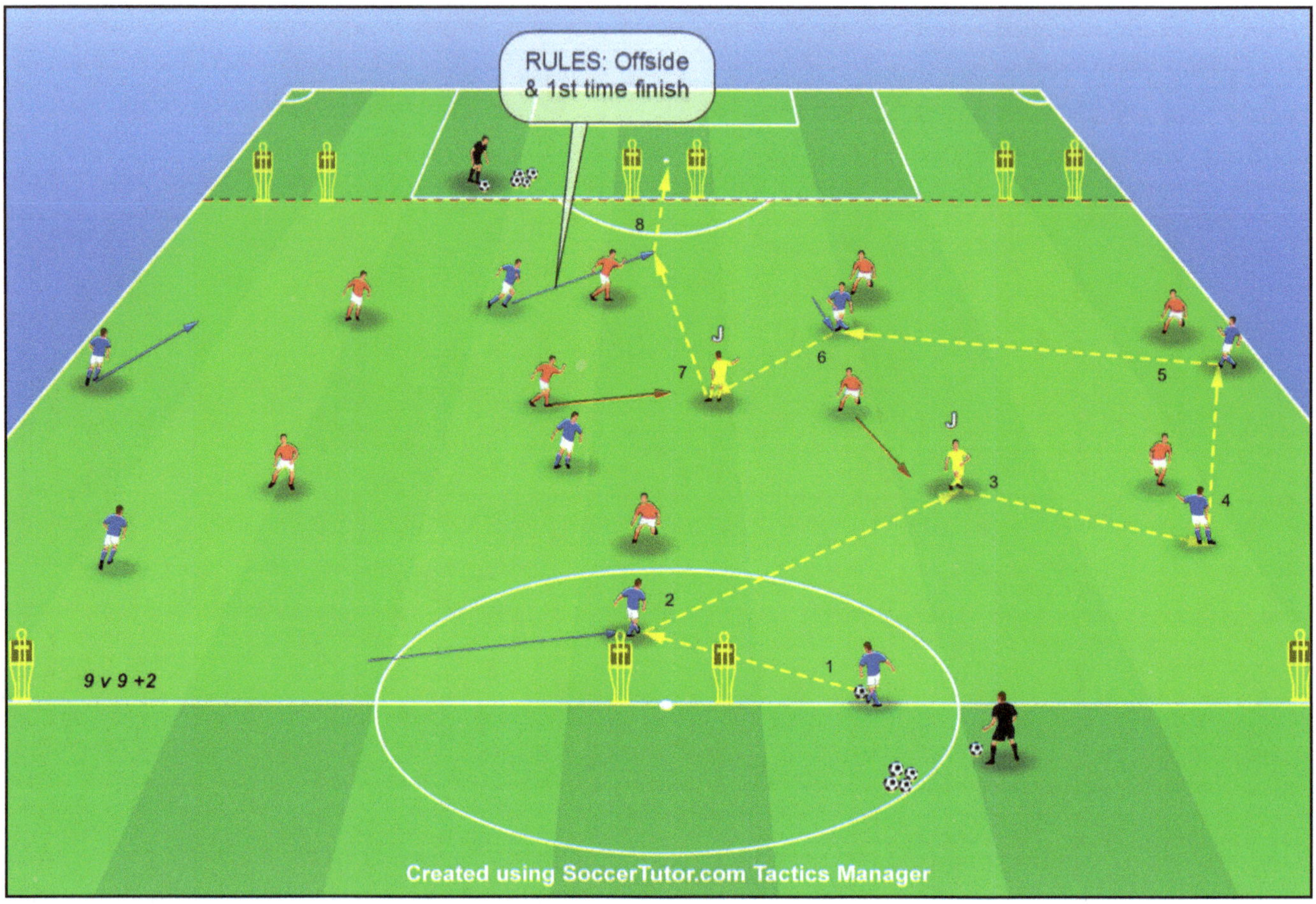

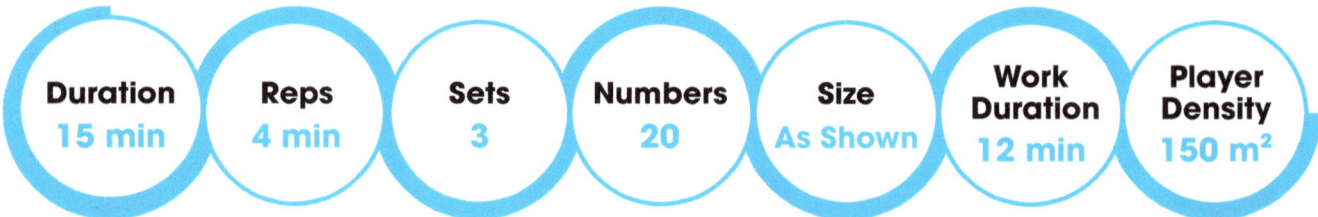

PRACTICE INFORMATION

Duration	Reps	Sets	Numbers	Size	Work Duration	Player Density
15 min	4 min	3	20	As Shown	12 min	150 m²

OBJECTIVE: Positional game with a tactical focus (offside rule and first time finishing)

Volume Metrics	Practice Total	Per Min. of Work
Total Distance (km)	1.599	0.13
High Speed Running (m)	41.23	3.44
Sprint Distance (m)	2	0.17
HML Distance (m)	167.55	13.96
Power Plays (HiActs)	8.9	0.74

Intensity Metrics	Practice Total	Per Min. of Work
Max Speed (m/s)	6.61	
Intensity (m/min)		85.79
Power Score (w/kg)	7.05	
Max Accel. Distance (m)	13	1.08
Max Decel. Distance (m)	23	1.92

The data shows the physical output per player based on research from elite level teams - see pages 81-83 for details

Adam Owen Performance Consultancy

As a highly regarded leading practitioner and coach educator within the area of performance coaching and football science, AO Performance continues to work with both European and continental based elite football and sports organisations, as well as grassroots based sports clubs, Universities and FIFA member associations across a range of levels. To find out more about how you, or your organisation can collaborate now or in the future...

 www.aoperformance.co.uk / Email: contact@aoperformance.co.uk

@adamowen1980

Additional Reading Reference

- Abrantes, C., Maças, V., & Sampaio, J. (2004). Variation in football players sprint test performance across different ages and levels of competition. Journal of Sports Science and medicine, 3(1), 44-49.
- Baldari, C., Videira, M., Madeira, F., Sergio, J. and Guidetti, L., 2004. Lactate removal during active recovery related to the individual anaerobic and ventilatory thresholds in soccer players. European journal of applied physiology, 93(1), pp.224-230.
- Barnes, C., Archer, D.T., Hogg, B., Bush, M. and Bradley, P., 2014. The evolution of physical and technical performance parametres in the English Premier League. International journal of sports medicine, 35(13), pp.1095-1100.
- Barreira, D., Garganta, J. and Anguera, M.T., 2011. In search of nexus between attacking game-patterns, match status and type of ball recovery in European Soccer Championship 2008. Research methods and performance analysis, 226, pp.226-237.
- Borges, P.H., Guilherme, J., Rechenchosky, L., da Costa, L.C.A. and Rinadi, W., 2017. Fundamental tactical principles of soccer: a comparison of different age groups. Journal of human kinetics, 58, p.207.
- Bosquet, L., Montpetit, J., Arvisais, D. and Mujika, I., 2007. Effects of tapering on performance: a meta-analysis. Medicine & Science in Sports & Exercise, 39(8), pp.1358-1365.
- Bowen, L., Gross, A.S., Gimpel, M. and Li, F.X., 2016. Accumulated workloads and the acute: chronic workload ratio relate to injury risk in elite youth football players. British journal of sports medicine, 51(5), pp.452-459.
- Bradley, P.S., Di Mascio, M., Peart, D., Olsen, P. and Sheldon, B., 2010. High-intensity activity profiles of elite soccer players at different performance levels. The journal of strength & conditioning research, 24(9), pp.2343-2351.
- Campos Vázquez, M.Á., Zubillaga, A., Toscano Bendala, F.J., Owen, A.L. and Castillo-Rodríguez, A., 2021. Quantification of high speed actions across a competitive microcycle in professional soccer.
- Casamichana, D. and Castellano, J., 2010. Time–motion, heart rate, perceptual and motor behaviour demands in small-sides soccer games: Effects of pitch size. Journal of sports sciences, 28(14), pp.1615-1623.
- Castellano-Paulis, J., Hernández-Mendo, A., Morales-Sanchez, V. and Anguera-Argilaga, M.T., 2007. Optimising a probabilistic model of the development of play in soccer. Quality & Quantity, 41(1), pp.93-104.
- Casarin, R.V., Reverdito, R.S., Greboggy, D.D., Afonso, C.A. and Scaglia, A.J., 2011. Model and play soccer in the process of education: global and specific principles. Movimento.
- Cerezo, E., 2000. Pre-temporada en el fútbol y acondicionamiento físico (Doctoral dissertation, Universidad del Salvador).
- Clemente, F., Couceiro, M.S., Martins, F.M. and Mendes, R.U.I., 2012. The usefulness of small-sided games on soccer training. Journal of physical education and sport, 12(1), pp.93-102.
- Clemente, F.M., Owen, A., Serra-Olivares, J., Correia, A., Bernardo Sequeiros, J., Silva, F.G. and Martins, F.M.L., 2018. The effects of large-sided soccer training games and pitch size manipulation on time–motion profile, spatial exploration and surface area: Tactical opportunities. Proceedings of the Institution of Mechanical Engineers, Part P: Journal of Sports Engineering and Technology, 232(2), pp.160-165.
- Coutts, A.J., Rampinini, E., Marcora, S.M., Castagna, C. and Impellizzeri, F.M., 2009. Heart rate and blood lactate correlates of perceived exertion during small-sided soccer games. Journal of science and medicine in sport, 12(1), pp.79-84.
- Chappuis, R. and Thomas, R., 1988. The sports team. The sports team.
- Da Costa, I.T., da Silva, J.M.G., Greco, P.J. and Mesquita, I., 2009. Tactical principles of Soccer: concepts and application. Motriz, 15(3), pp.657-68.
- Da costa I, Garganta J, Greco PJ, Mesquita I, Maia J. System of tactical assessment in soccer (FUt-SAt): development and preliminary validation. Motricidade. 2011;7(1):69–83; doi: 10.6063/motricidade.7(1).121.
- Delgado-Bordonau J, Mendez-Villanueva A. Tactical periodization: Mourinho's best kept secret. Soccer NSCAA J 3: 28–34, 2012.
- Dellal, A., Chamari, K., Owen, A.L., Wong, D.P., Lago-Penas, C. and Hill-Haas, S., 2011. Influence of technical instructions on the physiological and physical demands of small-sided soccer games. European Journal of Sport Science, 11(5), pp.341-346.
- Dellal, A., Wong, D.P., Moalla, W. and Chamari, K., 2010. Physical and technical activity of soccer players in the French First League-with special reference to their playing position. International SportMed Journal, 11(2), pp.278-290.

- Di Salvo, V., Baron, R., Tschan, H., Montero, F.C., Bachl, N. and Pigozzi, F., 2007. Performance characteristics according to playing position in elite soccer. International journal of sports medicine, 28(03), pp.222-227.
- Fanchini, M., Azzalin, A., Castagna, C., Schena, F., Mccall, A. and Impellizzeri, F.M., 2011. Effect of bout duration on exercise intensity and technical performance of small-sided games in soccer. The Journal of Strength & Conditioning Research, 25(2), pp.453-458.
- Fessi, M.S., Nouira, S., Dellal, A., Owen, A., Elloumi, M. and Moalla, W., 2016. Changes of the psychophysical state and feeling of wellness of professional soccer players during pre-season and in-season periods. Research in Sports Medicine, 24(4), pp.375-386.
- Gabbett, T.J., 2016. The training—injury prevention paradox: should athletes be training smarter and harder?. British journal of sports medicine, 50(5), pp.273-280.
- Gabbett, T.J. and Domrow, N., 2007. Relationships between training load, injury, and fitness in sub-elite collision sport athletes. Journal of sports sciences, 25(13), pp.1507-1519.
- Gabbett, T.J. and Mulvey, M.J., 2008. Time-motion analysis of small-sided training games and competition in elite women soccer players. The Journal of Strength & Conditioning Research, 22(2), pp.543-552.
- Garganta, J. and Gréhaigne, J.F., 1999. Systemic approach of Soccer game: a case of fashion or need. Movimento, 10, pp.40-50.
- Halouani, J., Chtourou, H., Gabbett, T., Chaouachi, A. and Chamari, K., 2014. Small-sided games in team sports training: a brief review. The journal of strength & conditioning research, 28(12), pp.3594-3618.
- Helgerud, J., Engen, L.C., Wisloff, U. and Hoff, J.A.N., 2001. Aerobic endurance training improves soccer performance. Medicine and science in sports and exercise, 33(11), pp.1925-1931.
- Hill-Haas, S.V., Dawson, B.T., Coutts, A.J. and Rowsell, G.J., 2009. Physiological responses and time–motion characteristics of various small-sided soccer games in youth players. Journal of sports sciences, 27(1), pp.1-8.
- Iaia, F.M., Fiorenza, M., Perri, E., Alberti, G., Millet, G.P. and Bangsbo, J., 2015. The effect of two speed endurance training regimes on performance of soccer players. PloS one, 10(9), p.e0138096.
- Issurin, V.B., 2010. New horizons for the methodology and physiology of training periodization. Sports medicine, 40(3), pp.189-206.
- Jaspers, A., Brink, M.S., Probst, S.G., Frencken, W.G. and Helsen, W.F., 2016. Relationships between training load indicators and training outcomes in professional soccer. Sports medicine, 47(3), pp.533-544.
- Jones, S. and Drust, B., 2007. Physiological and technical demands of 4 v 4 and 8 v 8 games in elite youth soccer players. Kinesiology, 39(2), pp.150-156.
- Köklü, Y., Ersöz, G., Alemdaroglu, U., Asç, A. and Özkan, A., 2012. Physiological responses and time-motion characteristics of 4-a-side small-sided game in young soccer players: The influence of different team formation methods. The Journal of Strength & Conditioning Research, 26(11), pp.3118-3123.
- Kyprianou, E., Lolli, L., Haddad, H.A., Di Salvo, V., Varley, M.C., Mendez Villanueva, A., Gregson, W. and Weston, M., 2019. A novel approach to assessing validity in sports performance research: integrating expert practitioner opinion into the statistical analysis. Science and Medicine in Football, 3(4), pp.333-338.
- Križaj, J., Rauter, S., Vodičar, J., Hadžić, V. and Šimenko, J., 2019. Predictors of vertical jumping capacity in soccer players. Isokinetics and Exercise Science, 27(1), pp.9-14.
- Kelly, D.M. and Drust, B., 2009. The effect of pitch dimensions on heart rate responses and technical demands of small-sided soccer games in elite players. Journal of Science and Medicine in Sport, 12(4), pp.475-479.
- Lievens, E., Klass, M., Bex, T. and Derave, W., 2020. Muscle fiber typology substantially influences time to recover from high-intensity exercise. Journal of Applied Physiology, 128(3), pp.648-659.
- Mallo, J., Mena, E., Nevado, F. and Paredes, V., 2015. Physical demands of top-class soccer friendly matches in relation to a playing position using global positioning system technology. Journal of human kinetics, 47, p.179.
- Mallo, J. and Navarro, E., 2008. Physical load imposed on soccer players during small-sided training games. Journal of sports medicine and physical fitness, 48(2), p.166.
- Malone, S., Owen, A., Mendes, B., Hughes, B., Collins, K. and Gabbett, T.J., 2018. High-speed running and sprinting as an injury risk factor in soccer: Can well-developed physical qualities reduce the risk?. Journal of science and medicine in sport, 21(3), pp.257-262.
- Malone, S., Owen, A., Newton, M., Mendes, B., Collins, K.D. and Gabbett, T.J., 2016. The acute: chonic workload ratio in relation to injury risk in professional soccer. Journal of science and medicine in sport, 20(6), pp.561-565.
- Matveyev, L. P. (1981). Fundamentals of Sports Training. (A. Zdornykh, Trans.) Moscow: Progress Publishers.
- Martín-García, A., Díaz, A.G., Bradley, P.S., Morera, F. and Casamichana, D., 2018. Quantification of a professional football team's external load using a microcycle structure. The Journal of Strength & Conditioning Research, 32(12), pp.3511-3518.

- Menuchi, M.R., Moro, A.R., Ambrósio, P.E., Pariente, C.A. and Araújo, D., 2018. Effects of spatiotemporal constraints and age on the interactions of soccer players when competing for ball possession. Journal of Sports Science & Medicine, 17(3), p.379.
- Mohr, M., Krustrup, P. and Bangsbo, J., 2003. Match performance of high-standard soccer players with special reference to development of fatigue. Journal of sports sciences, 21(7), pp.519-528.
- Morin, J.B., Gimenez, P., Edouard, P., Arnal, P., Jiménez-Reyes, P., Samozino, P., Brughelli, M. and Mendiguchia, J., 2015. Sprint acceleration mechanics: the major role of hamstrings in horizontal force production. Frontiers in physiology, 6, p.404.
- Nunes, N.A., Gonçalves, B., Davids, K., Esteves, P. and Travassos, B., 2021. How manipulation of playing area dimensions in ball possession games constrains physical effort and technical actions in under-11, under-15 and under-23 soccer players. Research in Sports Medicine, 29(2), pp.170-184.
- Otte, F.W., Millar, S.K. and Klatt, S., 2019. Skill training periodization in "specialist" sports coaching—an introduction of the "PoST" framework for skill development. Frontiers in Sports and Active Living, 1, p.61.
- Owen A., (2022). Football science & coaching performance. Meyer & Meyer Book publishing, Germany (submitted for publication).
- Owen, A.L., Wong, D.P., Paul, D. and Dellal, A., 2014. Physical and technical comparisons between various-sided games within professional soccer. International journal of sports medicine, 35(04), pp.286-292.
- Owen, A., Twist, C. and Ford, P., 2004. Small-sided games: The physiological and technical effect of altering pitch size and player numbers. Insight, 7(2), pp.50-53.
- Owen, A.L., Wong, D.P., Dunlop, G., Groussard, C., Kebsi, W., Dellal, A., Morgans, R. and Zouhal, H., 2016. High-intensity training and salivary immunoglobulin a responses in professional top-level soccer players: effect of training intensity. Journal of strength and conditioning research, 30(9), pp.2460-2469.
- Owen, A.L., Wong, D.P., McKenna, M. and Dellal, A., 2011. Heart rate responses and technical comparison between small-vs. large-sided games in elite professional soccer. The journal of strength & conditioning research, 25(8), pp.2104-2110.
- Owen, A.L., Djaoui, L., Newton, M., Malone, S. and Mendes, B., 2017. A contemporary multi-modal mechanical approach to training monitoring in elite professional soccer. Science and medicine in football, 1(3), pp.216-221.
- Owen, A.L., Wong, D.P., Paul, D. and Dellal, A., 2012. Effects of a periodized small-sided game training intervention on physical performance in elite professional soccer. The Journal of Strength & Conditioning Research, 26(10), pp.2748-2754.
- Owen, A.L., Lago-Peñas, C., Gómez, M.Á., Mendes, B. and Dellal, A., 2017. Analysis of a training mesocycle and positional quantification in elite European soccer players. International Journal of Sports Science & Coaching, 12(5), pp.665-676.
- Owen, A., Dunlop, G., Rouissi, M., Chtara, M., Paul, D., Zouhal, H. and Wong, D.P., 2015. The relationship between lower-limb strength and match-related muscle damage in elite level professional European soccer players. Journal of sports sciences, 33(20), pp.2100-2105.
- Owen, A.L., Newton, M., Shovlin, A. and Malone, S., 2020. The use of small-sided games as an aerobic fitness assessment supplement within elite level professional soccer. Journal of Human Kinetics, 71(1), pp.243-253.
- Rampinini, E., Coutts, A.J., Castagna, C., Sassi, R. and Impellizzeri, F.M., 2007. Variation in top level soccer match performance. International journal of sports medicine, 28(12), pp.1018-1024.
- Rechenchosky, L., Borges, P.H., Menegass, V.M., de Oliveira Jaime, M., Guilherme, J., Teoldo, I. and Rinaldi, W., 2017. Comparison of tactical principles efficiency among soccer players from different game positions. Human Movement Special Issues, 2017(5), pp.31-38.
- Sarmento, H., Clemente, F.M., Harper, L.D., Costa, I.T.D., Owen, A. and Figueiredo, A.J., 2018. Small sided games in soccer–a systematic review. International journal of performance analysis in sport, 18(5), pp.693-749.
- Swaby, R., Jones, P.A. and Comfort, P., 2016. Relationship between maximum aerobic speed performance and distance covered in rugby union games. The Journal of Strength & Conditioning Research, 30(10), pp.2788-2793.
- Tee, J.C., Ashford, M. and Piggott, D., 2018. A tactical periodization approach for rugby union. Strength & Conditioning Journal, 40(5), pp.1-13.
- Teoldo, I., Guilherme, J. and Garganta, J., 2021. Para um futebol jogado com ideias. Editora Appris.
- Travassos, B., Duarte, R., Vilar, L., Davids, K. and Araújo, D., 2012. Practice task design in team sports: Representativeness enhanced by increasing opportunities for action. Journal of sports sciences, 30(13), pp.1447-1454.
- Van Winckle, J. (2014). Fitness in Soccer. Routledge.

FREE TRIAL

Football Coaching Specialists Since 2001

TACTICS MANAGER
Create your own Practices, Tactics & Plan Sessions!

 www.SoccerTutor.com/TacticsManager
info@soccertutor.com

PC   Mac   iPad   Tablet   Web

Football Coaching Specialists Since 2001

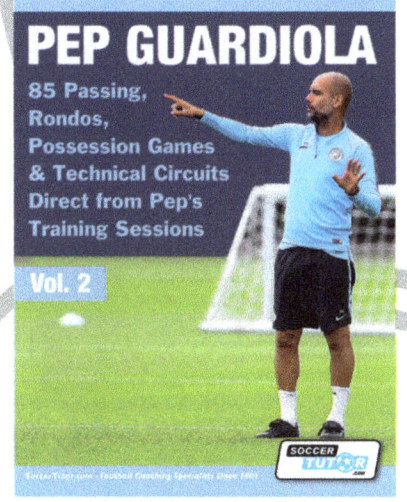
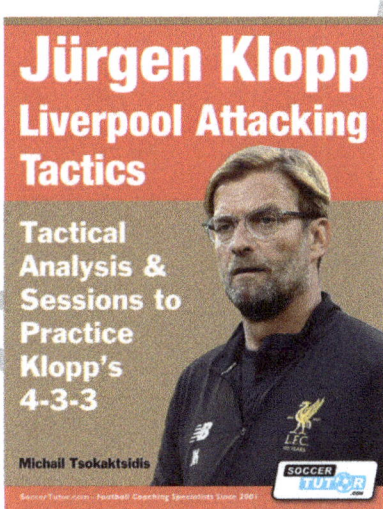
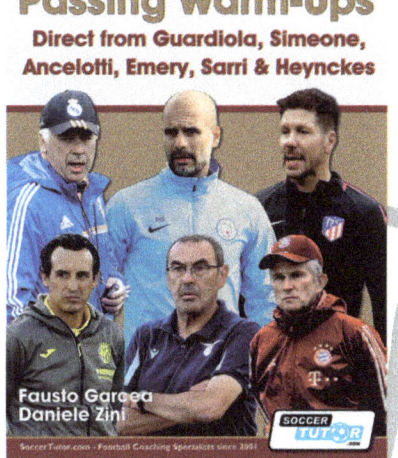

Coaching Books Available in Full Colour Print and eBook!
PC | Mac | iPhone | iPad | Android Phone / Tablet | Chromebook

FREE COACH VIEWER APP

www.SoccerTutor.com